Perspectives on Southern Africa

A Democratic
South Africa?

A Democratic South Africa?

Constitutional Engineering in a Divided Society

Donald L. Horowitz

University of California Press
Berkeley   Los Angeles   Oxford

University of California Press
Berkeley and Los Angeles, California

University of California Press, Ltd.
Oxford, England

© 1991 by
The Regents of the University of California

Library of Congress Cataloging-in-Publication Data

Horowitz, Donald L.
    A democratic South Africa? : constitutional engineering in a
divided society / Donald L. Horowitz.
        p.   cm. — (Perspectives on southern Africa ; 46)
    Includes bibliographical references and index.
    ISBN 0-520-07342-8 (cloth)
    1. South Africa—Politics and government—1978– 2. South Africa—
Race relations. 3. Democracy. I. Title. II. Series.
DT1963.H67   1991
320.968—dc20   90-44180
                                                              CIP

Printed in the United States of America
1 2 3 4 5 6 7 8 9

For Judy

Contents

Tables and Figures

Preface

Democracy is a popular destination, for which it is difficult to give directions. There is a wealth of knowledge on the characteristics of both democratic and authoritarian regimes, even on the sources of regime breakdown. But building the new regime—the process, the institutions, and the connections between them—forms the most uncertain part of an uncertain science. Small wonder that many countries take the wrong path, design the wrong structures, and get lost along the way.

Despite redoubled efforts to provide better answers, practice is quickly outrunning theory. Among the issues requiring attention are the following:

• How should constitution makers approach their task in order to enhance the prospects for a durable democratic order?

• What are the effects of ideological differences on the institutions a democratizing polity requires and on the process by which it reaches democracy?

• What happens if some forces in a polarized society reject the new system and the course chosen to reach it?

• In a situation fraught with dissensus, how should leaders choose among plans for new democratic institutions?

• What configuration of institutions is required by a democratizing country that is severely divided along racial and ethnic lines?

- What is the best way to induce minorities to take risks with majoritarian democracy and to protect them against permanent exclusion from power?

- What role can bills of rights, courts, and judges play in protecting minority rights?

- What electoral systems are likely to help reduce the conflicts that flow from racial and ethnic divisions and to foster cooperation across group lines?

- Is it possible to induce political actors who seem bent on undemocratic solutions, including their domination of the political system, to commit themselves to democratic power sharing and possible alternation in office?

- What is the effect of alternative modes of proceeding toward democracy on the nature and durability of the democratic product?

These ten questions make it clear that democratic innovators need to make careful choices among approaches and processes, as well as among institutions and arrangements, and they need to be attentive to the special problems posed by difference, division, and antipathy in a democratizing society.

A study of South Africa has a considerable contribution to make to the theory and practice of democratization. All the questions raised, and others as well, perplex South Africans. By most standards, South Africa cannot be considered among the most promising candidates for democracy. A racially and ethnically divided society, South Africa is also polarized along ideological lines within and across racial groups. Awareness of the potentially disintegrative effects of intergroup conflict has been muted by a frequently held belief that group identities are artificial constructs rather than genuine bases of social and political difference. The ideal of democracy is widely held, but it conjures up many conflicting images. An extremely unequal society, South Africa has practically no political institutions that command broadly acknowledged legitimacy. Instead, it has a significant band of extreme political tendencies, from White fascists to Black Leninists. Shaping an inclusive democracy is therefore a formidable task.

If democratic institutions do take hold in South Africa, they will still be threatened from several directions. At least some political forces at the extremes are likely to reject any democratic compromise. As in other countries, the armed forces might feel obliged to intervene in politics.

As in many other African countries in particular, the temptation will be strong for some political actors to preempt the democratic process and establish a one-party state. Conflicting racial and ethnic claims may also trigger undemocratic methods of responding to them. The legacy of apartheid is a residue of distrust that will be felt in the political system.

In the comparative perspective in which South Africa needs to be set, these inauspicious conditions make the attempt at democratization all the more interesting and important. A successful democratization would teach rich lessons in how to bridge cleavages, how to design appropriate institutions, how to foster conciliation, how to thwart an array of undemocratic impulses. If democracy endures in South Africa, more fortunately situated countries will have ground for greater optimism.

The special problems of racially and ethnically divided societies require more than the usual measure of democratic ingenuity. The political institutions that emerge must counter conflict and foster intergroup accommodation. At the same time, these institutions will bear the burden of securing consent from people and organizations whose experiences and opinions are utterly divergent. They will be faced with opposition from mobilized, even aroused, popular forces on all sides, inevitably disappointed either with the democratic arrangements or with their part in them. South Africa thus provides the quintessential challenge to democratic conflict management.

Confronted with this challenge, democratic innovators in South Africa will have to proceed with a keen sense of the magnitude of the task and also of the constraints within which it must be accomplished. Despite the need for a powerful set of political institutions to heighten cooperation and reduce conflict, the force of ideology places severe limits on the kinds of structure that have a chance of gaining acceptance. Consequently, the task of innovation is especially difficult in South Africa. This makes the substance of democratic innovation a subject of considerably greater importance than it has usually been in discussions of the transition to democracy.

The principal emphasis of democratization studies has been on political forces and processes. Here, too, South Africa provides a wealth of material. At the beginning of the process, the democratic prospect was not encouraging. The main participants entertained diametrically opposing visions of the appropriate institutions for a future regime.[1] Almost any way they were assessed, the interests of the parties also sug-

1. One view was based on group rights, another on undifferentiated majority rule. For a description of the unpromising character of these conflicting visions, see Donald L.

gested that if the process moved forward, South Africa could well follow other African countries in the ultimate establishment of an undemocratic single-party state. As the process began to unfold, however, some other possibilities opened up. The process itself seemed to change the structure of behavior and relations, but it did not enhance prospects for including all the major actors in a pro-democracy coalition. Such a development runs contrary to some theorizing, which postulates inclusiveness as an indicator, if not a determinant, of the success of a democratic transition.

One theme that emerges clearly from the South African evidence is the close relationship of process and substance in an attempted transition to democracy. The auspices under which change is initiated affect the willingness of actors to participate. The scope of participation in turn shapes emerging interests, relationships, and possible outcomes. The same is true for the effect of mode of constitutional policy making on the choice of institutions. Some procedures are conducive to the adoption of certain institutions, and others are not. This book was completed before negotiations began in South Africa, but even the prenegotiation phase made clear the close connections among who, how, and what.

It is hard to paint a moving train, and South Africa was a fast-moving train while this book was in progress. A great many people have helped keep me on track. Pierre du Toit was kind enough to send me invaluable material on several occasions and to provide me with incisive comments on the entire manuscript. Doreen Atkinson also sent me useful material and a critique of Chapter 7. David Welsh furnished helpful comments on a much earlier, now barely recognizable version of the manuscript. C. R. de Silva provided me with constructive reactions to Chapter 5, and Sande Churchill was generous with comments on Chapter 1.

At Duke University, I have had the benefit of abundant research assistance. Steven Wilkinson was diligent in searching out obscure data. Marta Campos and Brett Heavner helped keep me abreast of ongoing events. Jan Maarten Gerretsen and Mandisa Maya assisted with some difficult South African data.

As usual, I have been inordinately dependent on resourceful librarians. Fortunately, Janeen Denson has no "no" in her vocabulary. Betty

---

Horowitz, "Afrique du Sud: L'impasse après l'espoir?" *Le Monde* (Paris), December 7, 1989.

Hertel, Brenda Stephenson, Stephan Naudé, Bessie Carrington, Ilene Nelson, Jane Vogel, and Janet Sinder have all managed, at various times, simply to make information appear.

The manuscript was typed and retyped by Joan M. Ashley, with her customary dispatch and consummate skill. This book could never have been produced without her.

At the University of California Press, Richard Holway and William McClung were unsparing in encouragement, and Mary Pasti managed superbly the tricky task of editing the manuscript meticulously yet indulgently. Marilyn Schwartz and Pamela MacFarland facilitated the publication process at every point. So supportive a press has made everything easier.

Portions of the book were presented as the Maurice Webb Memorial Lectures at the University of Natal in Pietermaritzburg and Durban. A strong opponent of the policy of racial separation, Maurice Webb was the cofounder of the South African Institute of Race Relations, and 1989 marked the centenary of his birth. I am grateful to the trustees of the Webb Memorial Trust for inviting me, and I am particularly grateful to A. S. Mathews, a trustee of the trust, for his patience and efficiency in expediting the arrangements for my lectures. I am also indebted to Duchene Grice and Gavin Maasdorp for their extraordinary hospitality in Durban. At the University of Natal in Durban, I was very well received by Mervyn Frost and by Chaya Lokhani. At the University of Natal in Pietermaritzburg, I benefited—not for the first time—from the cool efficiency and warm welcome of Kushy Ramjathan.

While in South Africa, I gave a number of other lectures. I was fortunate to speak to the Liberal Democratic Association in Pietermaritzburg and to the Institute for a Democratic Alternative for South Africa (IDASA) in Durban. Both helped expose me to important currents in South African thought. I am also appreciative of the welcome accorded by H. J. Kotzé and Hermann Giliomee, respectively, when I spoke at the Universities of Stellenbosch and Cape Town.

Chapter 5 was presented at the Yale Legal Theory Workshop and at the MIT Peoples and States Seminar. The response at both helped clarify a number of points.

The Eugene T. Bost Research Professorship (funded by the Charles A. Cannon Charitable Trust) at the Duke Law School made time available for preparing the manuscript, and Dean Pamela Gann provided an atmosphere conducive to creative work. The University Research Council furnished a small stipend to facilitate the research.

To all of these colleagues and grantors, I owe a great debt of gratitude. To Judy Horowitz, practitioner of democracy and accommodation, I express my thanks for her usual mix of friendship, support, and constructive skepticism.

Donald L. Horowitz

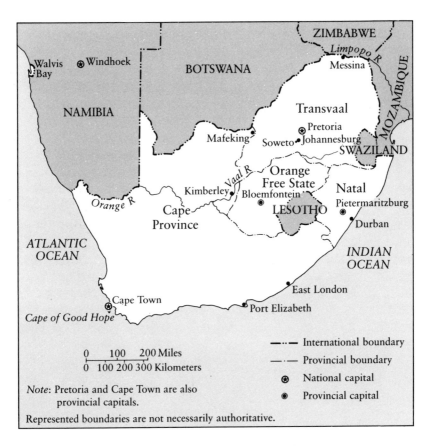

Map of the Republic of South Africa

CHAPTER ONE

The Conflict and the Conflict about the Conflict

There is a conflict in South Africa that has something to do with race. That is about as far as agreement runs among many of the participants and interpreters of the conflict. Beyond that, there is disagreement over the extent to which the conflict is really *about* race, as opposed to being about oppression merely in the guise of race, or about nationalism among groups demarcated by race, or about contending claims to the same land. There is disagreement over the identification and even the names of the racial categories. There is disagreement over the extent to which the conflict also involves ethnic differences within each of the racial categories. There is no consensus whatever about whether a future South Africa might also be divided along ascriptive (that is, racial and ethnic) lines and, if so, how severe such divisions might become. Even among those who acknowledge the possibility of ascriptive divisions, there is discord about what measures might be required to reduce future conflicts. There is further controversy over whether democracy is possible in such a future society and, if so, over what institutions might be required to foster a democratic outcome. Moreover, the common term *democracy* obscures fundamentally different visions of what a democratic regime might look like. In short, the basic description of South African society, present and future, is contested.

The more uncertain is the depiction of South Africa as a society divided along racial and ethnic lines, the more certain is the depiction of South Africa as a society divided along ideological lines—lines that de-

1

marcate fundamental differences in how the society ought properly to be understood and organized. Whereas in other settings knowledge about a society can proceed cumulatively, in South Africa virtually every interpretive effort involves some return to first principles, even to first facts. The plethora of contributions also means that every new contribution must struggle with nuances of difference in the understandings of its predecessors. South Africa is characterized by cognitive dissensus.

There is, then, not one conflict in South Africa, or even one type of conflict, but two. There is the conflict itself, and there is the metaconflict—the conflict over the nature of the conflict. Neither is coterminous with the other; neither can be reduced to the other.

In many severely divided societies, there are differences among participants and observers in characterizations of the conflict, but rarely are the differences as deep as they are in South Africa. The existence of a conflict over the conflict greatly complicates the problems of those who wish to plan for a democratic South Africa. In polities where all groups acknowledge the divided character of the society but disagree over the justice of their respective claims, there still remain the difficult tasks of specifying the terms of intergroup relations and the modes of handling conflict. But where the basic character of the society and the identity of its components are themselves disputed, even the need to make provision for future conflict is put in issue.

Any effort to engage in planning for democracy must begin with divergent understandings of South Africa. As I shall point out later, South Africa has many features in common with other severely divided societies. One of the most difficult tasks of putative constitutional engineers in such a setting is to take account of the pervasive dissensus without abandoning their own understanding of the conflict.

Many other societies are doubly divided, but not in the same way as South Africa is. In some societies, racial or ethnic divisions coexist, alternate, and compete for political attention with class, religious, or regional differences. In others, one set of racial or ethnic conflicts competes for attention with another set. Historically, South Africa itself has been doubly divided in this sense, for White Afrikaans and English speakers formed two contending groups, whose conflict in some ways exacerbated the racial conflict. The dual conflict I am referring to here is different, however, because the conflict of understanding does not in any sense alternate with the ascriptive conflict—it relates directly and exclusively to that conflict and thereby compounds it. Just how the conflict and the metaconflict relate to each other I shall attempt to explain after we have had a chance to examine some competing views, their origins, and the impact of the dissensus on even the terminology of the conflict.

TWELVE SOUTH AFRICAS

Practically no one in South Africa thinks it is a healthy society, but diagnoses of what ails it and prescriptions to cure it run a wide gamut. What is more, the divergent perspectives are fervently held. What I shall present are merely tendencies, rather arbitrarily selected capsule views typical of particular strands of thought but not necessarily representative of any single proponent. Virtually all strands are hctcrogeneous and evolving, so it would be a distortion to regard hybridized descriptions of them as anything more than paradigmatic. No doubt these capsule views do violence to nuances within each of the conceptions depicted. Even with these qualifications, a sample catalogue of this sort makes clear the scope and depth of the dissensus.

I shall enumerate the perspectives of participants and a few selected observers alike. Ordinarily, the views of participants should have priority in an exercise of this sort, but in the South African case the views of some observers either already represent a segment of more general South African opinion or are likely to form some part of the ongoing debate.[1] The sketches emphasize alternative descriptions of contemporary South African society, the end-states that are envisioned (including prospects for democracy), and the measures advocated to bring about the desired end-states. Some positions, of course, have changed over time. Some organizations and individuals could easily subscribe to parts of more than one of the views described here. Although twelve ideal-type perspectives are enumerated, there are many commonalities among clusters of these perspectives on one point or another. While it is important to elucidate the many ways of looking at South Africa, it is equally important not to exaggerate the differences either.

1.   *An Official View.* South Africa is a society divided into four racial groups (Whites, Coloureds, Indians, and Africans) and, within

---

1. Accordingly, the views depicted are not intended as a reflection of the state of academic theorizing about South Africa. Some major attempts to integrate South African experience into a wider framework, such as the theory of capitalist development or the theory of rational choice, are therefore completely omitted. See Stanley B. Greenberg, *Race and State in Capitalist Development* (New Haven: Yale University Press, 1980); Michael Banton, *Racial and Ethnic Competition* (Cambridge: Cambridge University Press, 1983).

these groups, into a number of distinct ethnic groups or nationalities. All of the racial groups need to participate in politics at the center, albeit on a group basis (as all groups do not participate now in the White-dominated regime). To create peace and democracy in such a divided society, however, maximum power over its "own affairs" should be devolved to each of the racial (and perhaps also the ethnic) groups, reserving to the center power over those matters that affect everyone. In addition, some or all of the nationalities may need their own territorial expression, in the form of self-governing, perhaps federated, homelands. (All of this is put in rather contingent terms. Within a few years of the 1983 Constitution, the government had become equivocal about the extent to which it continued to adhere both to the own affairs–common affairs dichotomy of that Constitution and to its policy regarding independent homelands. After the legalization of several opposition groups in 1990, these ideological commitments were weakened further.)

2. *A Charterist View.* According to the Freedom Charter, adopted at a public meeting in 1955 and subscribed to by the African National Congress (ANC), "South Africa belongs to all who live in it, black and white."[2] The charter did recognize the existence of several "national groups," which, it declared, "shall have equal rights!" These were to include "equal status in the bodies of state, in the courts and in the schools for all national groups and races . . . ."[3] In 1969, however, the ANC's Revolutionary Program rejected the idea of separate political institutions for racial minorities.[4] If South Africa manifests any racial or ethnic divisions, that is because of apartheid. Abolish apartheid, all forms of racial discrimination, and all manifestations of "separate development," and South Africa can have what is called a "nonracial [and nonethnic] democracy," although this will not necessarily be a "classical liberal democracy."[5]

2. *Freedom Charter,* preamble (adopted at the Congress of the People, Kliptown, South Africa, June 26, 1955), in Thomas G. Karis and Gwendolen M. Carter, eds., *From Protest to Challenge: A Documentary History of African Politics in South Africa,* vol. 3, *1882–1964* (Stanford: Hoover Institution Press, 1977), p. 205.

3. Ibid. For the background to the Freedom Charter, see Tom Lodge, *Black Politics in South Africa since 1945* (London: Longman, 1983), pp. 69–74. See also Thomas G. Karis, "Revolution in the Making: Black Politics in South Africa," *Foreign Affairs* 62, no. 2 (Winter 1983–84): 378–406.

4. See "African Nationalism in South Africa," in James Leatt et al., eds., *Contending Ideologies in South Africa* (Cape Town: David Philip, 1986), p. 102; Lodge, *Black Politics in South Africa since 1945,* p. 301.

5. Monty Narsoo, "Responses to the Report," in Charles Simkins et al., *The Prisoners of Tradition and the Politics of Nation Building* (Johannesburg: South African Institute of Race Relations, 1988), p. 88. For further evidence of hostility to liberal democracy, see Tom Lodge, "The United Democratic Front: Leadership and Ideology," in

3. *An Alternative Charterist View.* There is less of a plural society and more of a common society in South Africa than many people realize. Commonalities among South Africans have been obscured by apartheid. If only nature could take its course without the artificial constraints of apartheid, an unremarkable democracy would develop in a nonracial society. (In some such formulations, however, rigorous safeguards, including some based on group affiliation, are regarded as necessary to guarantee the democratic character of the nonracial society.[6])

4. *A People's Democracy View.* South Africa without apartheid can easily be a nonracial democracy, with no need for pernicious "group" protections. But mere representative democracy alone is inadequate. The future of South Africa can and will be shaped by the popular opposition to apartheid, out of which is growing a new form of people's democracy. That form is not limited to periodic elections or to a few spheres of political activity but is genuinely based on local organization by oppressed people, who are prepared to take every sphere of activity that concerns their lives directly into their own hands. (Such views are held by significant segments of the United Democratic Front [UDF], the Mass Democratic Movement, and the African National Congress.[7])

5. *An Africanist View.* South Africa is not an ordinary divided society but a colonial society, defined by colonial oppression in the form of racially based capitalism. The problem of South Africa is "settler colonialism."[8] Africans are the indigenous people and the sole legitimate owners of the soil. South Africa needs an anti-colonial revolution before it can become democratic and socialist. The resulting state will

---

John D. Brewer, *Can South Africa Survive? Five Minutes to Midnight* (New York: St. Martin's Press, 1989), p. 216.

6. See Heribert Adam and Kogila A. Moodley, *South Africa without Apartheid: Dismantling Racial Domination* (Berkeley and Los Angeles: University of California Press, 1986), discussed at much greater length in Chapter 4, below.

7. Paulus Zulu, "Resistance in the Townships—An Overview," in Fatima Meer, ed., *Resistance in the Townships* (Durban: Madiba, 1989), pp. 10–23; Andrew Boraine on Behalf of the United Democratic Front, "Democracy and Government: Towards a People's Struggle," Institute for a Democratic Alternative for South Africa, Occasional Paper no. 3 (1987); African National Congress, *Strategy and Tactics of the ANC* (1969), quoted in Roland Stanbridge, "Contemporary African Political Organizations and Movements," in Robert M. Price and Carl G. Rosberg, eds., *The Apartheid Regime: Political Power and Racial Domination* (Berkeley: University of California Institute of International Studies, 1980), p. 98.

8. For the Africanist tendency in the opposition movements, see, e.g., Lodge, *Black Politics in South Africa since 1945,* pp. 84–86; Karis, "Revolution in the Making," p. 382. On "settler colonialism," see, e.g., *Weekly Mail* (Johannesburg), November 17–23, 1989. On skepticism of parliamentary democracy, see Simkins et al., *The Prisoners of Tradition and the Politics of Nation Building,* pp. 25–26.

require no constitutional checks and balances. Rather than parliamentary democracy, South Africa needs representation on a class basis in a socialist society. (In some such formulations, "nonindigenous" peoples have no part to play in a future South Africa, whereas in others even Whites can become Africans, by means unspecified.)

6. *A Black Consciousness View.* South Africa is a society divided by the oppression of color. Once those oppressed by color find the means to overcome their oppression, South Africa can become a socialist, revolutionary state. (In some such formulations, Black Consciousness is merely a means of struggle, so that color becomes irrelevant once the struggle is won, whereas in others something like a Black state is envisioned.[9])

7. *A Racial Self-Assertion View.* South Africa is a severely divided society, in which democracy is improbable. But just as "racial dignity" has assumed priority over democracy in post-colonial African states, so may racial self-assertion be necessary in South Africa, even if democracy is not achieved.[10] "To some, freedom means the turning of the tables . . . ."[11]

8. *A Two-Nationalisms Partitionist View.* South Africa is fundamentally divided into Black and White. The interests of the two groups are so incompatible that territorial division is necessary. (There are many versions of this view circulating among dissident, sometimes exotic, White political organizations,[12] but it is also a view that was espoused by the African National Congress in the 1920s and the All-African Convention in 1936.[13])

9. See "Black Consciousness," in Leatt et al., eds., *Contending Ideologies in South Africa,* pp. 105–19.

10. David D. Laitin, "South Africa: Violence, Myths, and Democratic Reform," *World Politics* 39, no. 2 (January 1987): 258–79, at 259 n. 3, 279. Since it is extremely unfashionable to eschew democracy in South Africa, this view is rarely, if ever, articulated there; but it probably enjoys a fair amount of support. It has, of course, some affinity to the Africanist view identified previously.

11. Nomavenda Mathiane, *South Africa: Diary of Troubled Times* (New York: Freedom House, 1989), p. 117. For an interesting range of views, see ibid., pp. 115–20.

12. Such as the Afrikaner Weerstandsbeweging, the Vereniging van Oranjewerkers, and the Afrikaner Volkswag. See Carole Cooper et al., *Race Relations Survey, 1985* (Johannesburg: South African Institute of Race Relations, 1986), pp. 11–12. For an inventory, see Helen Zille, "The Right Wing in South African Politics," in Peter Berger and Bobby Godsell, eds., *A Future South Africa: Visions, Strategies and Realities* (Cape Town: Human & Rousseau Tafelberg, 1988), pp. 55–94.

13. Gwendolen M. Carter, "African Concepts of Nationalism in South Africa," in Heribert Adam, ed., *South Africa: Sociological Perspectives* (London: Oxford University Press, 1971), p. 118.

9. *A Two-Nationalisms Accommodationist View.* South Africa consists of several racial and ethnic groups, but the fundamental struggle is between White (or Afrikaner) and Black (or African) nationalism. Given time, these two nationalisms could accommodate each other and perhaps grow together into a nonracial society. For the time being, however, a binational state is the best that can be hoped for. With a dual set of largely autonomous institutions, such a state could be democratic.[14]

10. *A Consociational View.* South Africa is a severely divided society, with both racial and ethnic divisions. Democracy is rendered difficult to achieve by virtue of that fact—difficult but not impossible or even improbable if elaborate precautions are taken. To achieve democracy in a divided society, elites of the various groups must agree to share executive power and abide by a system of mutual vetoes and spheres of communal autonomy. (Over a period of nearly two decades, enormous energy has been invested in devising such model arrangements for South Africa.[15])

11. *A Modified Consociational View.* South Africa is a severely divided society, requiring some complex institutions if it is to function democratically. "Checks and balances" will be needed to protect minorities, including "black political minorities."[16] But a full-blown apparatus of mutual vetoes and delegations of communal authority would render it impossible for the new polity to solve some of its most pressing problems of inequality and perhaps also, therefore, to remain democratic.[17]

12. *A Simple Majoritarian View.* Whether South Africa is or is not

14. See Hermann Giliomee, "The Communal Nature of the South African Conflict," in Hermann Giliomee and Lawrence Schlemmer, eds., *Negotiating South Africa's Future* (New York: St. Martin's Press, 1989), pp. 114–29.

15. Most of these efforts are discussed in Arend Lijphart, *Power-Sharing in South Africa* (Berkeley: University of California Institute of International Studies, 1985), pp. 47–82. Among the major contributions are F. van Zyl Slabbert and David Welsh, *South Africa's Options: Strategies for Sharing Power* (New York: St. Martin's Press, 1979); Political Commission of the Study Project on Christianity in Apartheid Society, *South Africa's Political Alternatives*, SPRO-CAS Publication no. 10 (Johannesburg: Ravan Press, 1973); The Buthelezi Commission, *The Requirements for Stability and Development in KwaZulu and Natal*, vol. 1 (Durban: H & H Publications, 1982); KwaZulu Natal Indaba, *Constitutional Proposals Agreed To on 28 November 1986* (Durban: n.p., n.d.; pamphlet).

16. Charles Simkins, "Democracy and Government: A Post-Leninist Perspective," Institute for a Democratic Alternative for South Africa, Occasional Paper no. 1 (1987), p. 6.

17. Charles Simkins, *Reconstructing South African Liberalism* (Johannesburg: South African Institute of Race Relations, 1986; mimeo.), pp. 74–77.

a severely divided society is irrelevant. The problem is that it is un-democratic. To make it democratic, the majority must rule, and rule unimpeded. In the ordinary course of events, majority rule will produce a Black government.[18]

It might be possible to reduce these twelve views to four main tendencies—official, Charterist, Africanist, and consociational—but this would do violence to the range of perspectives and would omit some important strains, both articulate and inchoate. Even a fourfold division, however, would show just how polarized ideologies are, for it would not be possible to align them on a spectrum if the test were self-perceived proximity of one ideology to the next. Or, to make the point more graphically, organizations in the Charterist stream have been engaged for years in violence not only with the official instrumentalities of force but also with organizations aligned with the Africanist stream and with Inkatha, the organization led by Chief Mangosuthu Buthelezi, an avowed consociationalist.

If all or nearly all of these perspectives are to be taken seriously, as they should be, South Africa could easily be seen as a kind of riddle society, impossible to fathom. Even within the realm of similar general diagnoses of the society's condition, there are many different prescriptions for its treatment. But despite the plurality of conceptions about South Africa, it is no riddle. South Africa is a complex place, but the cleavages reflected in these divergent views are patterned and explicable.

It is conventional to regard ideological cleavages as the fallout of historical events, conflicts, or movements.[19] South African history contains the seeds of the ideological cleavages already identified, but with a special qualification. European South Africa was what Louis Hartz calls a "fragment society," an incipient whole society constructed out of merely a part of the European society of origin—or, in South Africa's case, out of two societies of origin, the Netherlands and Great Britain.[20]

18. This is sometimes the formulation of the ANC when it speaks of the "transfer of power from a white minority to a black majority." Quoted in Heribert Adam, "Exile and Resistance: The African National Congress, the South African Communist Party and the Pan Africanist Congress," in Berger and Godsell, eds., *A Future South Africa*, p. 104.

19. Thus, Seymour Martin Lipset and Stein Rokkan speak of "inherited cleavages." "Cleavage Structures, Party Systems, and Voter Alignments: An Introduction," in Seymour Martin Lipset and Stein Rokkan, eds., *Party Systems and Voter Alignments: Cross-national Perspectives* (New York: Free Press, 1967), p. 8.

20. Louis Hartz et al., *The Founding of New Societies* (New York: Harcourt, Brace & World, 1964).

As Hartz explains, the history of such societies entails working out the logic of the fragment ethos or culture as it encounters new conditions, new problems, and new people in the transplanted setting. The process of fragmentation, whereby a part becomes a whole, accounts, in Hartz's view, for the distinctive character of fragments such as French Canada or Dutch South Africa. The full social complexity of the home country was not transplanted, and so the fragments escaped social conflicts that occurred in the sending country after the migration. Eventually, however, the isolation of the fragments from world history broke down, and the distinctive fragment societies returned to worlds they thought they had eluded. "As the globe contracted, the Western revolution that the fragments escaped was spreading throughout it with increasing rapidity, so that ultimately it was bound to overtake them, if only from a distant place suddenly made near. If Holland was left behind, there was still Russia, China, the awakening African states." [21]

The concatenation of distinctively South African historical events and reverberations of events in world history is responsible, above all, for the proliferation of ideological currents. To make sense of what otherwise appears to be a kaleidoscope, to put back together the views I have pulled apart, and to capture the extent to which ideas have migrated across cleavages and over time, at least an abbreviated historical excursion is required.

ON UNDERSTANDING SOUTH AFRICAN CLEAVAGES

The conflict and the metaconflict have deep roots in South African history, particularly the history of the ruling Afrikaner group and its encounters with the British and the Africans who occupied the same space. Both nationalist aspiration and racial ideology formed prominent threads of Afrikaner history. [22]

The Cape Colony in South Africa was founded by the Dutch East India Company in the seventeenth century and finally taken over by the British in the early nineteenth century. In the interval, descendants of the first Dutch and other European settlers were well on their way to forming a distinctive group, the Afrikaners. Throughout their long conflicts with the Dutch East India Company and with the British, the Af-

---

21. Ibid., pp. 20–21.
22. Among useful histories of South Africa, see T. R. H. Davenport, *South Africa: A Modern History*, 3d ed. (Toronto: University of Toronto Press, 1987); C. E. de Kiewiet, *A History of South Africa* (London: Oxford University Press, 1957).

rikaners were also engaged in conflicts with the Africans around them. Practically every step the Afrikaners took to secure their precarious collective existence had elements of both struggles embedded in it. The Great Trek north from the Cape in the 1830s, for instance, was precipitated by the desire to escape some unpleasant features of British rule and threats to cattle and security from Africans on the eastern frontier.[23] The Afrikaners thought they were creating or preserving a nation out of a people threatened with "extinction,"[24] particularly by an increasingly powerful British colonialism, but they were simultaneously acting as conquerors of Africans.

For more than two centuries, Afrikaners (and later the British as well) subjugated Africans in the territories they controlled, and they developed racial attitudes typical of such relationships. Along their shifting frontiers, Afrikaners also fought the various Black ethnic groups, forming alliances with some against others, in struggles lasting until the late nineteenth century. While this process was winding down, events such as the British annexation of the Transvaal in 1877 gradually made Afrikaner relations with the British authorities and with English-speaking South Africans the overriding issue.[25]

For half a century after the Second Anglo-Boer War (1899–1902), there was an uneasy power-sharing arrangement within the British Empire and Commonwealth. Slowly, however, the fears of the socially inferior Afrikaners prevailed over appeals to unity with the far wealthier and culturally self-assured English-speaking South Africans. In 1948, the Afrikaner-based National Party came to power and began a process of Afrikaner upliftment. Within a few decades, Afrikaners were brought to virtual economic parity with their English-speaking compatriots.[26] Afrikaner nationalism had triumphed.

The National Party, in "its endeavor to make the country safe for Afrikanerdom . . . set up a bulwark of restrictive racial legislation."[27] Threatened by the Africans around them, as Afrikaners had been for 300 years, the Nationalists greatly extended previous policies of racial

23. See Hermann Giliomee, "The Growth of Afrikaner Identity," in Heribert Adam and Hermann Giliomee, eds., *Ethnic Power Mobilized: Can South Africa Change?* (New Haven: Yale University Press, 1979), p. 95.

24. Ibid., p. 103.

25. See Gwendolen M. Carter, *The Politics of Inequality: South Africa since 1948*, 2d ed. (New York: Praeger, 1959), pp. 27–38.

26. See Milton J. Esman, "Ethnic Politics and Economic Power," *Comparative Politics* 19, no. 4 (July 1987): 395–418, at 406–10.

27. Giliomee, "The Growth of Afrikaner Identity," p. 115.

segregation. In the 1950s, the government put in place a network of statutes to separate the races spatially and socially. The Population Registration Act (1950) assigned every person to a racial category. The misnamed Abolition of Passes and Coordination of Documents Act (1952) required all Africans to carry a wad of identifying papers. Over the next decades, hundreds of thousands were arrested annually for failing to produce the documents upon demand. The Reservation of Separate Amenities Act (1953) provided for segregation in public facilities. The Native Laws Amendment Act (1952) and the Natives Resettlement Act (1954) limited the rights of Africans to live in urban areas and permitted authorities to relocate those not authorized to be where they were living. The Group Areas Act (1950) was designed to segregate every locality by race.

In the 1960s, under the prime ministership of H. F. Verwoerd (1958–66), the apartheid system was refined, perfected, and—above all—enforced. Under the euphemism of "influx control," tough restrictions were placed on Black migration to cities. For those permitted to migrate, urban life was made unattractive. Large numbers of Black workers were forced to live in single-sex hostels far from their families, whom they got to visit only occasionally. There were restrictions on the movement of Indians and a complete ban on their residence in one province, the Orange Free State. Whole business and residential areas, declared "White" under the Group Areas Act, were eventually cleared of people who had worked or lived there for decades. Blacks were relegated to a standardized, inferior "Bantu education." Higher education was also segregated, and several separate universities were established. Verwoerd propounded an ideology of "separate development."

With the Bantu Self-Government Act (1959), the regime initiated a policy of consolidating eight "homelands" that might eventually become independent African states. Land ownership outside the homelands became virtually impossible for Blacks, all of whom were ultimately intended to become citizens of their respective homelands and hence foreign workers in South Africa proper. In the meantime, the citizenship of all except Whites had been devalued. The regime meticulously removed all but White voters from the electorate, in part to insure that Afrikaners were not outnumbered at the polls by English-speaking Whites and their "non-White" allies.

At its height, apartheid thus had two complementary thrusts: racial separation within South Africa proper and ethnic "self-determination" in the Bantustans. Both were out of step with international standards.

As segregation was being phased out in the United States, it was being reinforced in South Africa. As Britain, France, and Belgium were granting African independence within existing colonial boundaries, South Africa was contemplating balkanized independence for impoverished, disconnected dots on a map. As Hartz suggests, developments outside South Africa could no longer be ignored.

As the institutions of apartheid were being strengthened, the ideology supporting it was being undermined. The standards of the outside world had an insidious influence on apartheid even as they were being defied. Contact with those standards was intensified, ironically enough, by the very success of Afrikaner nationalism, which produced a class of Afrikaner academics, professionals, writers, and business people who understood emerging international norms and were, at the very least, embarrassed by the failure of South Africa to conform to those norms. At the same time, the economy engendered major changes in Black educational, occupational, and income status. Between 1960 and 1985, the number of African students in secondary school increased more than 20-fold, those in the highest primary-school standard more than 40-fold, and those in university more than 25-fold.[28] Between 1970 and 1980, Africans increased their share of higher-level professional and technical employees by more than a third and of administrative, managerial, and clerical workers by more than 50 percent.[29] Although average White income was still more than three times average Black income, Black incomes rose six times as fast as White incomes from 1970 onward.[30] Since surveys show that tolerance among Africans for the regime of apartheid declined sharply with increasing education,[31] the expansion of Black education—and probably also the increases in income—paved the way for widespread Black opposition. Just as apartheid was fully constructed, it had powerful forces arrayed against it.

Black opposition to White rule has a rich history, long antedating apartheid. Facing a regime that had largely excluded them from political participation, opposition organizations had to answer at least three

28. Hermann Giliomee and Lawrence Schlemmer, *From Apartheid to Nation-Building* (Cape Town: Oxford University Press, 1989), p. 118.

29. Ibid.

30. Ibid., pp. 125–26; Lawrence Schlemmer, "Change in South Africa: Opportunities and Constraints," in Price and Rosberg, eds., *The Apartheid Regime*, p. 238; Heribert Adam, "Three Perspectives on the Future of South Africa," *International Journal of Comparative Sociology* 20, nos. 1–2 (March–June 1979): 122–36, at 128–29.

31. Giliomee and Schlemmer, *From Apartheid to Nation-Building*, p. 119; John D. Brewer, "Black Protest in South Africa's Crisis: A Comment on Legassick," *African Affairs* 85, no. 2 (April 1986): 283–94, at 287–90.

interrelated questions: (1) Who properly belongs to South Africa? (2) Who should be included in the struggle against the regime? (3) What institutions are appropriate for a future South Africa? Answers to these questions, which constitute components of the metaconflict, have varied widely over time and across organizations. The answers, however, were not formulated in isolation but as part of a response to White, particularly Afrikaner, pretensions; and the answers affected White responses in turn.

As I have suggested, Afrikaner political behavior over the centuries was underpinned by two motivating and justifying forces: nationalist aspiration and racial ideology. Once contending African groups had been defeated, racial ideology might well have occupied the field alone, had it not been for the enduring struggle against the British, which had the effect of sharpening the keen Afrikaner sense of a precarious national destiny. Black opposition to White domination also had, in the first instance, two sides: African nationalism, on the one hand, and nonracial ideology, on the other.

As early as the nineteenth century, a movement had begun to keep "Africa for the Africans."[32] This was an enduring theme in the decades that followed, but it alternated with more inclusive conceptions of belonging. The African National Congress had operated on racially inclusive assumptions in choosing its allies and in advancing plans for a future South Africa. The Bill of Rights it published in 1923 went no further than to demand "equality of treatment and equality of citizenship in the land, irrespective of race, class, creed or origin."[33] By 1944, however, an "Africanist" tendency was discernible in the ANC Youth League, led by Anton M. Lembede. Lembede's Youth League Policy Statement declared that "Africa is a Black man's country."[34] The statement had implications at two levels. First, it implied that Blacks might have an exclusive or at least prior right to South Africa; perhaps others could stay only on sufferance. Second, it was critical of ANC cooperation with Whites, particularly with White communists, with whom the ANC was working. ANC leaders, in turn, saw the Africanists' thinking as a mirror image of Afrikaner nationalist ideology.

To the ANC's declaration in the Freedom Charter of 1955 that "South

32. "African Nationalism in South Africa," p. 89.
33. Quoted in ibid., p. 91. For the modest goals of the ANC's predecessor at its inception in 1912, see Brian Willan, *Sol Plaatje, South African Nationalist, 1876–1932* (Berkeley and Los Angeles: University of California Press, 1984), pp. 150–54.
34. Quoted in Lodge, *Black Politics in South Africa since 1945*, p. 21.

Africa belongs to all who live in it, black and white . . . ,"[35] the Africanists rejoined in their journal that "[t]he African people have an inalienable claim on every inch of the African soil. . . . The non-Africans are guests of the Africans . . . [and] have to adjust themselves to the interests of Africa, their new home."[36] In 1959, as one African country after another was receiving its independence, the ANC Africanists withdrew from the organization and founded the Pan Africanist Congress (PAC). The early Africanists did not quite resolve the oscillation in their pronouncements that implied at times that Whites did not belong in South Africa at all (or belonged as mere guests) and at other times that Whites were only disqualified from playing a part in the struggle for a South Africa that might nevertheless ultimately include them on equal terms. In general, however, the PAC's view has been to refer to Whites as colonial "settlers" in "occupied Azania."[37] At the end of 1989, a new Pan Africanist Movement, an internal counterpart to the PAC, was created. Its founding document declared that "colonialism in occupied Azania has over the years developed to be internal colonization of the African people by a white settler minority," and participants at its inaugural meeting chanted "One settler—one bullet!"[38]

In its choice of allies, the ANC also oscillated. Under Africanist influence, the organization adopted a militant Programme of Action in 1949 that espoused Black self-determination and eschewed cooperation with other racial groups, a position that was reversed at the time of the ANC's Defiance Campaign of 1952, following which the ANC returned to a policy of cooperating with the multiracial, but disproportionately White and Indian, South African Communist Party. Even the ANC, however, referred from time to time to the leading role Africans had to play in the liberation struggle, and some in the Charterist stream have spoken of "settlers," thieves who have "come and stolen my land."[39]

These debates continued in the 1960s and 1970s as new organizations proliferated.[40] Many of these wore the emblem of Black Con-

35. *Freedom Charter*, preamble, p. 205.

36. Quoted in "African Nationalism in South Africa," p. 98.

37. *Weekly Mail*, October 7–13, 1988, quoting the Pan Africanist Congress; Colin Legum, ed., *Africa Contemporary Record, 1986–87* (New York: Africana, 1988), p. B747, quoting PAC leader Johnson Mlambo. Azania is the Africanist name for South Africa.

38. Quoted in *New York Times*, December 27, 1989.

39. Winnie Mandela, *Part of My Soul Went with Him* (New York: Norton, 1984), pp. 42, 127.

40. See Stanbridge, "Contemporary African Political Organizations and Movements," pp. 77–92.

sciousness, which drew some inspiration from anti-colonial struggles and perhaps even more from Black struggles in the West. Like the Africanists, the Black Consciousness groups were ambiguous on the ultimate place of those who were not Black in South Africa. For those, such as Steve Biko, seeking to consolidate Black solidarity before the struggle began, Black Consciousness could be reconciled with the inclusion of Whites on equal terms once the struggle was over. The Azanian People's Organization (AZAPO), founded in 1978 and working within the Black Consciousness tradition, spoke, on the other hand, of "repossessing the land," and Black Consciousness leaders repeatedly described Azania as belonging exclusively to Blacks.[41] While AZAPO and its affiliate, the National Forum, incorporated strong elements of class analysis in their thinking, it was not the sort of orthodox class analysis that rendered thinking along racial lines illegitimate. Virtually all of the Africanist and Black Consciousness groups took the position that the struggle had to proceed without significant White participation.

In planning for a future South Africa, a full array of proposals was presented by the opposition over time. As I mentioned earlier, the ANC in the 1920s and the All-African Convention in 1936 advanced overtly partitionist positions, contemplating a division of South Africa into one Black and one White state. In the 1940s, the ANC recognized the existence of racial pluralism in a future, undivided South Africa and proposed parliamentary representation based on separate voters' rolls and reserved seats for various races. Later, the organization changed its position and demanded a single voters' roll.[42] Nevertheless, recognition of pluralism was present even in the Freedom Charter, for it promised, as we have seen, "equal status" for "all national groups and races." The possibility of a racially federated South Africa was thus opened, but since 1969 the ANC has set its face against separate political institutions for racial minorities. The government's emphasis on racial categories and groups had made group-based arrangements anathema to the opposition.

The first president of the PAC, Robert Sobukwe, declared as early as

41. "African Nationalism in South Africa," p. 113; Theodor Hanf et al., *South Africa: The Prospects of Peaceful Change* (London: Rex Collings, 1981), p. 285; "Tell No Lies . . . Claim No Easy Victories, a Position Paper of the Black Consciousness Movement on the Events Culminating in the United Democratic Front (UDF) and the Congress of South African Trade Unions (COSATU) Distancing Themselves from Mrs. Winnie Mandela" (1989; mimeo.), p. 3.
42. "African Nationalism in South Africa," p. 93.

1959 that the PAC would "guarantee no minority rights, because we think in terms of individuals, not groups . . . ."[43] Sobukwe equated multiracialism with "racialism multiplied."[44] On this score, the Black Consciousness organizations were largely in agreement: they favored the term *nonracialism* over *multiracialism,* because they, too, wished to avoid thinking, at least ultimately, in terms of ascriptive groups. Even now, AZAPO argues that race does not really exist except as an artifact of economic exploitation and political oppression.[45] With the infusion of class analysis, the prospect of liberal democracy has receded. AZAPO and the National Forum speak of the present system in terms of "racial capitalism"; AZAPO is committed to a "dictatorship of the proletariat," the PAC to African socialism. The PAC and AZAPO are both highly skeptical of multiparty democracy.[46]

Even this cursory survey demonstrates the extent to which the various movements have either oscillated or proved ambiguous on the three questions of membership in the South African community, inclusion in the struggle against the regime, and the nature of future South African institutions. The customary demarcation between Africanist and Charterist organizations and ideas identifies the latter as being nonracial and inclusive. In answering the three questions posed, however, so clear a demarcation is not possible. Ideas have traveled across organizational boundaries. The ANC, committed to nonracialism, nevertheless included non-Africans (Whites, Coloureds, and Indians) in its National Executive Committee only as late as 1985. The ANC has referred to the South African government as a "colonial regime," and individual United Democratic Front leaders have referred to White "settlers."[47] Sobukwe's dictum that the PAC thinks in terms only of individual rather than group rights has become an article of faith in virtually all extra-

43. Quoted in Carter, "African Concepts of Nationalism in South Africa," p. 116.
44. Quoted in Gail Gerhart, *Black Power in South Africa: The Evolution of an Ideology* (Berkeley and Los Angeles: University of California Press, 1978), p. 195.
45. Narsoo, "Responses to the Report," p. 84.
46. Simkins et al., *The Prisoners of Tradition and the Politics of Nation Building,* pp. 24–26.
47. *Proceedings of the Second National Consultative Congress of the ANC,* Lusaka, Zambia, June 16–23, 1985, quoted in F. van Zyl Slabbert, "The Dynamics of Reform and Revolt in Current South Africa," lecture 3, "The Dynamics of Reform: Patterns of Resistance and Revolt," Institute for a Democratic Alternative for South Africa, Occasional Paper no. 9 (October 1987), p. 4; Hanf et al., *South Africa: The Prospects of Peaceful Change,* p. 285, quoting an ANC leader; Donald L. Horowitz, "After Apartheid: How Majority Rule Can Work," *New Republic,* November 4, 1985, p. 23, quoting a UDF leader.

parliamentary opposition thinking, despite the willingness of the ANC, in particular, to think quite differently throughout a good part of its history. *Nonracial* has eclipsed *multiracial* as the norm for the entire extraparliamentary opposition. The early Africanist notion that Whites, although not automatically part of the political community, could be accepted as Africans if they made a proper adjustment has also had influence far beyond its origins. Even Afrikaners in the parliamentary opposition have been heard to say that Whites must learn to be, not White, but merely South African. The terminology of some Black Consciousness organizations, which used the word *Black* to include all those oppressed by color, has also spread very widely among the opposition, as I shall note later. In some ways at least, one can say that the ANC has been winning the organizational battle among the opposition but that the Africanists have been winning the ideological battle.

The completeness of racial exclusion under the Nationalists, coupled with the emerging doctrines of the Black opposition, had an impact on Whites who were opposed to the regime. As early as 1959, the then–Progressive Party, the largely English-speaking parliamentary opposition, began to think seriously about ways for excluded groups to participate in South African politics. The report of the party's Molteno Commission was the first of several efforts to provide a political framework in reaction to apartheid and in recognition of the plural character of South African society.[48] Over time, these efforts drew increasingly on theories of consociational democracy and emphasized formal devices to provide minority security. Their proponents were eventually joined by Chief Buthelezi, who, as a result of the government's homeland policy, had become chief minister of the Zulu homeland, although he refused the offer of independence for it. The effect was to provide a counterpoint to the undifferentiated majority rule propounded by the ANC and to the restrictive formulations of the Africanists. White politics and Black politics, often treated separately, do not exist in isolation.

The Soweto rising of 1976 and the introduction in 1984 of a new constitution that continued to exclude Africans from even limited parliamentary participation both produced surges of Black opposition. New organizational structures were created, and the opposition became a mass movement or, rather, several mass movements. The UDF, formed

48. See Donald B. Molteno et al., *A Report Prepared for the Progressive Party of South Africa by a Commission of Experts* (N.p. 1960 and 1962).

to oppose the constitution, consisted of some 600 organizations. The increasing breadth and depth of opposition helped elicit additional perspectives on South Africa.

The new activity coincided with a less self-confident apartheid. In the late 1970s, some features of "petty apartheid" (segregated facilities) began to disappear. White universities were again permitted to accept some Black students. In 1975, the South African Defence Force "announced that black soldiers would enjoy the same status as whites of equal rank, and that whites would have to take orders from black officers."[49] In the late 1970s, the regime set itself on a path leading to the recognition of Black trade unions. Some mixed residential areas were tolerated, although not fully legitimated until 1988. The anti-miscegenation acts were repealed in 1985. Influx control and the pass laws were abolished in 1986. Freehold title was made possible for Africans in the same year. Segregation in hotels, beaches, restaurants, and business districts declined rapidly in the late 1980s. The regime had embarked on an effort at "reform."

Complete racial separation was seen to be less and less feasible, and in the 1980s the regime began to speak, not of separate development, but of "cooperative coexistence," within "a system in which there is no domination of one population group over another, which in turn requires self-determination for each group over its own affairs and joint responsibility for and co-operation on common interests."[50] Not that the regime was consistent about any of this. Just as the regime was finally abandoning measures that would have relegated all Africans to homeland citizenship, further territories were being added to some of the homelands. Untouched by "reform apartheid" were the central pillars of the system: segregated primary and secondary education, the Group Areas Act (the cornerstone of segregated living), the Population Registration Act (which assigned everyone to a race), and—above all—the segregated political system, in which Africans had no significant voice.

49. Giliomee and Schlemmer, *From Apartheid to Nation-Building,* p. 124. The other changes recited in this paragraph are drawn from ibid., pp. 123–26, and from Hendrik W. van der Merwe, *Pursuing Justice and Peace in South Africa* (London: Routledge, 1989), p. 106. On the nonracial definition of "superior officer," see also Kenneth W. Grundy, *Soldiers without Politics: Blacks in the South African Armed Forces* (Berkeley and Los Angeles: University of California Press, 1983), p. 191.

50. P. W. Botha, "Speech by the State President, Mr. P. W. Botha, on the Occasion of the Opening of the Second Session of the Eighth Parliament of the Republic of South Africa, 25 January 1985" (mimeo.), p. 1.

At the height of the UDF protests of 1985, the government was as ambiguous about the future as the opposition was. A National Party pamphlet, entitled . . . *And What about the Black People?*[51] confessed to the bankruptcy of earlier plans to consign all Blacks to their homelands to find their political rights, but it rejected one person, one vote and a parliamentary chamber for Blacks. Having stated flatly that "[i]t has long been clear that political rights cannot be withheld from Black people forever," the pamphlet merely said that any future solution would have to take the "group nature of South African society . . . as the point of departure" and that no group could be placed in a position where it might be dominated by another.[52] Vague demands for a nonracial state had been met by a vague plan for a multiracial state.

Many Whites took up more conservative positions, some advocating a return to pure apartheid and others, convinced that White control over an undivided South Africa was untenable, devising a variety of schemes for partition along racial lines. Among White academics, the old regime of race relations had lost its legitimacy. Some became committed to Charterist positions; others, along with members of the business community, developed an interest in consociational thinking; and a few, unconvinced by the feasibility either of power-sharing plans in an undivided South Africa or of territorial partition, pursued the theme of two nationalisms and argued for a binational state. This last theme produced a strong reaction because of its contradiction of a fundamental tenet of opposition ideology—namely, that race does not demarcate a legitimate pluralism worth preserving after apartheid. On this view, race is purely a device for oppression, not an affiliation that could be transformed into a benign nationalism.

Currents of thought in the Black townships are rather more difficult to ascertain than are the elaborate programs of established organizations to which many, but not necessarily all, township residents subscribe. At least two strands, however, can be identified.

The first might be labeled majoritarianism coupled with deep suspicion of minority protection. "God made us the majority in South Africa. As soon as Blacks do what everyone else does [practice majority rule]," there will be objections.[53] "For centuries we have been oppressed, exploited and downtrodden both as individuals and as a peo-

---

51. Stoffel van der Merwe, . . . *And What about the Black People?* (Pretoria: Information Service of the National Party, 1985; pamphlet).
52. Ibid., pp. 12, 13.
53. Conversations with a youth group from Soweto, August 5, 1989.

ple. Now that whites fear the day of reckoning we hear all this moral-
istic nonsense. It's another attempt to maintain power."[54] On this view,
any form of minority protection is out of the question.[55] In some such
formulations, there is more than a hint of revenge.[56]

A second view might aptly be labeled Leninist. It is focused on revolutionary transformation, and it is quite prepared for things to get worse
before they get better. One example: a comrade from Soweto argued,
in terms reminiscent of Weimar Germany, that a Conservative Party
government, prepared to restore apartheid, would be preferable to the
status quo, because then "the people would know they are oppressed."[57] Leninism may be dead in Eastern Europe, but it is not dead
in the townships.[58]

I have not listed such revolutionary formulations separately, but there
is no doubt that many in several streams of the extraparliamentary opposition entertain transformative objectives. The ANC has said: "Victory must embrace more than formal political democracy. There must
be a return of the wealth of the land to the people. . . . The perspective
of a speedy progression from formal liberation to genuine and lasting
emancipation is made more real by the existence in our country of a
large and growing working class whose class consciousness comple-
ments national consciousness."[59] Leaving aside the Marxist teleology
implicit in the statement—that is, bourgeois nationalism can be converted more quickly to socialism because of the large working class—
there is the same dichotomy of "formal" democracy, presumably liberal
democracy, on the one hand, and "genuine liberation," "people's de-

54. Quoted from a group discussion reported in Paulus Zulu, "The Politics of Internal Resistance Groupings," in Berger and Godsell, eds., A Future South Africa, p. 147.
55. See Mandela, Part of My Soul Went with Him, p. 125:

It is not us, but the white man, who should be thinking about how he will fit into
our future society. It's his problem. He has the audacity to talk about the protection
of minority groups when he is oppressing the majority. The arrogance! That he sits in
power for over four hundred years, legislating against millions and millions of people
and oppressing us for all these generations, and now we must worry about the protection of minority rights, and of his property and his culture.

56. "There are many stories of what will happen when blacks take over. One woman
maintains she will hunt down all the whites who were responsible for black suffering,
lock them up at Voortrekkerhoogte [a military township] and be their warder. On Sunday, her prisoners will go without shoes, winter or summer. Similar stories are common,
half in jest and half serious." Mathiane, South Africa, p. 117.
57. Conversations with a youth group from Soweto, August 5, 1989.
58. See Robert K. Massey, Jr., "Great Expectations," New Republic, February 26,
1990, pp. 17–20, reporting township criticism, directed at two Soviet visitors, of the
Russian rejection of socialism under Gorbachev.
59. African National Congress, Strategy and Tactics of the ANC, p. 98.

mocracy," on the other. As Charles Simkins has noted,[60] in a racially stratified society, where capital is mainly White and labor is mainly Black, such formulations translate into racial revolution at least as readily as they do into class revolution.

I have also not listed separately a set of township orientations that is easier to infer from behavior than from documents. It is simultaneously militant and pragmatic, but otherwise difficult to categorize. It derives from the UDF protest activity of the mid-1980s and after. At the local level, UDF affiliates often undertook consumer boycotts of White businesses. These boycotts sometimes led to negotiations and agreements, often wide-ranging, with White merchants and local authorities. Since they did not produce anything like an articulated perspective, I shall reserve further treatment of them for a later discussion of models of accommodation.[61]

In the United Democratic Front, there is, in addition to majoritarian and Leninist strains, a strong current of support for what is called people's democracy, which is distinct from liberal democracy:

> . . . not only are we opposed to the present parliament because we are excluded, but because parliamentary-type representation *in itself* represents a limited and narrow idea of democracy.
>
> Millions of South Africans have for decades not only been denied political representation, but have also been oppressed and exploited. Our democratic aim therefore is control over every aspect of our lives, and not just the right (important as it is) to vote for a central government every four to five years.
>
> When we speak of majority rule, we do not mean that black faces must simply replace white faces in parliament. A democratic solution in South Africa involves all South Africans, and in particular the working class, having control over all areas of daily existence—from national policy to housing, from schooling to working conditions, from transport to consumption of food. This for us is the essence of democracy. When we say that the people shall govern, we mean at all levels and in all spheres, and we demand that there be real, effective control on a daily basis.
>
> This understanding of democracy tends to be fundamentally different from the various abstract constitutional models which tend to be put forward as solutions. Most of these are concerned with the question of how central political representation can be arranged so that "groups" cannot dominate each other, or how what is referred to as the "tyranny of the majority" can be avoided. . . .
>
> The rudimentary organs of *people's power* that have begun to emerge in South Africa (street committees, defence committees, shop-steward struc-

---

60. *The Prisoners of Tradition and the Politics of Nation Building*, p. 22.
61. See Chapter 4, below.

tures, student representative councils, parent / teacher / student associations) represent in many ways the beginnings of the kind of democracy that we are striving for.[62]

Formulations of this sort are very common.[63] Among the Black opposition, there is a large measure of distrust of representative democracy,[64] deriving from fear of cooptation and a long history of being far from the center of power. Needless to say, however, the transformative objectives of the opposition would require a very strong central government; there is tension between direct, bottom-up democracy and a strong center. There is also tension between direct democracy and multipartyism. As Simkins notes, when township street committees sprung up in 1984–86, they took one of two forms: either partisan differences were ignored or one organization took charge of an area and forcibly excluded all rivals.[65] Neither pattern resembles multiparty competition. The conflicts among direct popular democracy, Leninism, and liberal democracy have only begun to surface, but they are profound.

Many of these perspectives, including some only barely touched on here, will be analyzed more thoroughly in later chapters. So, too, will the quite different dimensions of consensus and dissensus that derive from sample surveys of popular attitudes. All that needs to be said for now is that nearly every historical source of ideology, internal and external, was structured to produce dissensus. In opposing the regime, it became routine to oppose its definitions, its categories, its assumptions, its visions. Theodor Hanf has pointed out that the ANC's rejection of group-based political thinking occurred as a reaction to the rigid formulations of the White regime. Previously, the ANC itself was organized "plurally: based on collaboration between Africans, Indians and Whites as different but like-minded groups. It was government policy— the unilateral definition of groups, the manipulation and ascription of ethnicity—that induced the ANC to reject all group formulas, regardless of their nature and reason, as expression and symbol of a system of oppression."[66] The very organizational structure of the opposition re-

62. Boraine on Behalf of the United Democratic Front, "Democracy and Government: Towards a People's Struggle," pp. 4–5 (emphases in the original).
63. See, e.g., Zulu, "Resistance in the Townships—An Overview," p. 17; "The Western Cape," in Meer, ed., *Resistance in the Townships*, p. 61.
64. See Simkins et al., *The Prisoners of Tradition and the Politics of Nation Building*, p. 24.
65. Ibid., p. 30.
66. Theodor Hanf, "The Prospects of Accommodation in Communal Conflicts: A Comparative Study," in Giliomee and Schlemmer, eds., *Negotiating South Africa's Future*, p. 108.

sponded, by 180-degree reversal, to official formulations, so inimical were the regime's conceptions to the interests of all but its White subjects.

To be sure, the independence of Africa had an effect that cut across several conflicting positions. After decolonization, a White regime looked anomalous, even to itself. After decolonization, equal White participation became problematic for the regime's antagonists. By raising the question of a settler-dominated polity, African developments simultaneously undermined regime exclusiveness and opposition inclusiveness. And Marxist revolutionary formulations, superimposed on racial classes, had an inescapable element of racial reversal about them. Yet, in the formulation of both cognitive and prescriptive positions, the shaping influence of the South African state and the experience of apartheid stand out most prominently, if only by virtue of negation. In such a setting, the very term *opposition* takes on a totalistic meaning.

THE TERMINOLOGY OF DISSENSUS

Terminological disputes reflect some of the basic differences of cognition. The government's division of the society based on racial groups generally yields four main categories: Whites, Coloureds, Indians (or Asians, thus including the very small Chinese minority), and Blacks (meaning Black Africans).[67] A division of the society based on the oppression of color, however, often yields only two categories: the privileged, who are White, and the oppressed, who are Black. The Black category can then embrace all who are oppressed on grounds of color—Coloureds, Indians, and Africans alike. The origin of the inclusive term *Black* lies in Black Consciousness thought of the 1970s. The inclusive usage is entirely congruent with an older, Eurocentric division of White-dominated societies into Whites and non-Whites—only now, of course, the conversion of *non-White* to *Black* signifies an opposite valence.[68]

The term *Coloured* is also a matter of sharp contention, reflecting

---

67. We shall review population statistics more fully in Chapter 2. The racial breakdown (including all the so-called national homelands) is approximately as follows: Black Africans, 74.0 percent; Whites, 15.0 percent; Coloureds, 8.4 percent; and Indians, 2.6 percent.

68. "... Black means anyone who is not White, anyone who is discriminated against because of colour." South African Students' Organization manifesto, quoted by Patrick Lawrence in *Star* (Johannesburg), February 16, 1972, and requoted in Brian M. du Toit, "Consciousness, Identification, and Resistance in South Africa," *Journal of Modern African Studies* 21, no. 3 (September 1983): 365–95, at 378.

unease with the externally determined name of the category but, for some, denial that the category should exist at all. The "Coloured" category is a complex product of contact among Europeans, Khoi, San, other Africans, and "Malays" brought by the Dutch from Indonesia. As in many other colonial societies with a significant number of Eurafricans, Coloureds were placed in a middle position between Europeans and Africans, their group boundaries, status, and prerogatives defined by the Europeans.[69] The minimalist objection to the name Coloured is expressed in alternative terminology: the "so-called Coloured community." Maximalists are more likely to refer to so-called Coloureds as merely Black.

Were there only an objection to the name, a new name would surely be adopted. New names commonly are adopted—and even more frequently proposed—for groups in conflict, always with political purposes and often reflecting an aspiration for an improved collective status or a different conflict alignment.[70] In South Africa, the term *Afrikaner* was originally employed as the rough equivalent of *Creole*—that is, locally born people—in contrast to the Europeans who administered the Dutch East India Company. The term *Boer* (farmer) was later used, but its backwoods, pejorative quality, when uttered by the British, rendered it obsolete for those who bore the designation, particularly since a movement to promote an "Afrikaans" language was then under way.[71] In the same way, the offensive term *Bantu* was abandoned in favor of *Black* or *African*;[72] and *European*, which might suggest a temporary status in South Africa, has given way to *White*. In the case of the so-

---

69. Borrowing terminology from J. A. Laponce, *The Protection of Minorities* (Berkeley and Los Angeles: University of California Press, 1960), Pierre du Toit and François Theron suggest that the Coloured population is a "minority by force" rather than a "minority by will." "Ethnic and Minority Groups and Constitutional Change in South Africa," *Journal of Contemporary African Studies* 7, nos. 1–2 (April–October 1988): 133–47, at 142–43. For the emergence and nonemergence of comparable categories in the Western Hemisphere, see Donald L. Horowitz, "Color Differentiation in the American Systems of Slavery," *Journal of Interdisciplinary History* 3, no. 3 (Winter 1973): 509–41.

70. See, e.g., Harold R. Isaacs, *Idols of the Tribe: Group Identity and Political Change* (New York: Harper & Row, 1975), pp. 77–92; Donald L. Horowitz, *Ethnic Groups in Conflict* (Berkeley and Los Angeles: University of California Press, 1985), pp. 33–34.

71. For the language movement, see Isabel Hofmeyr, "Building a Nation from Words: Afrikaans Language, Literature and Ethnic Identity," in Shula Marks and Stanley Trapido, eds., *The Politics of Race, Class and Nationalism in Twentieth-Century South Africa* (London: Longman, 1987), pp. 95–123.

72. For African resentment of the Bantu label, see Melville Leonard Edelstein, "An Attitude Survey of Urban Bantu Matric Pupils in Soweto, with Special Reference to Stereotyping and Social Distance: A Sociological Study" (M.A. thesis, University of Pretoria, 1971), pp. 47, 137.

called Coloureds, name change appears precluded, at least temporarily, because of the larger South African dissensus: as indicated, some putative group members deny that the group should exist separately from the Black category. This difference reflects the fundamental conflict over the identification of the racial categories and the conflict over the character of the conflict.

Now, for social scientists, such issues pose some problems of epistemology, but they are not insoluble. Take the question of political party affiliations or group attitudes. Using sample survey instruments, it is possible to determine whether, for example, so-called Coloureds or Indians hold distinctive patterns of affiliations or attitudes or are regarded distinctively by others. Racial or ethnic identity is a matter of the interplay between self-definition and other-definition. The epistemological problem is to determine, in the first instance, who among the respondents is Coloured or Indian. If identification becomes too difficult, because social convention makes it so, it is then unlikely in any event that distinctive patterns would emerge in the data. If, however, respondent identification is possible and if distinctive patterns do emerge, social scientists might conclude that these categories of respondent were acting *as if* they constituted distinctive groups.[73] As we shall see, research—including studies conducted by investigators located at widely distant points along the political spectrum—discloses some important, patterned differences among the four racial categories, which is why I need to retain separate terms for Coloureds and Indians.[74]

Nevertheless, this does not resolve the matter for participants, for although I have labeled the issue a cognitive one, it is by no means exclusively that. Group names, as I have suggested, have an aspirational

73. For the distinction between ethnic *category* and ethnic *group*, see Banton, *Racial and Ethnic Competition*, p. 105; R. D. Grillo, "Ethnic Identity and Social Stratification on a Kampala Housing Estate," in Abner Cohen, ed., *Urban Ethnicity* (London: Tavistock, 1974), p. 160. For the intricate relations between ethnic group labels and ethnic group behavior, see Frederik Barth, "Introduction," in Frederik Barth, ed., *Ethnic Groups and Boundaries* (Boston: Little, Brown, 1969), pp. 29–30.

74. For clarity, I shall also reserve the term *Black* for Africans, and I shall use these two designations interchangeably. In this work, I shall also use the words *race* and *racial* for the differences demarcated by color. I shall use the terms *ethnicity* and *ethnic* when referring specifically to Afrikaners, English-speakers, Xhosa, Tswana, etc. This is not because race and ethnicity are, by themselves, qualitatively separate phenomena but because this is the usage in South Africa, where differences along color lines have been the more important ones. In referring inclusively to groups based on race and ethnicity, I shall generally use the term *ascriptive*, although in parts of the theoretical discussion not confined to South Africa the term *ethnic* will also be used. Finally, I shall refer to North Sotho as Pedi, to South Sotho simply as Sotho, and to Shangaan or Tsonga by either designation interchangeably, as is conventional in South Africa.

aspect. The cognition that Coloureds and Africans share a common fate is bound up with the hope for solidarity among the oppressed.

I use these terminological disputes to illustrate the fundamental dissensus with which I began. Nor have I exhausted them: there are Afrikaners who object to the use of the term *African* for Black Africans alone, on the ground that Afrikaners are White Africans.[75] And, again, historical understanding is linked to group legitimacy, for to be called African is to belong, fully and properly, to Africa.

The possibility, raised by the Africanist stream, that Whites could ultimately become full members of the African community in South Africa has a close historical parallel in debates between Afrikaner leaders over who, among Whites, was a genuine Afrikaner. Many alternatives were advanced in the late nineteenth and early twentieth centuries.[76] Among the possibilities, one, proposed by J. H. Hofmeyr, was a conception that would embrace English-speakers who had settled permanently in South Africa. For the next century, a much narrower definition, based on ancestry and the Afrikaans language, prevailed. The newer White category may have roughly the same inclusive effect as Hofmeyr's version of Afrikanerdom. But in a severely divided society, as White society alone was for much of the twentieth century, identifying terminology that includes the contending ethnic groups is foreclosed.

Every society with ascriptive divisions, as I have suggested, has such terminological issues, but South Africa's are more severe than those of most other deeply divided societies. A glance at one terminological issue in one such society is sufficient to make the point.

After Malaysia was created out of Malaya and two former British colonies in Borneo, the term *Bumiputera* was adopted to embrace Malays and the various indigenous (but not Malay) peoples of the Borneo states, in contradistinction to the Malaysian Chinese and Indians. *Bumiputera* means "son of the soil," and the clear implication is that non-Bumiputera (Chinese and Indians) are immigrants and, on that account, entitled to fewer of the rewards and opportunities the state might dispense. What began as an effort to find an inclusive term for indigenes, only some of whom were Malays, also proceeded on the assumption

75. "After more than ten generations I regard myself as 'African' as any other African." Stoffel van der Merwe, "Not Just Two Groups," *Sunday Times* (Cape Town), August 9, 1987, reprinted in Giliomee and Schlemmer, eds., *Negotiating South Africa's Future*, p. 15.

76. Giliomee, "The Growth of Afrikaner Identity," pp. 101–03, 105, 111.

that the term would be exclusive of others, and it ended with an implicit declaration of differential legitimacy underpinning differential access to certain "Bumiputera privileges."[77]

How, then, is South Africa different? Not because of official categorizations: contrary to some popular South African myths, those are present in many countries, though rarely, if ever, with comparable disabilities attached to them. Rather, because official categorization in South Africa had much harsher results for life chances, the categories themselves came to be contested. In Malaysia, although Chinese and Indians always regarded the consequences of division into Bumiputera and non-Bumiputera categories as unfair, they acknowledged that the categories identified the main actors in a conflict-prone polity. While the argument was made, as it always is, that group leaders were merely using ethnicity to benefit from it, hardly anyone thought that this fact, if true, vitiated the operational significance of the categories for political and social life. In South Africa, by contrast, a strong body of opinion holds, as I have said, that the categories are incorrectly and illegitimately demarcated. The intensity of terminological dispute shows, above all, the unusual depth of cognitive and normative dissensus in South Africa.

THE BURDEN OF THE METACONFLICT

The conflict about the conflict makes at least three interrelated problems of severely divided societies more difficult in South Africa. First, the metaconflict places severe constraints on political discourse. Second, it contracts the range of acceptable innovations and future arrangements. Third, it increases the difficulty of finding ways for the parties to the conflict to seek accommodation and inclusion rather than hegemony and exclusion. In Hanf's apt words, "The real load of conflict, already burdened by the huge disparities in power and prosperity, is enormously increased by the fundamental ideological cleavage[s]."[78]

The most useful way to illustrate the constraints on discourse is to

77. The Malaysian Constitution has, since independence, provided that indigenous people enjoy a "special position" and are entitled to superior access to scholarships, licenses, and employment in the civil service. Even before the merger with the Borneo states, who was a Malay was specified by the Constitution. *Constitution of Malaysia*, article 153, in Albert P. Blaustein and Gisbert H. Flanz, eds., *Constitutions of the Countries of the World*, vol. 9 (Dobbs Ferry, N.Y.: Oceana, 1988), pt. 12, pp. 153–56. For the official definition of a Malay, see article 160, in ibid., pp. 161–62. For its rationale, see K. J. Ratnam, *Communalism and the Political Process in Malaya* (Kuala Lumpur: University of Malaya Press, 1965), pp. 78–79.

78. "The Prospects of Accommodation in Communal Conflicts," p. 111.

probe the significance of the term *nonracial*. The term arose in response to the emphasis of the government on ethnic divisions among Africans and racial divisions among everyone in South Africa. In assigning Africans to their national "homelands," the regime acted on the assertion that "there exist great differences between the Zulu and the Tswana, for example, or between the Xhosa and the Venda, differences more important than those between the Swedes and the Spaniards."[79] The government may also have created some further divisions, such as the division between the two Xhosa "homelands" of Ciskei and Transkei.[80] The whole policy of separate development assumes there is something separate to develop. The vision of a nonracial future is therefore diametrically opposed to the policy of divide and rule.

If the future is to be nonracial—not, it should be emphasized, multiracial, for *multiracial* is a term the regime has used—it must also be nonethnic. If nonracial merely meant nondiscriminatory, practically no one but avowed proponents of a return to pure apartheid would contest its usage. But it means more. At a minimum, it means that race and ethnicity can have no officially recognized part in public life and, for some, also that those affiliations should play no part, even informally, in political alignments or collective action. The nonracial society is the plural society's analogue to the utopian aspiration for a classless society. Both suggest so dramatic a transformation as to make the former society unrecognizable. The regime's contention that ascriptive groups are building blocks of the society is met with the contention that they cannot and should not be regarded as components of a good social order at all. So strong is the aversion to official group categories that the very existence of politically significant ethnic groups is denied. And denial is not too strong a term for describing the studied neglect of ethnicity that characterizes current discourse in South Africa.

Of course, South Africans are not alone in rejecting the significance of ethnicity. Western scholarship often sees ethnic affiliations as a mask for what are really class affiliations, as diversions from more important forms of conflict, as a cover for elites to secure support, as just about anything but ethnic affiliations—that is, anything but sources of com-

79. P. W. Botha, quoted in *Le Figaro* (Paris), December 5, 1986, as requoted in Marianne Cornevin, "Populations noires d'Afrique du Sud," *Afrique Contemporaine*, no. 141 (January 1987): 34–49, at 34.
80. See "Ethnicity and Pseudo-Ethnicity in the Ciskei," in Leroy Vail, ed., *The Creation of Tribalism in Southern Africa* (Berkeley and Los Angeles: University of California Press, 1989), pp. 395–413.

munity (as well as conflict), familiarity (as well as distance), and assistance (as well as discrimination). The reasons for this bias against ethnicity run deep. They relate to the general disfavor in which ascriptive affiliations of all kinds are held in the West and to the growth of materialist explanations for social phenomena. But the confluence of South African opposition with this more general stream of scholarship has produced something close to silence on ethnicity in South African scholarly and political discourse.

When scholars tread close to ethnicity, they deal in euphemisms or walk on eggs. The "Eastern Cape" is "an ANC stronghold"; the Xhosa who live there go unmentioned.[81] In 1976, *"a section* of the migrant worker population of Mzimhlope Hostel in Soweto"[82] killed young people in its path; Zulu go unmentioned.[83] The odd reference to ethnicity typically explains how it will be overcome: "the uniform exploitation of African workers at the bottom of the pay scale and labour hierarchy promises to become the binding grievance that bridges black heterogeneity."[84] Careful researchers who find ethnic phenomena in their data weave them skillfully, if obliquely, into their explanations, so that they will be available to sharp eyes and alert minds.[85] Rarely is there explicit discussion of even the possibility of protecting Black ethnic minorities.

As is common in divided societies, there is a belief that talking about ethnicity creates or reinforces ethnic divisions—in South Africa, that such talk does the government's dirty work for it—even when the talk is directed at how to prevent such divisions from overwhelming a future democratic state. This is a notion that, in some measure, spans the otherwise significant chasm between the extraparliamentary and the parliamentary opposition. When, in a speech at the Institute for a Democratic Alternative for South Africa (IDASA), an Afrikaner academic suggested

81. Karis, "Revolution in the Making," p. 391.
82. Lodge, *Black Politics in South Africa since 1945*, p. 329 (emphasis supplied).
83. To the same effect, see Martin E. West, "The 'Apex of Subordination': The Urban African Population of South Africa," in Price and Rosberg, eds., *The Apartheid Regime*, p. 140.
84. Heribert Adam, "Variations of Ethnicity: Afrikaner and Black Nationalism in South Africa," in Anand C. Paranjpe, ed., *Ethnic Identities and Prejudices: Perspectives from the Third World* (Leiden: E. J. Brill, 1986), p. 43.
85. Cf. William Beinart, "Worker Consciousness, Ethnic Particularism and Nationalism: The Experiences of a South African Migrant, 1930–1960," in Marks and Trapido, eds., *The Politics of Race, Class and Nationalism in Twentieth-Century South Africa*, p. 306.

that South Africa might actually house more than one nationalism that would have to be accommodated, he was advised that this kind of thinking was "exactly what IDASA was trying to get away from."[86]

In Chapter 2, I shall provide evidence that ethnic heterogeneity is likely to have some political significance in a fully democratic South Africa. There is now a fairly strong taboo on public discussion of whether such a forecast is accurate and, if it is, what the consequences might be.

The result of this taboo has been a paucity, albeit fortunately not a complete absence, of research on demographic, attitudinal, and behavioral differences among Ndebele, Pedi, Shangaan (Tsonga), Sotho, Swazi, Tswana, Venda, Xhosa, and Zulu. Research on this subject, elsewhere recognized as increasingly important, is in South Africa vulnerable to the suspicion that it could foment ethnic divisions where no significant divisions exist. From research on divided societies, it is well established that the context of interactions, including the political context, affects the operative level and felt intensity of group identities.[87] Under apartheid, race has been preeminent. After apartheid, this could change, and African ethnic identities could become more important. But the ideological reaction to apartheid has been such that the matter has not been considered in these terms. Ideology about the conflict presses in on understanding of the conflict at every level.

The metaconflict, then, can be a constraint on imagination and a constraint on innovation. The response of analysts to the two constraints should be different. As I shall suggest, to defer to ideas about the conflict, even mistaken ideas, in institutional innovation is to acknowledge the power of ideas to defeat the work of otherwise well-designed institutions. To defer to mistaken ideas about the conflict in analyzing the conflict—except to the limited extent that ideas about the conflict actually remake the conflict—is to perpetuate illusions. In the ethnicity example I have provided, these could turn out to be very dangerous illusions for the polity. And so the analyst who aims to ameliorate the conflict is confronted with the difficult task of combining relentless pursuit of the truth about the conflict—and persuasion of the participants that it is the truth—with deference to their sensibilities when the time comes for design.

As I have indicated, in the field of ethnic and racial conflict, the ideas

86. Alex Boraine, quoted in Pierre de Vos, "NP Shift Poses New Challenge," *Democracy in Action* (Cape Town), May 1989, pp. 1, 5, at p. 1.
87. See, e.g., Crawford Young, *The Politics of Cultural Pluralism* (Madison: University of Wisconsin Press, 1976), pp. 114–21.

of the participants have only limited ability to reshape the conflict. To demonstrate that point would require a volume in itself. An illustration of the repeated failure of a remarkably resilient idea will have to suffice.

The history of efforts to organize noncommunal socialist parties in divided societies—efforts based on the premise that the "real" divisions are class rather than ethnic divisions—testifies to the ability of ascriptive affiliations to overcome such ideas. The reason is, in part, that conceptualization exclusively in terms of class is disproportionately the propensity of educated elites. The participants, especially those at lower levels, also entertain other ideas, some of which are at odds with this conceptualization of the conflict. In the daily interactions that shape political cleavages, they are more likely to act on the basis of those other (smaller) ideas and on the basis of interests that hardly rise to the ideational level at all. And, cumulatively, a dynamic is set in motion, so that, before too long, socialist parties are either monoethnic, de facto ethnically based parties or they are out of electoral business altogether.[88] No taboo on discussion or research can change this dynamic where the ingredients for it are otherwise in place. The participants' views of the conflict feed into it, but the conflict cannot be reduced to what some of its more organized and articulate participants think it is about. The dynamics of the conflict, even apart from the discourse, place people in positions and relationships that exercise an independent influence on the course of politics.

If the metaconflict should not inhibit imagination, it nevertheless must, as I have said, constrain innovation. The feasibility of what might be desirable political arrangements is affected by the way interested parties understand and characterize the conflict. Some institutions that have operated well in environments more frankly hospitable to the legitimacy of group identities will be regarded as illegitimate ab initio in a South Africa where some of the major actors identify groups only with discrimination and are willing to accommodate difference only if it works no fundamental contradiction to their way of seeing the world.

No doubt some actors can and will modify their ideological predispositions. Learning takes place as events proceed. But it is fanciful to assume that ideologies developed over decades will be transformed during the shorter period in which the adoption and implementation of fundamental constitutional change takes place. That does not obviate

88. The evidence is assembled in Horowitz, *Ethnic Groups in Conflict*, pp. 9–10, 334–40.

the need to argue the merits of conflict-reducing institutions. Without a good deal of candid argument and a generous measure of persuasion, the South African future will almost surely be very bleak. But it would be a grave mistake, even if it were possible, to force those institutions on unwilling participants as the price of change or the price of peace, for that is virtually to invite them to delegitimize the institutions, to accept them insincerely, to play against their rules, and to overthrow them when they can. I shall suggest later that the first set of inclusively democratic institutions is likely to assume inordinate importance for the future of democracy. If that is so, grudging acceptance as the prelude to something else is not good for democracy. To insure durability, institutions to effectuate democratic consent need to aim at, among other things, genuine consent in the adoption.

It follows that those who propose institutional innovations for South Africa bear an unusual burden. It is not adequate to be correct about the conflict. That is difficult enough in divided societies. In addition, it is necessary to be correct in relation to the metaconflict—that is, to propose nothing that is at the center of the conflict of visions, for that, like the conflict of races, needs to be ameliorated. This emphatically does not mean that innovations should somehow split the difference, for such an approach could produce a grotesque combination of institutions, ineffective for accommodating the underlying conflict. What is required is the design of institutions drawn from the realm of what is acceptable.

To take a crude example of the extra constraints imposed by the metaconflict, I shall note in Chapter 5 that the former Lebanese electoral system, based on seats reserved for candidates of particular ascriptive identities, performed accommodative functions in Lebanon. The usual argument against ethnically reserved seats in divided societies is the a priori assertion that such arrangements entrench or perpetuate the divisions they seek to heal. In the case of Lebanon and in many other such societies, the argument is without substance. Lebanon disintegrated despite, rather than because of, these arrangements. But no Lebanese-style electoral system could perform similarly accommodative functions in a South Africa that has had more than enough of officially designated, group-based institutions.

Innovations always must meet the dual standards of aptness and acceptability. In no society are the two coterminous, but in South Africa, the gap between what would be apt and what would be acceptable is often very wide. Constitutional engineers should tell South Africans which bridges will and will not stand, but in designing bridges for South Africa they will need to take the idiosyncratic South African institutional aesthetics into account. This, of course, is not easily done, since the aesthetics are themselves in conflict: for example, one is averse to official formulations based on ascriptive groups, while another is averse to the abandonment of group identities. This is a central burden of the conflict over the nature of the conflict.

All of this leads to the final and most serious potential burden of the metaconflict, which is perhaps best stated as a question. Does the formidable degree of ideological dissensus incline the participants in the ideological contest to hegemonic rather than accommodative aspirations, rendering democracy even more difficult to attain?

A willingness to share power or alternate in power is necessary for democracy to succeed. In a very important paper, Pierre du Toit argues that such a willingness is not likely to emerge in South Africa.[89] In severely divided societies, he suggests, contenders for power are engaged in a contest for hegemony based on competing models of the regime they prefer. If the models are incompatible, as they are in South Africa, no constitutional scheme alone will be sufficient to insure democratic outcomes. The aim is simply to capture the state for one's own side. Examples might be the government's recurrent efforts to share power without losing it or the ANC's oft-stated position that it was prepared to negotiate only the transfer of power to itself, as agent for "the people."

The appropriate analogy for du Toit is the international system. There regulatory regimes can gain the consent of contending actors once the application of strategic rationality leads them to "a common perceptual frame about the nature of the conflict, which complies with the requirements of cooperation theory . . . ."[90] In severely divided societies, there is no "community of consent about the basic structure of society," and "the opposing parties do not share a common perceptual frame through which to assess societal conflict"[91]—which is to say that they are engaged in a conflict about the conflict. This is because no learning process, comparable to that which produces international cooperation, has taken place. What is needed, therefore, is a process of what du Toit

89. Pierre du Toit, "Contending Regime Models and the Contest for Hegemony in Divided Societies" (University of Stellenbosch, 1989; unpublished paper).
90. Ibid., p. 14.
91. Ibid., p. 19. In du Toit's formulation, the lack of a common perceptual frame is a feature of all divided societies, but I would argue that the extent to which this is so is a variable and not a constant in such societies.

calls, significantly, "meta-bargaining, or 'bargaining about bargaining,'" to produce "a joint commitment by all contenders to the view that the conflict cannot be won by either party on its own terms but instead, that a mutually profitable, and therefore mutually acceptable, settlement should be sought."[92] Without that commitment, the antagonists will see the choice as being merely to dominate or to be dominated and so will engage in behavior that aims at hegemony.

As the term *metabargaining* suggests, it is not, for du Toit, the mere existence of serious racial or ethnic divisions that creates the special problem, but the contending regime models, which in South Africa he reduces to liberal democracy or polyarchy, with its emphasis on procedure, versus "populist democracy," including "the deployment of authoritarian methods by a pro-active state, or even the establishment of an authoritarian regime, in the pursuit of substantive justice in the post-apartheid South Africa . . . ."[93] The difficulty, in short, derives from the conflict compounded by some version of the metaconflict, the conflict of ideologies and visions. No settlement is likely, even if there is formal agreement, so long as one contender suspects another of harboring an incompatible vision.

How, then, to achieve what du Toit calls a community of consent about the threshold question of the regime model entertained by the contenders? The process he advocates entails a blend of learning, deterrence, and confidence building. In international metabargaining, the adversaries begin to understand the high costs of a contest with an uncertain outcome; they slowly create a zone of overlapping rather than zero-sum agendas; and the contest for hegemony is ultimately dissolved. On this view, the task of the constitutional engineer, even before devising arrangements to make liberal democracy work in the face of ethnic or racial conflict, is to unravel for the participants the social costs of hegemonic aspirations—to facilitate, in other words, the learning that leads to deterrence, which leads in turn to a widened zone of agreement. The constitutional engineer is perforce engaged in "demystification"— a task that should not be impossible, since "rewards for cooperation, and the inability to escape the retaliatory consequences of extremism and unilateral actions, ought to be even more compellingly obvious within divided societies than within international society."[94]

Perhaps they ought to be, since the contenders live at closer quarters.

92. Ibid., p. 20.
93. Ibid., p. 17.
94. Ibid., p. 23.

Yet, the experience of South Africa suggests that these lessons will not be easy to learn. The argument can easily be made to sound tautologous. The society is severely divided because the actors believe the myths; if the myths could be dissolved, the society would not be severely divided in the first place, so a learning model simply wishes away the problem.

Moreover, there are other models of how liberal democracy can come into being in a society as severely conflicted as South Africa. The growth of international regimes in an otherwise anarchic environment itself suggests a different account. There the contenders learn to modify their goals through long and bitter experience, not through mere counsels of demystification. If the international analogy is truly apt, it might imply the unavailability of any rapid path to a democratic outcome in South Africa. It seems doubtful that the learning process can be short-circuited. Alternatively, perhaps engineering has a design role to play, rather than a demystification role, on these ideological issues as well as on those that derive from ethnic divisions per se. Perhaps institutions can be designed to prevent hegemony or to make it very costly to attain once a contender subscribes to the institutions. If so, potential hegemons could become cooperating democrats in spite of themselves.

As these speculations imply, models of the transition to democracy are indeed various. In Chapter 7, where we return to this question, we shall examine some alternative models. The point here is to raise the crucial community of consent issue as separate and to underscore that it arises as much from the metaconflict as from the conflict itself.

THE PATH FROM SUBORDINATION AND THE FUNCTIONS OF ETHNICITY

Up to this point, we have concentrated more on the metaconflict than on the conflict itself. When we focus on the conflict in comparative perspective, the gap between the two becomes apparent.

South African society is not difficult to classify. It is characterized, above all, by what is appropriately called *ascriptive ranking*. There are superordinates and subordinates, largely defined by birth criteria. To be sure, within the ranks of each stratum, there are also cleavages that divide, in some variable measure, Afrikaans speakers from English speakers, Zulu from Xhosa and Tswana, and so on. But the overall design of the society is predicated on racial hierarchy, and the significance of those alternative cleavages is, at least temporarily, suppressed.

We can identify other societies organized along similar lines, and we can trace their similar behavioral propensities: the enforcement of an etiquette of subordination, the denial of prestige and mobility opportunities to ranked subordinates, the social impermissibility of intermarriage and interdining, and what Max Weber calls the "acknowledgment of 'more honor' in favor of the privileged caste and status groups."[95]

In the United States South and the West Indies, as in South Africa, the indicia of difference were color and physiognomy, but in caste-ridden India, a more complex set of indicia of birth-based membership is employed. In Japan, differences between the subordinated Burakumin and other Japanese can be detected only through clues about family origin, which led to the description of the Burakumin as Japan's "invisible race."[96] In Rwanda and Burundi, yet other indicia of differences are employed.[97] Color is a powerful differentiator, to be sure, but in analyzing systems of subordination one should not fall victim to the parochial fallacy that mistakes the indicator of group identity for the relationship itself. Many differentiating attributes will do just as well as color, as the victims of caste violence in India or of ethnic violence in Burundi will attest. One should not succumb to the assumptions of the system of subordination in reverse and fall prey to what I call the figment of the pigment.

Slavery on an ascriptive basis, an institution formerly well known in South Africa, has been far more widespread than we might like to think. In many places, it forms the basis for post-emancipation superior-subordinate relations.

A somewhat obscure example is enough to demonstrate the persistent regularities that characterize such relationships. Among the Ibo of Eastern Nigeria, two different kinds of slavery were practiced until fairly recently.[98] One involved the Osu, slaves serving deities that protected villages. The other involved the Ohu, whose servitude originated in con-

---

95. H. H. Gerth and C. Wright Mills, eds., *From Max Weber: Essays in Sociology* (New York: Free Press, 1958), p. 189.

96. George De Vos and Hiroshi Wagatsuma, eds., *Japan's Invisible Race* (Berkeley and Los Angeles: University of California Press, 1966).

97. See René Lemarchand, *Rwanda and Burundi* (New York: Praeger, 1972). See also Reginald Kay, *Burundi since the Genocide* (London: Minority Rights Group, 1987); René Lemarchand and David Martin, *Selective Genocide in Burundi* (London: Minority Rights Group, 1974); Leo Kuper, *The Pity of It All: Polarization of Racial and Ethnic Relations* (Minneapolis: University of Minnesota Press, 1977).

98. M. M. Green, *Ibo Village Affairs*, 2d ed. (New York: Praeger, 1964), pp. x, 12, 23, 50–51, 58, 62, 158–59; W. R. C. Horton, "The Ohu System of Slavery in a Northern Ibo Village-Group," *Africa* 24, no. 4 (October 1954): 310–36.

quest (or sometimes conquest and payment). In both cases, slavery was intergenerational. Osu and Ohu alike were residentially segregated, either in peripheral areas of a village or in separate villages. Intermarriage was strictly forbidden and regarded with utter repugnance by other Ibo. Ohu and Osu were treated as property rather than persons, and Osu were occasionally used as human sacrifices. When the system was formally abolished in 1956, proponents of the abolition explicitly drew the parallel to South African apartheid. After abolition, escaping the subordinate identity still proved virtually impossible, even by migration to more anonymous, urban communities. Even where Ohu had served as priests or where Osu had amassed wealth, they were denied the respect generally accorded ordinary Ibo. Much to the discomfort of progressive Ibo, the stigma of subordination has endured.[99]

At various times in the modern period, slavery and subordination based on ascriptive criteria have been present on every inhabited continent except possibly Australia. None of this mitigates racial domination in South Africa or elsewhere; but there is no basis at all for the view that Whites have a monopoly on this kind of behavior. No one familiar with even the outlines of, for example, Burundian ethnic relations could entertain such a view. René Lemarchand has described Burundi as "the one state in Africa that displays the most systematic and blatant violations of human rights," a state in which the Tutsi minority of 14 percent (about the same percentage as Whites in South Africa) controls well over 90 percent of all high governmental, political party, foreign service, private sector, educational, judicial, and health care positions, not to mention its 99.7 percent of all military positions, top to bottom.[100] In this setting, the assertion that Tutsi do not "claim the right to dominate power, still less to monopolize it" but "are ready to share power with their Hutu brothers, if the act of sharing does not constitute a threat to their own safety,"[101] has a familiar, Pretorian ring to it. There

---

99. See, e.g., Igwebuike Romeo Okeke, *The "Osu" Concept in Igboland: A Study of the Types of Slavery in Igbo-speaking Areas of Nigeria* (Enugu, Nigeria: Access, 1986). For the debate on abolition in the former Eastern Region House of Assembly, see ibid., pp. 142–59.

100. René Lemarchand, "Burundi: The Killing Fields Revisited" (University of Florida, 1989; unpublished paper), pp. 1, 4.

101. Juvénal Mugiraneza [pseud.], *The Origins of the Ethnic Problem in Burundi* (Bujumbura, Burundi: n.p., 1988; pamphlet), p. 6. In this twelve-and-one-half-page, progovernment pamphlet, the apprehension of a Tutsi genocide by Hutu is pervasive. The word *extermination* appears at least eight times, synonyms like *final solution, genocide,* and *massacre* many more times. Compare the Afrikaner apprehension of extermination; see note 24, above, and accompanying text. I am indebted to René Lemarchand for a copy of this pamphlet, but the interpretation is my own.

is, then, a common behavioral tendency to subordinate others, a tendency that bitterly reaffirms the common humanity and the common failings of Whites and Blacks—and Asians as well.

Rudimentary knowledge of the common phenomenon of ascriptive subordination may be of small comfort to those who are subordinated. But it ought at least to enable us to think more coolly than has generally been done so far about how to change the status quo in ways that promise decent, peaceful relations in the future. One thing it means is that we can learn from the experience of those who have tried to move to a different system. When we do this, we shall see that learning to live without predictable relations of superordination and subordination is not the same as living without ascriptive groups at all.

The rather antiseptic description I have provided to this point serves the purpose of countering the inevitable parochialism that comes with immersion in a particular conflict. South Africa is certainly not unique in enduring a harsh system of ranked subordination, but it has had a far more elaborate legal apparatus deployed in the service of ranking than other systems have. With respect to the Burakumin, the Japanese have never had a formal apparatus of discrimination comparable to apartheid, although a cynic might say that the tight structure of Japanese society hardly requires legal sanctions. There are, for instance, published directories of Burakumin names available to employers who wish to discriminate against them. In Burundi, where the oppression of ranked subordinates has been far more lethal than almost anywhere else, South Africa's efficient legalism has nevertheless been absent.

Once we place South Africa in the category of ranked systems, we can see why it is in a process of change. Above all, the source of change lies in the realm of ideas. The spread of conceptions of human equality around the globe has made ascriptive stratification ideologically obsolete. Those who practice it must pretend that they do not. Even in the Jim Crow American South, the claim was not "separate and appropriately inferior"; rather it was "separate but equal." The importance of the international diffusion of ideas is attested by the adoption of the tactics of the American Civil Rights Movement—with a good many Japanese refinements!—by the Buraku Liberation League in Japan,[102] and it is reaffirmed by the very name of such groups of Indian ex-Un-

102. Frank Upham, *Law and Social Change in Postwar Japan* (Cambridge: Harvard University Press, 1987), pp. 78–153.

touchables as the Dalit Panthers, obviously modeled on the Black Panthers.

Several paths lead away from relations of ascriptive subordination, but the path leading to a wholly nonascriptive society is the path least traveled, even when it is the path on which many wish to journey. Far more common is an improvement in the status, wealth, and power of the formerly subordinate group, so that now it encounters other groups, not from a fixed position of submission and inferior ranking, but from a more fluid position, in which individual group members may rank low or high but in which the groups themselves are unranked in relation to each other. The relations between groups have changed from ranked to unranked, but groups still exist.

It is easy to see why the shift from ranked subordination to unranked group relations is so common. When subordination on a birth-determined basis is undermined, subordinated people challenge the system of ranking by collective action, by action on the basis of group identity, even as they deny its importance. Group networks are not abolished with a change of ethnic status, particularly as endogamy, which perpetuates group identity and recruitment by birth, is unlikely to change over the short term. Moreover, in post-subordination encounters among members of various groups, intergroup stereotypes, divisions of labor, and divergent patterns of political interest all persist.

In the United States and in India, there have been considerable changes in systems of ascriptive subordination. Although the officially declared aim for race relations in the United States and for caste relations in India was an end to public action on the basis of ascriptive identity—in American parlance, a color-blind society, and, in Indian terms, a society free of casteism—the pursuit of equality has taken a rather different form. Although subordination is no longer the norm, or at least it is no longer the exclusive norm, ascriptive identities have not been abolished. Race and caste groups still encounter other race and caste groups as groups, but the behavior, the rights, the claims of the former subordinates, are no longer limited and rigidly specified.

The paths to status enhancement in India and the United States have been somewhat different.[103] But in both, intergroup interactions are

103. For recent American trends, see Howard Schuman et al., *Racial Attitudes in America* (Cambridge: Harvard University Press, 1985); Reynolds Farley, *Blacks and Whites: Narrowing the Gap?* (Cambridge: Harvard University Press, 1984). For two aspects of the complex trends in India, see Marc Galanter, *Competing Equalities: Law and the*

more complex and less predictably unequal than they formerly were. Groups have more autonomy than before, and now they function in a system of unranked relations that has far greater legitimacy than the former system of subordination could have in the egalitarian ideological climate of the present day. Race and caste groups remain self-conscious entities capable of political mobilization and collectivities to which members can repair for mutual support.

Since not everyone believed that race and caste groups were truly equal, the initial consensus that race and caste should disappear was far from complete in the United States and India. The persistence of race and caste groups owes something to the incompleteness of the consensus and to the persistence of discriminatory behavior.[104] But continuing inequality is not the whole explanation for the durability of ascriptive groups. For virtually everywhere—and especially in a mobile society like South Africa's—ethnicity serves a number of useful functions. These range from assistance far from home to a sense of familiarity and neighborliness, even fictive kinship, and diffuse obligations in what can otherwise be a rather unfriendly and impersonal world. More than this, there is a strong human tendency in a common environment for people to define themselves by contrast and to seek confirmation of their collective worth. It is no accident that, given an opportunity to evaluate themselves on a survey instrument, virtually all ethnic groups everywhere rank themselves first.[105] Nor is it surprising that, in the quest for collective well-being, ethnic groups should stereotype themselves and others, should feel closer to some groups, further from others, and even hostile to others.

These tendencies have been documented in scores of environments. They are as applicable to South Africa as to other countries, and they will persist long after apartheid is gone. No doubt the creation of the homelands has induced a good many Black South Africans to react by relegating their ethnic identity to the equivalent of their mental attic, putting it in deep storage. They reject the stigma of belonging to a "tribe,"

Backward Classes in India (Berkeley and Los Angeles: University of California Press, 1984); Owen M. Lynch, *The Politics of Untouchability: Social Mobility and Social Change in a City of India* (New York: Columbia University Press, 1969).

104. For surveys on White attitudes to racial integration in the United States over time, see Schuman et al., *Racial Attitudes in America*, pp. 74–75. For the early movements to abolish caste distinctions and the civil rights legislation that followed, see Galanter, *Competing Equalities*, pp. 23–44.

105. For perfect South African consistency with the general rule, see J. W. Mann, "Attitudes towards Ethnic Groups," in Adam, ed., *South Africa: Sociological Perspectives*, pp. 53–54. Further South African evidence on this is reviewed in Chapter 2.

an affiliation regarded as premodern, even "primitive." In this respect, apartheid has ill prepared South Africans for the future. Ethnic affiliations coexist very nicely with modernity all around the world. If the Québecois, the Basques, the Walloons, the Sinhalese, the Berbers, the Yoruba, the Ilocano, and the Kikuyu can all retain their ethnicity, why cannot South Africans equally belong to an array of ethnic groups, recognizing full well that, without precautions, interethnic competition can turn to severe conflict? The only reasons I can think of are the regime's effort to use such affiliations for its own purposes and the overarching present significance of color and race rather than ethnicity per se.

Nevertheless, affiliations now in the attic can be dusted off. Politics all over Africa—and nearly all over the world—has a strong ethnic component. With some qualifications, what is true of Zimbabwe, Nigeria, Zambia, Kenya, and Mauritania is also likely to be true of South Africa.

If that is so, is the aspiration to a nonracial, nonethnic South Africa doomed? If that aspiration requires that racial and ethnic groups disappear from the social and political landscape, this they will surely not do. If, however, the aspiration means that no official categories and no state institutions based on racial and ethnic groups shall be erected, that is an aspiration quite compatible with life even in a thoroughly plural society. As we shall see, it is possible to devise a range of political innovations apt for South Africa's ascriptive conflicts and located well within the narrower range of acceptability dictated by South Africa's ideological conflicts. There are nonracial, nonethnic institutions available to serve the multiracial, multiethnic society that South Africa will be for the foreseeable future.

CHAPTER TWO

A Divided Society

South Africa is appropriately viewed, I said earlier, as a society characterized by ascriptively determined superior-subordinate relations. That
is the nature of racial domination. South African society is also characterized by ethnic cleavages within the racial categories. Underpinning
both sets of cleavages are distinctive intergroup attitudes and orientations. Although I shall spend more time here on the neglected cleavages
within the various racial groups, it is worth emphasizing as well that
interracial differences are also likely to persist.

BLACK AND WHITE: SOME PRELIMINARIES

In a survey of White elites conducted in the late 1960s, Heribert Adam
found decidedly negative attitudes toward Africans. Strong majorities
of Afrikaner officials and English entrepreneurs labeled "true" statements to the effect that there are important differences between "Bantu"
and Whites, that the "average Bantu is a child, some hundreds of years
behind the white man in development," and that some Black-White
differences are biologically determined.[1] Agree-disagree questions have
some methodological problems attached to them; however, there is no
mistaking the bigoted character of most of the replies. A decade later, a

1. Heribert Adam, "The South African Power Elite: A Survey of Ideological Commitment," in Heribert Adam, ed., *South Africa: Sociological Perspectives* (London: Oxford
University Press, 1971), pp. 73–102.

large-scale study by Hanf, Weiland, and Vierdag, which generally asked different questions, nevertheless suggested the emergence of somewhat more flexible attitudes and, on the one question overlapping Adam's—racial job reservations that excluded Blacks—produced dramatically different results.[2]

Change, then, was occurring on some dimensions, but virtually every study shows unfavorable White attitudes toward Blacks.[3] Afrikaner attitudes are more unfavorable than English attitudes are. Blacks generally reciprocate Afrikaner hostility—indeed, to an extreme degree—although, as we shall see, they are far more favorably disposed toward English-speaking Whites.

We shall review these studies shortly. The best place to do so is in the consideration of African attitudes, because the attitudes of groups toward each other are closely interrelated. For example, we shall observe that, even as Black hostility to Afrikaners was growing, Black views of English-speaking Whites were remarkably friendly. Some categories of Black respondents evaluated the attributes of English speakers more favorably than those of any other group, including other Black groups. By the same token, as Afrikaner views of Africans hardened, their views of White English speakers, Coloureds, and Indians softened. All of this shows the interplay of interracial and interethnic attitudes and relations in South Africa. The results also show that White and Black (especially if Black includes Coloureds and Indians) are not quite the categories in which respondents think. The strongest reciprocal hostility is between Afrikaners and Africans.

In any case, for the moment, it is obvious that, if attitudes are any guide, a nonracial society is not around the corner. Neither is a nonethnic society. Much of the future of South Africa lies in the interplay of race and ethnicity and in responses to these affiliations that do not wish them away.

2. Theodor Hanf et al., *South Africa: The Prospects of Peaceful Change* (London: Rex Collings, 1981), pp. 127–241. On job reservations, compare ibid., pp. 133–34, 213, with Adam, "The South African Power Elite," pp. 87–88.

3. Ans E. M. Appelgryn and Johan M. Nieuwoudt, "Relative Deprivation and the Ethnic Attitudes of Blacks and Afrikaans-speaking Whites in South Africa," *Journal of Social Psychology* 128, no. 3 (June 1988): 311–23; J. M. Nieuwoudt and C. Plug, "South African Ethnic Attitudes: 1973 to 1978," *Journal of Social Psychology* 121, 2d half (December 1983): 163–71; Graham C. Kinloch, "Racial Attitudes in South Africa: A Review," *Genetic, Social, and General Psychology Monographs* 111, no. 3 (August 1985): 261–81; Patrick C. L. Heaven, "A Historical Survey and Assessment of Research into Race Attitudes in South Africa: 1930–1975," *South African Journal of Sociology* 16 (September 1977): 68–75.

A NEW CONTEXT

In Asia and Africa, prior to independence, ethnic differences among the subject peoples generally were muted. Following independence, however, the context and the issues changed. With independence secured, the question was who in the new state would control it. At that point, ethnic differences became relevant, contradicting the expectations of those who saw in anti-colonial movements the makings of enduring transethnic nationalisms. As Anderson, von der Mehden, and Young have written, ". . . the transcendent obligation of resistance to the colonizer did largely obscure the vitality of ethnicity as a basis of social solidarity. Only in the cold dawn of independence did the potency of this factor begin to become clear." All over Africa, they point out,

> scholars, highly sympathetic to the aspirations of African nationalism, looked naturally for the factors of cohesion rather than for elements of potential discord. "Tribalism" was a retrograde force of merely historical interest; the future belonged to the "detribalized." The inevitable urbanization and industrialization would create a social system dominated by economic classes . . . . "Class formation," wrote one distinguished anthropologist, "tolls the knell of tribalism."[4]

For a brief but intense period in the 1960s, a literature on "nation building" emerged. The problems of nation building were generally conceived as entailing construction of an institutional infrastructure, creating symbols of national identity, fostering economic development, and closing the perceived gap between "modern" elites and "traditional" masses. The problems posed by ethnic, racial, religious, and linguistic pluralism that often came to dominate post-colonial politics were largely neglected.[5]

The same flavor of neglect is now in the South African air. The struggle against apartheid has created illusions about the homogeneous character of a future South Africa. Part of the problem derives from linear,

4. Charles W. Anderson et al., *Issues of Political Development*, 2d ed. (Englewood Cliffs, N.J.: Prentice-Hall, 1974), p. 29, quoting Daniel F. McCall, "Dynamics of Urbanization in Africa," *Annals* 298 (March 1955): 151–60, at 158.

5. This depiction, of course, has a certain element of caricature about it, but it also resembles the writing of the period under discussion. See, e.g., Karl W. Deutsch and William J. Foltz, eds., *Nation-Building* (New York: Atherton Press, 1963); Wendell Bell and Ivar Oxaal, *Decisions of Nationhood: Political and Social Development in the Caribbean*, Social Science Foundation and Department of International Relations Monograph Series (Denver, Colo.: University of Denver, 1964); Leonard Binder, "National Integration and Political Development," *American Political Science Review* 58, no. 3 (September 1964): 622–31.

Ethnic divisions will become more important, coexisting with and, for some purposes, even superseding racial divisions. That has certainly been the experience of those Caribbean societies that were doubly divided—first on the basis of a color hierarchy like South Africa's and second on the basis of African or East Indian ancestry. When universal suffrage undercut the position of Whites, the focus of conflict shifted rapidly to tensions between Afro-Caribbeans and East Indians.[8]

As I have indicated, the underlying logic is the logic of context. Who else is in the common environment? Which collectivities are similar, and which are different? Whose interests seem similar, and whose seem incompatible? Through half-perceptual, half-conscious judgments of this sort, group affinities and disparities are discerned, and group alignments and juxtapositions are established. South Africa is beginning a period of rapid change that will alter the context but will not render obsolete judgments like these, which lie at the core of ethnic group formation and re-formation and the ethnic politics that follows.

Second, the arguments that have been made are based on the behavior of selected sectors: certain urban areas but not others (Soweto but not the Durban or Pretoria townships, for example), trade unionists but not dwellers in the so-called homelands, and so on.[9] Research on rural South Africans is difficult, but they are far more likely, as we shall see, to have retained their ethnic loyalties at this stage than are urban Blacks, who have been on the front lines against apartheid.

Third, the data available on Black ethnicity throughout South Africa, when pieced together, suggest that it is generally similar to ethnicity elsewhere in Africa and in much of Asia. On the whole, ethnicity is a fairly strongly held affiliation that is reflected in a variety of attitudinal and behavioral measures of group difference, an affiliation that can, under certain circumstances, give rise to serious conflict.

Fourth, the argument predicated on the artificial character of some Black South African ethnic divisions is based on a non sequitur—that contrived groups cannot become serious antagonists.[10] In the discourse

8. See, e.g., Ralph R. Premdas, "Politics of Preference in the Caribbean: The Case of Guyana," in N. Nevitte and P. Kennedy, eds., *Ethnic Preference and Public Policy in Developing States* (Boulder, Colo.: Lynne Rienner, 1986), pp. 155–87.

9. For the suggestion of a fairly strong rural-urban cleavage based on a study of self-rankings, see A. A. Dubb et al., "African Attitudes in Town: The Search for Precision," *African Studies* 32, no. 2 (1973): 85–97. For further evidence of anti-urban ideology, see P. A. McAllister, "Political Aspects of Xhosa Beer Drink Oratory," *English in Africa* 15, no. 1 (May 1988): 83–95.

10. The assumption that, but for the South African state, there might not be any ethnic groups in South Africa is widespread in South African academic discourse. For a

developmental thinking, rather than contextual thinking about identity. Philip M. Mayer's view of urban African identity is rather shared. "The evidence suggests that it is too late for [homeland] cal ethnicity" to take hold among Africans in town, he conten place is likely to be taken more and more by Black ethnicity." the context changes, however, alternative levels of identity can I more relevant. Similarly, it is argued that the emergence of c cultural norms in urban areas precludes the emergence of ethnic on the implicit but certainly unproved assumption that a stron of cultural difference is a necessary condition for such rivalry. Africa could well enter a period of fundamental change with tl mind-set that prevailed at the time of African decolonization, pared for the ethnic diversity that will undoubtedly be one of spicuous characteristics.

To be sure, there are bits and pieces of evidence that sup position that Black ethnicity is unlikely to have significant poli lience. Progressive South Africans, steeped in the anti-aparthei ment, point especially to the nonracial, nonethnic ideology of th to the solidarity of various groups in the movement, to nonco tendencies in places like Soweto, and to the contrived nature c identities in South Africa, resulting from the regime's manipul ethnicity for its own ends.

The evidence, however, is not convincing, for four reasons. rests on the logic of changing contexts. The second relates to tl tive character of the data on which the conclusions are based. T derives from the thrust of the data that a more wide-rangin elicits. The fourth in lies the propensity for even invented ider develop their own resonance. I shall take these reasons up briefly

First of all, in South Africa today, the overriding issue is, o race. The context of White domination is hardly the best test division. While racial divisions are highly salient, every incentiv to Black solidarity, and even then Black solidarity is incomplet White domination is past, a different set of incentives will ta

6. Philip M. Mayer, "Class, Status, and Ethnicity as Perceived by Johann ricans," in Leonard Thompson and Jeffrey Butler, eds., *Change in Contempo Africa* (Berkeley and Los Angeles: University of California Press, 1975), p. 15 dorsement, see Martin E. West, "The Urban African Population of South / Robert M. Price and Carl G. Rosberg, eds., *The Apartheid Regime: Political I Racial Domination* (Berkeley: University of California Institute of Internation 1980), pp. 141–45.
7. Mayer, "Class, Status, and Ethnicity," p. 155.

of the South African regime, there has been a tendency to describe ethnic differences among Black groups as if they were given and immutable. At an earlier stage, ethnic affiliations might well have been depicted as deriving from God's plan, the same plan that ostensibly divided the world into races. Research on ethnicity makes it abundantly clear that ethnic groups are by no means given, that ethnic identities have an element of malleability, that groups form and re-form their boundaries.[11] In South Africa, for example, the Afrikaners are an amalgam of several European components; the long-standing boundary between the English and Afrikaans groups shows increasing signs of porosity, as I shall note below; the "Coloured" category is assuredly a human product, frequently described as "an artificial community created by the official race classification policies of South Africa";[12] and various Black ethnic groups are also "very much a human construct, a social product . . . ."[13]

Race, too, is a construct, but in South Africa it is, nonetheless, highly significant. It is a conceptual mistake to leap from an understanding of ethnicity as a construct to a conclusion that ethnicity is politically insignificant. In many parts of Africa, there are ethnic groups whose identity can be traced to official policies, missionary categorizations, and encounters with neighboring groups. These "artificial" creations are often significant political actors.[14]

The same can be true in South Africa. Tsonga (Shangaan) ethnicity, for example, was initially a product of early European classification, missionary work, later government policy, the desire of members of the category to benefit from largess distributed along ethnic lines, mobilization to counter that of more powerful and centralized groups (such as Zulu and Swazi), and the establishment of a Tsonga Bantustan named Gazankulu, created in 1973 and eventually involved in border disputes with a neighboring Pedi homeland, Lebowa. The Tsonga are neither a group existing from time immemorial nor a merely ephemeral product

---

fairly typical taste, see Wilmot G. James, "Reinforcing Ethnic Boundaries: South Africa in the 1980s," in Susan Olzak and Joane Nagel, eds., *Competitive Ethnic Relations* (London: Academic Press, 1986), pp. 137–50.

11. See, e.g., Frederik Barth, ed., *Ethnic Groups and Boundaries* (Boston: Little, Brown, 1969).

12. Albert J. Venter, "The South African Plural Society: Reflections and Musings towards Its Understanding," *Plural Societies* 19, no. 1 (September 1989): 1–20, at 7.

13. Patrick Harries, "Exclusion, Classification and Internal Colonialism: The Emergence of Ethnicity among the Tsonga-Speakers of South Africa," in Leroy Vail, ed., *The Creation of Tribalism in Southern Africa* (Berkeley and Los Angeles: University of California Press, 1989), p. 83.

14. See, e.g., the classic treatment of the emergence of the Bangala by Crawford Young, *Politics in the Congo* (Princeton: Princeton University Press, 1965), chap. 11.

of Bantustan politics. In the judicious view of Patrick Harries, "it is unlikely that the abandonment of apartheid and the Bantustan system will end the regional underdevelopment which, through the politicization of cultural differences, is one of the major causes of ethnic exclusivism."[15] Neither will the end of apartheid diminish the political significance of ethnicity among other Black groups.

In 1978, a sample of Black men in Soweto with at least mid-high-school education was asked: "What problems do you think might arise in the future if black people should rule South Africa?" Soweto is the most successful Black ethnic melting pot in South Africa, and better educated respondents, such as these, are generally less likely to provide ethnic responses to identity questions. Soweto after the 1976 violence was an angry place. Pan-Africanism and other versions of transethnic Black affiliations held considerable sway. It is all the more remarkable, therefore, that, for this open-ended question, the largest fraction of respondents, 37 percent, named intra-Black ethnic tensions as a future problem.[16]

These results are discussed by Hanf, Weiland, and Vierdag,[17] who postulate that apprehension of Black ethnic conflict underlies the frequently expressed Black rejection of unqualified Black majority rule options in sample surveys—a survey result we shall examine in Chapter 3. Here, however, the aim is not to explore this possible relationship. Instead, in most of the remainder of this chapter, I simply wish to inquire into evidence bearing on the perception of the Soweto respondents who anticipated Black ethnic tensions. How is Black ethnicity manifested, and how might it be manifested in a future South Africa?

AFRICAN ETHNIC ATTITUDES

In 1986, the estimated population of South Africa, including all of the homelands, was about 33 million, consisting of approximately 24.0 million Africans, 2.8 million Coloureds, 0.9 million Indians, 3.0 million Afrikaners, and 1.9 million other Whites (principally British, but also Portuguese, Jews, Germans, and Greeks). The African population was divided into nine main, linguistically based ethnic groups. Very rough, rounded figures for the nine groups are provided in Table 1.[18]

15. Harries, "Exclusion, Classification and Internal Colonialism," p. 110.
16. Lawrence Schlemmer, "Change in South Africa: Opportunities and Constraints," in Price and Rosberg, eds., *The Apartheid Regime,* p. 278.
17. *South Africa,* pp. 439–41.
18. That these are estimates, rather than conclusive figures, can be ascertained by

TABLE 1. ESTIMATED AFRICAN POPULATION OF
SOUTH AFRICA BY ETHNIC GROUP, 1986

Ethnic Group	Number (in millions)	Approximate Percentage of Total African Population
Zulu	6.5	27
Xhosa	5.5	23
Tswana	3.3	14
Pedi (North Sotho)	3.0	13
Sotho (South Sotho)	2.0	8
Tsonga (Shangaan)	1.5	6
Swazi	1.0	4
Venda	0.7	3
Ndebele	0.5	2
Total	24.0	100

The enumerated categories are by no means perfectly demarcated, either externally or internally. Boundaries between them are not always sharp. Like ethnic groups elsewhere, most of the South African groups could easily be subdivided into segments. Subgroup identification with the overarching group is frequently imperfect,[19] and conflicts among subgroups are often serious. The Xhosa speakers, for example, would include Xhosa, Pondo, Thembu, and Mfengu, among others. But this is not unusual in ethnicity. The category of English-speaking Whites, for example, also embraces considerable heterogeneity, but that does not render the category politically insignificant.

From Table 1, it is obvious that the two largest amalgams, Zulu and Xhosa, alone comprise about half of the African population, with, respectively, 27 percent and 23 percent of the total. In politics, these two groups are especially important. They also have relatively homogeneous

consulting different estimates, such as those contained in Marianne Cornevin, "Populations noires d'Afrique du Sud," *Afrique Contemporaine,* no. 141 (January 1987): 32–49, at 36. For present purposes, however, these estimates are sufficient.

19. For an example, see Jean Comaroff, *Body of Power, Spirit of Resistance: The Culture and History of a South African People* (Chicago: University of Chicago Press, 1985), pp. 38–39. For historical heterogeneity at the subgroup level and below, see Peter Delius, *The Land Belongs to Us: The Pedi Polity, the Boers and the British in the Nineteenth-Century Transvaal* (Berkeley and Los Angeles: University of California Press, 1984).

home areas, so that surveys in those areas yield responses that are more or less ethnically identifiable.

Consider first an unpublished but important survey administered in 1986 to a large female African sample in four areas: Soweto; Pretoria and the industrial Reef; Durban; and the Eastern Cape.[20] Although their ethnic mix is different, Soweto and Pretoria, both in the Transvaal, are heterogeneous areas, with many migrants. Durban, in Natal, is about 90 percent Zulu, and the Eastern Cape is Xhosa.[21]

The sample was asked an identity question, "Would you say you are first of all . . . ," and there followed three choices: an ethnic group response such as Zulu or Xhosa, a "Black" response, and a nonracial "South African" response. The responses differed markedly by area. In Soweto, the most frequent response, provided by 46.0 percent, was "South African," followed by "Black" (33.6 percent) and then various ethnic responses (20.4 percent). On the Reef and in the Pretoria townships, the rank order of responses was completely different: 40.9 percent said "Black," 29.9 percent ethnic, 29.3 percent "South African." The rank order in Durban was different from these two, and it was different again in the Eastern Cape.

Since Durban and the Eastern Cape are largely homogeneous, it is instructive to contrast their responses, depicted in Table 2. The largely Zulu respondents of Durban gave an ethnic response about three times as frequently as the largely Xhosa respondents of the Eastern Cape. (The Zulu figures may actually have been higher, because the small non-Zulu minority in Durban, which is mainly Xhosa-speaking, may have provided responses more like those of the Eastern Cape.) For the Xhosa respondents of the Eastern Cape, the "South African" response was over three times as frequent as for the Durban Zulu respondents, and the "Black" response was significantly higher as well.

This pattern was repeated in responses to a question asking, "To which of these regional groups do you feel you belong?" The choices ranged from one's township to one's homeland, to one's city, to South Africa as a whole, and to Africa as a whole. The pan-African response was three to four times as frequent in the Eastern Cape as anywhere else (23.3 percent, compared to 3.7 percent to 6.7 percent elsewhere).

20. This survey was administered by Markinor to a sample of 800 respondents in the various metropolitan areas. I am indebted to Nick Green of Markinor for making a copy of the results available to me.
21. For figures on the ethnic composition of Soweto, Durban, and Pretoria, see Hanf et al., *South Africa*, p. 266.

TABLE 2.   GROUP IDENTITY AMONG FEMALE
AFRICANS IN FOUR METROPOLITAN AREAS OF
SOUTH AFRICA, 1986
(N = 800)

Response to Identity Question	Durban (%)	Reef / Pretoria (%)	Soweto (%)	Eastern Cape (%)
Ethnic	55.0	29.9	20.4	19.2
Black	33.9	40.9	33.6	43.3
South African	11.0	29.3	46.0	37.5
Total	99.9	100.1	100.0	100.0

SOURCE: Adapted from Markinor, "Lifestyle for Markinor" (1986; unpublished survey).
NOTE: Totals may not equal 100 because of rounding.

The Durban sample was at the lowest end here, with only 3.7 percent naming Africa as a whole. More than a quarter of the Durban respondents gave their homeland, compared to about 10 percent of the remainder of the sample. Only 15.6 percent of the Durban people named South Africa as a whole, compared to 43.4 percent in Soweto, 47.5 percent in Pretoria and on the Reef, and 36.7 percent in the Eastern Cape.

Too much weight should not be put on any one survey. The exclusively female sample is one limitation. Another is the urban focus. Like many surveys of Black South Africans, this one does not tap rural responses. For present purposes, however, this is no real shortcoming. On the contrary, the findings can be interpreted to suggest that, even among those with a similar urban experience, ethnic differences in response patterns stand out. Such differences would likely stand out more decisively among rural respondents. A hint to this effect is that poorer and older respondents in this sample tended to give more parochial and more ethnically focused responses.

Especially prominent in the survey is a degree of polarity between Xhosa in the Eastern Cape and Zulu in Durban. Zulu responses are markedly more parochial, more place oriented, assuredly more ethnically focused, and less universalistic. Xhosa responses are more South African, more pan-African, less tied to locality. It is notable that Xhosa responses in the Eastern Cape mention homeland ties only about as often as do all respondents in Soweto or the Pretoria-Reef area, even though Xhosa in the Eastern Cape are in or near what some might plausibly consider their home areas, whereas many of the Transvaal respondents live far from what they might consider their home areas, and many of their home-place ties are greatly attenuated by now.

This is not, of course, to equate Zulu ethnic-identity and locality responses to the two questions with Zulu ethnocentrism or necessarily to exempt Xhosa from ethnocentrism on the basis of their responses that refer to a wider identity and a wider field. The responses, however, do suggest different approaches to these questions, different conceptions of correct answers to them, perhaps different foci of identity.

As I shall point out, the Eastern Cape, with its long history of intense and often hostile contacts with White invaders, is the center of resistance movements and the center of ANC-UDF ideology. Natal has generally been peripheral to these movements. The Natal Indian Congress (NIC), rather than any African organization, has been perhaps the most important component of the UDF in that province.[22] Natal is the center of what has become a separate, Zulu-based mass organization, Inkatha—albeit an organization that does not necessarily command an uncontested hold on Zulu loyalty, particularly in urban areas and certainly not in urban areas of the Transvaal. One consequence is that the survey tells us nothing about what Zulu responses are in the Transvaal, where there are many Zulu, or what Xhosa responses are in the Transvaal, although there are many fewer Xhosa there. Despite these reservations, the polarity of the responses is a revealing piece of evidence that needs to be matched against other pieces of evidence: it is no more, but it is no less either.

This survey put the choices more explicitly than most others, but its results are congruent with others, including one that asked an open-ended question of a sample of Transvaal township students: "When asked what group do you belong to, what do you answer?" Zulu gave the highest proportion of ethnic responses, 24 percent, and Xhosa the lowest, 7 percent, with the median of all groups in the mid-teens.[23]

22. A circumstance that occasioned the remark of Mangosuthu Buthelezi, leader of Inkatha, that prominent among the UDF affiliates in Natal was the NIC, composed of "a brand of Indian who is poison to the black struggle for liberation." Quoted in Carole Cooper et al., *Race Relations Survey, 1987 / 88* (Johannesburg: South African Institute of Race Relations, 1988), p. 33.

23. Mark Orkin, " 'A Divided Struggle': Alienation, Ideology, and Social Control among Black Students in South Africa," *Journal of Intercultural Studies,* 4, no. 3 (1983): 69–98, at 76.

Again, the contrast is marked, although the total range of difference is relatively modest.

The matter goes considerably beyond questions of identity. There are also Xhosa-Zulu attitudinal contrasts revealed by surveys. On some central political issues, Zulu and Xhosa are out of step with each other.

Giliomee and Schlemmer present the results of a survey of a sample of Black coal miners in 1987, in which respondents were asked whether they preferred undifferentiated majority rule or either of two "arrangements for multiracial power sharing."[24] Although most of the sample preferred majority rule over power sharing, by an average of 27 percent, Zulu were below average, at 18 percent, and Xhosa were considerably above average, at 39 percent. This does not imply that Zulu are more conservative, for when a sample of Black industrial workers in seventeen locations was asked to choose a description of their feelings about the South African political situation, 62 percent of Zulu respondents, compared to 44 percent of Xhosa, 45 percent of Sotho, and 30 percent of other groups, chose the "angry and impatient" label.[25] Controls for education, urbanization, age, or other variables did not change the results by ethnicity. It would not be amiss to conclude that Zulu, Xhosa, and perhaps Sotho have the highest levels of political consciousness, but that consciousness is expressed differently by the two largest groups.

An important qualification relates to location. Given an ethnic or Black alternative, the results vary in Soweto. The question was, "If all black people voted in South Africa, [name of respondent's group] would be small in number and other groups might have more power in government. Would people like you feel weak and insecure or do you agree with the statement 'blacks are all one people—it would not matter at all'?" Only 24 percent of Soweto Xhosa and 21 percent of Soweto Zulu took the "weak and insecure" option. (Zulu are by far the largest group in Soweto, about a third of its population.) Rural Xhosa, Eastern Cape Xhosa, and rural Zulu, however, selected that option at between 44 percent and 50 percent—a significant fraction given both the counter-ideological wording of the choice and the homogeneous (presumably secure) area in which those respondents lived. But 64 percent of Zulu migrant workers chose the "weak and insecure" response, rather than the "blacks are all one people" response.

24. Hermann Giliomee and Lawrence Schlemmer, *From Apartheid to Nation-Building* (Cape Town: Oxford University Press, 1989), p. 167.
25. Ibid., p. 168.

ORGANIZATIONAL AFFILIATIONS
AND AFRICAN ETHNICITY

Another matter on which ethnic differences emerge relates to partisan and leadership preferences among Blacks. These, however, cannot be understood fully without understanding the ethnic composition of parties and movements.

It is, of course, well known that Inkatha is largely a Zulu organization centered on the nonindependent KwaZulu homeland. Led by Chief Mangosuthu Buthelezi, it is the lineal descendant of the Zulu National Congress, founded in 1928, but it has had wider ambitions. Increasingly, however, Inkatha seems unable to secure support from other homeland leaders and members of Black ethnic groups that gave Buthelezi strong support previously: Ndebele, Swazi, Tswana, and Venda.[26]

Much less well known is the ethnically skewed leadership composition of two of the main panethnic extraparliamentary organizations, the African National Congress and the Pan Africanist Congress. In both cases, Xhosa speakers have been disproportionately represented at the top.

Despite its nonracial ideology, the ANC, as noted in Chapter 1, had no non-African members on its National Executive Committee until 1985. After 1985, it had two Whites, two Coloureds, and two Indians. Of the remaining twenty members, as of mid-1989, ten were Xhosa, five Tswana, four Pedi, and one Zulu. In short, fully half the Black leadership of the ANC was Xhosa-speaking, which means that Xhosa were overrepresented by a factor of about 2.2. Zulu were dramatically underrepresented, by a factor of more than 5.[27]

The most conspicuous ANC leaders are also disproportionately Xhosa. Nelson Mandela, Walter F. Sisulu, Oliver Tambo, Govan and Thabo Mbeki, Chris Hani, and Pallo Jordan are all Xhosa speakers. Of the major future contenders for power, only Joe Modise and one or two others are not Xhosa. This imbalance and the factionalism related to it

26. See Hanf et al., *South Africa*, p. 355.
27. These calculations, and those that follow on the PAC, are mine. Data were supplied by several South African informants. I am particularly grateful to Pierre du Toit and W. J. Breytenbach for coordinating the data gathering and to Steven Wilkinson for double-checking ethnic affiliations from written and oral sources. Since Black ethnicity in politics is rarely discussed, and data on identity are hard to come by, it is possible that I have mislabeled the identity of one or two leaders, who, for example, may be products of mixed marriages. But the overall tendencies are undeniable.

have been subjects of concern within the ANC.[28] There is thus support for the rather casual—and, even then, rarely stated—judgment that the ANC "has been dominated by Xhosas . . . ."[29] Following coups in the two Xhosa "homelands," Transkei and Ciskei—the latter shortly after the release of Nelson Mandela from prison in 1990—the new military rulers made clear their alignment with the ANC.[30]

The leadership composition of the PAC is roughly similar to that of the ANC. Taking its Central Committee and principal foreign representatives together, there were, as of mid-1989, a total of nineteen members, two of whom were Coloured and one of whom was Indian. The remaining sixteen were as follows: ten Xhosa, three Zulu, two Tswana, and one Venda. A clear majority was Xhosa—nearly a threefold overrepresentation. Xhosa are also prominent in AZAPO.[31]

As I shall explain later, there are important historical reasons for Xhosa to be in the forefront of radical anti-regime activity. For now, the situation is unlikely to change dramatically within either of these movements.

After a long period of factional disputation, culminating in an upheaval in its Central Committee in 1987, the PAC settled into a more stable period, during which it increased its standing with foreign governments.[32] Further upheaval would be very costly.

The ethnic balance of leadership in the ANC was also related to the balance of new recruits who moved across the border. This in turn was largely a function of developments inside South Africa, which provided waves of recruits. These waves were, in some degree, ethnically differentiated, depending on the location of the key events propelling the move into exile. After the Soweto rising of 1976, there was an exodus of youth from Johannesburg townships to ANC training camps. In the mid-1980s, there was another flow of recruits, this time disproportion-

28. See *Africa Confidential* (London), January 12, 1990, p. 3; ibid., February 23, 1990, p. 4; ibid., April 20, 1990, p. 3.

29. Graham Leach, *South Africa: No Easy Path to Peace* (London: Routledge & Kegan Paul, 1986), p. 111.

30. See *Argus* (Cape Town), March 5, 1990.

31. Of the AZAPO officers elected in 1990, seven were Africans, three of them Xhosa. The PAC has reportedly made a point of emphasizing its diverse composition, contrasting it with alleged Xhosa domination of the ANC. *Africa Confidential,* April 6, 1990, p. 8.

32. Gary van Staden, "Return of the Prodigal Son: Prospects for a Revival of the Pan Africanist Congress" (paper presented at the Research Colloquium of the Political Science Association of South Africa, October 6–7, 1988). For the background, see Tom Lodge, *Black Politics in South Africa since 1945* (London: Longman, 1983), pp. 305–17. See also *Africa Confidential,* October 16, 1985, p. 7.

TABLE 3.   AFRICAN SUPPORT FOR POLITICAL
TENDENCIES IN THREE AREAS OF SOUTH AFRICA, 1986

Political Tendency Supported	Zulu in Natal (%)	Zulu in the PWV (%)	Non-Zulu in the PWV (%)	Non-Zulu in the Cape (%)
Buthelezi and Inkatha	34	11	3	0
Mandela and the ANC	19	29	27	62

SOURCE: Adapted from Mark Orkin, *Disinvestment, the Struggle, and the Future: What Black South Africans Really Think* (Johannesburg: Ravan Press, 1986; pamphlet), p. 40. The original version contains choices for Bishop Desmond Tutu and for the UDF and radical groups, including the PAC.

NOTE: PWV refers to the large industrial area of Pretoria-Witwatersrand-Vereeniging, located in the Transvaal.

ately from the Xhosa-speaking townships of the Cape Province. The Cape was the location of the school and rent boycotts that triggered the 1984–86 resistance movement. There the UDF also emerged most strongly.[33] It has been asserted that rivalries within the second echelon of the ANC, particularly between Joe Modise and Chris Hani, involve to some extent their mobilization of, respectively, "the Jo'burgers" and other Transvaalers, on the one hand, and the newer militants from the Cape, on the other.[34] In considerable measure, these would be ethnically differentiated support bases. How reliable such accounts are is open to question, but there seems little doubt that the influx of the 1980s was disproportionately Xhosa.

Against this background, Xhosa and Zulu responses to survey questions about identity are more comprehensible. When Xhosa respond that they are Black or South African, they are providing an answer very much in line with the officially declared policy of the ANC and the PAC, with either of which it is easy for Xhosa to identify, given their leadership composition. More than that, of course, such a response re-

33. See Steven Friedman, "Black Politics at the Crossroads," South African Institute of Race Relations, PD1 / 86 (Johannesburg, January 2, 1986; mimeo.), p. 9.

34. W. J. Breytenbach, *The ANC: Future Prognosis,* University of Stellenbosch Institute for Futures Research, Occasional Paper no. 4 (July 1989), pp. 24–26; Belinda Barrett, "A Profile of the African National Congress (ANC)" (Inkatha Institute of South Africa, May 1989; mimeo.), pp. 24, 60–63; *Africa Confidential,* August 12, 1988, pp. 1–3. See also *Africa Confidential,* July 6, 1983, pp. 1–4; ibid., December 11, 1985, pp. 1–5.

TABLE 4.   AFRICAN SUPPORT FOR POLITICAL
TENDENCIES IN SOUTH AFRICA BY ZULU AND
XHOSA ETHNICITY, 1977

Political Tendency Supported	Durban Zulu (%)	Xhosa (%)
Buthelezi	78	23
ANC	8	25

SOURCE: Adapted from Theodor Hanf et al., *South Africa: The Prospects of Peaceful Change* (London: Rex Collings, 1981), p. 355.

flects the exigencies of the present struggle—including the preeminence of race over ethnicity—and its obvious battle lines, the state versus the mainly Black resistance. When Zulu provide a different response, it presumably signifies that they are, for understandable reasons, less wholly identified with ANC or PAC positions and that there may be more than one struggle and more than one set of cleavage lines.

The same contrasting responses are revealed in surveys that tap support for various political organizations. Consider support for Buthelezi and Inkatha versus support for Mandela and the ANC among Zulu in Natal and non-Zulu (essentially, Xhosa) in the Cape, as revealed in the 1986 survey depicted in Table 3. The ANC seems to have about as much support among Zulu in the Transvaal as it does among non-Zulu there. But drop out the two middle columns, and the contrasts between Zulu and Xhosa are striking. For Zulu in Natal, the ANC has some resonance, but much less than Inkatha has. For Xhosa in the Cape, Inkatha is anathema; and the ANC is supported by a strong majority.[35] Polarity is not too strong a word to use in characterizing these responses, which range from zero to 34 percent and from 19 percent to 62 percent.

The percentages just quoted show Buthelezi's support in decline, but this does not mitigate the Xhosa-Zulu difference. In the late 1970s, Buthelezi had more support in Natal, and the ANC had less in Natal. But Xhosa support was almost equally divided between Buthelezi and the ANC, as the 1977 comparison in Table 4 shows.

Although the respondent categories are not exactly the same, still the two tables together show that the exclusivity of Xhosa identification

35. See also Martin Meredith, "The Black Opposition," in Jesmond Blumenfeld, ed., *South Africa in Crisis* (London: Croom Helm for the Royal Institute of International Affairs, 1987), p. 87.

with the ANC has grown dramatically in a decade. The distance between the Xhosa position and the Zulu position is, despite growth in
ANC support in Natal, certainly no less than it was, particularly because Inkatha support has fallen off so completely in the Cape. In per-
centage-difference terms, the two groups were further apart in preferences in 1986 than in 1977. The average difference on each item was
36.0 points in 1977 and 38.5 in 1986. (The 1977 difference might have
been larger if, instead of Durban Zulu, the respondent category had
been Zulu in all of Natal.) And, as usual, the political preferences of
every other African ethnic group—Tswana, Pedi, Sotho, Tsonga, Swazi,
Venda, and Ndebele—fall in between those of the Durban Zulu and the
Xhosa.[36]

A survey conducted in 1984–85 by the Institute of Black Research
at the University of Natal confirms the Zulu-Xhosa divergence and adds
some further regional qualifications as well. A question about organizational support divided Africans into three cities and one township,
each of which represented a major region: Durban (Natal), Langa
(Western Cape), Johannesburg (Transvaal), and Port Elizabeth (Eastern
Cape). Inkatha received 55.5 percent support in Durban but 3.1 percent
in Johannesburg and virtually none anywhere else. The UDF had 51.0
percent in Port Elizabeth, 30.8 percent in Langa, 21.3 percent in Durban, and 12.7 percent in Johannesburg. The Eastern Cape was clearly
the most pro-UDF area. The three Black Consciousness or Africanist
groupings, AZAPO, the PAC, and the National Forum, were weak
everywhere (with a combined percentage share of 6.8 percent in Port
Elizabeth and Langa, practically no share in Durban) except the Johannesburg townships, where the three organizations received support of
15.6 percent, 15.2 percent, and 3.3 percent, respectively. ANC figures
were lower than in other recent surveys—their high was 27.1 percent in
Langa—but it is uncertain from the question whether respondents would
have felt free to name a then-illegal organization as an appropriate response.[37] Again, the difference between Natal and the Eastern Cape
stands out above all other differences.

Leadership ratings are an indication of consensus or dissensus. In the

36. With a single exception, the Pedi, who are slightly below even the Xhosa in their
enthusiasm for Buthelezi, but only by 3 percentage points. On every other response relating to the ANC or Buthelezi, Zulu and Xhosa form the extremes within which other
groups fall. See Hanf et al., *South Africa*, p. 355.

37. Though some, as indicated, named the PAC, which was then illegal. Institute of
Black Research, University of Natal, Durban, tables, based on a 1984–85 survey, from
an untitled forthcoming manuscript, table 2. Some figures are subject to final correction.

Eastern Cape, Mandela, the Reverend Allan Boesak, and Bishop Desmond Tutu are all "admired" by at least 94.6 percent of respondents, with "disliked" ratings of less than 5.0 percent each. In Durban, although Mandela still leads the pack, admiration for these three declines to an average of 67.0 percent. In Durban, Buthelezi is "admired" by 76.0 percent; elsewhere, he scores much lower, and, by now predictably, lowest by far in Port Elizabeth, with only 6.3 percent positive ratings and 65.4 percent negative. To put the point in terms of ratios of "admired" ratings to "disliked" ratings: in Durban, Buthelezi's ratio is + 4.3; in Port Elizabeth, it is − 10.4.[38]

Finally, a question asked how unfair laws could be changed. African responses varied enormously by city. In Durban, nine respondents out of ten chose "dialogue," "government reform," or "peaceful opposition." Only one in ten chose "extraparliamentary peaceful" or "violent" strategies. In Port Elizabeth, these preferences were turned upside down: more than nine out of ten chose the latter two responses (83.5 percent chose "extraparliamentary peaceful" and 10.2 percent "violent"). In Langa and in Johannesburg, responses were, once again, in-between, although Langa respondents tended to prefer softer options and Johannesburg respondents produced a 43.6 percent plurality for violence.[39]

All of these data illustrate what Mark Orkin has called "a divided struggle," and they show with special sharpness how the Xhosa and Zulu heartlands anchor two ends of a spectrum. The data on which I have drawn in this section are derived from surveys conducted by researchers of varying political inclinations. In addition to a market research organization, the data come from the work of Theodor Hanf and his colleagues, Lawrence Schlemmer, Mark Orkin, and Fatima Meer and her colleagues—researchers who are otherwise often at odds. Some of them have fought survey wars over whether Blacks prefer foreign investment or divestment and over whether Buthelezi still has a strong support base.[40] That their results are so congruent on ethnicity and political preference is, therefore, all the more significant.

The results are, moreover, congruent with long-standing patterns of

38. Ibid., table 68b.
39. Ibid., table 8.
40. See, e.g., Mark Orkin, *Disinvestment, the Struggle, and the Future: What Black South Africans Really Think* (Johannesburg: Ravan Press, 1986; pamphlet), pp. 5–28, 37–44, 62–67; Fatima Meer and Alan Reynolds, "Sample Survey of Perceptions of the Durban Unrest—August 1985," in Fatima Meer, ed., *Resistance in the Townships* (Durban: Madiba, 1989), p. 276.

organization. The Eastern Cape is the historic heartland of ANC organization. Although it had nationwide objectives, the ANC's best-organized protest, the Defiance Campaign of 1952, drew nearly three-quarters of its participants from the townships of the Eastern Cape, especially around the two main cities of Port Elizabeth and East London.[41] Port Elizabeth was, according to Tom Lodge, "consistently the strongest centre of ANC mobilization," and East London was "the second most important centre of the civil disobedience campaign in the country."[42] By contrast, the Defiance Campaign "had only limited success among Africans in Natal. There, the ANC still had few branches . . . ."[43] Although the ANC did manage to penetrate Natal in the next several years, no doubt aided by the election of a Natal Zulu, Albert Luthuli, as ANC national president in 1952, its following in the Eastern Cape has been consistently much stronger and better organized.

Underlying such patterns, and comparable patterns in Zimbabwe, Angola, Namibia, and Nigeria, where anti-colonial movements were divided along ethnic lines, is the intertwining of rational and affective elements in ethnicity. These elements affect followers as well as leaders, as Masipula Sithole has pointed out for Zimbabwe:

> It is the masses who respond negatively or positively to tribal ideology, otherwise politicians would not use this resource. The masses calculate that they stand to benefit one way or the other from "our leader" or "our son," or "our homeboy," or indeed "our tribesman" in power, or representing "us" in the corridors of power. Indeed the tribesman politician might appeal to the masses in this way, but the response is not based on simple emotional false-consciousness; the masses do give thought to the promises made and the base of their credibility. It all makes rational sense to them in the same way they would rationalize an economic argument. A homeboy will deliver the goods.[44]

That, despite such considerations, the extraparliamentary organizations have thus far achieved the degree of interethnic solidarity that they have

41. Tom Lodge, "Political Mobilization during the 1950s: An East London Case Study," in Shula Marks and Stanley Trapido, eds., *The Politics of Race, Class and Nationalism in Twentieth-Century South Africa* (London: Longman, 1987), p. 318.

42. Ibid., pp. 315, 323.

43. William Beinart, "Worker Consciousness, Ethnic Particularism and Nationalism: The Experience of a South African Migrant, 1930–1960," in Marks and Trapido, eds., *The Politics of Race, Class and Nationalism in Twentieth-Century South Africa*, p. 298.

44. Masipula Sithole, "The Salience of Ethnicity in African Politics: The Case of Zimbabwe," in Anand C. Paranjpe, ed., *Ethnic Identities and Prejudices: Perspectives from the Third World* (Leiden: E. J. Brill, 1986), p. 57.

is a measure of the overwhelming urgency of the struggle against apartheid.

EXOGAMY, SOCIAL DISTANCE, AND STEREOTYPES

So far, all we know is that the two largest groups, which are also disproportionately important in politics, occupy polar positions on some key questions of ethnic identity, ideology, organizational affiliation, leadership preferences, and strategic inclinations, and that one of these groups is significantly overrepresented and the other underrepresented in the leading extraparliamentary opposition organizations. Polarity may reflect or ripen into antipathy, but it is not necessarily the same thing.

The strongest case that ethnic differences will not ripen into recurrent ethnic conflict is made by examining data on Africans living in certain urban areas, above all Soweto. We have already seen that Soweto Zulu do not share a number of attitudes held by Durban Zulu. The passions against Inkatha and its leader can run rather deep among Zulu in Soweto. But a broader point can be made about Soweto. Africans in Soweto tend to hold quite liberal views toward ethnic intermarriage and toward ethnic differences in general.[45]

Historically, around Johannesburg, interethnic marriage has been a variable rather than a constant. As early as the 1930s, Ellen Hellmann found that nearly half of all marriages in Rooiyard, a small slum area in a Johannesburg suburb, were interethnic.[46] In the early 1950s, however, a much more wide-ranging and rather careful local government survey showed exogamy to be decidedly a minority trend in several townships on the west side of Johannesburg. Most people then married not only within their own language group but within their own subgroup as well. The exceptions concerned some specific patterns of intermarriage: Pedi men marrying Tswana women, Swazi men marrying Zulu women, and Shangaan marrying members of several other groups. For the rest, endogamy was practiced with considerable consistency.[47] Even today, exact rates of marrying out are hard to come by. As William

45. Hanf et al., *South Africa*, pp. 339–41.
46. Ellen Hellmann, *Rooiyard: A Sociological Survey of an Urban Native Slum Yard*, Rhodes-Livingstone Papers, no. 13 (Cape Town: Oxford University Press, 1948), p. 13.
47. See "Report of a Sample Survey of the Native Population Residing in the Western Areas of Johannesburg" (Non-European Affairs Department, City of Johannesburg, 1951; mimeo.), pp. 74, 78. For some later West African comparisons, see Margaret Peil, *Cities and Suburbs: Urban Life in West Africa* (New York: Africana, 1981), pp. 149–51.

Beinart says, they have been "little studied."[48] Nevertheless, within a generation, attitudes toward intermarriage have changed. Estimates put exogamy in Soweto in the range of one-third to one-half of all marriages.[49] Melville Leonard Edelstein's Soweto sample in 1971 consisted of elite pupils, 42 percent of whose parents had married exogamously.[50] These are very high rates indeed, but not incompatible with the persistence of ethnic identities.[51] Similarly, the extent to which actual political behavior reflects norms of interethnic accommodation is an open question. In precept, at least, "exclusive tribal patriotism seems to have almost died in Soweto," replaced by an ideology of the melting pot: "We are all Africans here, suffering from the same malady—the injustice of Government."[52] Although the results were not uniform, Edelstein's study showed that children of exogamous marriages generally displayed slightly less social distance toward racial and ethnic outgroups than did children of endogamous marriages.[53]

Even in Soweto, there has been lethal behavior at variance with these norms, as we shall see later; and, as of the early 1970s, the various groups in Soweto held significantly more favorable in-group than outgroup stereotypes and associated more frequently with in-group than with out-group members.[54] Outside of Soweto, social distance studies show significant amounts of ethnocentrism and some patterns of intergroup hostility. As exogamy is understudied, so are ethnic attitudes among Africans,[55] but they are far from being wholly unstudied.

In the Johannesburg township of Dube (part of Soweto), Zulu, Sotho, and Xhosa were asked to rank several groups on an adjectival scale representing a wide variety of desirable personal attributes.[56] Groups

48. "Worker Consciousness, Ethnic Particularism and Nationalism," p. 295.
49. A. A. Dubb, "The Impact of the City," in W. D. Hammond-Tooke, ed., *The Bantu-speaking Peoples of South Africa* (London: Routledge & Kegan Paul, 1974), p. 465.
50. Melville Leonard Edelstein, "An Attitude Survey of Urban Bantu Matric Pupils in Soweto, with Special Reference to Stereotyping and Social Distance: A Sociological Study" (M.A. thesis, University of Pretoria, 1971), p. 108.
51. See Donald L. Horowitz, "Conflict and Accommodation: Mexican-Americans in the Cosmopolis," in Walker Connor, ed., *Mexican-Americans in Comparative Perspective* (Washington, D.C.: Urban Institute, 1985), pp. 81–84.
52. Mayer, "Class, Status, and Ethnicity," pp. 152, 153.
53. Edelstein, "An Attitude Survey of Urban Bantu Matric Pupils in Soweto," pp. 110, 130–31.
54. Melville Leonard Edelstein, *What Do Young Africans Think?* (Johannesburg: South African Institute of Race Relations, 1972), p. 116.
55. See J. W. Mann, "Attitudes towards Ethnic Groups," in Adam, ed., *South Africa: Sociological Perspectives*, p. 66.
56. Dubb et al., "African Attitudes in Town."

to be ranked included the respondent's own, the two other African groups, and Whites. Majorities of all the respondent groups had either been born in town or, if not, had scant contact with rural birthplaces. As expected, respondents in each group ranked their own group highest. Both Sotho and Xhosa ranked Whites higher than they ranked Zulu; Xhosa ranked Whites above both Zulu and Sotho. Zulu ranked Whites last, but, for Zulu respondents, there was not much to choose. The three groups, apart from the subjects' own, formed a "compact set."[57] For Zulu and Sotho, the distances between subject groups and target groups were not very great, but Xhosa respondents emerged in this study as more ethnocentric. They evaluated other groups "a good deal less favourably than themselves . . . ."[58]

Subjects in a nationwide study of positive and negative qualities, conducted under the auspices of the Human Sciences Research Council (HSRC), were Afrikaans-speaking Whites, English-speaking Whites, Coloureds, Sotho, and Zulu.[59] The instrument employed semantic differential scales.[60] Respondents were asked to characterize groups in terms of 32 sets of adjective antonyms, such as *courteous* or *rude, kind* or *cruel, aggressive* or *submissive*. Differences in group evaluations are revealed by degree of agreement among subjects on positive and negative adjectives that characterize a given target group. These evaluations were based on research from the early 1970s to the early 1980s. Over this time span, the intergroup rankings are reported to have been quite consistent. A graphic depiction of the values over time, for all subject and target groups, is displayed in Figure 1.

From the figure, it is obvious that all respondent groups had the most positive views of themselves. The greatest spread in evaluations of other groups was displayed by Afrikaners. While they evaluated themselves only modestly favorably, Afrikaners held less positive views of Blacks and Coloureds than any other subjects in the sample displayed toward any group. The range of difference between in-group evaluations and out-group evaluations displayed by English-speaking White and by Coloured subjects was markedly narrower. The range of evaluations by Zulu respondents was in-between, but the evaluative range exhibited by

57. Ibid., p. 89.
58. Ibid., p. 90.
59. HSRC Investigation into Intergroup Relations, *The South African Society: Realities and Future Prospects* (Pretoria: Human Sciences Research Council, 1985), pp. 81–82.
60. On the logic of semantic differentiation, see Charles E. Osgood et al., *The Measurement of Meaning* (Urbana: University of Illinois Press, 1957).

Figure 1. Average Semantic Differential of Own and Other Groups in South Africa, 1973–82

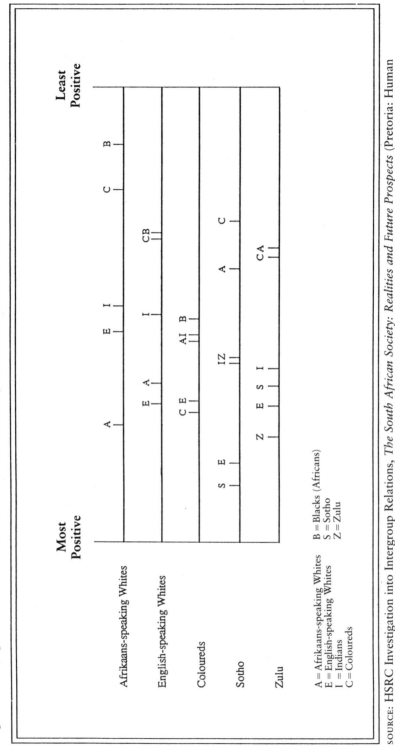

SOURCE: HSRC Investigation into Intergroup Relations, *The South African Society: Realities and Future Prospects* (Pretoria: Human Sciences Research Council, 1985), p. 82. © HSRC 1985. Reproduced by permission.
NOTE: Sample sizes varied with respondent group and year, but were very large. For example, the Sotho sample in 1979 consisted of 1,199 respondents; the Zulu sample in the same year consisted of 1,168 respondents.

Sotho was close to that shown by Afrikaners. Both Sotho and Zulu gave English-speaking Whites the most positive evaluations, second only to their own, and both gave Afrikaners and Coloureds the least positive. English-speaking Whites, however, did not reciprocate the positive views held of them by Sotho and Zulu. For Sotho, Zulu and Indians ranked in the middle; both of these groups were placed by Sotho respondents at a substantial distance from the positive evaluations by Sotho subjects of their own group. For Zulu, Sotho and Indians occupied the middle ground, not far behind Zulu evaluations of English-speaking Whites. As in the study of Dube, out-group evaluations, on the whole, were not powerfully negative. But it is very clear that Black South Africans are as keenly aware of ethnic differences as of racial differences.

Perhaps the most important findings are the sharp evaluative distinctions made by Zulu and Sotho respondents between Afrikaans and English speakers—a result found in other studies of Black respondents[61]—the least positive evaluations accorded by those respondents to Afrikaners and Coloureds, and the fact that both Zulu and Sotho evaluated each other less positively than either evaluated the English speakers. This last, despite the prevalence of color discrimination in the society.

The negative attributes imputed to Afrikaners by majorities of Sotho and Zulu are politically relevant ones. The adjectives used by Sotho were *snobbish, unjust, fickle,* and *stubborn;* those used by Zulu were *stubborn, aggressive, prejudiced,* and *quarrelsome.*[62] In an earlier Soweto social distance study of four African respondent groups, Afrikaners were uniformly seen as the most distant group, as we shall see.

In KwaMashu, a satellite town outside Durban, Zulu respondents were asked a variety of social distance and stereotype questions.[63] The vast majority of the respondents had been born in town or had lived there for more than twenty years. Social distance scales gauge attitudes

61. See, e.g., Nieuwoudt and Plug, "South African Ethnic Attitudes: 1973 to 1978," pp. 168–69.
62. S. J. Kruger, *Sienswyses wat Suid-Sotho's oor hulself en ander Suid-Afrikaanse bevolkingsgroepe gehuldig het, 1979–1982* (Pretoria: Human Sciences Research Council, 1984), p. 21; S. J. Kruger, *Sienswyses wat Zoeloes oor hulself en ander Suid-Afrikaanse bevolkingsgroepe gehuldig het, 1979–1982* (Pretoria: Human Sciences Research Council, 1984), p. 19. The three target groups eliciting the largest number of majority responses (Sotho, Zulu, and English) also received higher percentages of agreement on group characteristics than did the remaining target groups. The same is true for Zulu evaluations of English speakers and Sotho versus Zulu evaluations of Afrikaners and Coloureds. I am indebted to G. A. Thiele for making these reports available to me.
63. Brian M. du Toit, "Ethnicity, Neighborliness, and Friendship among Urban Africans in South Africa," in Brian M. du Toit, ed., *Ethnicity in Modern Africa* (Boulder, Colo.: Westview Press, 1978), pp. 143–74.

toward others by measuring the willingness of respondents to join with those others in activities involving varying degrees of intimacy, from occasional visits to residence in the same neighborhood, to friendship, to work relationships, and to marriage. As intimacy increased in the activity postulated by the question, so did reluctance to engage in that activity with ethnic strangers. For these respondents, as for other Zulu in Durban townships,[64] marriage with a member of any out-group was regarded as nearly unthinkable.[65] The groups that seem to respondents to be most distant from them, by far, were Indians, Whites, and Coloureds (in that order).[66] Fairly elaborate stereotypes were held of all the out-groups. Strongly negative characterizations were provided for the most distant African groups. Ndebele were "backward," Tsonga were "loose-living," and Xhosa were "clever" people who would make the Zulu feel "lost" and "inferior" or would cheat them.[67] In fact, "Zulu really get their ire up when they refer to the Xhosa," whom they described as "too clever," "crooks," "scheming," "very cunning," "crafty," and "stiffheaded."[68] Among males, the most highly educated respondents displayed the greatest social distance.[69]

Although KwaMashu, like other Durban townships, is overwhelmingly Zulu in composition, it contains non-Zulu minorities, among whom Xhosa speakers are predominant. The articulated stereotypes, then, are not based on an absence of intergroup contact. Some of the contact is not particularly friendly, as we shall see.

The reliability of such findings can be gauged by matching them against what other studies find. For all the differences between Durban and Soweto, young, educated Zulu in Soweto display roughly the same rank order of distance from various groups as those in Durban do.[70] In Soweto, as in Durban, Xhosa and Shangaan are seen by Zulu as somewhat distant, while Swazi are seen as close. In Soweto, both Zulu and Xhosa agree, as do all categories of respondent, that Zulu are "hardworking,"

64. See Hanf et al., *South Africa*, p. 341.

65. Du Toit, "Ethnicity, Neighborliness, and Friendship among Urban Africans in South Africa," pp. 151–52.

66. Ibid., p. 153.

67. Ibid., pp. 158, 153.

68. Ibid., p. 158.

69. Ibid., p. 161. So did the oldest respondents, but below age 54 little difference was observable. Among females, the most highly educated respondents—those with tertiary education—displayed the least social distance, but the numbers in that cell were very small. Ibid., pp. 162, 149.

70. Edelstein, *What Do Young Africans Think?* p. 106.

while Xhosa, the most educated group in Soweto, are "intelligent."[71] And, finally, Soweto Xhosa do not reciprocate Zulu feelings of distance; on the contrary, they see themselves as close to Zulu, Tswana, and Sotho and—like Soweto Zulu, only more so—most distant from Coloureds, Indians, and Whites.[72]

It is worth a closer look at the Soweto social distance study. The data, gathered in 1971, are rather old, but they are quite consistent (especially in the Zulu and Sotho responses) with the HSRC data, which were gathered into the 1980s. Moreover, the Soweto respondents were then matriculation pupils—those qualifying for some form of higher education and, therefore, future elites—in their teens.

Where respondents are asked to scale the distance of a variety of both ethnic and racial groups, one can ask whether other racial groups are seen to be more distant from the respondent than other ethnic groups are. In South Africa, the answer to this is generally "yes." In this respect, as we have seen, the results are different from stereotype studies, which often show more favorable evaluations of at least some other racial groups. But a further question can be asked: Are the groups ordered continuously or discontinuously? Does the distance separating the cluster of ethnic groups from the cluster of racial groups indicate a great gap between the two? An answer to this question for South African Black elites lurks in Edelstein's Soweto data. As one might have hypothesized from the Dube township and nationwide HSRC studies, the results vary by the ethnicity of the respondent, even in Soweto.

Edelstein breaks the results out for four groups of respondents: Zulu, Xhosa, Tswana, and Sotho. Figure 2, which diagrams his results, shows that Zulu and Sotho see other ethnic and racial groups as being placed at various points on a single continuum. For Zulu, it is a narrower continuum overall than for Sotho, who, in the HSRC study, also spread their evaluations out more than Zulu did. Tswana create a bit more distance between the furthest African group and the nearest non-African group than either Zulu or Sotho do. For Tswana respondents, there are at least three clusters: the three African groups they see as being very close to them, then the four more distant African groups, followed by the non-African groups. Xhosa also group Africans into two clusters—the extremely close and the fairly close—but, unlike Tswana, they

71. Ibid., pp. 107, 110.
72. Ibid., p. 106.

Figure 2. Social Distance Evaluations of South African Ethnic Groups by Soweto Matriculation Pupils, 1971 (*N* = 200)

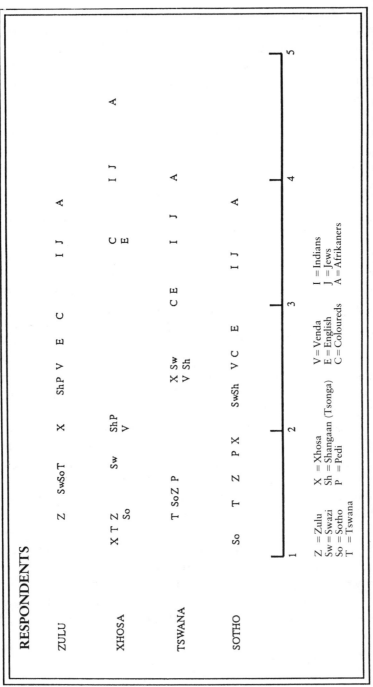

SOURCE: Based on data in Melville Leonard Edelstein, "An Attitude Survey of Urban Bantu Matric Pupils in Soweto, with Special Reference to Stereotyping and Social Distance: A Sociological Study" (M.A. thesis, University of Pretoria, 1971), p. 132.
NOTE: On the scale from 1 to 5, 1 denotes least distance and 5 denotes greatest distance from the respondent.

TABLE 5.   MEAN SOCIAL DISTANCE EVALUATIONS
OF AFRICAN AND NON-AFRICAN GROUPS BY
SOWETO MATRICULATION PUPILS, 1971

Ethnicity of Respondents	Mean Distance from African Groups	Mean Distance from Non-African Groups	Difference
Zulu	2.0	3.26	1.26
Xhosa	1.66	3.94	2.28
Tswana	2.04	3.48	1.44
Sotho	1.96	3.18	1.22

SOURCE: Computed from the same data as in Figure 2.

place the non-Africans in a completely different category. For Xhosa, there is a great gap between Africans and non-Africans. For all four respondent groups, the ranking of the non-Africans is close to the same: Afrikaners are furthest by far, English and Coloureds are closest. But the average distance varies enormously by respondent group, as Table 5 shows.

Edelstein concludes that while "Zulu respondents associate more readily with Venda than [with] South African English there is not a great difference between their attitudes to these two outgroups," and he makes the same point for the proximity of the least favored African and most favored non-African group for Sotho. (In all cases, the most favored non-Africans are either Coloured or English.) But Xhosa, he notes, place fully 1.4 points on a scale of only 1.0 to 5.0 between the furthest African group and the nearest non-African groups.[73] And, as Table 5 shows, Xhosa mean distance ratings are markedly different from those of other respondents.

All of this is really another way of saying that, for Xhosa respondents, the definition of the situation seems different. For them, racial differences are so much greater that they are discontinuous from intra-African ethnic differences. The location of Afrikaners on the Xhosa response scale is truly extraordinary, and this is before the Soweto rising of 1976. The 4.6 distance rating on the scale, together with the overall bimodal pattern of Xhosa responses, indicates clearly that, for Xhosa, racial antipathy supersedes ethnic antipathy. When Xhosa provide a nonethnic response to an identity question on a sample survey, they are

73. Edelstein, "An Attitude Survey of Urban Bantu Matric Pupils in Soweto," pp. 114, 116, 115, respectively.

reflecting their view of South African society. Given this view, it is no wonder that Xhosa are so strongly identified with militant movements.

In several of these studies, taken together, are hints of some sources of the different political alignments of Xhosa and Zulu. The antipathy toward Xhosa, coupled with fear of Xhosa craftiness, expressed in the KwaMashu study, suggests reasons why Natal Zulu might steer clear of organizations that seem to be controlled by Xhosa. The significantly greater distance between Xhosa subjects and Whites than between Zulu subjects and Whites may mean that, for Xhosa, the struggle for racial equality outweighs African ethnic differences to a greater degree than it does for Zulu. The frequent finding that Africans of various groups believe at least some Whites to possess more desirable attributes than those possessed by Black groups other than their own—and this finding holds even for Xhosa in the Dube township study—suggests rather strongly that there is potential for intra-African conflicts to supersede Black-White conflicts at some stage, for some purposes.

Against these findings, it is easier to understand the variety of settings in which Black interethnic attitudes crystallize. In Soweto and possibly a few other heterogeneous townships, the initial residential segregation by ethnic group has broken down; and, although "ethnic categories do still have considerable resonance in daily interaction," nevertheless, intra-African ethnocentrism, while not absent, meets with social disapproval.[74] In more homogeneous urban or rural areas, a good deal of ethnocentrism is expressed,[75] but it might or might not find a behavioral outlet. In heterogeneous areas composed of migrants from several home areas, the setting is conducive to ethnic exclusiveness. Most well documented are mines and factories where migrants comprise a multiethnic work force.[76] Housing is often ethnically segregated, social life is largely conducted within ethnic groups, and intergroup hostility is in evidence. In such settings, the potential for interethnic violence is great,

74. Mayer, "Class, Status, and Ethnicity," p. 152.
75. See, e.g., Philip M. Mayer, *Townsmen or Tribesmen?* 2d ed. (Cape Town: Oxford University Press, 1971), pp. 40–41.
76. See, e.g., J. K. McNamara, "Brothers and Work Mates: Home Friend Networks in the Social Life of Black Migrant Workers in a Gold Mine Hostel," in Philip M. Mayer, ed., *Black Villagers in an Industrial Society* (Cape Town: Oxford University Press, 1980), pp. 305–40; Dunbar Moodie, "Mine Culture and Miners' Identity on the South African Gold Mines," in Belinda Bozzoli, ed., *Town and Country in the Transvaal: Capitalist Penetration and Popular Response* (Johannesburg: Ravan Press, 1983), p. 185; Philip Bonner and Rob Lambert, "Batons and Bare Heads: The Strike at Amato Textiles, February 1958," in Marks and Trapido, eds., *The Politics of Race, Class and Nationalism in Twentieth-Century South Africa*, pp. 341–48; Beinart, "Worker Consciousness, Ethnic Particularism and Nationalism," pp. 292–93.

and indeed it frequently occurs, sometimes with considerable loss of life. In 1985, for example, 119 people were killed in fighting between Xhosa and Sotho miners at a gold mine.[77]

Attitudinally, the Soweto rising of 1976 was a watershed in Black-White relations. There is good evidence that White attitudes toward Blacks hardened and Black hostility to Afrikaners in particular increased substantially after Soweto.[78] Even in the early 1970s, however, as we have seen, interracial social distance studies among African respondents showed Afrikaners as the most distant group and English speakers (or, occasionally, Coloureds) as the closest, with Indians and Coloureds generally at various points in between.[79] White attitudes toward Indians, and Afrikaner (but not English) attitudes toward Coloureds as well, grew more favorable after Soweto.[80] This may reflect an implicit economy of antipathy (it is difficult to be equally hostile to all groups simultaneously) or contrast effects resulting from the nonparticipation of Indians and Coloureds in the main events of 1976.[81] What we do not have are complete measures over time for rising and declining intra-African ethnic attitudes. Soweto may have had a slight softening effect on them as well—it certainly helped close the attitudinal gap between English- and Afrikaans-speaking Whites.[82] As long as White-Black conflict is preeminent, there are limits to intra-White ethnic differences. For the time being, presumably, there are similar limits to intra-Black ethnic antipathy.

ETHNICITY, VIOLENCE, AND "HOMELAND" POLITICS

Despite the obvious binding force of White rule on Black cohesion, modern South Africa has experienced a great deal of intra-Black vio-

77. Carole Cooper et al., *Race Relations Survey, 1985* (Johannesburg: South African Institute of Race Relations, 1986), p. 169. For other accounts of violence, see the works cited in note 76, above.

78. Nieuwoudt and Plug, "South African Ethnic Attitudes: 1973 to 1978."

79. H. G. Viljoen, "Stereotipes en sosiale afstand as dimensies van ethniese vooroordeel by Bantoe- en Indiërstudente" (Ph.D. diss., University of Pretoria, 1972), pp. 131, 137, 143; Edelstein, "An Attitude Survey of Urban Bantu Matric Pupils in Soweto," pp. 113, 132.

80. Nieuwoudt and Plug, "South African Ethnic Attitudes: 1973 to 1978," p. 167.

81. For the perceptual basis of contrast effects, see Muzafer Sherif and Carl I. Hovland, *Social Judgment: Assimilation and Contrast Effects in Communication and Attitude Change* (New Haven: Yale University Press, 1961); H. Tajfel, "Quantitative Judgement in Social Perception," *British Journal of Psychology* 50, pt. 1 (February 1959): 16–29.

82. Nieuwoudt and Plug, "South African Ethnic Attitudes: 1973 to 1978," pp. 168–69.

lence, some of it between competing Black extraparliamentary organizations and some between Black ethnic groups.[83]

When the multiracial United Democratic Front was formed in 1983 to oppose the new Indian and Coloured legislative chambers, it immediately came into conflict with the Azanian People's Organization.[84] The UDF and AZAPO saw themselves as rivals for support in the Black townships, especially in the Eastern Cape. Up through 1987, there was violence between the two, with the UDF generally emerging triumphant. Violence between Africanists and Charterists continued sporadically thereafter, accelerating in 1990, when the ANC clashed with the PAC as well as with AZAPO.[85]

The balance of power was different in Natal, where UDF efforts to expand met with armed resistance from Inkatha. With its strength especially concentrated in the Cape, the UDF was surely seen by some in Natal as a non-Zulu movement.[86] From 1986 through 1989, more than 2,000 people were killed in the townships around Pietermaritzburg, which had become the center of uncontrollable violence. From 1986 to 1988, 3,000 houses were burned, and 30,000 people were left homeless. More of the victims were UDF supporters than Inkatha supporters. In some cases, the police appeared more sympathetic to Inkatha, to judge by police inactivity, the appointment of some Inkatha activists as auxiliary constables, and the pattern of arrests.[87] Interspersed in the Natal inci-

83. For present purposes, I leave aside violence in 1985–86 at the Crossroads settlement outside Cape Town between so-called *Witdoeke* (white cloths, after strips of cloth by which they identified themselves) and generally younger comrades. With the apparent connivance of the security forces, a very large number of homes were destroyed. Some of those left homeless moved to Kaiyelitsha, a Black settlement near Stellenbosch. For an account of the violence, see Lawyers Committee for Human Rights, *Crisis in Crossroads* (New York: Lawyers Committee for Human Rights, 1988). For comparable episodes in the Eastern Cape, see Cooper et al., *Race Relations Survey, 1987/88*, pp. 47–49.

84. See Barney Mthombothi, "Introduction," in Meer, ed., *Resistance in the Townships*, pp. 5–6; Colin Legum, ed., *Africa Contemporary Record, 1986–87* (New York: Africana, 1987), p. B744.

85. See Carole Cooper et al., *Race Relations Survey, 1986* (Johannesburg: South African Institute of Race Relations, 1987), pt. 1, pp. 142–43; *Cape Times* (Cape Town), February 14, 1990.

86. See, e.g., the letter to the editor of *Argus*, April 26, 1990.

87. The Pietermaritzburg violence has been well documented in Wendy Leeb, "Death, Devastation and Destruction—Refugees in Natal" (Pietermaritzburg: Centre for Adult Education, University of Natal, 1989; unpublished paper); J. W. W. Aitchison, "The Pietermaritzburg Conflict—Experience and Analysis" (Pietermaritzburg: Centre for Adult Education, University of Natal, July 7, 1989; unpublished paper); J. W. W. Aitchison, "Numbering the Dead: Patterns in the Midlands Violence" (Pietermaritzburg: Centre for Adult Education, University of Natal, 1988; unpublished paper). On the so-called *Kitson-konstabels*, see Colin Legum and Marion E. Doro, eds., *Africa Contemporary Record, 1987–88* (New York: Africana, 1989), p. B732.

dents was also some violence between UDF and Black Consciousness youth.

As the violence spread in Natal in the late 1980s and in 1990, it became more difficult to decompose its elements. In some areas, political violence was intertwined with conflict between old and young, migrants and residents, extended families, Zulu subgroups *(Iziwe)*, Zulu tribal authorities and their opponents, and local gangs.[88]

It is difficult to say whether organizational rivalries have any clear ascriptive underpinnings within Zulu society or elsewhere. There is no doubt that subgroup divisions are occasional sources of violent conflict. In 1978, 260 people were killed in clashes between Madondas and Majolas in KwaZulu; and, in 1984, 70 people were killed in comparable fighting in Natal.[89]

Much clearer have been episodes of outright interethnic violence. In 1976, during the Soweto revolt, Zulu migrants emerged from their hostel and killed a good many youth on the streets.[90] At the end of 1985, Zulu outside Durban attacked Xhosa-speaking Pondo migrants who worked in the sugar industry, killing many and driving the rest out.[91] Around the same time, homeland boundaries provoked violence—first in 1985 between Shangaan and Pedi over the boundary between Gazankulu and Lebowa[92] and then in early 1986 between Ndebele and Pedi over a South African government plan to incorporate the largely-Pedi Moutse area outside Pretoria into KwaNdebele.[93] Finally, in 1990, there was widespread violence between Zulu hostel dwellers, and Xhosa in Transvaal townships, resulting in many, many deaths.

To be sure, some of this violence appears to have been manipulated or encouraged by state authorities, and their role was even more direct when they used Zulu or Tswana police to remove Xhosa squatters, as

88. Interviews, Botha's Hill, Natal, August 3, 1989.

89. For the 1978 events, see Ernest Harsch, *South Africa: White Rule, Black Revolt* (New York: Monad Press, 1980), p. 67. For the 1984 violence, see Leach, *South Africa*, p. 111. For similar events, see Cooper et al., *Race Relations Survey, 1985*, pp. 309, 318.

90. *Times* (London), August 26, 1976; Colin Legum, ed., *Africa Contemporary Record, 1976–77* (New York: Africana, 1977), pp. B792–93.

91. For a helpful account, see "Umbumbulu," in Meer, ed., *Resistance in the Townships*, pp. 165–76; see also *Los Angeles Times*, December 27, 1985. For the flavor of Pondo-Zulu antipathy in the Natal cane fields, see Beinart, "Worker Consciousness, Ethnic Particularism and Nationalism," pp. 289, 293.

92. "Umbumbulu," p. 166. For the background, see Harries, "Exclusion, Classification and Internal Colonialism," pp. 106–07. For an account of the dispute, see Cooper et al., *Race Relations Survey, 1985*, p. 284.

93. *Financial Times* (London), January 3, 1986; *Los Angeles Times*, January 3, 1986. For background, see Cooper et al., *Race Relations Survey, 1985*, pp. 284–86.

they did, with lethal results, in Crossroads in 1985.[94] But ethnic strangers were sent in for police duty precisely because it was known they would be reliable. The fact that ethnic affiliations were available for manipulation or encouragement suggests that ethnic violence is not just the product of the state's action in setting one group against another but reflects the continuing importance of ethnicity.

A similar point can be made about the so-called African homelands. They are creations of the apartheid regime, but they nonetheless reveal some important patterns of ethnic politics.

As I indicated earlier, a contextual view of ethnicity suggests that intra-African divisions would be muted while White-Black conflicts are preeminent but that they would become salient as White-Black conflicts recede in importance. Universal suffrage is likely to produce just such a change in context. To appreciate the increased role of ethnicity in these circumstances, a glimpse at politics in the various homelands is instructive.

Although the homelands were designed for each of the major African ethnic groups, several homelands contain significant minorities. In the Pedi homeland, Lebowa, Ndebele form a minority. In turn, Pedi are a large minority in the Tswana homeland, Bophuthatswana. There are Swazi in KwaZulu and Sotho in the two Xhosa Bantustans, the Transkei and Ciskei. In none of these have minorities been politically well represented. Early on, leaders of the dominant group generally did the equivalent of what the chief minister of Bophuthatswana did—namely, insist on a strongly Tswana identity for the territory.[95] That, after all, was the ostensible raison d'être for the homeland. There was also a general suppression of party competition at an early stage in homeland development. In a single-party context, it was easy to neglect ethnic strangers, prevent them from securing legislative representation, and keep them out of the cabinet.

In most homelands, subethnic rivalries have also played a major role in politics. In the Ciskei, the long-standing rivalry between two major Xhosa-speaking subgroups formed the leitmotiv of political conflict. The Rharhabe, who fought the Europeans for more than a century, were

94. See Lars Waldorf, "Life in Crossroads," *New Republic*, August 25, 1986, pp. 17–19. See also "Affidavits—Orange Free State," in Meer, ed., *Resistance in the Townships*, p. 127, reporting that township councillors in Thaborg in the Orange Free State are protected by vigilantes "drawn from migrants, thugs in the township and some Zulu people from Natal."

95. See D. A. Kotzé, *African Politics in South Africa, 1964–1975* (New York: St. Martin's Press, 1975), pp. 47–48.

aligned against the Mfengu, who had migrated to the Ciskei 150 years earlier. The political dispute in the Ciskei reflects a variety of underlying group-based differences.[96] Comparable subgroup or lineage divisions are to be found in other homelands.

In Bophuthatswana, both ethnic and subethnic divisions are simultaneously important. In 1988, the precariously placed chief minister, Lucius Mangope, announced that he would sooner merge the homeland into neighboring Botswana than reincorporate it into South Africa in accordance with the views of the extraparliamentary opposition. After the legalization of the ANC and the PAC in 1990, demonstrations demanding reincorporation into South Africa were put down by the homeland police and army. Non-Tswana were particularly fearful of a connection with Botswana, with its overwhelming Tswana majority. In addition, Mangope had excluded the Bafokeng subgroup, located in the east of the homeland, from any real power, and that triggered coup attempts, clashes with villagers resisting integration into the homeland, and an alignment between the regionally based dissenters and the ANC.[97]

South Africans have tended to think in terms of fixed rather than fluid categories and alignments. What homeland politics shows is that there is a substructure of allegiances and divisions available for activation when a new context brings African politics into the foreground.

THE HISTORY OF RACIAL AND ETHNIC ENCOUNTERS

In many African colonies, the encounter between colonizers and colonized involved warfare during the initial conquest, the later "pacification," and the periodic suppression of rebellion. The dislocations caused by colonial occupation also produced population movements and conflicts among the colonized peoples themselves and did not necessarily prevent the continuation of warfare begun before the colonial occupation.

The patterns of colonial warfare, however, were varied. In Nigeria, a southward march by Fulani was interrupted by the British arrival.

96. See "Ethnicity and Pseudo-Ethnicity in the Ciskei," in Vail, ed., *The Creation of Tribalism in Southern Africa*, pp. 395–413; C. W. Manona, "Ethnic Relations in the Ciskei," in Nancy Charton, ed., *Ciskei: Economics and Politics of Dependence in a South African Homeland* (London: Croom Helm, 1980), pp. 97–121; M. G. Whisson and C. W. Manona, "Maqoma and Ciskeian Politics Today," in Charton, ed., *Ciskei*, pp. 214–27. Cf. David J. A. Edwards, "Political Identity among South African Blacks in and near a Contemporary Homeland," *International Journal of Psychology* 22, no. 1 (February 1987): 39–55.

97. See *Africa Confidential*, February 23, 1990, p. 6.

Later protected by the British, Hausa-Fulani were slow to join the independence movement. Conflict between them and southern ethnic groups occurred, but it had little to do with pre-colonial warfare.[98] The same was not true in Gabon, where the Fang were on the move, conquering and absorbing other groups on their way to the coast, when the French stopped their advance. Rivalry between Fang and coastal peoples continued during the colonial period. After independence, the Fang, seen by others as domineering and ethnocentric, assumed leadership roles in every area of Gabonese life.[99] In Zaire, a series of revolts by Lulua against Belgian rule began in the 1890s and lasted up to the 1940s. With much of the countryside decimated, non-Lulua fled to the towns. By 1930, Baluba constituted a majority of the urban population. As the Belgians departed, Lulua hostility was redirected toward Baluba, who in 1959 were victims of massive violence.[100] Sometimes interethnic warfare was not resumed, sometimes it was, and sometimes anti-colonial violence was channeled into ethnic conflict.

Warfare in South Africa was unusually bitter and protracted. The first colonists at the Cape owed allegiance to the Dutch East India Company, which had a skeletal organization and a limited capacity to reach into the territory. As the frontier grew away from the Cape peninsula, the company had little impact. It was nearly two centuries before the British consolidated their control over South Africa. During this interval and even after, there was warfare between Afrikaners on the move northward and the Africans they encountered along the way, as well as warfare among the Africans themselves. Until the British consolidated their hold, there was no single overwhelming force to crush opposition and impose a colonial peace.[101]

In the Cape, as the Boers moved eastward toward the Fish River, they encountered the Xhosa. A series of raids back and forth matured into hostilities that lasted on and off for more than a century. Officially, nine wars were fought between Whites and Xhosa in the nineteenth century. As late as 1920, a strong Xhosa uprising was put down by the White government.

98. See C. S. Whitaker, Jr., *The Politics of Tradition: Continuity and Change in Northern Nigeria, 1946–1966* (Princeton: Princeton University Press, 1970).

99. See Brian Weinstein, *Gabon: Nation-Building on the Ogooué* (Cambridge: MIT Press, 1966), pp. 32–69.

100. See Thomas Turner, "Congo-Kinshasa," in Victor A. Olorunsola, ed., *The Politics of Cultural Sub-Nationalism in Africa* (Garden City, N.Y.: Anchor Books, 1972), pp. 218–24.

101. See, e.g., T. R. H. Davenport, *South Africa: A Modern History,* 3d ed. (Toronto: University of Toronto Press, 1987).

Zulu, meanwhile, were in an expansionist phase in the early nineteenth century. Having undergone considerable subgroup amalgamation and centralization, the Zulu moved out in every direction, in a massive dispersion often called the *mfecane,* subjugating a variety of groups—Swazi, Sotho, and Pondo—and causing many to migrate from their home areas, including those Ndebele who fled to what is now Zimbabwe. Only the British occupation of Natal put an end to Zulu expansion.

It would be inaccurate to attribute all or most intra-African differences to this history, but the unusual turbulence of the eighteenth and nineteenth centuries certainly has contemporary reverberations. There is still, for example, a martial spirit revived from time to time among the Zulu. In 1949, when Zulu attacked Indians in Durban, the attackers were organized into *impis,* or regiments.[102] Relations between Mfengu and Rharhabe Xhosa are colored by the fact that, although the Mfengu fled Natal from the *mfecane* in the early nineteenth century and found shelter among Xhosa, they then proceeded to ally with Whites against Xhosa in the various frontier wars from 1834 to 1879, for which they were well rewarded. The persistence of Zulu vocabulary in the Mfengu dialect of Xhosa also remains an irritant.[103]

Among the Xhosa, too, there is a strong strand of exclusive, anti-White nationalism, found particularly among so-called Red Xhosa, those who adhere to a consciously traditional subculture reflecting a rejection of the White conquest:

> The happy past to which the Red person looks back is the period . . . when there were no White men; the dream he would entertain for his future is getting away from the White men again—away into Xhosa independence and dignity. Meanwhile no inconsistent cultural aspirations complicate the straightforward political opposition. "There is nothing I like about them or their way of life. There can never be any peace between a Xhosa and *Umlungu* [the White man]."[104]

Although the Red tradition is in decline,[105] both it and the more acculturating "School" tradition among the Xhosa reflect "the different reactions of an earlier generation to a particular conquest situation over

---

102. Maurice Webb and Kenneth Kirkwood, *The Durban Riots and After* (Johannesburg: South African Institute of Race Relations, 1949); Union of South Africa, *Report of the Commission of Enquiry into Riots in Durban* (Cape Town: Cape Times, 1949).

103. Manona, "Ethnic Relations in the Ciskei," p. 103.

104. Mayer, *Townsmen or Tribesmen?* p. 33.

105. R. Hunt Davis, "School vs. Blanket and Settler: Elijah Makiwane and the Leadership of the Cape School Community," *African Affairs* 78, no. 310 (January 1979): 12–31, at 13.

a hundred years ago." [106] One part of that conquest was the dispossession of Blacks by Whites. Another part was the participation of some groups in helping to subjugate others. Both components are remembered.[107]

It is not surprising in such an environment that both nationalism and ethnicity should have claims on the loyalties of Black South Africans. The intensive contact and protracted warfare between Xhosa and Whites make Xhosa overrepresentation in the ranks of militant movements understandable.[108] Some recrudescence of Zulu historical pride helps explain an organization like Inkatha, with its paramilitary trappings. The Zulu-Pondo Wars of the 1820s are perhaps in the distant background of recent Zulu-Pondo violence. Throughout the twentieth century, "Zulu ethnic nationalism" has been widespread in Natal, and among its sources were "the ways in which a pre-colonial past provided military metaphors for mobilization."[109] And if some groups, like the Pedi, have a degree of enthusiasm even for their government-created homeland, that, too, can be understood, in part, by reference to the turbulent history of their relations to their neighbors.[110] Ethnicity may be no more keenly felt than in other African countries, but historical recollections as a component of ethnic sentiment may be more powerful in South Africa.

FURTHER COMPLEXITY: WHITES, INDIANS, COLOUREDS

The initial apartheid vision of a four-segment society—of Whites, Coloureds, Indians, and Africans—is confounded by the social complexity, not merely of the African category, but of the Indian, Coloured, and White categories as well. The picture of ideological and ascriptive divisions among Africans is mirrored by similar divisions within each of the other categories.

Political differences among Whites are greater now than they have

---

106. Mayer, *Townsmen or Tribesmen?* p. 293.

107. See Hanf et al., *South Africa*, p. 246; Cornevin, "Populations noires d'Afrique du Sud," p. 43. For the roles of historical memory and warfare in ethnic relations, see Anthony D. Smith, *The Ethnic Origins of Nations* (Oxford: Blackwell, 1986), pp. 30–31, 37–41.

108. See Winnie Mandela, *Part of My Soul Went with Him* (New York: Norton, 1984), p. 48: ". . . you tell yourself: 'If they failed in those nine Xhosa wars, I am one of them, and I will start from where those Xhosas left off and get my land back.' "

109. Shula Marks, "Patriotism, Patriarchy and Purity: Natal and the Politics of Zulu Ethnic Consciousness," in Vail, ed., *The Creation of Tribalism in Southern Africa*, p. 233.

110. See Delius, *The Land Belongs to Us.*

been since before 1948.[111] The most obvious difference is in the realm of party competition and the divergent opinions it reflects. Between the 1987 and 1989 elections to the White chamber of parliament, the political spectrum spread out considerably. The Conservative Party moved from 27 percent of the vote in 1987 to 31 percent in 1989. In 1987, the liberal opposition consisted of the Progressive Federal Party (PFP). Together with the small New Republic Party, the PFP had 16 percent of the vote. By 1989, the liberal opposition became consolidated in a new Democratic Party (DP), consisting of the former PFP and a number of defectors from the Nationalists. In the 1989 elections, the DP gained 20 percent of the vote. Quite correctly, the National Party had pointed out in its campaign that the Democrats were not committed to a White minority veto in a future South Africa. For the first time, moreover, an anti-apartheid party in parliament had more than a token share of Afrikaner support.[112] Reciprocally, a great many English-speaking Whites gave their support to the National Party.[113] Ethnicity is no longer the firm predictor of political attitudes within the White category that it once was. This, a mere dozen years after Black South Africans had begun to make sharper distinctions between Afrikaner and English Whites.

Changes among Afrikaner elites are palpable. In 1985, a "Stellenbosch '85" discussion group was formed at the Afrikaans-language university that has nurtured a large number of South African cabinet ministers. Out of its discussions came an acrimonious meeting of some 28 leading Afrikaner intellectuals with then-President P. W. Botha. The disaffection of these intellectuals coincided with the defection of several Afrikaner politicians from the National Party in 1987. These streams fed directly into the new Democratic Party.

The roots of Afrikaner liberalism, particularly in the Cape, go back much further, but its political significance is traceable more immediately to the declining legitimacy of the old regime of race relations among many educated Afrikaners.[114] Among such people, there was a good

111. For a denial of any change, based on an eccentric reading of the evidence, see Bruce W. Nelan, "Changes in South Africa," *Foreign Affairs* 69, no. 1 (January 1990): 35–51.

112. For some of the sources of this change, see John D. Brewer, "Black Protest in South Africa's Crisis: A Comment on Legassick," *African Affairs* 85, no. 2 (April 1986): 283–94.

113. See Hennie Kotzé, "A Whole New Poll Game for '89 Nats," *Sunday Times* (Johannesburg), August 6, 1989. In 1977, by contrast, only 28 percent of English speakers were Nationalist supporters. H. Lever, "Public Opinion and Voting," in Anthony de Crespigny and Robert Schrire, eds., *The Government and Politics of South Africa* (Cape Town: Juta, 1978), p. 153.

114. For an example, see the HSRC Investigation into Intergroup Relations, *The South African Society*, p. 162, which called for "the establishment of public institutions that are

deal of impatience with the government's reluctance to commit itself to fundamental change.

There can be no more graphic demonstration of this shift than the changing position of the secret society called the Afrikaner Broederbond. The Broederbond has historically numbered among its members virtually the entire Afrikaner political leadership, including the cabinet and three-quarters of the National Party members of parliament, and it has been described as "a secret communication channel between the government and the Afrikaner elite."[115] Its 1986 confidential document, "Basic Political Values for the Survival of the Afrikaner," had a conventional title, but its content was anything but conventional. Reflecting a certain blurring of ethnic lines, the document equated the political interests of the Afrikaner with those of "the white man" in general.[116] More remarkably, the paper went on to assert that the "abolition of statutory discrimination measures must not be seen as concessions but as a prerequisite for survival," that "there can no longer be a white government," that Christian principles require that a government "must govern fairly and justly in respect of all its subjects," and that "the exclusion of effective black sharing in political processes at the highest level is a threat to the survival of the white man, which cannot be countered by maintaining the status quo or by a further consolidation of power in white hands."[117] And, to be sure that the message had been received, the Broederbond paper noted, almost *en passant,* that "the head of government does not necessarily have to be white . . . ."[118]

Not surprisingly, these statements produced a storm of right-wing invective. By South African standards, they are revolutionary formulations, illustrating both the growing social convergence between English and Afrikaans speakers[119] and the now-legitimate occupation by Afrikaners of positions all along the spectrum of White political opinion.

To both of these tendencies, there are limits. Although the boundary

---

worthy of trust and acceptance." At the meeting called in 1985 to discuss this report, there were repeated denunciations of the government's race relations policies by Afrikaner academics. Five years earlier, P. W. Botha had been heckled by students at the University of Stellenbosch.

115. Hermann Giliomee, "The National Party and the Afrikaner Broederbond," in Price and Rosberg, eds., *The Apartheid Regime,* p. 41.

116. Afrikaner Broederbond, "Basic Political Values for the Survival of the Afrikaner" (N.p., 1986; unpublished paper), pp. 1, 2, 7.

117. Ibid., pp. 6, 8, 6, 7, respectively.

118. Ibid., p. 7.

119. "A common white South African nationalism is well on the way to replacing the historical group identities." Adam, "The South African Power Elite," p. 99. Cf. Hanf et al., *South Africa,* pp. 169–73.

between English and Afrikaners is less firm than it once was, it has not been obliterated. Recollections of the Anglo-Boer Wars and of divergent attitudes toward European fascism in the 1930s and 1940s have been muted but not wholly transcended. A 1989 survey of members of the Democratic Party, which had not yet chosen a leader, showed that English-speaking party members supported Denis Worrall, an English speaker, for the leadership position, over Wynand Malan, an Afrikaner, by 52 percent to 15 percent. Among Afrikaners, 44 percent chose Malan, while only 28 percent chose Worrall.[120] Even in the Democratic Party, ethnic differences among Whites have political significance. Moreover, the two groups are not evenly distributed along the political spectrum. Afrikaners are a decided minority among Democrats, and English speakers are a rarity in the Conservative Party, which, while the Democrats were opposing apartheid, was attempting to reinstate segregation in Boksburg, a municipality whose town council the Conservatives controlled.[121]

The limits of Afrikaner liberalism are emphasized in a series of papers based on sample surveys of university students, conducted by Jannie Gagiano.[122] Gagiano identifies a number of important differences between Afrikaner Democratic Party and Afrikaner National Party supporters—including the firm rejection by the former of a White-controlled government—and he documents the extent to which White students are groping for an alternative to the status quo. Nevertheless, he is at pains to underscore the extent to which Afrikaner students remain symbolically attached to the institutions of the polity, despite the ferment around them.

If Whites present a picture of some interethnic convergence coupled with ideological divergence, somewhat analogous trends are present among both Indians and Coloureds. Both of these groups are ideologically conflicted, and the Indians are ethnically divided as well.

Indians are nearly everywhere a socially divided community, and South Africa is no exception. Between the descendants of the initial inden-

120. *Sunday Times* (Johannesburg), August 6, 1989.
121. *Daily News* (Durban), August 2, 1989.
122. Jannie Gagiano, "The Scope of Regime Support: A Case Study," in Hermann Giliomee and Lawrence Schlemmer, eds., *Negotiating South Africa's Future* (New York: St. Martin's Press, 1989), pp. 52–62; Jannie Gagiano, "Ruling Group Cohesion in South Africa: A Study of Political Attitudes among White University Students" (paper presented at the Biennial Conference of the Political Science Association of South Africa, October 9–11, 1989); Jannie Gagiano, "Meanwhile, Back on the 'Boereplaas,' " *Politikon* 13, no. 2 (December 1986): 3–23.

tured laborers and the later merchants, there are predictable class differences. To some extent, these are compounded by overlapping ascriptive divisions of language, caste, and religion. A working-class person
is more likely to be Tamil, Hindu, and low caste. A businessman is more
likely to be Gujarati, perhaps Muslim, and not low caste. To some extent, such differences translate into political positions, for the Indians
are a polarized community. Following Gandhi, many of them have joined
the Natal and Transvaal Indian Congresses and aligned with the UDF.
On the other hand, the serious Durban anti-Indian riots of 1949, and
some much milder but threatening episodes in 1974, 1985, and 1990,
have served to remind many Indians of the dangers that have befallen
Asian communities elsewhere in Africa. We have seen that Coloureds
and Indians usually are ranked by Africans as rather distant on social
distance scales. But there are differences. In the nationwide HSRC study,
Coloureds and Afrikaners received the least positive adjectival ratings,
and Indians placed closer to the middle of the scale.[123] However, in the
study of Durban, where most Indians live, social distance was greatest
from Indians.[124]

Indians, therefore, have reasons for a certain conservatism, and there
is no doubt that the unrest of the mid-1980s accelerated it. In a 1985
Durban survey that asked the respondents' choice of South African leader,
most Indians (53.4 percent) selected none other than P. W. Botha; none
chose Tutu, only 3.7 percent chose Mandela, and 3.1 percent chose
Boesak. The African figures are in stark contrast, with a majority for
Mandela, 11.9 percent for Tutu, 13.6 percent for Boesak, and none for
Botha.[125]

These results do not mean that Indians rushed to embrace their new
legislative chamber. On the contrary, only about 20 percent of registered voters cast a ballot in 1984, dividing their support between two
parties. Perhaps a better measure of Indian allegiance comes from a
question on organizational support in the same 1985 survey. Half of all
Africans gave their support to the UDF, and only 18.5 percent professed
support for no organization. By contrast, only 8.7 percent of Indians

    123. HSRC Investigation into Intergroup Relations, *The South African Society*, pp.
81–82.
    124. Du Toit, "Ethnicity, Neighborliness, and Friendship among Urban Africans in
South Africa," p. 153. See also Mann, Attitudes towards Ethnic Groups," p. 64.
    125. Meer and Reynolds, "Sample Survey of Perceptions of the Durban Unrest," p.
262.

supported the UDF, and another 8.7 percent supported the Indian parliamentary chamber. Half of all Indians professed support for no organization.[126] Bifurcated between pro-UDF activists and pro-system moderates, the Indians are a community divided, in-between, and heavily apolitical.

To some extent, the same applies to the so-called Coloured community, which derives from a variety of sources: ex-slaves in the Cape, people of mixed Khoi or San and European ancestry, and "Malays" brought by the Dutch from Indonesia. For some purposes, the differences between the largely-Muslim Malays and other Coloureds are significant, but they do not coincide with firm political lines. The watershed events for Coloureds appear to have been their disfranchisement in the early apartheid years and their massive forced removal in the 1960s, under the Group Areas Act, from parts of Cape Town in which they had long resided.[127] Two-thirds of those removed under the Group Areas Act were Coloured, and nearly one-third was Indian.[128] These were traumatic, bitter experiences that formed the prelude to increasing militancy, some identification with the plight of Africans, and growing rejection of the Afrikaans language, the mother tongue of most Coloureds.

In the 1984 elections to the Coloured chamber of parliament, only 30 percent of eligible voters turned out. They overwhelmingly elected members of Allan Hendrickse's Labour Party, which has repeatedly emphasized the illegitimacy of the tricameral constitutional arrangements and threatened not to participate in further elections if the system is not transformed.[129] The University of the Western Cape, officially a Coloured campus, has opened its doors to Africans and has been a center

126. Ibid., p. 264.

127. For the bitterness of this episode, see the novel by Richard Rive, *"Buckingham Palace," District Six* (Cape Town: David Philip, 1986).

128. See Hendrik W. van der Merwe, *Pursuing Justice and Peace in South Africa* (London: Routledge, 1989), p. 29. In a study that followed the removals by only a few years, H. G. Viljoen found that, despite religious differences between the two groups, Indians displayed less social distance from Coloureds than from any other group. "Stereotipes en sociale afstand," p. 150. Since Viljoen had no group of Coloured respondents, we do not know whether the sentiment was reciprocated, but the finding is testimony to the power of common situation and official definitions in shaping affinities.

129. For Labour Party noncooperation with government initiatives in the (Coloured) House of Representatives, see Cooper et al., *Race Relations Survey, 1987 / 88*, pp. xxxv–xxxvi. See also Hennie Kotzé, "Adapting or Dyeing: Parliamentary Political Parties, Reform and Reaction in South Africa," in D. J. van Vuuren et al., eds., *South Africa: The Challenge of Reform* (Pinetown, South Africa: Burgess, 1989), pp. 150–52.

of radical anti-government activity. Many Coloureds have joined the UDF, and the community as a whole is somewhat more anti-government than is the Indian community.

At the same time, there are crosscurrents, as might well be expected, given the strongly negative social distance evaluations of Coloureds by African respondents.[130] Asked in the 1985 Durban survey for their leadership choice, 31 percent, a plurality, still chose Botha, and 25 percent chose Frederik van Zyl Slabbert, then PFP leader of the parliamentary opposition. Mandela received only 11 percent support, Tutu 5 percent, and Boesak 3 percent.[131] Likewise, Coloureds in Natal did not opt for a radical line. While half of Natal's Africans professed to support the UDF, only 7 percent of the Coloureds did. A clear majority of Coloured respondents (56 percent) said they supported no organization.[132] In sample surveys, Coloureds show significantly higher levels of life satisfaction than Africans do—by levels of nearly 2 to 1.[133] The Coloured levels (81 percent) are close to those reported by both Indians and Whites (89 percent). The judgment seems inescapable that the unrest of the mid-1980s produced, in Fatima Meer's words, "a radicalization of African political sentiment, and a marked shift towards conservatism on the part of Coloured and particularly Indian people."[134] In recent years, more than a few Coloureds have emigrated to Canada and Australia.

Among students, moreover, Coloured responses to survey options

130. Even in Brian du Toit's study "Ethnicity, Neighborliness, and Friendship among Urban Africans in South Africa," p. 153, conducted in Durban, which has few Coloureds, Coloureds were evaluated as the third most distant group from Zulu respondents, after Indians and Whites, in that order. In the HSRC study, Coloureds were seen as more distant than Afrikaners by Sotho respondents and just about as distant as Afrikaners by Zulu respondents. HSRC Investigation into Intergroup Relations, *The South African Society*, p. 82.

131. Meer and Reynolds, "Sample Survey of Perceptions of the Durban Unrest," p. 262.

132. Ibid., p. 264.

133. V. Moller et al., "Quality of Life and Race in South Africa: A Preliminary Analysis" (Centre for Applied Social Sciences, University of Natal, Durban, September 1985; unpublished paper), pp. 8, 22.

134. Meer and Reynolds, "Sample Survey of Perceptions of the Durban Unrest," p. 261. For general surveys of the two groups, see Kogila A. Moodley, "Structured Inequality and Minority Anxiety: Responses of Middle Groups in South Africa," in Price and Rosberg, eds., *The Apartheid Regime*, pp. 217–35; Anil Sookdeo, "The Transformation of Ethnic Identities: The Case of 'Coloured' and Indian [South] Africans," *Journal of Ethnic Studies* 15, no. 4 (Winter 1988): 69–83; Karl P. Magyar, "The Permanent Minority: Politicization of South Africa's Indian Community" (paper presented at the Congress of the Political Science Association of South Africa, September 20, 1985). For an argument that Indians were united and mobilized into the struggle against apartheid, see Pushpa Hargovan, "Apartheid and the Indian Community in South Africa: Isolation or Cooperation," *Journal of Asian and African Affairs* 1, no. 2 (December 1989): 155–73.

are notably different from those of African students. As we shall see in Chapter 3, African university students in the Western Cape overwhelmingly chose a "hard nationalist" option among possible future arrangements, and only 5.8 percent chose "a society in which group identity has ceased to be crucial in determining who governs."[135] Among Coloured students in the Western Cape, this liberal option was chosen by literally ten times as many respondents: 59 percent.[136]

THE POLITICAL SIGNIFICANCE
OF ETHNICITY AND RACE

What we have seen is the continuing importance of racial, ethnic, and subethnic identities in South Africa. In all the racial categories, there are divisions along lines of ethnicity and ideology. Some intergroup cleavages have considerable conflict-producing potential. Eliminate White domination, and intra-African differences will be particularly important. They are very much on the order of the cleavages that in some countries translated into the serious post-independence conflict and violence. To ignore them in planning for a future South Africa would be to repeat the same fallacy of assuming in the 1950s and 1960s that an inclusive "nationalism" would be the universal solvent of differences in post-colonial Africa, a fallacy for which many people paid dearly. It is a fallacy the Nigerians, among others, want no part of, as their ventures into preventive measures attest.

It is not at all my purpose to paint a worst-possible-case scenario. All that needs to be said is that ethnic conflict is a recurrent phenomenon, that the ascriptive character of affiliations puts a strain on democratic institutions unless precautions are taken, and that having been through a long bout of White-Black conflict constitutes no inoculation against other varieties. Put simply, that is why South Africa's politics will not be nonracial and nonethnic but multiracial and multiethnic, and that is also why preventive arrangements should appeal to everybody in South Africa, regardless of color.

It might be thought that no African ethnic group is large enough to advance a claim to domination by itself; none even approaches 50 percent of the African population. Such arithmetic speculations would be quite misconceived in comparative perspective. To begin with, South

135. Peter Collins, *The Ethnic Factor in South Africa's Politics* (University of Cape Town, n.d.; mimeo.), p. 95.
136. Ibid.

African Whites, a small minority, maintained their domination for a very long time. In Nigeria, the Hausa comprised not more than 30 percent of the population, the Ibo and Yoruba 16–17 percent each; yet all three were major actors in an ethnic politics that, in the First Republic, produced essentially a Hausa-Ibo showdown. Likewise, the Kikuyu, with about 20 percent of the Kenyan population, managed to dominate Kenyan politics and exclude others for decades. Once the democratic process cracks under the strain of ethnic conflict and of parties aligned with particular ethnic groups—whether the crack comes from a military coup or the inauguration of a single-party state—the way is open for much smaller minorities to rule behind the facade of an allegedly inclusive military or an allegedly inclusive single party.[137] That possibility cannot be excluded for South Africa unless powerful precautions are taken. Would it not be ironic, after all the struggle that has passed, for South Africa to end up, as other countries have, with simply another form of minority rule?

137. For a description of how this can happen, see Donald L. Horowitz, *Ethnic Groups in Conflict* (Berkeley and Los Angeles: University of California Press, 1985), pp. 429–37, 486–508.

CHAPTER THREE

Obstacles to Democracy

When the old order dies, the future will not necessarily be secure. Several features of South Africa's structural situation put the democratic future in doubt. One of these is the need for carefully designed institutions to mitigate the conflicts of any severely divided society. Another derives from the possibly hegemonic aspirations of some of the contenders for power. Both of these problems I shall discuss in subsequent chapters.

Here I intend to treat impediments of a different sort. Some, such as dissensus on the means required to produce a democratic system and the sense of differential legitimacy resulting from a claim to indigenousness, form part of the ideological dissensus described in Chapter 1. Others, such as wishful thinking about the future and widespread suspicion about the intentions of other actors, are reactions to the harshness of the apartheid regime. Another impediment is a serious set of misconceptions about the nature of majority rule. The misconceptions are not confined to South Africa, but they can be fatal to democracy in a divided society. Finally, the fact that democratization was delayed so long has made dramatic rather than gradual change essential, but the very rapidity of the required change vastly increases the chance that some important social supports of democracy will not emerge in time to do their job. The multiple sources of these obstacles can either feed discouragement or motivate herculean efforts to build carefully.

THE PERILS OF WISHFUL THINKING

The very first obstacle to democracy is the common tendency to think it will be easy to attain, that the hard part is eliminating the apartheid regime. There is a sense that what is needed is a transfer of title, when in fact the house is not yet built.

One truism not heard sufficiently in South Africa is that every solution creates new problems. Many eloquent volumes have been devoted to depicting apartheid in all of its ugly manifestations. With a few notable exceptions, hard, and hardheaded, thinking about a post-apartheid South Africa has been much rarer. But a good cause does not assure a good result. It is a pernicious myth that all struggles are over when *the* struggle is over. South Africa may be pregnant with a new order, but it has had no political amniocentesis to check for birth defects.

Confronted with foreboding, even justifiable foreboding, a common reaction is to look on the bright side, to search for neglected, positive elements. This can be a useful exercise, but it frequently results, not in a more balanced assessment, but in an unbalanced prognosis in an opposite, unjustifiably optimistic direction.

There is a particularly strong propensity to such wishful thinking when it comes to democratic futures. At the height of *glasnost* and *perestroika,* when many observers thought Mikhail Gorbachev's future leadership in the Soviet Union imperiled, it was suggested that Gorbachev and the reformers could draw upon powerful democratic currents in the Russian past. The implication of the argument was that these traditions, plus a strong reformist leader, together were likely to produce a democratic outcome in the Soviet Union.[1] Since each of the democratic movements being invoked had been suppressed, however, one might have thought the contemporary power equation in the Soviet Union was a better guide to the outcome than was a vague collective memory of repeated failures. Admittedly, this example is far from South Africa, but it illustrates clearly the tendency to confront difficult political problems wishfully. The aspiration to a democratic future requires more than imagining it, but profound, psychologically induced distractions get in the way.

There have been good psychological reasons for the nearly exclusive emphasis on the present. If the current structures are evil, then their

1. S. Frederick Starr, "A Usable Past," *New Republic,* May 15, 1989, pp. 24–47.

abolition will bring about good. To the extent that we engage in foreboding, do we not then implicitly cast doubt upon the unmitigated justice of the present struggle? While these are good psychological reasons to repress the future, they are not good reasons. The present may be bad, but that fact does not tell us whether the future will be good or bad. It is, in short, very common to expend energy on thinking about ways to achieve "a fundamental reversal of race policies in South Africa" without the least idea—or with confused, contradictory, inchoate ideas—of what the replacement regime would look like.[2]

It is natural to think that it detracts from the revolutionary goals of the struggle to plan for the future. Planning may mean playing at least a hypothetical role as a future "insider," and this may seem contaminating.[3] But that is exactly the sort of "contamination" required for democracy to emerge. It is sobering to reflect that, at least since 1789, hardly ever, if at all, has revolution alone "produced a stable democratic regime in an independent state."[4] Revolutions require the use of undemocratic methods and the consolidation of undemocratic leadership. Both are inimical to the development of democracy later. If a democratic South Africa is desired, a future orientation is required.

Only recently has a future orientation emerged. In 1988, the African National Congress inaugurated the latest and most serious phase of the indispensable constitutional debate with the publication of its *Constitutional Guidelines for a Democratic South Africa.*[5] I shall say more about these guidelines later. All I want to say now is that they came not a moment too soon.

Yet the future has been slighted.[6] Again, South Africa is not unique.

2. A splendid example of this approach is provided by John A. Marcum, "Africa: A Continent Adrift," *Foreign Affairs* 18, no. 1 (January 1989): 159–79, at 176, from which the quotation in the text is drawn.

3. "[Allan] Boesak seems uncomfortable when it comes to the specifics of what should be done in South Africa. Those are 'insiders' questions,' he feels, and Boesak does and does not want to be an insider." Richard John Neuhaus, *Dispensations: The Future of South Africa as South Africans See It* (Grand Rapids, Mich.: Eerdmans, 1986), pp. 194–95.

4. Samuel P. Huntington, "Will More Countries Become Democratic?" *Political Science Quarterly* 99, no. 2 (Summer 1984): 193–218, at 213. To the same effect, see Guillermo O'Donnell and Philippe C. Schmitter, "Tentative Conclusions about Uncertain Democracies," in Guillermo O'Donnell et al., eds., *Transitions from Authoritarian Rule: Prospects for Democracy* (Baltimore: Johns Hopkins University Press, 1986), pt. 4, p. 11; Alfred Stepan, "Paths toward Redemocratization: Theoretical and Comparative Considerations," in ibid., pt. 3, p. 79.

5. The text is contained in the *Weekly Mail* (Johannesburg), October 7–13, 1988.

6. With some notable exceptions, some of which I shall discuss below. Some interesting contributions, worthy of note at the outset, are Peter L. Berger and Bobby Godsell,

Even where the goal is policy planning, practically nobody does it. In responding to a problem, the modern democratic state behaves like a voyeur: it adopts a wait-and-see attitude.

In fact, the advantages of planning are widely touted and largely true. Solving a problem earlier is better. There will be more accumulated obstacles to success later; a deliberative process is likely to be less prone to error than is a crisis-driven process; lead time is valuable in coping with complexity; and early action allows phasing in, a form of gradualism conducive to adaptation but foreclosed once crisis has struck.

Despite all these advantages, many of the most important policy decisions are taken at exceptional times—times of crisis, times when there is a strong demand for change, times when unusual events have immobilized obstacles to new policy or made proponents of innovation suddenly seem more credible.[7] This tendency has two serious implications for severely divided societies.

First, there is a good chance that it will be too late by then for the innovation to have a significantly positive effect on ethnic relations. The crisis probably means that measures that would have been ample to alter a conflict situation at an earlier period will be insufficient at the later period. Anyone who doubts this proposition should compare the two very modest devolution schemes for the Tamils proposed in Sri Lanka in 1957 and 1968—schemes that nevertheless produced a Sinhalese backlash that prevented their implementation—with the far more sweeping scheme ultimately put in effect but inadequate to stop the warfare.

Second, delaying policy making until after disaster has struck means that the time for deliberation is foreshortened. When serious conflicts exist, the pressure to settle builds up over a long time, but the actual settlement process tends to occur in a short time and is usually less considered and less future oriented than it should be. This is a particularly important disadvantage for ethnically divided societies, because the institutional arrangements they require to preserve harmony and

---

eds., *A Future South Africa: Visions, Strategies and Realities* (Cape Town: Human & Rousseau Tafelberg, 1988); Hermann Giliomee and Lawrence Schlemmer, eds., *Negotiating South Africa's Future* (New York: St. Martin's Press, 1989); F. van Zyl Slabbert and David Welsh, *South Africa's Options: Strategies for Sharing Power* (New York: St. Martin's Press, 1979).

7. See John W. Kingdon, *Agendas, Alternatives, and Public Policy* (Boston: Little, Brown, 1984), pp. 17–18. See also the issue "Policymaking in Developing Countries," *Policy Sciences* 22, nos. 3–4 (November 1989).

civility are often complex; they are best not improvised but precision engineered.

Not surprisingly, states that took explicit account of their ethnic heterogeneity at the outset have so far done better, even with worse problems, than those that failed to do so. Malaysia, with some of the world's most difficult ethnic problems, adopted institutions that moderated their behavioral manifestations. Sri Lanka, with more modest problems, exacerbated them.[8] Earlier is better, but later is much more common; and that is ground for concern.

MAJORITY RULE AND DEMOCRACY

If there has been insufficient attention to the future, one might guess that the attention that has been given has not produced a rich array of models. Scholarly observers and independent commissions have produced their share of plans. But to focus on political actors is to recognize that most of the already-stated visions of the South African future are at best merely precatory, at worst utterly impoverished.

Before the legalization of the African National Congress and other resistance organizations in 1990, A. S. Mathews summed up the regime's positive aspirations in a concise, discouraging, but altogether accurate formula: ". . . the rhetoric of the political reform policy of the government goes no further than sharing power without losing it."[9] "White domination" and "discrimination," it was said, "must go,"[10] but the regime's most sophisticated theorists of constitutional reform habitually envisioned "democratic decisionmaking" only "as far as possible" and specifically rejected what they called "the erroneous equation of democracy with majority rule."[11] Majority rule, they said, is appro-

8. See Donald L. Horowitz, "Incentives and Behaviour in the Ethnic Politics of Sri Lanka and Malaysia," *Third World Quarterly* 11, no. 4 (October 1989): 18–35.

9. A. S. Mathews, "National Security, Freedom and Reform in South Africa" (January 27, 1988; unpublished paper), p. 20.

10. Acting President Jan Chris Heunis, quoted in the *Durham Morning Herald* (N.C.), February 16, 1989; F. W. de Klerk, speech in parliament, May 9, 1989 (mimeo.), p. 4.

11. Fanie Cloete, "Constitutional Change in South Africa," (August 1988; unpublished paper), p. 10. Cloete was then chief director for constitutional planning. See also Jan Chris Heunis, "Finding a Formula for Constitutional Reform," in S. Prakash Sethi, ed., *The South African Quagmire* (Cambridge, Mass.: Ballinger, 1987), pp. 73–83. Heunis was, for several years, the minister of constitutional development. For a similar formulation, emphasizing a Black role in decision making, without universal suffrage, see the National Party's five-year Plan of Action, issued in Pretoria on June 29, 1989.

priate to homogeneous societies but inappropriate to heterogeneous societies like South Africa.

Leaving aside the fact that most of the world, including that part of the world that practices majority rule, is heterogeneous, this position, I shall argue momentarily, is based on a misconception about the nature of majority rule. The misconception is not unique to the South African government. For the moment, it is sufficient to point out that democracy cannot be achieved in the modern world without universal suffrage. Although many countries countenance deviations from equal apportionment of legislative seats and many require special majorities of one kind or another for various purposes, very few qualify the franchise with education, property, or literacy requirements.[12] The franchise is a necessary—but not a sufficient—condition for democracy in conditions of mass society.[13] South Africa, no less than other societies, partakes of those conditions. In such conditions, without universal suffrage elections, there cannot be representation; without representation, there cannot be democracy.

The National Party's five-year Action Plan, prepared for the 1989 general elections, did not rule out universal suffrage, but it emphasized the need for group protection.[14] Cabinet ministers dropped heavy hints of separate electoral rolls for Whites.[15] When President F. W. de Klerk finally acknowledged the need for one person, one vote in February 1990, he coupled the concession with the usual formulation about the need to prevent group domination and to protect minority as well as individual rights.[16] Universal suffrage did not necessarily imply majority rule.

What long troubled the regime's reformers about majority rule is, of

12. Vernon Van Dyke, "One Man One Vote and Majority Rule as Human Rights," *Revue des Droits de l'Homme* 6, nos. 3–4 (1973): 447–66.

13. See Robert A. Dahl, *A Preface to Democratic Theory* (Chicago: University of Chicago Press, 1956), pp. 63–75; Harry Eckstein, *Division and Cohesion in Democracy* (Princeton: Princeton University Press, 1966), p. 229. Compare Carole Pateman, *Participation and Democratic Theory* (Cambridge: Cambridge University Press, 1970), p. 14; Benjamin Barber, *Strong Democracy* (Berkeley and Los Angeles: University of California Press, 1984), p. 266.

14. National Party, *Plan of Action of the National Party, Election of 6 September 1989* (Pretoria: Federal Information Service, n.d.), pp. 2–4. See F. W. de Klerk, "Address Introducing the Debate on the NP's Plan of Action," (Pretoria, June 29, 1989; mimeo.), p. 3.

15. See *Citizen* (Johannesburg), July 24, 1989.

16. The text of the speech is contained in the *Cape Times* (Cape Town), February 3, 1990.

course," their equation of majority rule with Black rule and White subordination, just as minority rule is White rule with Black subordination.
Unfortunately, some opponents of the regime agree with this prescription wholeheartedly, if almost absentmindedly. Nadine Gordimer, for
example, has written of a "black republic," of "the black majority which
will rule," and of "the black state that is coming."[17] Even the *Economist* of London speaks of the need to accept what it calls "black rule"[18]
in South Africa, though, so far as I am aware, it has never spoken of
the need to accept either Catholic rule in undivided Ireland or Protestant rule in Northern Ireland.[19]

In its understanding of the future, the *Economist* is very much in line
with what a great many Western Europeans and North Americans re-
flexively believe the concept of majority rule implies, even requires, in
South Africa. It is, they believe, the natural meaning of the words *majority rule*. And unwittingly, of course, this notion hardens the determination of the South African government not to embrace the conception.

If we are to be completely honest, if this is the inevitable implication
of majority rule, why should the regime embrace it? What is the ethical
foundation for requiring minority oppressors to submit to majority oppressors? Reviewing Gordimer's essays, Denis Donoghue remarks
pointedly that what she proposes could not be "anything more or better
than the present [system] turned upside down."[20] The American theo-
logian Richard John Neuhaus, hardly a friend of apartheid, expresses a
similar thought and goes a step further when he notes that, between
what he calls "the extremes" of Afrikaner nationalism and Black nationalism, "moderation and wisdom" are thought to reside. "But I think
it more likely," he continues, "that wisdom, and reason for tempered
hope, is to be found not on middle ground but on quite different ground.
No lasting dispensation can be established by splitting the difference

17. Nadine Gordimer, *The Essential Gesture: Writing, Politics and Places* (New York:
Knopf, 1988), pp. 32, 264. In her confusion, she calls the "black state" she foresees "nonracial." Ibid., p. 278. Winnie Mandela writes, "Our future South Africa will be multiracial. It will accommodate all of us." In the very next paragraph, she adds that the White
opposition parties should help Whites "adjust to the inevitable black government of to-
morrow," and she later refers to "a black-ruled South Africa." *Part of My Soul Went
with Him* (New York: Norton, 1984), pp. 123, 144.
18. "White South Africa," *Economist*, May 20, 1989, p. 24.
19. See "Soldiering On in Ulster," *Economist*, August 12, 1989, pp. 19–20.
20. Denis Donoghue, "The Essential Posture," *New Republic*, November 28, 1988,
p. 29.

between the white oppression of blacks and the black oppression of whites."[21] This insight, which Neuhaus does not develop, is, I shall suggest, full of possibility.

The unsatisfactory quality of theorizing about the nature of majority rule in South Africa can be illustrated very easily by turning it around in the United States. The United States is assuredly governed by principles of majority rule, but it would be totally unacceptable to declare, merely because there are many more Whites than Blacks, that the United States is or ought to be subject to "White rule." The very notion of White majority rule carries strong connotations of minority exclusion and discrimination.

In recent years, the United States Congress and the courts have not been wholly content to let numbers take their course in the electoral process. In 1982, the Voting Rights Act was amended; and, as interpreted, the act now makes it easier to carve out legislative constituencies in which minority representatives are likely to emerge. The notion is that, so long as voters of given ethnic or racial groups vote cohesively, deliberate action needs to be taken to forestall minority exclusion from political power, defined, in this case, in terms of elected minority representatives.[22] The burden does not fall on American Blacks to, as South Africans say, "become part of the majority." So long as the groups tend to have different interests, provision is made to insure against the permanent neglect of minority interests.

The same logic applies in South Africa. If majority rule means Black majority rule and White minority exclusion, something has gone wrong. It need not and should not mean that; and, at the threshold, if it does mean that, Whites will have no reason to choose an inclusive democracy for South Africa. Apart from altruism, that is one of several good reasons why Blacks should not prefer "Black rule."

The moral duties of ethnic groups to one another constitute largely uncharted territory. In the United States, there has recently been a de-

21. *Dispensations*, p. 293.
22. See Abigail M. Thernstrom, *Whose Votes Count? Affirmative Action and Minority Voting Rights* (Cambridge: Harvard University Press, 1987). I do not mean to imply here my agreement with all that has been done under the amended act, particularly the definition of power in terms of the identity of elected representatives alone. See Donald L. Horowitz, "The Voting Rights Act," in J. Jackson Barlow et al., eds., *The New Federalist Papers* (Lanham, Md.: University Press of America, 1988), pp. 314–17. Rather, my aim is simply to stress the strong impulse to prevent majority domination and minority exclusion. For elaboration, see Chapter 5, pp. 165–66, below.

bate on the ethics of excluding aliens from free entry into the country. The debate shows the issues to be at least murky and at best difficult; but the most liberal arguments for open boundaries are premised on the morality of sharing, the fortuity of the status quo ante, and "the equal treatment of individuals in the public sphere."[23] On the other hand, several Lockean, liberal, and communitarian socialist thinkers—respectively, Peter H. Schuck and Rogers M. Smith, Bruce Ackerman, and Michael Walzer—contend that the exclusion of immigrants can be justified to protect what they call, in turn, civic "homogeneity," "the process of liberal conversation," and the distinctiveness of the "political community" and its social life.[24] As I understand the debate, however imperfectly, no one would be prepared to argue for unrestricted immigration if it were likely to result in political subordination of the population already in place. Precisely such objections underlay the ultimate liberal Western consensus against colonialism.[25]

I do not intend to extrapolate any positive principles from the ethics of immigration to the ethics of ethnic politics.[26] All I need to say for now is that I share the reservations of Donoghue and Neuhaus on this matter. I do not believe that any group is under a moral duty to legislate itself into a position of political subordination. I use the phrase "all I need to say for now" advisedly, because I do not believe that the inevitable result of universal suffrage is majority domination or, for that matter, that majority rule is necessarily the same as Black majority rule.

Before I explain what I mean, let me note that the ANC certainly does not equate majority rule with Black rule. Upon his release from prison, Nelson Mandela flatly opposed the government's insistence on group rights and in the same breath added: "We are aware of the fears of whites in this country of being dominated by blacks, and we are addressing that very seriously."[27] The ANC wants a "non-racial state"

23. Joseph H. Carens, "Aliens and Citizens: The Case for Open Borders," *Review of Politics* 49, no. 2 (Spring 1987): 251–73, at 268.

24. The quotations are, in order, from Peter H. Schuck and Rogers M. Smith, *Citizenship without Consent* (New Haven: Yale University Press, 1985), p. 28; Bruce Ackerman, *Social Justice in the Liberal State* (New Haven: Yale University Press, 1980), p. 95; Michael Walzer, *Spheres of Justice* (New York: Basic Books, 1983), p. 39. Compare Sanford Levinson, "Constituting Communities through Words That Bind: Reflections on Loyalty Oaths," *Michigan Law Review* 84, no. 8 (June 1986): 1440–70, at 1445–46.

25. Cf. Rupert Emerson, *From Empire to Nation* (Cambridge: Harvard University Press, 1960), p. 295.

26. Nor even to advert to the voluminous literature on the ethics of affirmative action (positive discrimination).

27. Quoted in the *New York Times,* February 15, 1990.

based on "one person / one vote," though, in its *Constitutional Guidelines*, the ANC does not prescribe any specific electoral system.[28] The omission is not inadvertent, since the ANC had before it a quite comprehensive description of electoral alternatives.[29]

There are, then, two theoretical positions: (1) majority rule produces majority domination; or (2) majority rule produces something else. The ANC calls the something else a "non-racial state." As I have explained, it is more appropriate to envision a multiracial state with nonracial institutions.

I have said that the first position—majority domination—is not inevitable. But it certainly is a common result. One only needs to stipulate a few conditions to make it the most probable outcome by far. Suppose in a given state there are two groups, A and B, with, respectively, 60 percent and 40 percent of the population and the voters who vote.[30] Suppose, in this polarized society, that Group A is a majority in 60 percent of the territorially demarcated single-member parliamentary constituencies and that the rule of election is the British rule of first-past-the-post or plurality election. This is the rule according to which the victorious candidate is the one who has managed to obtain the largest number of votes (a plurality), even if that number is less than 50 percent. The plurality rule is one which, I note with parenthetical irony, both the government and many of its most serious opponents believe to be the appropriate one for a future South Africa.[31] Make one further assumption, richly supported by the comparative experience of divided societies—namely, that, under conditions of free elections, groups in polarized societies will line up behind ethnically based political parties representing their respective groups. If overwhelming majorities of Group A vote for candidates of Party A and majorities of Group B vote for candidates of Party B, the result is a predictable and permanent en-

28. *Constitutional Guidelines*, ¶ E: "In the exercise of their sovereignty, the people shall have the right to vote under a system of universal suffrage based on the principle of one person / one vote."

29. Kader Asmal, "Electoral Systems: A Critical Survey" (paper presented at the In-House Seminar, African National Congress, Lusaka, Zambia, March 1–4, 1988).

30. The example is taken from Donald L. Horowitz, *Ethnic Groups in Conflict* (Berkeley and Los Angeles: University of California Press, 1985), pp. 83–86. The same problem was identified earlier in J. A. Laponce, "The Protection of Minorities by the Electoral System," *Western Political Quarterly* 10, no. 2 (June 1957): 318–39, at 325–26, and for South Africa by Slabbert and Welsh, *South Africa's Options*, p. 85.

31. Which is one reason the government drew the unfortunate conclusions that it did about universal suffrage. For an influential Black view, see, e.g., Dr. Nthato Motlana, quoted in Neuhaus, *Dispensations*, p. 267. Motlana wants the present South African constitution "minus race."

trenchment of Group A in power. As a matter of fact, because first-past-the-post is a plurality rule, even if Group A gave its support to more than one party, Party A might still end up with a firm majority of seats.[32]

Such polarizing elections have been very much more common in Asia and Africa than we might like to think. It is quite possible that, in the first instance, South Africa's universal suffrage elections under such a system would turn out that way, too. As I have shown elsewhere,[33] such elections are a major (though not the only) source of the decline of democracy in both continents. Polarizing elections have divided such countries as Nigeria, Uganda, the Sudan, Chad, Congo (Brazzaville), Burkina Fasso (then Upper Volta), Mali, Zambia, Togo, Ghana, Sierra Leone, and, most recently, Zimbabwe. In the first four countries on this list, such elections were the indispensable prelude to civil war, as they were also in Pakistan and Sri Lanka. In the remaining countries, military coups or the institution of a one-party state replaced democratic elections with authoritarian regimes, sometimes more or less benign, more often highly oppressive, almost always ethnically less than fully inclusive. A common initial response to polarized election results of this sort is for Group B—the permanent minority—to engage in violent strategies of resistance. These include riots and, if Group B is well represented in the armed forces officer corps, military coups (Nigeria, January 1966, being merely one example) or, if Group B is territorially concentrated, secessionist movements. None of these possibilities can be ruled out for South Africa.

And so there are two kinds of majority rule. Democratic theory demands that they be distinguished from each other. Ascriptive majority rule, with few if any floating voters, is one kind. It is the kind found in polarized societies, of the sort South Africa would be the day after universal suffrage based on the present electoral system. The election is

---

32. By winning pluralities in repeated three-way contests or by winning in repeated four-way contests if Group B were also divided. Sri Lanka's elections until the electoral reforms of 1978 approximated this situation. In the 1948 and 1953 elections in South Africa—and again in 1989—the National Party (together with an allied party in 1948) won a majority of seats on less than half the votes—a very common result in first-past-the-post systems, as witness Margaret Thatcher's own electoral victories in Great Britain, whence the system emanated. For vote-seat relationships in South Africa, see Gwendolen M. Carter, *The Politics of Inequality: South Africa since 1948*, 2d ed. (New York: Praeger, 1959), pp. 448–52; Richard Hodder-Williams, "South Africa: Democratic-Centralism versus Elite-based Parties," in Alan Ware, ed., *Political Parties: Electoral Change and Structural Responses* (Oxford: Blackwell, 1987), p. 25.

33. *Ethnic Groups in Conflict*, pp. 473–86.

tantamount to a census, and it locks out the minority from any significant political power, save what it can pry loose by violence or disruption. And there is the other kind of majority rule, associated with stable democracies, where marginal voters choose—that is, elect in the true sense—among competing parties and where the outcome is not foreordained by demography. If democratic alternatives were available, I have never understood why anyone would choose institutions that would produce the first kind of election—the census-type election—except, of course, because of the common failure to distinguish between the two types.

In point of fact, after 1948, Afrikaner political domination of English-speaking Whites was based on an electoral system conducive to minority exclusion. Only recently, as intra-White social and political differences have declined, has democratic choice within all segments of the White electorate been enhanced. Albie Sachs's scathing indictment of White hypocrisy is, on this score, wide of the mark. "Now that the majority is going to be black," he says,

> South African whites suddenly believe majority rule is a terrible thing. They've been very happy with the idea until now—South Africa has had majority rule since it was formed in 1910—but that's because it's been reserved for the whites. Now that the majority stands to change color, you no longer hear people talking about majority rule but about "majoritarianism," which sounds worse than Marxism-Leninism.[34]

If English-speaking Whites were happy with the particular form of majority rule that gave them Afrikaner domination, they certainly did not show it. And the problem of the future is neither majority rule nor majoritarianism, both of which are essential to democracy, but ascriptive majority rule, which kills democracy by turning elections into censuses and locking minorities out.

Beneath this confusion lie fundamental misconceptions about democracy and majority rule. If democracy is defined as "a system of rule by temporary majorities,"[35] rule by permanent majorities is plainly incompatible. If democracy is characterized by "the quality of being completely or almost completely responsive to all its citizens,"[36] then per-

---

34. Albie Sachs, "Post-Apartheid South Africa: A Constitutional Framework," *World Policy Journal* 6, no. 3 (Summer 1989): 503–29, at 513.

35. Dankwart A. Rustow, "Transitions to Democracy: Toward a Dynamic Model," *Comparative Politics* 2, no. 3 (April 1970): 337–63, at 351.

36. Robert A. Dahl, *Polyarchy: Participation and Opposition* (New Haven: Yale University Press, 1971), p. 2.

manent exclusion of minorities is a disqualifying condition. If democracy requires the creation of a majority out of "shifting temporary alliances,"[37] the pre-formed racial or ethnic majority is not democratic.

In the most comprehensive consideration of the concept of majority rule, Elaine Spitz takes cognizance of the special problems posed by permanent minorities. Constituencies are ordinarily organized by geography, she notes, because of the assumption that territorial contiguity creates bonds among people; but that assumption is highly doubtful in the case of racially or ethnically divided societies.[38] In seriously divided societies, where minorities cannot "coalesce to form a majority,"[39] attention must be focused on the method "of organizing the representative system in general . . . . The opportunities for organizing and becoming a majority or a minority become critical. No group that feels it has a fair chance to dominate or influence importantly the outcome of the political process will be likely to feel permanently excluded."[40] Put succinctly, community is a prerequisite for majority rule. Where community exists, minorities acquiesce "in hopes that they will someday become majorities."[41] Severely divided societies are short on community, and the problem is to organize the system of representation so that those hopes are not doomed in advance.

One way to approach the problem of representation, suggested by Robert A. Dahl and other writers, is to limit the majority principle whenever people of different languages, races, religions, or national origins "with no firm habits of political cooperation and mutual trust" are to unite in a single polity.[42] A distinguished historian, Hermann Giliomee, has argued for such an approach, because of the likelihood of a census-type election—in South Africa. The conflation of majority rule with ascriptive majority rule and the census-type election, in his view, leaves only one alternative: the "shelving (for the time being) of the concept of majority consent."[43] One common possibility is to constitute each

37. Elaine Spitz, *Majority Rule* (Chatham, N.J.: Chatham House, 1984), p. xiii.
38. Ibid., pp. 56–58.
39. Ibid., p. 58.
40. Ibid.
41. Ibid., p. 163.
42. Robert A. Dahl, *After the Revolution* (New Haven: Yale University Press, 1970), p. 89.
43. Hermann Giliomee, "South Africa, Ulster, Israel: The Elusive Search for Peace," *South Africa International* 19, no. 3 (January 1989): 140–51, at 150. But see the somewhat different formulation in Hermann Giliomee and Lawrence Schlemmer, *From Apartheid to Nation-Building* (Cape Town: Oxford University Press, 1989), which I shall discuss in Chapter 4, below.

such group a subpolity and then apply the majority principle to it and a different linking principle between groups.

In my view, however, there is no alternative to majority consent, and the division into subpolities is neither the only nor the best way out of the problem, which is to avoid a system that produces racially or ethnically defined majorities and minorities. There are ways of thawing frozen majorities and minorities within a single polity without providing for concurrent majorities and—most important of all—without doing violence to the principle of one person, one vote, one value.

THE DISSENSUS ON MEANS

Democratic alternatives are available, as the Nigerians, among others, have shown. The major questions are (1) whether they are acceptable to South Africans and (2) whether, if they are, they can actually be made to work in South Africa. These are separate questions.

When I ask whether they are acceptable, as I have already said, I do not mean to imply that they entail any dilution of the principle of universal suffrage. Among the options that can and should be eliminated at the outset are the qualified franchise (that is, qualified by property, tax payment, literacy, or any other requirement besides age and citizenship), ethnically or racially demarcated houses of parliament, and so-called communal (ethnic or racial) electoral rolls. It needs to be said, as emphatically as possible, that every vote should count for one and none should count for more than one.

As I shall indicate later, the institutions I am referring to entail a revision of the first-past-the-post electoral system, under which the candidate who receives the largest number of votes (even if less than a majority) wins the election. The plurality system is not, in any event, accepted in most Western democratic countries outside the Anglo-American orbit or, for that matter, even in such British-derived parliamentary systems as Austrialia's or Ireland's. Moreover, the plurality system is under attack in two of its historical bastions: in Great Britain and in New Zealand, where a Royal Commission in 1986 recommended proportional representation.[44] The problem of acceptability is

44. See Arend Lijphart, "The Demise of the Last Westminster System? Comments on the Report of New Zealand's Royal Commission on the Electoral System," *Electoral Studies* 6, no. 2 (August 1987): 97–103; Jonathan Boston, "Electoral Reform in New Zealand: The Report of the Royal Commission," *Electoral Studies* 6, no. 2 (August 1987): 105–14; Vernon Bogdanor, "Electoral Reform and British Politics," *Electoral Studies* 6, no. 2 (August 1987): 115–21.

not that any alternative to plurality election in single-member constituencies is a ruse for cheating the majority out of its due. The problem
is that South Africans of all colors seem to equate first-past-the-post
with majority rule and majority rule with first-past-the-post.

I cannot help but mark the special irony that Afrikaner politicians
and intellectuals (but not only they) were, for so long, fixated on British
institutions and the further irony that the principal impetus for adopt-
ing continental electoral systems came initially from English speakers in
Natal. Of course, the irony may have something to do with the benefit
the National Party has historically derived from plurality elections and
the benefits the former Anglophone opposition might have gained from
a different system. It took a civil war in Nigeria and the threat of one
in Sri Lanka to overcome, at least in part, the intellectual power of
British colonial institutions. Will it take the same in South Africa?

Constitution making is not an a priori exercise in taking principles
from on high and parachuting them into any environment but a matter
of starting with certain democratic objectives and choosing among constitutional principles to secure those objectives in a particular environment. There is nothing wrong with borrowing institutions. After all,
how can any people be expected to invent everything from scratch? The
trick is to borrow the right institutions, those that are apt for the predicament of the borrowers. As we shall see later, one test of aptness is
to see how various institutions have functioned elsewhere.

As I read the South African evidence, there is a large paradox involved in the question of the acceptability of democratic alternatives. It
is this: In sample surveys, majorities of all groups, and particularly majorities of Blacks, appear firmly committed to an inclusive South African polity, based on majority rule but not on Black domination. At the
same time, the means to achieve such results are viewed with understandable suspicion by that same majority. Whites, on the other hand,
are prepared to abandon White rule, but they equate majority rule with
Black rule. There is some consensus on ends but not on means.

In 1986, an urban South African sample was asked about various
possible future governments.[45] Overwhelming majorities of all groups
professed support for a future government in which "no group dominates." This is perhaps unsurprising, given the motherhood-and-apple-
pie character of the question, but it is worth pointing out that even 58

45. C. P. de Kock, "Revolutionary Violence in South Africa: 1,000 Days after 3 September 1984," in D. J. van Vuuren et al., eds., *South Africa: The Challenge of Reform*
(Pinetown, South Africa: Burgess, 1988), pp. 343–405.

percent of the Whites thought such a future government would be good, despite the fact that the question probably was interpreted to suggest major regime changes so far as Whites were concerned. (On the other hand, perhaps not. For several years, the South African government had been touting the idea of "no domination" in a way that might suggest only marginal changes.) More revealing in my view are the responses to the question asking about a future under a "Black majority government." Less than 6 percent of every group except Blacks thought such a future would be good. This is no surprise. The surprise, if there is one, consists of the urban Black response. Only 25 percent of Black respondents approved of such a future—a decline of 60 percentage points from Black respondents approving of a future government in which no group dominates. Can it be that urban Black respondents were making a sharp distinction that had eluded both Nadine Gordimer and the editors of the *Economist?*

I do not regard this survey as conclusive evidence of anything: the hypothetical and aspirational character of such questions is a problem in survey research. As we shall see shortly, Black opinion may ultimately be more equivocal than it is depicted here. Black students—future elites—certainly seem to provide rather different responses. Nevertheless, this survey is suggestive of support for measures to break the impasse that results from the prospect of the census-type election, in which majority rule comes down to Black rule, and it is supported by the results of other surveys of Black opinion.[46]

46. Similar results to the de Kock results were obtained in surveys reported by Theodor Hanf et al., *South Africa: The Prospects of Peaceful Change* (London: Rex Collings, 1981), p. 439, with substantial majorities of Whites accepting a government that included all groups but in which none dominated the others and only 35 percent of Soweto Blacks in 1978 favoring a government "in which blacks as the majority rule the whites," compared to 57 percent of that sample preferring "equal numbers of blacks and whites in [the] Cabinet." There are other surveys in which Black respondents indicate a strong preference for equality rather than Black control, even in sectors apart from politics (such as industry). See, e.g., Lawrence Schlemmer, *Black Worker Attitudes: Political Options, Capitalism and Investment in South Africa* (Durban: Centre for Applied Social Sciences, University of Natal, 1984), pp. 31–32. See also Lawrence Schlemmer, "Build-up to Revolution or Impasse?" in Heribert Adam, ed., *South Africa: The Limits of Reform Politics* (Leiden: E. J. Brill, 1983), p. 77, reporting a survey conducted for the Buthelezi Commission in which 70 percent or more of Black respondents "not only would oppose discrimination *against* whites but . . . valued white participation in South African society . . . ." (emphasis in the original); KwaZulu Natal Indaba, "Black Attitudes in KwaZulu Natal" (September 1988; mimeo.), p. 18, reporting that only 11 percent of the sample favored Black-only rule in a future South Africa, compared to 40 percent favoring rule by "all races together" and 15 percent favoring rule by Blacks and Whites, with support for the "all races" option increasing steadily with education level. For even stronger and more recent survey results in the same direction, see Giliomee and Schlemmer, *From Apartheid*

A 1989 survey of White university student preferences points in a similar direction. Among six options for a future South Africa, the "White control" option came in third, with the support of only 16.6 percent of the students, and actually came in a very distant fourth (3.2 percent)—far below an undifferentiated majority rule option (20 percent)—among English-speaking students.[47] These results obtained even though the White students responded quite candidly that they would expect to experience positive "conditions and quality of life" under a White-controlled government and negative conditions and quality of life under a Black-controlled government.[48] Either their candor on the one question is marred by hypocrisy on the other, or, very much more likely, they actually prefer alternatives to White domination, despite the privileges that come with it.

These results are not very different from adult White opinion expressed in other surveys asking about preferred options. Although very few Whites want a single, majority-controlled parliament, only a minority favors White rule or the current three-chambers variant of White rule. Most Whites—in fact, close to two-thirds—prefer some form of power-sharing accommodation of Blacks (though the options to which the respondents subscribe have been framed by researchers in a variety of ways).[49] Majorities of Whites appear to be ready for an end to apartheid in schools, group residential areas, and public accommodations.[50] There is also considerable support for fundamental political change. In 1988, two-thirds of White voters in Natal agreed with the statement "Until black people are included in Parliament, I don't think there will be peace in South Africa"; only one-fifth disagreed.[51]

There is, then, some fairly persuasive evidence that many Whites would

---

to *Nation-Building*, pp. 214–15, 223. But compare the rather different results reported in Mark Orkin, *Disinvestment, the Struggle, and the Future: What Black South Africans Really Think* (Johannesburg: Ravan Press, 1986; pamphlet), p. 51.

47. Jannie Gagiano, "Ruling Group Cohesion in South Africa: A Study of Political Attitudes among White University Students" (paper presented at the Biennial Conference of the Political Science Association of South Africa, October 9–11, 1989), pp. 41–42.

48. Ibid., pp. 57–58.

49. See the summaries of three surveys, administered between 1986 and 1989, in Giliomee and Schlemmer, *From Apartheid to Nation-Building*, pp. 156–58.

50. Michael Sutcliffe, "The Integration of Facilities: Results and Conclusions from a Survey of Residents of Durban" (Institute for a Democratic Alternative for South Africa, Durban, 1989; mimeo.), pp. 9, 13, 15; KwaZulu Natal Indaba, "New Indaba Survey Shows That Most White Natal Voters Reject Apartheid," KwaZulu Natal Indaba Press Release (Durban, February 3, 1988; mimeo.), tables 1, 2, 3, 6. The Durban site of the surveys is, of course, an important limitation

51. KwaZulu Natal Indaba, "New Indaba Survey Shows That Most White Natal Voters Reject Apartheid," table 4.

like a change from White rule and that many Blacks would not like a change to Black rule.

Still, there are obstacles to electoral engineering. To enumerate them is to complete the paradox.

On the White side, the main obstacle is simply stated. The assumption is that universal suffrage will produce Black domination. Consequently, in the same year as 58 percent of White respondents expressed support for a government in which no group dominates, only 30 percent of White respondents in a different survey professed support for equal suffrage.[52] The apparent inconsistency between the White desire for Black participation and the absence of support for majority rule is explicable by the inability of most Whites to square majority rule with anything other than a straight reversal of the present system.

This obstacle is reinforced by another, solidly grounded in much of White opinion. It is that African-led governments are not likely to be democratic. The objection has two forms: a crude, bigoted one and a more substantial one. The crude version is typified by the remark of a superintendent of local administration in a Black township. Explaining the violence in the township, the official told a researcher: "You must forget about elections and democracy among Africans. The ones who stand in your way you eliminate—it's normal in the African way."[53] The more substantial objection is based on the very poor record of democracy in most of independent Africa thus far—a record scrupulously noted and well publicized, albeit without any careful causal analysis, by South African officials.

With respect to the excluded majority, the source of the obstacles to electoral engineering lies, initially, in the history of franchises and parliaments in South Africa. That history has given rise to a perfectly understandable Black suspicion of electoral manipulation. Since at least 1960, liberal South African Whites have been attempting to persuade Black leaders to focus on alternatives to plurality electoral formulae. The efforts include reports by the Molteno Commission and the Political Commission of the Study Project on Christianity in Apartheid Society.[54] With the notable exception of Mangosuthu Buthelezi, Blacks generally have been unconvinced. Black suspicion helps explain why.

52. *Times* (London), August 3, 1986. See also Gagiano, "Ruling Group Cohesion in South Africa," pp. 42–43, reporting that most White students choose an option other than undifferentiated majority rule. Most of the alternatives involve some sort of group protection. Giliomee and Schlemmer, *From Apartheid to Nation-Building*, pp. 156–58.

53. Quoted in Colin Legum, ed., *Africa Contemporary Record, 1986–87* (New York: Africana, 1987), p. B748.

54. Donald B. Molteno et al., *Final Report of the Commission Set Up by the Pro-*

The extraordinary fact is that, over the last 150 years, while the franchise was expanding in the West and even in parts of the then-colonial world—Sri Lanka, for example, had universal suffrage by 1931—it was contracting in South Africa. When the Cape Province first received representative government, in 1853, the franchise had, in fact, been "color-blind."[55] By 1910 and the Act of Union, Blacks had already been stripped of their right to be elected to parliament,[56] although some 7,000 Blacks and 14,000 Coloureds still held the franchise in the Cape Province at that time. When the franchise was extended to all White adults, in 1930–31, property qualifications were left intact for other groups. In 1936, Blacks in the Cape were deprived of the common roll vote they had had and were placed on a separate electoral roll, from which they could choose three White representatives. Throughout the Union, Blacks were allowed to elect four White senators.[57] After a five-year legal struggle that included a packing of the Senate, so-called Coloured voters in the Cape were also placed on a separate electoral roll in 1956. And, finally, in 1959, the White representatives of Black voters were removed from parliament and from the Cape Provincial Council, so that, with the exception of the four Whites elected by Cape Coloureds, all voters, as well as all representatives, were White.

Most recently, in 1983, two new chambers of parliament were created, one for Coloureds and one for Indians, both with limited powers. Both were inaugurated over the boycott of majorities of those who were to be represented in those chambers and over the flat opposition of the Black majority that was not to be represented. In the light of all this history, can anyone wonder that the vast majority of South Africans might be suspicious of fancy franchises and might prefer for themselves the same first-past-the-post system that White South Africans have chosen for themselves?

The suspicion is pervasive. It manifests itself, for example, in an otherwise highly sophisticated survey of electoral alternatives prepared for the ANC, in which the tendency to wonder whether proportional rep-

gressive Party to Make Recommendations on a Revised Constitution for South Africa, vol. 1 (N.p. 1960), pp. 7–28; Political Commission of the Study Project on Christianity in Apartheid Society, South Africa's Political Alternatives, SPRO-CAS Publication no. 10 (Johannesburg: Ravan Press, 1973), pp. 144–73.

55. See Carter, The Politics of Inequality: South Africa since 1948, pp. 19, 21, 120.

56. See Tom Lodge, Black Politics in South Africa since 1945 (London: Longman, 1983), p. 2; D. A. Kotzé, "African Politics," in Anthony de Crespigny and Robert Schrire, eds., The Government and Politics of South Africa (Cape Town: Juta, 1978), pp. 116–17.

57. Paul Maylam, A History of the African People of South Africa: From the Early Iron Age to the 1970s (London: Croom Helm, 1986), p. 166.

resentation might be a superior electoral system for a future South Africa is identified with "the ineluctable need of the racial oligarchy to maintain its power . . . ." [58]

I shall lay out later some of the details of the electoral innovations that seem to me to give South Africa a chance for majoritarian democracy with universal suffrage and without racial bifurcation. It suffices to say here that an electoral system in South Africa should provide every inducement to candidates and to political parties to reach out across racial and ethnic lines for support. If the parties do this, they will tend to interracial and interethnic compromise. To make such a system work, a plurality of political parties—a multiparty system—is better than just two parties, which would tend to bifurcation; and first-past-the-post elections in single-member constituencies will not produce the desired result.

Indeed, it may also be desirable to have a separately elected president, rather than a prime minister, so that the election of the president can be accomplished by an electoral system that provides strong incentives—as the Nigerian presidential system of 1979 did—for the candidates to reach out to groups other than their own or risk losing the election. And, finally, if there is to be multipolar fluidity in the party system, instead of bifurcation, a federal system of government may be preferable to a unitary system.

As soon as we say this, of course, we have evoked yet another understandable suspicion. The so-called Black homelands created by the regime of apartheid have made federalism a dirty word among many South Africans. They see federal states as a way of perpetuating divide and rule, of compartmentalizing people.[59] Federal proposals have been described by the ANC as " 'manoeuvres' to perpetuate Bantustans under new guises . . . ." [60] All "compartments," in the words of a UDF leader, are unacceptable.[61] And so, as majority rule can mean two things, a

58. Asmal, "Electoral Systems: A Critical Survey," p. 2. Inexplicably, the paper ends by asserting that proportional representation systems "have a built-in mechanism to ensure that no party obtains over 50% of the seats; they inevitably give rise to coalitions through the over-representation of minority interests." Ibid., p. 14. Both halves of the sentence are erroneous; and the whole statement is extremely curious, since the author displays elsewhere in the paper a knowledge of electoral systems, including proportional systems.

59. See, e.g., *Democracy in Action* (Cape Town), May 1989, p. 5.

60. Heribert Adam, "Exile and Resistance: The African National Congress, the South African Communist Party and the Pan Africanist Congress," in Berger and Godsell, eds., *A Future South Africa*, p. 104.

61. Interview, Johannesburg, September 20, 1985.

unitary South Africa can mean two things. Either it can mean one South Africa devoid of secessionist and partitionist schemes, or it can mean something more: one South Africa without federal components. To many people, unfortunately, it means the latter as well as the former.

Federal units, of course, need not be ethnically homogeneous or resemble the homelands in any way. It is not well recognized that divided societies can gain benefits even from federal units that are heterogeneous.[62] Perhaps that difference might change some minds, as well it should. But I do not think there is any blinking the deep suspicion of federalism that is entertained by many Black South Africans.

If this is where things stand, one of the major obstacles to a democratic South Africa may be that, while South Africans of all groups devoutly will the end, they do not necessarily will the required means to that end. Many White South Africans reject universal suffrage on a common roll—exactly the sort they have prescribed for themselves—and many Black South Africans seem to reject any institutions other than those borrowed by Whites from Great Britain. If that is so, the South African tragedy may be even sadder than we think.

It is worth noting that the suspicions of Black South Africans to which I advert are directly traceable to apartheid—to the apartheid of White-only elections and of Black exclusion, as well as to the apartheid of the Bantustans. And so the deeper irony is that the White regime, in its policy of separate development, has created resentments that may spill over and taint even some of the best prospects for living, not separately, but together.

THE BURDEN OF ALIENATION
AND THE MYTH OF INDIGENOUSNESS

Two further obstacles derive from the sense of being excluded and of having had one's land stolen. One is a common heritage of rigidly authoritarian societies; the other is common to many plural societies.

A particular kind of political learning seems to take place among those long excluded from political participation. The late Merle Fainsod pointed out many years ago that the tsarist autocracy helped create the conditions for the Soviet autocracy that followed. In his words, tsarist policy "alienated substantial sections of the vital and creative forces

62. Compare the recommendations in Arend Lijphart and Diane R. Stanton, "A Democratic Blueprint for South Africa," in S. Prakash Sethi, ed., *The South African Quagmire*, p. 92.

in society. They denied these forces experience in self-government, and where they could not deny, they limited such experience to the narrowest possible range. By damming up the constitutional channels for the expression of social grievances, they helped create a situation in which popular disaffection overflowed into revolutionary turbulence."[63]

Like the tsars, colonial regimes in Asia and Africa often taught their subjects that politics was the art of domination. In a few colonies, a form of limited, but not meaningless, democracy was practiced for some years or decades before independence. The association is not susceptible of proof, but it appears to be more than coincidence that three of those ex-colonies that practiced pre-independence self-government—India, Sri Lanka, and the Philippines—have maintained (or lost and then restored) vigorous democracies in the face of considerable obstacles, whereas others have generally done less well.

South Africans, deprived of democratic participation, have assuredly developed a keen sense of suspicion. They may also have learned lessons in domination. The fear, however well or ill founded it may prove to be, argues for the most careful design of institutions to foster democratic outcomes. To some extent, they will have to substitute for the trust that helps sustain most of the world's democracies.

The general obstacle is not unique to South Africa but is quite common in ethnically divided societies that have experienced international or interregional migration. It is a claim by some groups to legitimacy, to priority in the polity—even to the exclusion of others—by virtue of indigenousness, by having arrived first. In Malaysia, the Malays claim to be the sons of the soil and claim that the Chinese are mere immigrants. Assamese in India make similar claims against the Bengalis in their state. In the Nigerian First Republic of 1960–66, northern Nigerians made such claims against Ibo, who migrated from the south. Where claims to priority by virtue of indigenousness are made, interethnic compromise is far more difficult. Not that indigenousness is an unshakable fact. On the contrary, it is a feeling, a social construct. Wherever claims to indigenousness are heard, there is a large measure of fiction about who arrived when.[64]

63. Merle Fainsod, *How Russia Is Ruled,* 1st ed. (Cambridge: Harvard University Press, 1953), p. 5.
64. In Sri Lanka, for example, where Sri Lankan Tamils arrived, on the average, about a thousand years ago, they are nonetheless occasionally called by Sinhalese *kallathoni,* a term referring to recent, illegal Indian immigrants. In Malaysia, many Malays actually arrived significantly later than many Chinese.

Such claims are now occasionally heard in South Africa, where Whites are, from time to time, referred to as colonial "settlers" like those in Kenya or Zimbabwe. In the background, of course, is a powerful history of land grabbing, relegation of "natives" to "reserves," and creation of impoverished Bantustans. There is both an organizational component and an underlying popular-attitudinal component to these claims.

As we saw in Chapter 1, the place of Whites (and other minorities) in South Africa has been a frequent source of friction among the extra-parliamentary opposition. The ANC has itself been somewhat ambiguous on the question. Adhering to the racially inclusive Freedom Charter,[65] the ANC has also referred to the leading role of Africans in the struggle and to the South African government as a "colonial regime," a diagnosis that implies that Whites are mere colonists. For its part, the Black Consciousness Movement and the Pan Africanist Congress call South Africa "occupied Azania." The United Democratic Front, with a good many White and Indian members, is a loose confederation of organizations professing allegiance to the Freedom Charter, but individuals entertain a variety of views on the relative connections of groups to the territory. "We are the indigenous people of the country," a strongly committed, well-educated, African UDF leader stated in 1985.[66]

No doubt the "people's history" currently being taught by the resistance movement embodies a view of the conquest and warfare that took place in South Africa that is diametrically opposed to the White regime's view of wide open spaces, to which Black and White groups migrated. The "people's history" view will likely strengthen conceptions of Black indigenousness. In his inaugural address, the rector and vice-chancellor of the University of the Western Cape, a bastion of "people's history," referred to "the settler-dominated social order" in South Africa.[67]

Already, popular conceptions of Black indigenousness are strong. A survey among Black high school and university students, conducted in 1985, revealed racial sentiments far more exclusive than those elicited from random samples of the African population. Offered a "Black hegemony" option and a "majority rule" option, the former was chosen

65. See, e.g., *Sechaba, Official Organ of the African National Congress, South Africa,* July 1983.
66. Interview, Johannesburg, September 20, 1985.
67. Jakes Gerwel, "Inaugural Address by Professor Jakes Gerwel at His Installation on 5 June 1987 as Sixth Vice-Chancellor and Rector of the University of the Western Cape" (1987; pamphlet), p. 4.

by half of the respondents, nearly twice as many as chose the latter. Only seven of 119 Blacks in the sample preferred a future "society in which group identity has ceased to be crucial in determining who governs."[68] By contrast, large majorities of Coloured and English-speaking White respondents preferred such a society.[69] "Moreover," concluded the principal investigator, "it is clear from interviews that most black students perceive all 'Whites,' English and Afrikaans, in the role of immigrants who have illegally seized the land of their birth and reduced them to the condition of a subject people."[70] And 40.5 percent of the African respondents in a 1983 survey answered "Don't know" to a question about the meaning of human rights, compared to only 14.2 percent of Coloureds, 7.7 percent of Indians, and 6.8 percent of Whites who gave such a reply.[71] Such results are disquieting in the light of comparative evidence from divided societies, because they augur distinctions (or worse) based on perceived indigenous or immigrant status.

In the larger society—as opposed to student society—according to a 1986 survey, an overwhelming majority of Africans (78 percent) believe that Whites should continue to live in a future South Africa,[72] but there is no good evidence on what the acceptable terms of political interaction might be or on what the significant minority of respondents who gave a different answer were thinking.[73] This much is clear: claims to indigenousness always make democratic accommodation more difficult. Rarely, as I have indicated, are they historically supportable in the form in which they are made—any more than official White historical claims are supportable—particularly in a country where so many people have historically moved around so much. All over the world, the truth is that virtually all peoples come from somewhere else, and the history of migration and conquest that is propagated is usually highly selective. How important that history, and the claims to priority that flow from it, will be in South Africa remains to be seen, but it certainly has a chance of becoming a dominant strand in African political discourse.

68. Peter Collins, *The Ethnic Factor in South Africa's Politics* (University of Cape Town, n.d.; mimeo.) p. 95.
69. Ibid.
70. Ibid., p. 96.
71. Ibid., p. 98.
72. *Times* (London), August 3, 1986.
73. But see the studies reported in note 46, above.

CONSTITUTIONAL CHANGE: GULPS OR SIPS?

Both gradual constitutional change and dramatic constitutional change create risks for the future of South African democracy. Gradual change, accomplished much sooner, would have reduced the risks. There is now no alternative to dramatic change, and this stark fact, as I shall suggest, means that some of the most important supports for democracy will be, at best, imperfectly developed.

It is, of course, possible to acquire democratic institutions slowly, as Great Britain did. Moreover, students of the process of democratization suggest that democratic stability is enhanced where democratic rights, including suffrage, are institutionalized before mass claims are made on the political system.[74] Gradual incorporation of social groups by stages into the political system is generally a good formula for durable democracy. This statement alone should indicate the problematic future of a country in which the opposite course was followed.

It has been said that democracy can come in parts, in fragments, that it is always under construction.[75] No doubt there is a sense in which this is true, but it is more true of some times and places than of other times and places. Whatever good opportunities there were, twenty or even ten years ago, for South Africa to get its full democracy by a process of gradual but politically shrewd reform,[76] South Africa will not now get its democracy in parts or in small increments. It will get it, if at all, in a few spurts, rather like those that characterized decolonization in most Asian and African countries.[77]

I say this, not because I think great leaps into democracy are the best way, for, as I remarked earlier, under ideal conditions the Indo–Sri Lankan–Philippine way is the better way, as recent work on democratization attests.[78] Rather I say it because, as Disraeli pointed out, one

74. Seymour Martin Lipset, "Political Cleavages in 'Developed' and 'Emerging' Polities," in Erik Allardt and Yrjö Littunen, eds., *Cleavages, Ideologies and Party Systems* (Helsinki: Academic Bookstore, 1964), pp. 34–35.

75. Richard L. Sklar, "Developmental Democracy," *Comparative Studies in Society and History* 29, no. 4 (October 1987): 686–714.

76. See Samuel P. Huntington, "Reform and Stability in South Africa," *International Security* 6, no. 4 (Spring 1982): 3–25.

77. In using the decolonization analogy, I am not at all suggesting that South Africa is a colonial situation, as I shall make clear below. The analogy relates only to the issue of pacing.

78. See Larry Diamond, "Beyond Authoritarianism and Totalitarianism: Strategies for Democratization," *Washington Quarterly* 12, no. 1 (Winter 1989): 141–63, at 144–47.

cannot cross a great chasm in several leaps. There is a great chasm to be crossed in South Africa. Psychologically, a clean break with the past is necessary, because no change will be fully legitimate, given all that has transpired over the apartheid decades, without a sense that something momentous has occurred. For Black attachment to any new regime, the change must be palpable. The advantage of gradual change—its smoothness—is precisely its disadvantage in South Africa.

Even from the regime's standpoint, a strategy of change in big gulps rather than small sips is probably desirable. Perhaps with some justification, the government complained that it received no credit, either internationally or domestically, for reforms undertaken in the 1970s and 1980s. The parliamentary and extraparliamentary opposition simply pocketed them and went on to make new demands. To take one of many examples, protests at segregated sport finally produced integrated teams, at which point South Africa was met with continued boycott on the ground that there could be no normal sport in an abnormal society. The same goes for influx control, pass laws, freehold land ownership, and so-called residential gray areas, among others.[79] The government's changes went unreciprocated, partly because they were accomplished in a manner conducive to "salami tactics," one slice at a time, until, imperceptibly, the whole salami is gone.[80]

Moreover, gradual change risks a loss of control that may not be in the interest of the public in general. For example, Whites who prefer to stay in South Africa but are fearful of the uncertain end-state toward which the government is leading them may be able to use the time accompanying protracted change to find ways to export their capital and emigrate. This they might do in greater proportions than they would if more rapid changes took place in a surefooted way that provided assurance of a stable future. It is not clear at all that "radical change in incremental steps" is more likely to be "orderly."[81]

Perhaps the most important reason of all to prefer big gulps is that, at this point, small sips will be tainted by their association with the government in power. We have already seen that the regime's history of disenfranchisement and territorial division has placed a cloud over promising innovations in the electoral system and in federalism. Be-

79. For the regime's reforms of the 1970s and 1980s, see Giliomee and Schlemmer, *From Apartheid to Nation-Building*, pp. 114–49.

80. Cf. Thomas C. Schelling, *Arms and Influence* (New Haven: Yale University Press, 1966), pp. 66–69.

81. Hendrik W. van der Merwe, *Pursuing Justice and Peace in South Africa* (London: Routledge, 1989), pp. 110–12.

cause of their gradualness, even more substantial and genuine incremental reforms risk more of the same effect that Eugene Lourens and Hennie Kotzé have identified for the regime's earlier perversions of potentially promising ideas:

> One gains the impression that the National Party has appropriated the form of concepts like consociation and confederation while simultaneously rejecting their substantive contents. This may in the long run have unfortunate results for more committed proponents of these ideas. By using their form but perverting their contents the NP may be vitiating federalism and consociationalism as political alternatives . . . .[82]

A future South Africa will need some fairly complex institutions. Those institutions can stand on their own merits. They ought not to be put at risk by becoming the property of a government whose legitimacy is far from universally recognized.

Whether to proceed by sips or gulps is a question that cannot easily be finessed. There are tensions between the two methods.[83] And, of course, there is the ever-present question of which forces, on each side, will be strengthened, and which weakened, by one strategy or the other. There is a substantial risk that incremental reforms will strengthen the hand of those forces on both sides most interested in revolutionary solutions and least amenable to compromise.[84]

To suggest that the time for gradual change has passed does not mean that everything has to happen at once. If it did, that would be a prescription for failure. There is no prospect that White opinion would take the requisite risks or, even if it did, that a wide array of new institutions could all be made to work at once. To advocate big gulps is not to advocate choking to death. Nor does what I have said imply that the more dramatic, nonincremental strategy is free of difficulty. Quite the contrary. Securing and maintaining democracy will not be easy. There are problems of enactment and problems of maintenance. Speaking comparatively, there may be a tradeoff between getting democracy and keeping it. Those states that came to democracy more slowly may have less trouble maintaining it.

If we look at the difference between democracy achieved in incre-

---

82. Eugene Lourens and Hennie Kotzé, "South Africa's Non-unitary Political Alternatives," in A. Venter, ed., *South African Government and Politics* (Johannesburg: Southern, 1989), p. 327.

83. See Samuel P. Huntington, "Whatever Has Gone Wrong with Reform?" *Die Suid-Afrikaan* (Cape Town), Winter 1986, pp. 19–22, at p. 21.

84. See generally Samuel P. Huntington, *Political Order in Changing Societies* (New Haven: Yale University Press, 1968), pp. 362–69.

ments and democracy achieved in bold strokes, we can see exactly what the maintenance problems are for the latter. The difficulty of maintaining democracy achieved in bold strokes lies in the frequent absence of some conditions that support democracy. By supporting conditions, I mean two things: propitious sequencing of political change and the growth of social complexity.[85]

Propitious sequencing has full participation as the culmination of a process of building national identity and legitimate authority, rather than the reverse.[86] Poor sequencing has something to do with the general failure of democracy in Africa thus far. Where sequencing has been favorable, democracy has done better, as the cases of Botswana and Senegal show. In their comparative study of *Democracy in Developing Countries*,[87] Diamond, Linz, and Lipset employ a minimal conception of democracy, embracing nonviolent competition for power at regular intervals, inclusion of all major social groups in the selection of leaders and policies, and maintenance of basic civil and political liberties. Using that standard, their edited volume for Africa covers a mere six countries of the approximately 36 countries below the belt of North African states. Of the six, four are not democracies. Zimbabwe became, unofficially, a one-party state while the book was in press; Uganda and Ghana have been democracies for no more than 20 percent of their 30 years of independence; and Nigeria has twice seen democratic regimes overthrown by military coups. Of the remaining two, Senegal is described as a "semi-democracy," and Botswana is called a "paternalistic democracy" or, less kindly, "a *de facto* one-party state."[88] Nevertheless, these two states, with some continuous history of reasonably free elections and respect for liberty, provide some interesting contrasts with likely patterns of political participation in South Africa.

85. These are hardly new ideas with me. See Diamond, "Beyond Authoritarianism and Totalitarianism," p. 148; Huntington, "Will More Countries Become Democratic?"

86. This is the theme of much writing on the subject. See Dahl, *Polyarchy*, p. 36. See generally Leonard Binder et al., *Crises and Sequences in Political Development* (Princeton: Princeton University Press, 1971).

87. Larry Diamond et al., eds., *Democracy in Developing Countries*, vol. 2, *Africa* (Boulder, Colo.: Lynne Rienner, 1988). The study might have included the two mini-democracies of Mauritius and the Gambia; but, any way the computation is done, African democracies can be counted on the fingers of one hand.

88. The quotations in the text are drawn, in sequence, from Christian Coulon, "Senegal: The Development and Fragility of Semidemocracy," in Diamond et al., eds., *Democracy in Developing Countries*, vol. 2, *Africa*, pp. 141–78; John D. Holm, "Botswana: A Paternalistic Democracy," in ibid., pp. 179–215; Louis A. Picard, *The Politics of Development in Botswana: A Model for Success* (Boulder, Colo.: Lynne Rienner, 1987), p. 142.

Both Botswana and Senegal are one-party-dominant systems, in which alternation of government has never taken place. The same is true of the Gambia, which, though more or less democratic, is not included in the Diamond, Linz, and Lipset volume. In the three African countries with regular elections, opposition parties can be permitted to operate relatively freely, because they pose no threat of defeating the ruling party in a general election. The axiom that toleration of an opposition is likely to increase as the costs of toleration decrease is entirely apposite here.[89]

The basic reason for the uneven distribution of support is the same in Botswana and Senegal. In Botswana, there is a dominant ethnic group, the Tswana, which comprises about 90 percent of the population. Opposition parties have support among two non-Tswana minorities and among a dissident Tswana subgroup fearful of others. In the Tswana heartland, the ruling party commands about 90 percent of the vote, and the support of two large Tswana subgroups is alone almost sufficient to gain a majority of parliamentary seats.[90] In Senegal, the ruling party can generally count on the support of two large blocs: Wolof, who constitute more than 40 percent of the population, and Muslims (including Wolof and other ethnic groups), who constitute about 90 percent. As in Botswana, opposition strength has been located disproportionately in a few ethnic and religious minority areas, especially in the non-Muslim Casamance region, dominated by the Diola ethnic group.[91] Neither Botswana nor Senegal represents the likely pattern in South Africa, which is a much more thoroughly heterogeneous society.

More to the present point of sequencing of participation, elections in Senegal go back at least to 1871 in the four main *communes.* During the Fourth French Republic, Senegalese sat in the French parliament. Parties flourished before independence, and political mores had roots before the period of mass participation.[92] In Botswana, elections came late, but mobilized mass participation came even later. Initially, low levels of education meant that demands on the system were very mod-

---

89. Dahl, *Polyarchy*, p. 15.

90. Holm, "Botswana," p. 181–92; John D. Holm, "Elections in Botswana: Institutionalization of a New System of Legitimacy," in Fred M. Hayward, ed., *Elections in Independent Africa* (Boulder, Colo.: Westview Press, 1987), pp. 123, 133, 137–39; Picard, *The Politics of Development in Botswana*, pp. 148, 152–54, 158, 171; W. A. J. Macartney, "Botswana Goes to the Polls," *Africa Report*, December 1969, pp. 28–30.

91. Coulon, "Senegal," pp. 163–65; Fred M. Hayward and Siba N. Grovogui, "Persistence and Change in Senegalese Electoral Processes," in Hayward, ed., *Elections in Independent Africa*, pp. 263–64, 269 n. 74.

92. Coulon, "Senegal," pp. 142–43; Hayward and Grovogui, "Persistence and Change in Senegalese Electoral Processes," pp. 240–43.

est. Elites have had time to get the rules of contestation straight, to establish norms, even as participation has gradually been expanding.[93] In short, Senegal's early elections and Botswana's late participation both allowed time for elites to be socialized into politics before they had to contend with mobilized mass participation. Such conditions will surely not obtain in South Africa, as they have not obtained in many other African countries.

Writers on Senegal and Botswana stress the peaceful, accommodative political cultures of most Senegalese groups and of the Tswana.[94] These make political contests less violent and more amenable to compromise than in some other African countries. The South African political cultures are more various; some are assuredly more contentious; and the long history of internecine warfare is hardly forgotten. Again, more to the point, in both Senegal and Botswana, participation has been highly structured and controlled by intermediaries. The Senegalese mediators are the marabouts, leaders of the important Muslim brotherhoods, under whose auspices followers were integrated into the political system.[95] In Botswana, the political class has been largely continuous with traditional rulers, and participation has been mediated by the chiefdoms to whom voters owe allegiance.[96]

Considering all of these conditions, John D. Holm concludes that if "Botswana succeeds in establishing elections as a means for transferring government power when other African polities have failed . . . the critical reason may be the fact that elections were already institutionalized before the full force of modernization took hold." [97] The same can certainly not be said for South Africa, where mass mobilization has preceded the expanded franchise.

The importance of social complexity refers to the state-society balance. There needs to be time for the growth of a middle class—or, in a plural society, broadly distributed middle classes—the group that recurrently demands democratic participation and a return to democracy when authoritarianism periodically creeps in. In fact, democracy is fostered by the development more generally of autonomous social forces, of vol-

93. Holm, "Elections in Botswana," pp. 143–45.
94. Hayward and Grovogui, "Persistence and Change in Senegalese Electoral Processes," p. 240; Holm, "Botswana," p. 196.
95. Coulon, "Senegal," pp. 171, 173; Hayward and Grovogui, "Persistence and Change in Senegalese Electoral Processes," p. 239.
96. Picard, *The Politics of Development in Botswana*, pp. 121–44; Holm, "Botswana," p. 190.
97. Holm, "Elections in Botswana," p. 144.

untary associations and interests,[98] of a civil society that stands apart from the state, of forces that can balance each other in utilizing the future state machinery for political ends.

There is now a large literature on the process of democratization in Latin America and southern Europe. One thing it shows very clearly is the utility of social complexity.

In Brazil, for example, there was a growing middle class with a stake in democracy. The working class, politicized by the Catholic church, by barrio organizations, and by trade unions, also demanded a voice. Business wanted a more open system that might provide influence over sources of credit controlled by the state and protection against international competition. Although Brazil had a strong tradition of the domination of civil society by the state, the "gradual decompression"[99] that took place over more than a decade provided time for social groups to re-dress much of the balance. Once it began, Brazil's "slow road to democratization"[100] produced something like a balance among the state, political parties, and civil society.[101]

Portugal did not have the same long transition: its democracy followed a military coup. At first, the Communist Party took advantage of its traditional strength. Slowly, the Socialists, the Centrists, and the Conservatives caught up, because they were supported by a strong peasantry and a strong bourgeoisie. Within two years, the Socialists had an electoral plurality, and the authoritarian right and left had been defeated by the complexity and balanced forces of a differentiated society.[102] The Portuguese experience shows that a rapid transition is not necessarily fatal, but only because organized sectors of the society with a stake in a democratic order took steps to protect their interests.

Will the plurality of forces be sufficient to sustain democracy in South

98. Such as the growing South African trade union movement. See, e.g., C. R. D. Halisi, "The Political Role of the Trade Union Movement," in Anthony G. Freedman and Diane B. Bendahmane, eds., *Black Labor Unions in South Africa* (Washington, D.C.: Center for the Study of Foreign Affairs, 1986), pp. 37–44.

99. Bolivar Lamounier, "*Authoritarian Brazil* Revisited: The Impact of Elections on the *Abertura*," in Alfred Stepan, ed., *Democratizing Brazil: Problems of Transition and Consolidation* (New York: Oxford University Press, 1989), p. 45.

100. Thomas E. Skidmore, "Brazil's Slow Road to Democratization, 1974–1985," in Stepan, ed., *Democratizing Brazil,* pp. 5–42. See also Maria do Carmo Campello de Souza, "The Brazilian 'New Republic': Under the 'Sword of Damocles,' " in ibid., p. 381.

101. Scott Mainwaring, "Grassroots Popular Movements and the Struggle for Democracy: Nova Iguaçu," in Stepan, ed., *Democratizing Brazil,* pp. 189–95.

102. Kenneth Maxwell, "Regime Overthrow and the Prospects for Democratic Transition in Portugal," in O'Donnell et al., eds., *Transitions from Authoritarian Rule,* pt. 1, pp. 109–37.

Africa? By limiting Black social mobility, apartheid has prevented the emergence of a strongly differentiated Black civil society. By insuring that the racial issue transcends others, the regime has repressed differences among those who oppose it. There are many ideological streams, to be sure, but at least in the Black townships the complaint of thoughtful participant-observers is that opposition to the regime should not, but generally does, produce conformity, often coerced conformity, to a single line.[103] Apart from racial and ethnic cleavages, which have a tendency in any event to preempt other forms of social differentiation, it is difficult to foresee a post-apartheid South African version of the Brazilian or Portuguese counterbalancing complexity.

Writing of the oscillating Nigerian experience of democracy, Sam C. Nolutshungu, a South African, has emphasized a major difference between the emergence of democracy in western Europe and in Africa. Whereas in Europe a preexisting bourgeoisie resisted state power and sought influence over it, the nascent Nigerian bourgeoisie has had no special need to limit the power of the state but rather a desire to enlarge it and live off its largess. There has been little sense of "empowering the people against the state" and no "equilibrium of power between classes, but a balance of weakness."[104] In a post-apartheid South Africa, there is an excellent chance that emergent Black middle-class interests will also see the state as a source of largess rather than as an impediment to be kept in a limited sphere. In addition, the depressed African peasantry might well have differentiated interests to assert against the state, given the proclivity of African states to extract a surplus from agriculture and to subsidize urban food consumption at the expense of the peasantry.[105] But Black South African peasants and wage laborers, now subordinated in White rural areas or pushed aside in the homelands,[106] have hardly been heard from in the struggle thus far. There is considerable doubt whether, given their economic debility and ethnic fragmentation, rural

103. See Nomavenda Mathiane, *South Africa: Diary of Troubled Times* (New York: Freedom House, 1989).

104. Sam C. Nolutshungu, "Fragments of a Democracy: Reflections on Class and Politics in Nigeria," *Third World Quarterly* 12, no. 1 (January 1990): 86–115, at 110, 111.

105. Robert H. Bates, *Essays on the Political Economy of Rural Africa* (Cambridge: Cambridge University Press, 1983).

106. The South African economy no longer has a sizable sector of traditional agriculture. Stephen R. Lewis, Jr., *The Economics of Apartheid* (New York: Council on Foreign Relations Press, 1990), p. 129. Cf. Colin Bundy, *The Rise and Fall of the South African Peasantry* (Berkeley and Los Angeles: University of California Press, 1979), pp. 221–47.

Africans could be organized to play a role strongly supportive of democracy, along Portuguese lines. The peasant sector in Portugal was much stronger and politically dynamic. The South African resistance organizations have been mainly urban in focus, rural leaders are few, and most (though not all) homeland leaders are discredited.

Some of these social conditions would surely have been different if democracy had been given a chance to evolve in South Africa. South Africa needs more time, but South Africa does not have much more time.

As I intimated earlier, there is a vast difference, for democratic prospects, between having political organizations that oppose for a time and then are pulled into government to practice democracy before independence and having political organizations forced to oppose to the bitter end. As Juan J. Linz has said, conflicts within the political elite that hamper cooperation between government and loyal opposition

> are not so great when the democratic political system has evolved slowly out of a more restricted political system like a semiconstitutional monarchy with representative institutions, an oligarchic democracy in which democratic reformers had already participated in a minority role, or a system of dual authority like that of India before independence. They are exacerbated when the instauration of democracy follows a prolonged period of authoritarian rule that provided no opportunity for the emergence of counterelites, and the[ir] interaction in certain political arenas such as legislatures, municipal governments, or interest-group bargaining.[107]

Clearly, this would have been an argument for the gradualism and incorporation of the opposition for which the time has long since passed in South Africa. How tempting it looks in retrospect to have enlarged the functioning South African parliamentary system in stages to embrace the dispossessed and excluded, along the lines of the British Reform Acts or the Senegalese *communes* during the French period, and how tragic it is that the opposite course was followed instead, with the disfranchisement of those few who were already at the edges of democratic participation.

White South Africa has had functioning parliamentary institutions, but I do not see any way of enlarging them in phases to secure the advantages of gradualism. Indeed, it could well be argued that, for Whites, democracy, insofar as it means electoral competition, has grown in re-

---

107. Juan J. Linz, "Crisis, Breakdown, and Reequilibration," in Juan J. Linz and Alfred Stepan, eds., *The Breakdown of Democratic Regimes* (Baltimore: Johns Hopkins University Press, 1978), pt. 1, p. 34.

cent years: the electorate has more options than it had when White politics was defined in clear terms of Afrikaner inclusion and English exclusion. The White electorate has the Conservative Party and the Democratic Party, in addition to the Nationalists and the small Herstigte Nasionale Party. But this helps the cause of fully inclusive democracy not at all, because the main issue in the competition among the White parties has been what posture to adopt toward the aspirations of all other groups. Plainly, the growth of *intragroup* democracy by no means implies the growth of *intergroup* democracy. Electoral competition among Whites has involved a fair amount of outbidding for the exclusivist White vote, to the detriment of the participation of everyone else.

Anyone who thinks that this is a unique feature of the South African system, having no implications once that system is dissolved, needs to look carefully at the comparative evidence. From 1956 on, the growth of party competition in Sri Lanka made the system more responsive to Sinhalese aspirations. Their fulfillment came at the expense of the Tamils. From the early 1970s on, the growth of party competition in Northern Ireland made more options available to Protestants but impeded the accommodation of Catholics. From 1970 on, Malaysia became somewhat less democratic overall, but the Malays were offered significantly more choices, resulting ultimately in unprecedented intra-Malay contests for deputy prime minister and prime minister.[108] Divided societies, in short, tend toward segmented electorates and toward within-group party competition that makes democratic accommodation more difficult.

Indeed, there is frequently an inverse relationship between intragroup democracy and intergroup democracy. Intergroup accommodation may be easier where ethnically based parties do not need constantly to be looking over their shoulders to see which of their competitors might make political gains as a result of compromises made across group lines.

I have digressed a bit from my point that South Africa will need, for the most part, to attain its full democracy in large gulps, rather than small sips, but that there are grave perils accompanying such a strategy. Along the way, we have noted that segmented electorates and ethnically

108. See Donald L. Horowitz, "Cause and Consequence in Public Policy Theory: Ethnic Policy and System Transformation in Malaysia," *Policy Sciences* 22, nos. 3–4 (November 1989): 249–87, at 273–74.

based parties are likely to further conflict in divided societies. It is a point that can hardly be emphasized too often.

One more word about the transition to full democracy. Several of those post-colonial states that received their independence without fighting for it—India, Sri Lanka, Malaysia, and the Philippines—have done better in maintaining democracy than some near neighbors who engaged in warfare to secure independence (Indonesia, Bangladesh). There are, it seems to me, clear advantages in a peaceful transition.

When, then, is the time right? I said that earlier is generally better, but once an obvious juncture, such as the attainment of independence, has passed, not every moment is equally propitious. The best time is after a common disaster, such as those that have befallen Nigeria and Uganda and have given rise to desires not to repeat the disaster. But disaster can hardly be recommended on the ground that it might create a sense of community later. If, short of disaster, serious conflict is already well along, the participants will not be motivated to move if they think they are winning. Perhaps fortunately for South Africa, neither the government nor the forces of opposition can feel secure about the future—the government for the obvious reason that there is a clock ticking on White-only rule, the opposition for the equally obvious reason that the government's control of the instrumentalities of force is thus far overwhelming. So the government is vulnerable in the long term, and the opposition is vulnerable in the short and perhaps the medium term. As the settlement of a decade-and-a-half-long Sudanese civil war in 1972 shows, mutual vulnerability can provide an occasion for accommodation.

It may be objected that the Sudanese settlement lasted only about ten years. The impermanency of the arrangements, however, has much to do with their substance—specifically, the asymmetrical devolution that was imposed, with only one regional authority for the entire south but several for the north—and nothing to do with the propitiousness of the occasion. This reinforces a point I shall make more forcefully later— namely, that it is not enough for the parties merely to reach agreement but is necessary to inquire carefully into the content of the agreement.

Now it may well be that the asymmetry between the government and the extraparliamentary opposition will be conducive not to action but, at the crucial moment, to great caution on the part of Whites. If the government is not vulnerable in the short and medium term, and if, in addition, what is demanded are some great leaps, Whites may ultimately be reluctant to take a risk.[109] This risk aversion would be most unfortunate.

The misfortune for the whole society is obvious. The misfortune from the standpoint of the self-interest of Whites alone needs to be stated. It seems unlikely that the passage of time will greatly improve the bargaining position of Whites and quite likely that it will erode that position. Precisely such a sense that "continued resistance may lose them even more ground in the end"[110] underlies a number of historical decisions by regimes to incorporate those excluded from the democratic process. It is no longer a question of the best time but of the least-bad time. Sheer self-interest suggests the desirability of overcoming the misplaced risk aversion of Whites. Despite the enormous obstacles to democracy inherent in rapid political change, gulps are necessary.

AGAINST THE ODDS

This grab bag of obstacles to democracy can, to some extent, be explained in terms of the metaconflict described in Chapter 1. Wishful thinking derives from a sense that the only problem is apartheid. The equation of majority rule with Black rule, the dissensus on the means to democracy, the alienated and suspicious opposition, and the sense of African indigenousness all form part of the contested description of the future South Africa. Only the problems that attend the need for rapid political change can really be described as more structural than ideological.

For present purposes, the source of the obstacles is less important than the scale of the obstacles. They are considerable. Nevertheless, it should not be thought that the structure of the South African problem includes every conceivable problem of democratic legitimacy that besets the most severely divided societies. Despite the obstacles I have enumerated, South Africa has one advantage not enjoyed by, for example, Northern Ireland. Once South Africa reverses the homelands policy, it will not run afoul of what Adrian Guelke calls "international legiti-

109. For the view that the state of affairs in South Africa does not give rise to propitious timing, see Steven Friedman, *Reform Revisited* (Braamfontein: South African Institute of Race Relations, 1988), p. 28. If that is true, it is discouraging, for it is hard to envision a set of conditions, short of disaster, under which timing will be more propitious. See also Huntington, "Whatever Has Gone Wrong with Reform?" p. 22: "In a sense, South Africa today has a government too weak to impose reform from above—assuming it wanted to—and opposition groups which are too weak to compel reform from below through negotiation."

110. Rustow, "Transitions to Democracy," p. 357.

macy," a norm which, after World War II, came to mean self-determination within the boundaries of the undivided state.[111] Whereas the partition of Ireland violates this norm, the unitary South Africa that even the regime now seems to accept means that the problem loses its intractable territorial aspect and comes down to the (still intractable) matter of engineering arrangements for multiracial, multiethnic democracy within the agreed boundaries.

Whether the requisite engineering can be accomplished will depend very much on whether South Africans can shed some of their acquired biases against the arrangements that are most apt to ease their predicament and whether they can summon the moral courage to will the means to the amelioration of the group tensions that cloud the South African future. About the odds for this, only a seasoned gambler could be sanguine.

111. Adrian Guelke, "The Political Impasse in South Africa and Northern Ireland: A Comparative Perspective" (paper presented at the International Political Science Association World Congress, Washington, D.C., August 28–September 1, 1988).

CHAPTER FOUR

Models and Pitfalls

When I said earlier that, for a democratic, accommodative regime to emerge, it is necessary to will the means as well as the ends, I meant to imply that what looks like a surprising degree of interracial consensus on goals in South Africa can be defeated by dissensus on specific measures that might actually achieve those goals. Small mistakes have large consequences in this field. It is useful to remember the remark of the Confucian Hsün-tzu: "Yang Chu, weeping at the crossroad, said, 'Isn't it here that you take a half-step wrong and wake up 1,000 miles away?' "

Right at this point, there is an important difference between engineering, the design of physical structures, and constitutional engineering, the design of political structures. In engineering, as in constitutional engineering, there are multiple potential sources of failure. Consequently, engineers create redundancy (backup systems) and factors of safety (overbuilding) to counter failures and mid-course correction features to reverse them when they occur.[1] In constitutional engineering, mid-course correction is extremely difficult, because interests quickly crystallize around whatever arrangements are adopted; and so, even if the institutions fail in their public objectives, there are actors whose private success depends on the maintenance of the arrangements. South Africa cannot count on mid-course correction. This puts the burden of

---

1. See Henry Petrosky, *To Engineer Is Human* (New York: Free Press, 1985). On stress and factors of safety, see J. E. Gordon, *Structures, or Why Things Don't Fall Down* (Harmondsworth, Eng.: Penguin Books, 1978), pp. 64–65.

averting failure on precision at the outset, on safety factors, and on redundancy, but in a divided society it is fortunate if there is initial consensus on reasonably apt institutions. Consensus on precisely apt institutions, let alone overbuilt or redundantly apt institutions, will be very hard to reach.

All of this counsels against the advice frequently heard in divided societies—that if it is wrong at the outset, it can be fixed later[2]—and argues strongly for efforts to enhance initial agreement on institutional objectives, rather than on constitutional provisions that the parties can merely tolerate. A deliberate process can invest the participants in the product of their own hands, instead of being merely a necessary prelude to the contest for power.

These cautions make clear why Yang Chu's apprehension frequently applies in constitution making across the board—in careless borrowing of institutions, in citing the wrong examples and drawing the wrong lessons, in choosing one mode of decision making rather than another, and in choosing one set of institutions over another. All of these are problems in South Africa.

A particularly helpful way to see this is to review some of the major plans that have been considered for South Africa. Some are much more elaborate than others. They run the gamut, from doing very little except expand the franchise, to structuring extraordinary safeguards, to dividing up the state. As I intend to show, virtually all of the main models that have been advanced are inapt for the conflict, and most are also inapt for the metaconflict. More than this, they tend to overlook some very important distinctions relating both to the formulation of plans for accommodation and to the content of those plans. Failure to attend to these distinctions renders constitutional plans vulnerable to some predictable pitfalls. These I shall present later in the chapter.

BINATIONALISM

The prevalence of racial discrimination makes it easy to conceive of South African society as characterized by what I called in Chapter 1 ascriptive ranking and subordination. The tendency to view the society that way is powerfully reinforced by the whole history of European colonialism in Africa and by some of its important by-products, such as

2. I have encountered such views in South Africa a number of times, particularly among members of the extraparliamentary opposition.

slavery and segregation in the Western Hemisphere. There is, of course, no doubt that the Western, and particularly North American, focus on South African issues is at least as heavily determined by the experience of race relations in North America as it is by South African conditions and events. There is a strong element of projection of home-country guilt onto South Africa, which accounts for much of the importance of the South African issue in American (or British or French) politics.

This element of projection makes it difficult to conceive of the South African conflict in terms other than those of racial subordination. There have been numerous attempts, for example, to explain the history of Afrikaner nationalism to Western publics,[3] but they have largely fallen on deaf ears. More often than not, Afrikaners are portrayed as unreconstructed racists, throwbacks to the bad old days of Jim Crow and White supremacy.[4] The internalization of this same image—and the guilt consequent upon it—is largely responsible for the steady growth of Afrikaner liberalism in the post–World War II period.

There is, however, an alternative way to conceptualize the conflict, one that has long come naturally to Afrikaners themselves. An amalgam of Dutch, French, and German strands, the Afrikaners, even in the eighteenth century, saw themselves abused by and cut off from the Netherlands. "By 1795 the European roots of the white South African community were almost completely severed. Most of its members were South Africans of at least the third generation. Very few of them had even visited Europe, or were in communication with anyone in Europe. They were white Africans."[5] Later, of course, they considered themselves oppressed by British colonialists. All along, they fought battles with neighboring Black ethnic groups. Afrikaner victories and defeats burned themselves into a sharply defined ethnic consciousness.[6] Slowly, in the twentieth century, there has also been some further merger of the Afrikaner and the English-speaking populations, including increasing rates

3. For one such attempt, see Marq de Villiers, *White Tribe Dreaming* (New York: Viking, 1988). The most sophisticated effort to place Afrikaner settlement in a comparative framework is that of Louis Hartz et al., *The Founding of New Societies* (New York: Harcourt, Brace & World, 1964).

4. Cf. George M. Fredrickson, "Can South Africa Change?" *New York Review of Books,* October 26, 1989, p. 48: "If Johannesburg of the 1970s was like Birmingham [Alabama] in the 1950s, then Johannesburg of the late 1980s was, on the surface at least, strikingly like the Birmingham of the early 1970s."

5. Leonard M. Thompson, "The South African Dilemma," in Hartz et al., *The Founding of New Societies,* p. 187.

6. See Hermann Giliomee, "The Growth of Afrikaner Identity," in Heribert Adam and Hermann Giliomee, eds., *Ethnic Power Mobilized: Can South Africa Change?* (New Haven: Yale University Press, 1979), pp. 83–127.

of exogamy. In politics, for example, the National Party draws support almost equally from both White groups.

Conceived in this way, the current struggle can easily be regarded as involving Afrikaner nationalism or, more broadly, the nationalism of both White groups, on the one hand, and Black nationalism, on the other. Two important consequences follow from such a conception of what is happening in South Africa. The first is that the aspirations of the Whites become far more legitimate. Now they are not—or at least not merely—racist oppressors seeking to preserve privilege but nationalists struggling not to be swallowed up in a larger, competing nationalism. The second is that, if this characterization is accurate, political formulae might well take account of it. Needless to say, racial discrimination would not be countenanced, but nationalists, White and Black, may be entitled to a degree of self-determination.

If there are, for the sake of argument, just two nationalisms—one White, one Black—in South Africa, then perhaps South Africa does not resemble Mississippi in 1950 so much as it resembles Canada in 1980. In short, if there is a White nationalism and a Black nationalism, then the appropriate accommodation might be one that builds political institutions, as the Canadians have, on recognition of two "founding nations" that must live together in a single state but can only do so decently if the design of the state prominently reflects what is called "dualism."[7]

To be sure, the outcome in Canada is by no means certain. The "patriation" of the Canadian Constitution in 1982 established something like a loose federation, but this Quebec saw as insufficient. In 1987, the Meech Lake Accord attempted to secure the accession of Quebec by recognizing that "Quebec constitutes within Canada a distinct society."[8] The provinces remain more or less equal, but a province would have been permitted to declare a provision of the Charter of Rights inoperative, and Meech Lake would have allowed a province to opt out of certain federal programs. It also would have expanded the category of constitutional changes requiring unanimous approval of the provinces and required the courts to interpret the Constitution to take the binational character of the country into account. In 1990, amidst considerable Anglophone bitterness, the Meech Lake Accord lapsed with-

7. Mason Wade, *Canadian Dualism* (Toronto: University of Toronto Press, 1960).
8. See Peter M. Leslie, "Bicommunalism and Canadian Constitutional Reform," *Publius* 18, no. 2 (Spring 1988): 115–29. See also Carolyn McAskie, "The Meech Lake Accord," *Thatched Patio* 2, no. 3 (May 1989): 29–33.

out securing the required assent of all the provinces. Nevertheless, slowly and haltingly, Quebec has been pushing Canada toward a confederation that recognizes the state as having, not just an Anglophone majority and a Francophone minority, but "two majorities," each of which will have some sovereign powers. The tortuous path toward any such recognition is a sign of how great the obstacles to binationalism might be in South Africa.

Nevertheless, a somewhat analogous plan for South Africa has been advanced for a ten-year transitional period by Hermann Giliomee and Lawrence Schlemmer. Judging the struggle to be "primarily between Afrikaner and African nationalists,"[9] they argue that the most sensible change for the time being is to a binational state, probably with three electoral rolls—White, Black, and open[10]—and a dual set of symbols for the state, to allay the fears of Whites that political change will necessarily entail a "symbolic reversal."[11] At the center, they envision a joint Black-White government of national unity based on the requirement of concurrent majorities for action.

All of this they see as transitional. As confidence is built, what they call "nation-building" can take place. The long-term future, in their view, will be based on majority rule, following a dissolution of the binational system, a dissolution that will take place by mutual consent.

Of course, South Africa would not be alone if it adopted such arrangements. Not only Canada but also Belgium has elements of a binational polity; other Western European countries, of the consociational variety, have arrangements for decision making by consent of all groups. Czechoslovakia has dual symbols, including two national anthems, one Czech and one Slovak. In short, there are precedents for these proposals, although generally the binational solution is based on nations that have separate territorial homelands. The overarching Black and White groups occupy the same single homeland.

In this respect, there is an interesting distinction between traditional and contemporary conceptions of political community. Whereas kinship alone might frequently have been sufficient to constitute traditional polities, modern political systems are based heavily on inclusive conceptions of territorial proximity. No doubt there have been departures from

9. Hermann Giliomee and Lawrence Schlemmer, *From Apartheid to Nation-Building* (Cape Town: Oxford University Press, 1989), p. 211. This is also the formulation in Charles Simkins et al., *The Prisoners of Tradition and the Politics of Nation Building* (Johannesburg: South African Institute of Race Relations, 1988), p. 12.

10. Giliomee and Schlemmer, *From Apartheid to Nation-Building*, pp. 215–16.

11. Ibid., pp. 238–39.

this notion, but the idea of territorial sovereignty, which is now world-wide, is difficult to square with a full-blown division of sovereign authority based on origins rather than on territory. Skepticism about such approaches is epitomized in a scathing characterization of the government's emphasis on group autonomy and "own affairs": "it permits you to carry your own border around with you."

Apart from what I shall soon say about group rights and consociationalism—some of which might apply to the Giliomee-Schlemmer proposals if they were spelled out in more detail—there are two main additional objections that could be raised. The first relates to the temporary character of the arrangements. If there really are contending Black and White nationalisms, do nationalisms disappear in a decade? The second relates to the identification of the nationalisms in question. Leave aside the incomplete merger of Afrikaners and English into a White group. What of the merger of Zulu, Sotho, Tswana, and Xhosa into a Black group? If the polity is to be divided along sub–South African national lines, then Zulu nationalism, as represented by Inkatha and KwaZulu, might have a claim to recognition, but such claims are denied at the threshold by the binational character of the scheme. It is not clear that, once binationalism is to be recognized, some Black ethnic groups will not make strong demands for multinationalism.

Again, Canada comes to mind. The effort, in the 1960s, to foster bilingualism and biculturalism ended by promoting bilingualism and multiculturalism, as various non-British, non-French groups questioned the legitimacy of biculturalism.[12] The same might well happen in an initially binational South Africa.

The temporary character of the plan appears explicable in terms of its proponents' commitment to a nonracial society and to untrammeled majority rule, even as they recognize alternative ways to view the polity. Or, to put it more sharply, South African elites find divisions of the future polity so thoroughly illegitimate—reacting as they are against the past divisions of the polity—that proposals like these are difficult to justify, to oneself and to others, except as transitional. There are, in short, ideological crosscurrents in South Africa, some based on previous experience, some based on assessments of the present and future, and they sit most uneasily with each other.

The same point can be made about the boundaries of Black nation-

---

12. See John Porter, "Ethnic Pluralism in Canada," in Nathan Glazer and Daniel P. Moynihan, eds., *Ethnicity: Theory and Experience* (Cambridge: Harvard University Press, 1975), pp. 282–88.

alism. To recognize Zulu or Ndebele or Sotho nationalism might be to confirm the South African government's prior recognition of these nationalisms and its embodiment of that recognition in the form of the so-called homelands. To recognize nationalism below the level of an inclusive Black nationalism is to run afoul of an important South African taboo.

Once constitutional planners think in terms of contending nationalisms in South Africa, they will inevitably be faced with major obstacles of precisely the sort that confront Giliomee and Schlemmer. It remains true, however, that, over the short and medium term, no constitutional progress can be made without White assent. Perhaps Whites will be willing to assent to a scheme like this, and to no other. Of course, we do not know that this will be the case, since no proposed schemes have been put to the test. Nevertheless, if that does prove to be the inclination of Whites, Blacks will have to think long and hard before rejecting a scheme of this sort. South Africa, it needs to be emphasized, is not assured of either an easy transition or a democratic result. Any arrangement that can make both more likely has to be considered seriously.

There is, however, a good chance that Black leaders will reject such a scheme out of hand—so strong is the power of certain, relatively fixed ideas in South Africa. These ideas form part of the metaconflict described in Chapter 1. They were expressed by Walter F. Sisulu, the long-imprisoned ANC leader, in February 1990, when he noted that President F. W. de Klerk "still speaks of Black representation on an ethnic basis: Black people must elect Black people. The ANC will not even think of taking part in an election for Black representatives—it is a step back to ethnicity." [13] But suppose for the sake of argument that Blacks do not reject the plan for a binational state at the outset. Will the proposed arrangements make the transition and a democratic result more likely, if they are adopted?

There are grounds for a negative answer. If the plan is accepted by Blacks because, given White apprehensions, it is the only way Whites can be induced to agree to any substantial changes, that is scarcely a basis for optimism about the durability of the plan. There is a good chance then that the plan will be overthrown by resentful Black leaders at the earliest opportunity, and there is no assurance that what is put in

---

13. Quoted in Hermann Giliomee, "Stemmepoel: Nuwe voorstel vir 'n konstitusionele deurbraak," *Die Suid-Afrikaan*, February 1990, pp. 12–15, at p. 13.

its place will be at all apt for South Africa's divided society. Even if the plan is not overthrown, it merely postpones the debate over the choice of institutions that are ultimately going to be appropriate for South Africa, including, for example, the kind of electoral arrangements discussed at length earlier. In the meantime, South Africans will become habituated to completely different arrangements, building up a new set of inhibitions and taboos. And if the Giliomee-Schlemmer plan is adopted in order to make constitutional progress but is then overthrown, the postponed institutional debate may never take place.

Here, then, may be a concrete case of some caveats I shall enter in more detail later. Any agreement is not necessarily better than no agreement, and the existence of an agreement is no evidence whatever of its probable durability.

PARTITION

Needless to say, if binationalism is ideologically unacceptable to a good many influential South Africans, partition of the country into more than one state is anathema. The sources of this reaction are several: the common antipathy of politicians to the prospect of losing territory in which power can be exercised; the conception of partition as another form of divide and rule, comparable to cutting the Black homelands out of South Africa and declaring their inhabitants to be noncitizens; and suspicion that a partition plan will give the predominantly White successor state the major share of good land and natural endowment, particularly mineral resources and rainfall—a suspicion solidly grounded in experience with the boundaries of the crowded, resource-poor homelands.

The comparative experience with partition in the post–World War II period has generally been unhappy, not in the sense that the alternatives to partition were necessarily superior but in the sense that partition was costly in lives and in protracted, post-partition conflict. The examples of India-Pakistan, Israel and the rest of Palestine, Cyprus after 1974, and Ireland after 1968 (although it was partitioned almost a half-century earlier) are all pertinent here.[14] Partition may, in the end, be unavoidable, but for a great many reasons it is generally not the policy of choice.[15]

14. For brief discussions of these cases and comparisons to South Africa, see Newell M. Stultz, "On Partition," *Social Dynamics* 5, no. 1 (June 1979): 1–13.

15. For a fuller assessment of the consequences of partition for ethnic conflict, see Donald L. Horowitz, *Ethnic Groups in Conflict* (Berkeley and Los Angeles: University of California Press, 1985), pp. 588–92.

Still, South Africa is a society so divided that fallback positions can hardly be excluded a priori. Possible partition plans have been assessed in South Africa for a very long time.[16] Among the various plans, the most carefully considered, from the standpoint of history, economic integration, demography, and—especially—fairness in the allocation of resources, is the one described (but not advocated) by Gavin Maasdorp.[17] Maasdorp's plan is particularly generous, in terms of resources, to the part of the bisected state that would have an African majority. But to examine briefly even this careful design is to see the ethnic problems that would be left afterward.

The successor state with the larger White percentage—"Capeland"—would be centered on the Western Cape, extending eastward to, roughly, the Fish River (east of Port Elizabeth), and would also include two districts in the southwestern area of the Orange Free State. On the basis of the 1970 census, Africans would constitute only 23.6 percent of the population. The remainder of South Africa—"Capricornia"—would have a strong African majority. Nearly all Indians would be in Capricornia, and nearly all Coloureds would be in Capeland. More Whites would be in Capricornia than in Capeland, but since Capeland would have less than 20 percent of the total South African population, Whites would form a larger share of the Capeland population.[18]

Despite the effort to disentangle populations, Whites would still form a minority of only 27 percent in Capeland (and of 15 percent in Capricornia). Coloureds would make up nearly half the Capeland population, and Africans would be (even as of 1970) almost as numerous as Whites there. Neither state would be free of the same sort of conflict that now troubles South Africa.

No doubt it is true that there was once a possibility of solidifying the links between Whites and Coloureds in the Cape, but those links have been weakened and, in a good many cases, broken since the apartheid policy of the National Party disfranchised and forcibly displaced many Coloureds from their residences in the 1950s. Segments of the Coloured community remain quite conservative. As I noted in Chapter 2, in a 1985 survey in Natal, 31 percent of Coloureds chose President P. W.

16. For an excellent survey, see Eugene Lourens and Hennie Kotzé, "South Africa's Non-unitary Political Alternatives," in A. Venter, ed., *South African Government and Politics* (Johannesburg: Southern, 1989), pp. 294–331.

17. Gavin Maasdorp, "Forms of Partition," in Robert I. Rotberg and John Barratt, eds., *Conflict and Compromise in South Africa* (Lexington, Mass.: Lexington Books, 1980), pp. 107–46.

18. See ibid., p. 130.

Botha as their preferred South African leader, nearly three times the number that chose Nelson Mandela.[19] But a great many Coloureds have identified with the struggle of Africans against the White regime. In Capeland, there is little doubt that, in place of intergroup harmony, there would be considerable political conflict between Coloureds and Whites. Moreover, the end of influx control and pass laws in the mid-1980s has produced enormous growth in the African population around Cape Town, so that it is no longer a foregone conclusion that Whites would even constitute the second largest population group in Capeland. Capeland would be an especially severely divided, triethnic society.

About 80 percent of the population in Capricornia would be African. The White minority there would presumably have relatively little political power. Capricornia would, after all, be designed to be the African-dominated successor state of South Africa. If Whites had grievances, the presumption would be that they might move to the "non-African" successor state, Capeland, where, as we have just seen, their position might also be precarious. And to the extent that White power was diminished in Capricornia, conflicts among Black groups could be expected to emerge there, uninhibited by the comfort they would otherwise have given to powerful Whites. In fact, in Capricornia, as in Capeland, a few large groups would compete for power. Ironically, this would alter one of undivided South Africa's only favorable conflict conditions—the existence of a multiplicity of ethnic groups, no one of which could, under democratic conditions, easily capture power by itself.[20]

It seems obvious that partition along these lines would not solve the problems of intergroup conflict—though it would rearrange the conflict somewhat—or the problems of Whites, or the problems of anyone else. Any partition that stood a chance of solving such problems would require a massive population transfer, principally of Whites to the Cape, which might not be able to support them.[21] Even if a transfer could be arranged, its impact would be to turn the Coloureds, almost a majority under Maasdorp's plan, into a minority under the domination of Whites, who have not exactly been solicitous of their interests in the past. Partition cannot be ruled out, but it is not a promising idea.

19. Fatima Meer and Alan Reynolds, "Sample Survey of Perceptions of the Durban Unrest—August 1985," in Fatima Meer, ed., *Resistance in the Townships* (Durban: Madiba, 1989), p. 262.

20. For the conflict advantages of many dispersed groups, as opposed to a few centralized ones, see Horowitz, *Ethnic Groups in Conflict*, pp. 36–41.

21. Between 1947 and 1950, some 12 million to 15 million people crossed the borders between India and Pakistan in a population transfer that cost perhaps a million lives.

THE ZIMBABWE MODEL: MAJORITY RULE, MINORITY OVERREPRESENTATION

The so-called lessons of Zimbabwe are much discussed in South Africa. Whites in Zimbabwe feared for their future under majority rule. As is well known, no major calamity has befallen them. On the contrary, they prosper as farmers and business people under a regime that understands their contribution to the gross national product. In fact, within a few years after independence, some former Rhodesian diehards were returning to the country from South Africa. In a moment, I shall have something to say about what Zimbabwe teaches with respect to the controversial question of group rights. At this point, three other lessons can be derived from Zimbabwe.

The first is that, whatever the economic virtues of political quiescence, Zimbabwe is essentially a one-party state and not a democratic one. Political parties in Zimbabwe broke fairly neatly along ethnic lines, and under first-past-the-post elections the Shona majority could easily outvote the Ndebele minority. Repression was the dominant mode of nation building in Matabeleland until the capitulation of Joshua Nkomo and the institution of a de facto single-party system in 1987.[22] So the first lesson of Zimbabwe is to confirm the tendency, to be described more fully in Chapter 5, toward census-type elections and majority domination in divided societies unless appropriate precautions are taken. This is indeed a lesson of considerable relevance to South Africa.

The second lesson relates to the indigenousness question I have touched on previously. Dutch settlement in South Africa began at roughly the same time as Dutch settlement in New York, in the seventeenth century. The survivors of a wrecked Dutch ship began a sojourn near what is now Cape Town in 1647, the same year that Peter Stuyvesant arrived at Fort Amsterdam in what is now Manhattan. By contrast, the majority of Rhodesian Whites actually arrived in Zimbabwe after World War II.[23] Quite apart from the tiny fraction of the Zimbabwe population consisting of Whites, it seems appropriate to use the term *settler* for

22. See Richard W. Hull, "Overcoming Zimbabwe's Vulnerabilities," *Current History* 87, no. 526 (May 1988): 197–226; Barry M. Schutz, "Political Change and the Management of Ethnic Conflict in Zimbabwe," in Joseph V. Montville, ed., *Conflict and Peacemaking in Multiethnic Societies* (Lexington, Mass.: Lexington Books, 1990), pp. 433–47.

23. Mordechai Tamarkin, "The White Political Elite in Rhodesia's Decolonization Crisis, 1975–79" (paper presented at the Leonard Davis Institute 1989 annual conference, "Decisions at Historical Crossroads," June 5–7, 1989), p. 13.

such recent immigrants. One can readily understand, then, why Whites in Zimbabwe abandoned the aspiration to a real share of political power in order to preserve untouched their economic power. One could hardly envision a similar transaction in South Africa, where Whites aspire to retain a share of political power and Blacks aspire to attain a share of economic power. The second lesson of Zimbabwe is, then, that the Whites got it backward—perhaps not for Zimbabwe but for South Africa.

The third lesson of Zimbabwe takes us back to a theme discussed earlier: timing and planning. Following its Unilateral Declaration of Independence (UDI) in 1965, the Ian Smith regime took every opportunity to delay reaching a settlement. Mordechai Tamarkin has shown that, from 1974 onward, Smith had the possibility of negotiating power-sharing arrangements that would not only have been favorable to Whites but, more important, were supported by President Kenneth Kaunda of Zambia, by the West, and by the Soviet Union.[24] The settlements that were offered were certainly durable, at least over the short and medium term. Whether the institutional arrangements would have been conducive to a democratic, multiracial, multiethnic Zimbabwe is difficult to say in retrospect. What is clear is that the bad faith of the UDI regime precluded any such possibilities, accelerated guerrilla activity, and ultimately forced an international settlement that disadvantaged not so much the Whites as the Ndebele, who suffered violence in the countryside for years after independence in 1980. As is customary in such matters, when the time is propitious, the urgency seems absent. When the urgency is present, the time may no longer be propitious.

What was ultimately provided in the 1980 Constitution of Zimbabwe was temporary White overrepresentation in the legislature.[25] For a period of seven years, 20 House of Assembly members were to be elected by Whites on a "white roll," while the remaining 80 House of Assembly members were to be elected on a common roll consisting of other voters.[26] Less than 2 percent of the population thus held 20 percent of the parliamentary seats. At the earliest lawful moment, in 1987, the Zimbabwe government abolished these reserved seats and joined White voters to the common roll.[27] The 20 seats were converted to seats to be held by nominated members of any race.

To be sure, the government then nominated Whites to most of the

24. See ibid.
25. *Constitution of Zimbabwe*, 1980, as amended, § 60(2).
26. There were also ten reserved White seats in a Senate consisting of 40 members.
27. Constitution of Zimbabwe Amendment (No. 7) Act, September 21, 1987.

converted seats.[28] Nevertheless, the experience with reserved White seats shows that guaranteed disproportionate representation was seen to be reversible, that it created a desire to reverse it (despite the need for White capital), and that it did not create any real power that the White community did not in any event enjoy.

No doubt, as has been pointed out, South African Whites would not be content with the Zimbabwe arrangements.[29] But the lines along which much thinking has gone come down to minority guarantees, safeguards, and special rights.[30]

From what I have already said, it is not difficult to see the deficiencies of most versions of group rights—or, really, special group privileges. They provide illusory security, easily pierced. Even if they continue to function, they consign minorities to minority status. Unless they offer a minority veto—in which case the urge to abolish them will grow—they ratify the exclusion of the minority from power. So, in the first respect, group rights provide too much—benefits that are disproportionate and are, on that account, unlikely to survive. And, in the second respect, group rights provide too little, for they do not aim at minority participation at the seat of power. The overrepresentation of Whites in the 1980 Constitution of Zimbabwe had both of these vices.

In Zimbabwe, as in a number of other countries, minority overrepresentation was anchored to nothing. No doubt, overrepresentation served as a symbolic assurance by the incoming regime that it bore no special ill will toward Whites, despite the past. It was a transitional, confidence-building measure, not a provision that can help produce democracy in divided societies.

If one is looking for African democracy in a divided society, the place to look is not Zimbabwe but Nigeria. In 1978–79, despite severe ethnic conflict, military coups, civil war, and a long period of military rule, the Nigerians proceeded to design a sound regime for managing their het-

---

28. See *Times* (London), October 10, 1987.

29. Steven Friedman, *Reform Revisited* (Braamfontein: South African Institute of Race Relations, 1988), p. 27: "Whites don't want safeguards against the effects of majority rule—they want safeguards against majority rule itself." Friedman is quoting a White member of parliament.

30. See, e.g., *Financial Mail* (Johannesburg), August 4, 1989. See also John Dugard, "The Influence of Apartheid on the Development of the Law Governing the Protection of Minorities" (paper presented at the Conference on Ethnic Conflict, Human Rights, and the U.N. System, Oxford, March 30, 1989), pp. 10, 25, 31. Meanwhile, with little knowledge of ethnic relations, international lawyers have been creating a whole new set of understandings about group rights in international law. For some specimens, see James Crawford, ed., *The Rights of Peoples* (Oxford: Clarendon Press, 1988).

erogeneity in a democratic fashion. When that experiment was interrupted by a military coup on the last day of 1983, the Nigerians still
did not give up. In the late 1980s and early 1990s, they began the process of returning once again to democratic rule, and once again they
have designed institutions to foster interethnic accommodation. That is
where many of the African lessons are, but they seem far away, little
known, and less understood in South Africa.

CONSOCIATION

What divided societies like South Africa are likely to get is the worst of
both worlds. Majorities may ultimately get majority rule, but without
genuine inducements to accommodate minorities. Minorities may demand and receive guarantees of protection that, in the end, will protect
nothing worth protecting.

Consider, for example, the admittedly rough sketch of a future South
Africa drawn up by Heribert Adam and Kogila A. Moodley.[31] Adam
and Moodley argue that "factors unique to South Africa suggest that
the dream of a relatively democratic society has a better chance of being
realized in an integrated South Africa than elsewhere." [32] These unique
factors are said to be (1) minority rather than majority claims to exclusion;[33] (2) the noncorrespondence of racial divisions with cultural or
linguistic divisions; and (3) the economic interdependence of all groups.

It should be said in passing that none of these conditions is unique
to South Africa. Excluded groups often make claims to inclusive principles, and dominant groups reject them—whatever the numerical status of the groups. In many severely divided countries, religion and language span group boundaries. And the economic interdependence of
South Africans is hardly different from the interdependence that characterized many societies later shattered by ethnic violence, among them
Lebanon, Cyprus, Uganda, and Sri Lanka. If South Africa is to be saved,
it will hardly be saved by suggesting that it may not even be a thoroughly plural society. It will be saved by overcoming the obstacles in
the way of a democratic future.

31. Heribert Adam and Kogila A. Moodley, *South Africa without Apartheid: Dismantling Racial Domination* (Berkeley and Los Angeles: University of California Press,
1986).
32. Ibid., p. 196. The claim is reiterated at ibid., p. 248.
33. The authors point out that only the White minority wants anything other than "a
common nonracial citizenship in a polity that supports individual merit as the criterion
of privilege." Ibid., p. 196.

At some level, Adam and Moodley must realize this, for they advance the outlines of a scheme predicated on overcoming difficulties. What, then, is their plan? Their preferred outcome would be consociational democracy—a form of collective decision making that is said to mitigate unbridled majoritarianism in divided societies by requiring the concurrence of all groups in all major decisions and the delegation of decisions involving only the interests of particular groups to those groups themselves. It is, its most persuasive proponents say, the best, even the only, democratic system for severely divided societies.[34]

But, Adam and Moodley suggest,[35] it is too late for consociationalism in South Africa. Consociational systems in Switzerland and elsewhere in Western Europe antedate industrialization. Industrialization in South Africa has made "a more democratic means of representation of interests" necessary.[36] Consequently, their scheme envisions universal suffrage, but under a system that can guarantee "the influence of minority political parties . . . through proportional representation—or even overrepresentation—as well as veto rights."[37] As a matter of fact, they even contemplate "corporate federalism"[38]—that is, nonterritorial, group-based federalism that might even be represented in the upper house of the central legislature—a good measure of cultural autonomy, even group self-policing through local police forces, group proportional representation in the armed forces, perhaps even overrepresentation for minorities in the military.[39] A society with allegedly excellent raw prospects turns out in the end to require extraordinary precautions.

There is no need to dwell on the disjunction between Adam and Moodley's benign diagnosis and the strong medicine they prescribe. South Africa is a severely divided society; it needs a prescription.

If one person, one vote is required—and it is—then special rights for particular groups, rights designed to detract from the effects of universal suffrage, will not work. The contradiction between the two principles will be visible, and the former will win out. If the universal suffrage

---

34. See Arend Lijphart, *Democracy in Plural Societies* (New Haven: Yale University Press, 1977).
35. *South Africa without Apartheid,* pp. 207, 242–43.
36. Ibid., p. 243.
37. Ibid., p. 208.
38. Ibid., p. 219.
39. Ibid., p. 227. For a somewhat different two-chambers notion, see Hermann Giliomee, "The ANC, the Soviet Union and South Africa," *South African Foundation Review,* December 1988, p. 4. For another configuration, see The Buthelezi Commission, *The Requirements for Stability and Development in KwaZulu and Natal,* vol. 1 (Durban: H & H Publications, 1982), pp. 104–16.

that is contemplated seems conducive to majority oppression, ask not what can be done to counter universal suffrage but whether the right electoral system has been adopted.

Although Adam and Moodley deny that their prescription is consociational, the medicine has a strong aroma of consociation about it. The most elaborate consociational scheme for South Africa consists of several elements that add up to what its author, Arend Lijphart, calls "power-sharing."[40] (Just to keep the terminology clear, I do not mean *consociation* in the former South African government's sense of officially defined groups, enforced segregation, and cooptation of unrepresentative elites, but in Lijphart's sense.) These elements include a broadly inclusive coalition; an executive that represents all the significant groups; "internal autonomy for groups that wish to have it," embodied in federalism if the groups are geographically separate and in the nonterritorial, group equivalent of federalism if they are intermixed; "minority veto on the most vital issues"; a system of election based on proportional representation; and proportional allocation of civil service positions and public funds to the significant groups.[41] Since Adam and Moodley also espouse proportional representation, group vetoes, nonterritorial federalism, cultural autonomy for groups, and group proportionality in the armed forces, if not in the entire civil service, how their scheme differs from consociationalism is difficult to say.

I have enumerated elsewhere several reasons to doubt the applicability of consociational models to severely divided societies in Asia and Africa.[42] Here I only want to underscore a few points of immediate relevance to South Africa.

Perhaps the most important is that the consociational model contains no mechanism. The consociational idea has been aptly described as government based on a "cartel of elites."[43] But there is no reason to think that politicians—especially electorally minded politicians—will behave in accordance with its rules and form such a cartel across ascriptive lines. There are good reasons to think that they will not.

40. Arend Lijphart, *Power-Sharing in South Africa* (Berkeley: University of California Institute of International Studies, 1985).

41. See especially ibid., pp. 6–9, 80–81.

42. For a critique of Lijphart's earlier studies of consociation, see Horowitz, *Ethnic Groups in Conflict*, pp. 568–76.

43. This term is used by Arend Lijphart, "Consociational Democracy," *World Politics* 4, no. 2 (January 1969): 207–25, at 213, 215, 222. It was borrowed from Ralf Dahrendorf, *Society and Democracy in Germany* (Garden City, N.Y.: Doubleday, 1967), p. 276.

In divided societies, there are some studies indicating that elites are less ethnocentric than their followers, but there are more showing that ethnocentrism increases with education.[44] There is little or nothing in the available South African studies to suggest a different conclusion. There is direct evidence from several studies that increased education is generally associated with negative attitudes on the part of Black South Africans toward out-groups. Research conducted in KwaMashu, near Durban, found that the most highly educated male respondents displayed the greatest interethnic and interracial social distance.[45] A study of African interracial attitudes concluded that "a higher educational qualification was significantly associated with a negative attitude toward Afrikaans-speaking Whites . . . ."[46] A survey found African students at universities in the Western Cape to be racially exclusive "hard nationalists."[47] In a fourth study, based on an earlier Soweto sample, increasing parental education was associated with slightly reduced social distance between Black respondents and most other racial groups.[48] The

44. Myron Weiner, *Sons of the Soil: Migration and Ethnic Conflict in India* (Princeton: Princeton University Press, 1978), pp. 274–93; Mary Fainsod Katzenstein, *Ethnicity and Equality: The Shiv Sena Party and Preferential Policies in Bombay* (Ithaca: Cornell University Press, 1979), pp. 63–81; Maurice Pinard and Richard Hamilton, "The Class Bases of the Quebec Independence Movement: Conjectures and Evidence," *Ethnic and Racial Studies* 7, no. 1 (January 1984): 19–54; Craig Baxter, "The Jana Sangh," in Donald Eugene Smith, ed., *South Asian Politics and Religion* (Princeton: Princeton University Press, 1966), chap. 4; Erwin C. Hargrove, "Nationality, Values, and Change: Young Elites in French Canada," *Comparative Politics* 2, no. 3 (April 1970): 473–99, at 474 n. 1; George Henry Weightman, "A Study of Prejudice in a Personalistic Society," *Asian Studies* (Quezon City) 2, no. 1 (April 1964): 87–101, at 96; Rodolfo A. Bulatao, *Ethnic Attitudes in Five Philippine Cities* (Quezon City: University of the Philippines Social Science Research Laboratory, 1973), pp. 126, 129; Robert M. Price, "The Pattern of Ethnicity in Ghana," *Journal of Modern African Studies* 11, no. 3 (September 1973): 470–75; Roberta E. Mapp, "Cross-national Dimensions of Ethnocentrism," *Canadian Journal of African Studies* 6, no. 1 (Winter 1972): 73–96; R. D. Grillo, "Ethnic Identity and Social Stratification on a Kampala Housing Estate," in Abner Cohen, ed., *Urban Ethnicity* (London: Tavistock, 1974), p. 173; William John Hanna and Judith Lynne Hanna, "Polyethnicity and Political Integration in Umuahia and Mbale," in Robert T. Daland, ed., *Comparative Urban Research* (Beverly Hills: Sage, 1969), p. 179.

45. Brian M. du Toit, "Ethnicity, Neighborliness, and Friendship among Urban Africans in South Africa," in Brian M. du Toit, ed., *Ethnicity in Modern Africa* (Boulder, Colo.: Westview Press, 1978), pp. 161–62. Different results were found for the small number of most educated females in the sample.

46. Ans E. M. Appelgryn and Johan M. Nieuwoudt, "Relative Deprivation and the Ethnic Attitudes of Blacks and Afrikaans-speaking Whites in South Africa," *Journal of Social Psychology* 128, no. 3 (June 1988): 311–23, at 320–21. To the same effect, see the older studies cited in J. W. Mann, "Attitudes towards Ethnic Groups," in Heribert Adam, ed., *South Africa: Sociological Perspectives* (London: Oxford University Press, 1971), p. 63.

47. Peter Collins, *The Ethnic Factor in South Africa's Politics* (University of Cape Town, n.d.; mimeo.), pp. 95–96. Compare Chapter 3, note 46, above.

48. Melville Leonard Edelstein, "An Attitude Survey of Urban Bantu Matric Pupils

results were the same for social distance between the Zulu subsample of 75 respondents and most other racial groups; but the modestly increased levels of parental education reflected in the subsample produced an average *increase* in social distance between Zulu respondents and other African groups, a substantial one in the case of distance from the Xhosa.[49] Among Whites, although increased education might be thought to produce greater interracial tolerance, the South African results are at best equivocal.[50] Even if tolerant leaders could "bring the tendentiously hostile masses to accept coexistence," notes Theodor Hanf, ". . . this begs the question of how hostile and intolerant masses are going to produce such tolerant and open-minded leaders."[51]

Since the mute equation of educated elites with accommodative attitudes is unsupported, there is no reason to think automatically that elites will use their leadership position to reduce rather than pursue conflict. Analysts need to avoid projecting their own accommodationist impulses onto political leaders, who may entertain other ideas and whose behavior, in any event, will be governed not just by what they believe but by the situation they face.

If anything is to induce politicians to play by conflict-limiting rules, it lies in the structures in which they find themselves. By far the most important of these is the electoral system. I shall have much more to say later about the version of proportional representation (PR) that has been advanced as part of a consociational model for South Africa. Suffice it to indicate at this point that proportional representation makes a multiparty system, and therefore government by coalition, more likely than the present South African electoral system would, but it provides no

---

in Soweto, with Special Reference to Stereotyping and Social Distance: A Sociological Study" (M.A. thesis, University of Pretoria, 1971), pp. 111–12, 130.

49. Ibid., p. 131. Some social distance evaluations toward other African ethnic groups decreased slightly with parental education, while others increased. As indicated, the largest increase was with respect to the Xhosa, evaluated by Zulu respondents with slightly higher parental education as being as distant from them as the Pedi and the English-speaking Whites, and not much closer than the Afrikaners. On the last point, it should be noted that the study was performed before the hardening in African attitudes toward Afrikaners that followed the Soweto rising of 1976. It should also be underscored that differences in Zulu parental education represented in the study were relatively minor. The Zulu subsample was the only one reported separately.

50. Graham C. Kinloch, "Racial Attitudes in South Africa: A Review," *Genetic, Social, and General Psychology Monographs* 111, no. 3 (August 1985): 261–81, at 267, 269; Henry Lever, "Education and Ethnic Attitudes in South Africa," *Sociology and Social Research* 64, no. 1 (October 1979): 53–69.

51. Theodor Hanf, "The Prospects of Accommodation in Communal Conflicts: A Comparative Study," in Hermann Giliomee and Lawrence Schlemmer, eds., *Negotiating South Africa's Future* (New York: St. Martin's Press, 1989), p. 100.

assurance whatever that all the significant groups will be embraced in the coalition. Like other electoral systems, PR is conducive to government and opposition. Those parties that, individually or in coalition, have a majority of seats proceed to form the government, while those that have a minority of seats form the opposition. That is, after all, the way PR systems function in the Irish Republic, in Germany, in Scandinavia, in Australia, and even in Israel, whenever one of the major parties and its allies have a clear majority of seats. To obtain a broadly inclusive consociational coalition, one that routinely embraces all the major groups and tendencies, requires agreement to much more than a PR electoral system.

The same goes for group autonomy, consensus decision making, minority veto, and group proportionality in the bureaucracy. These features amount to a full-blown scheme of government that does indeed require agreement among a cartel of elites. But notably lacking in this prescription is any reason, anchored in electoral politics, for leaders to support such a system, to make such an agreement, or more generally to foster intergroup compromise. Even if leaders committed themselves to such a plan at the outset, under democratic, competitive conditions, centrifugal forces from among their own followers and from among their more extreme electoral competitors would easily undermine the durability of the agreement.

There have been other versions of consociational proposals for South Africa, perhaps most notably those of Frederik van Zyl Slabbert and David Welsh, who advocate a system based on the "principle of coalescent politics," which seeks to be "maximally representative [of parties and of groups] while operating on a broadly consensual basis."[52] Like Lijphart, Slabbert and Welsh propose a power-sharing executive, inclusive of all the major parties and groups, proportional representation elections, a minority veto, and group-based proportionality in the civil service, armed forces, and police. Unlike Lijphart, they do not advocate group autonomy on either a territorial or nonterritorial basis, and they hope that parties will have reason to appeal for support across group lines.[53] They, too, however, are counting on enlightened leadership to take steps to avoid "mutual destruction."[54] Of course, if such

52. F. van Zyl Slabbert and David Welsh, *South Africa's Options: Strategies for Sharing Power* (New York: St. Martin's Press, 1979), p. 147.
53. Ibid., p. 148.
54. Ibid., pp. 130, 150.

leadership could be counted upon consistently, consociational arrangements would be much less necessary in the first place.

In many ways, proposals like these entrench group rights, although Lijphart is careful to insure that the only groups whose rights will be recognized are those that emerge voluntarily in the electoral process. In this respect, his proposals are quite different from the practices of the apartheid government, which specified the identity of groups from above and assigned individuals to official group categories. Nevertheless, there is no gainsaying the ultimate group character of the protections. Cultural autonomy, for example, cannot be accorded to political parties but only to ethnic or racial groups.

The same problem attaches even more prominently to consociational plans or devices that are explicitly based on group identity. The proposals of the KwaZulu Natal Indaba (discussed in Chapter 5) and of the Soviet academic Gleb Starushenko[55] envision an upper chamber of the legislature based on racially demarcated seats, in equal numbers for each racial group. They would not meet the criterion I articulated in Chapter 1 of nonracial institutions suitable for a multiracial society.

This becomes a serious sticking point in South African opinion. As we have seen,[56] there is considerable support for arrangements that preclude majority or minority domination. However, this support turns soft when the arrangements contain safeguards for named groups. A survey question that elicited 53 percent White approval for special White voting privileges received only 1 percent Black approval.[57] A study conducted for the KwaZulu Natal Indaba asked whether "power-sharing between all races in South Africa" was the "best solution." Ninety percent of African respondents agreed. When, however, the question was framed in terms of "minority protections," only 20 percent agreed on the need for them, 38 percent disagreed, and 42 percent responded "Don't know."[58] Given the dissensus on means, arrangements based ultimately on group rights have a doubtful future. They run afoul of the metaconflict. They also run afoul of strongly held conceptions of territorial sov-

55. The Starushenko proposal of 1986 is described in G. R. Berridge, "The Role of the Superpowers," in John D. Brewer, ed., *Can South Africa Survive? Five Minutes to Midnight* (New York: St. Martin's Press, 1989), p. 18. In this plan, the upper house would have a veto.

56. See Chapter 3, note 46, above.

57. *Times* (London), August 3, 1986.

58. KwaZulu Natal Indaba, "Black Attitudes in KwaZulu Natal" (Durban, September 1988; mimeo.), pp. 19–21.

ereignty, which, around the world, have eclipsed earlier ideas of sovereignty or autonomy on a group or personal basis.[59] Perhaps unfortunately, proximity has displaced kinship as the fount of government, thus throwing the idea of self-determination into great confusion and undermining group rights.

Entrenched minority group vetoes would seem particularly precarious. It was pointed out by an unofficial South African study commission in 1973 that, for consociational plans to survive, the segments represented must be fairly equal in population.[60] It is one thing to have each of three or four substantial groups enjoy a mutual veto; it is another to confide such power to two or three racial minorities which together constitute less than a quarter of the population.

There is experience with these matters. Minority guarantees were an integral part of the consociational Cyprus Constitution of 1960. It required concurrent majorities for legislation; a division of the two top offices (one Greek, one Turk), with mutual veto powers; and quotas that generally overrepresented the Turkish minority in everything from the cabinet to the civil service, the armed forces, and the police.[61] Formal guarantees are virtually always resented by the group on which they are imposed in the same measure as they are insisted upon by the group seeking to benefit from them. Because they are resented, they are not likely to prove durable, unless, of course, they accidentally create an accommodative feature from which politicians can gain and which outweighs the resentment. That did not happen in Cyprus, and the arrangements were soon demolished.

An important source of durability for constitutional arrangements in severely divided societies is that they must work well and be seen to work well from the beginning. This is most likely if they create interests across group lines. Then there will be inhibitions on altering the arrangements. Group rights for the minority, however, are likely to appear temporary, as a thorn to be excised as soon as possible, as they were in Zimbabwe. But even if they were permanent, special rights would do nothing about the problem to which they are ostensibly addressed—the ability of ascriptive majorities to ignore interests other than their

59. See Yoram Dinstein, "Autonomy," in Yoram Dinstein, ed., *Models of Autonomy* (New Brunswick, N.J.: Transaction Books, 1981), p. 292.

60. Political Commission of the Study Project on Christianity in Apartheid Society, *South Africa's Political Alternatives*, SPRO-CAS Publication no. 10 (Johannesburg: Ravan Press, 1973), pp. 165, 168.

61. See Thomas Ehrlich, "Cyprus: The 'Warlike Isle': Origins and Elements of the Current Crisis," *Stanford Law Review* 18, no. 5 (May 1966): 1023–42.

own. If that is the problem, institutional designers will have to do better than reinvent wheels on which Zimbabweans were riding in 1980 and Cypriots were riding as early as 1960.

BOTTOM-UP

All of the plans reviewed thus far presuppose agreement at the center. By contrast, there has been a recurrent tendency in South Africa to suggest that, as long as progress was stymied at the center, local-level negotiations might create "nodes of interracial co-operation and accommodation" [62] from which political structures might grow, in spite of intransigence at the center. While top-down plans were merely being discussed, bottom-up action might actually be taken.

This idea was first mooted in 1973 by the Political Commission of the Study Project on Christianity in Apartheid Society, which urged the vigorous use of the governmental structures of apartheid against the aims of those structures, so as to produce "power centres capable of forcing change throughout South Africa at a greater pace." [63] The aim was not to succumb to immobilism but to use separate development to expand opportunities, improve Black social welfare, increase security of land tenure, reduce restrictions on free speech, phase out petty apartheid, encourage trade unionism and collective bargaining, and place segregated local authorities in ongoing relations with each other—in short, to adjust the existing system in order to reduce drastically the power of a stubborn central government, even before moving into a second phase, consisting of consultation and negotiation. [64] A variety of plans for multiracial, bottom-up cooperation were advanced in the 1970s and 1980s. [65]

Such an incremental strategy was of limited utility as time passed, for the same reason as gulps, rather than sips, became essential to the process of political change. Moreover, boring from within was not really possible so long as many major Black organizations declined to partic-

62. Slabbert and Welsh, *South Africa's Options,* p. 129.
63. *South Africa's Political Alternatives,* p. 220. Although cast in the mold of separate development, the work of the Tomlinson Commission of the 1950s was, in some ways, a precursor, for it recommended bottom-up political development of consolidated Black areas. For a summary, see L. J. Boulle, *Constitutional Reform and the Apartheid State* (New York: St. Martin's Press, 1984), pp. 127–29.
64. Slabbert and Welsh, *South Africa's Options,* pp. 201–37.
65. See, e.g., Ciskei Commission, *The Quail Report* (Pretoria: Conference Associates, 1980), pp. 123–25; Paul Malherbe, *Multistan: A Way Out of the South African Dilemma* (Cape Town: David Philip, 1974).

ipate in what they saw as utterly illegitimate governmental structures. A suggestion that the multiracial Regional Services Councils might, for example, provide such "nodes" of cooperation[66] was met with the obstacle that the councils were based in turn on racially based local authorities.

The possibilities, however, seemed greater with the mass activity of the United Democratic Front in the mid-1980s. At the local level, there were frequent consumer boycotts of White businesses, sometimes leading to negotiations with White merchants and to resolution of local grievances. In a number of cases, the negotiations were more wide-ranging. In the course of the negotiations, some considerable local understanding appears to have been built up on both sides. It is exemplified by a statement issued during a 1985 consumer boycott by a Black civic organization in Port Alfred, in the Eastern Cape:

> We emphasize our desire to make Port Alfred a pleasant place to live, for its own sake, and as an example to the rest of the country—after all, Jesus Christ wasn't born in the biggest city of Israel. This committee will always act responsibly in its dealings with its "counterpart" in the white section of our community. It is our greatest wish that this community will, in the very near future, be able to look back at these troubled times and see them as a good omen rather than the opposite . . . . The call of this committee is a simple one: We want a single non-racial local authority for Port Alfred. We are not blind nor wilfully deaf to the Government's new deal; we do not doubt the Government's good faith in seeking to resolve the political problems of our country. What we are doing is trying to contribute, in a positive way, to the search for solutions. We are well aware of the fact that our white "counterparts" have no direct powers to control what the Government does. However, we appeal to the white community as a whole to support this initiative, if only for the future of this particular area and, who knows, for South Africa as a whole.[67]

This statement had followed a number of productive meetings, and it illustrates the good will that was still present at the local level, even as conflict was reaching new heights at the national level.

Such local-level efforts at political change had various origins. In East London, as in Port Alfred, there was a request by a township residents'

66. See Lawrence Schlemmer, "Requirements for and Possibilities of Successful Constitutional Negotiation in South Africa," in Giliomee and Schlemmer, eds., *Negotiating South Africa's Future*, pp. 39–40.

67. Quoted by Doreen Atkinson, "Local Government Restructuring: White Municipal Initiatives, 1985–1988," Institute of Social and Economic Research, Development Studies Unit, Rhodes University, Grahamstown, South Africa, Working Paper no. 44 (April 1989; mimeo.), p. 71.

association for a takeover of the Black township administration by the White local authority, which proved receptive. In Pietermaritzburg, there was a planning exercise designed to reduce inefficiencies resulting from racially fragmented local governments. In Cape Town, the White city council began a dialogue with Black and Coloured civic groups and sought ways to restore the equivalent of the former nonracial franchise. In the main, therefore, the negotiations either followed a Black boycott or a White attempt to find a formula to transcend racially based local authorities.

These efforts failed for several reasons.[68] In some cases, bureaucratic rivalries among governmental units came into play. In others, the central government thwarted the proposals, which ran afoul of its own master plan for racially separate local authorities as part of the devolution of power over "own affairs" to the respective groups. In still others, the UDF declined to participate, or the initiatives were overtaken by local violence. And in some localities, Black civic activists were arrested as the negotiations were in progress.

By and large, it proved impossible to do what was intended—to use existing structures for purposes opposite to those the regime had when it created the structures. The bottom-up relations that were established were not unimportant, because they created the chance for some people to work together across group lines for the first time.[69] In a new period of change at the center, these understandings can be useful building blocks. For the most part, however, fundamental political change cannot come out of a bottom-up strategy.

THE MODELS: TOO LITTLE OR TOO MUCH

The models reviewed thus far can be grouped into categories. Some plans presuppose consent on the part of participants; others elide the issue of consent. The bottom-uppers and the partitionists assume that those who participate in their ventures agree on the need to proceed in the ways they propose. There is no point in even discussing a nonconsensual partition in South Africa. In both cases, however, even assuming mutual consent, the likely accomplishments of the plans fall far short

68. The ventures are well described and analyzed in Atkinson, "Local Government Restructuring," and in Doreen Atkinson and Chris Heymans, "The Limits and Possibilities of Local Initiatives for Change: The Case for Participatory Planning," *Politikon* 15, no. 1 (June 1988): 31–44.

69. This is a point to which I shall return in the discussion of federalism in Chapter 6, below.

of what would be required to achieve democracy in an environment of reduced conflict. In fact, drastic though partition would be, it might actually make the conflicts in the successor states more stark and serious than in an undivided South Africa. The same cannot quite be said of binationalism and consociationalism. Given the consent of the participants, perhaps they would have some of the desired effects. The problem is that consent is most unlikely to be forthcoming. In the case of group rights or overrepresentation on the Zimbabwe model, both defects are present. Neither consent nor effectiveness is likely. Bottom-up and partition plans accomplish too little; binationalism and consociationalism attempt too much; and overrepresentation achieves both too little and too much.

Ironically, the models that lay out plans for consensual rather than adversary politics do not explain how to obtain consent to a consensual plan. Slabbert and Welsh, for example, acknowledge that "African nationalism has not viewed the constitutional provision of guarantees for minority ethnic or racial groups with much favour."[70] In South Africa, there is a strong ideological aversion to guarantees on the part of Charterists and Africanists. Slabbert and Welsh also refer to "the strongly competitive and zero-sum conceptions of politics in South Africa, and its corollary that South Africa's political system must embody either white minority rule (under the guise of separate development) or black majority rule," which means that "the adoption of a more coalescent style of politics would require a substantial modification of attitudes."[71] In some countries, attitudes have been modified, but only after disaster has struck. Short of that, the modification of attitudes in the time required would seem highly unlikely.

Although they propose consociation despite this problem, Slabbert and Welsh also note that "the best possible safeguard for minority groups" is one "woven into the operation of the political system itself by making the votes of minority members important."[72] In Chapter 5, I shall show that the electoral system they recommend will not accomplish this, but the insight remains useful. Weaving concern for the interests of others into the fabric of political calculations is completely different from prescribing altruism ex cathedra. Much of the remainder of this chapter and of this book in general emphasizes this distinction, which is vital to the survival of severely divided societies.

70. *South Africa's Options*, p. 117.
71. Ibid., p. 116.
72. Ibid., p. 148.

CONTRACTS AND SOCIAL CONTRACTS

By and large, those Asian and African states that have done best at managing their divided societies in a democratic fashion have done so at one of two junctures: at independence or after a civil war. The European and North American states that have made similar accommodations (Belgium and Canada) tend to fall in between—they did not make appropriate plans at the outset for democratic conflict management, but they did not wait for civil war either. Since each of these times of innovation has a characteristic set of procedures, policies, and pitfalls attached to it, I want to deal with them separately.

First, in a minority of post-colonial societies, accommodations were reached at independence—not by the departing colonialists but by the local groups that would have to spend the future together. The most important cases are the Malaysian constitutional bargain of 1956 and the Lebanese National Pact of 1943, both of which saved conflict-prone societies from early disintegration.

Notice that they are "bargains," "pacts," "contracts." They are treaties between semisovereign peoples based on reciprocity, and they have all the characteristic problems all contracts have: the preferences of the parties change over time; conditions also change; the returns to the parties from the deal are uneven; and the deadlines laid down inevitably arrive. There is typically a good bit of splitting the difference when the contracts are made. Certain characteristic provisions, assuaging aspirations when adopted, create discontent later. If group quotas are used, changing demography may render them obsolete, but they are frozen into the agreement. If some issues are postponed to a date certain in the future, the firm target becomes a new date of reckoning, a new occasion for conflict. If incommensurables are traded—X in return for Y—and if X proves more valuable over the long term, the party that received Y may nurse a sense of grievance. Unless provision is made for amendment, contract alone is not a lasting basis for accommodation. Intergroup contracts tend to be their own undoing.[73] The problem with intergroup pacts, in a word, is that to endure they need to be flexible; but to be formed they must be, in principle, permanent, since the ripe moment may never come again.

Contrast with these problems the completely different assumptions,

---

73. These pitfalls, illustrated by the Malaysian and Lebanese arrangements, are explained in Horowitz, *Ethnic Groups in Conflict,* pp. 580–88.

procedures, and provisions of the Nigerian return to democratic rule in 1979—and again a decade later.[74] This is a second innovative juncture—after a civil war.

The Nigerians had been through severe conflict and civil war, and they did not want a repetition. Since no one could be sure which group might be on the receiving end in any future round of ethnic conflict and civil strife, the Nigerians made, not a bargain but a real constitution, not a contract among groups that knew what their interests would be but a social contract among groups that were not sure what their interests might be next time around. They made a blind, Rawlsian contract.[75]

Mirabile dictu, the Nigerian social contract worked according to plan. The president, elected by a formula that put a premium on multiethnic support, became a panethnic figure. The new federal system made everything, including ethnicity, more complex. In ethnic conflict terms, the Second Republic was different from the First.

If everything went so well, why, then, was it necessary to go through the same exercise again a decade later? To answer this question, it is necessary to recall that the Nigerians did not have the sober insights of 1978–79 at the time of independence in 1960. In the interval, they developed corrupt regimes, military coups, a civil war, and bloated, greedy armed forces. All of these problems, the indirect result of the ethnic conflict Nigerians failed to anticipate and avert the first time around, came back to undo what the Nigerians did the second time around.[76] As I said previously, earlier is better, in the sense that more obstacles are arrayed against democratic arrangements that are instituted later. Nevertheless, there is a tradeoff here: the bitter experience on which the later innovations are based may be costly and painful, but it is more likely to give rise to enduring institutions of conflict reduction.

That is because bitter experience is more likely to produce public policy making through the social contract mode than to produce treaty

74. I have described the Nigerian constitutional proceedings of 1978 in "About-Face in Africa: The Return of Civilian Rule in Nigeria," *Yale Review* 68, no. 2 (Winter 1979): 192–206. The proceedings of a decade later are recounted by Naomi Chazan, "Planning Democracy in Africa: A Comparative Perspective on Nigeria and Ghana," *Policy Sciences* 22, nos. 3–4 (November 1989): 325–57.

75. That is, one based on original-position reasoning, not present-position reasoning. See John Rawls, *A Theory of Justice* (Cambridge: Harvard University Press, 1971).

76. See Larry Diamond, "Nigeria: Pluralism, Statism, and the Struggle for Democracy," in Larry Diamond et al., eds., *Democracy in Developing Countries*, vol. 2, *Africa* (Boulder, Colo.: Lynne Rienner, 1988), pp. 33–91.

making through the simple contract mode. By public policy, I mean arrangements that do not merely reflect transient group interests but a design for living together premised on incentives for accommodative behavior transcending group interests at the moment of enactment.

Group rights tend to be negotiated as part of the simple contract mode. They therefore are prone to many of the problems I have identified as being inherent in contract as a tool of accommodation.

South Africa is neither starting completely fresh, as countries on the threshold of independence were, nor sobered by civil war fought to victory. South Africa is neither in the position of Lebanon in 1943 or Malaysia in 1956 nor in the position of Nigeria in 1978. It is somewhere in-between. This middle position may not be an altogether bad thing. South Africa may be able to avoid the civil war needed to reach the Nigerian sobriety and public policy making that followed, but it may be sufficiently chastened by its current prospects to reject mere intergroup horse trading in favor of public policy making.

That is not to imply that group interests are irrelevant or that some intergroup trades are not part of public policy. In the making of the United States Constitution, for example, there was a large element of reciprocity, especially in the trades that were made between small states and large states. But some of the central innovations of the Constitution, such as a strong federation and a separately elected president, had little or nothing to do with anything other than what was thought to be sound public policy. South Africa is a severely divided society, which can become even more severely divided in the future. Groups will need self-interested reasons even to adopt public policy measures. The difference between treaty making and public policy making does not lie in the absence of altruism in the one and its presence in the other. The motive for both is self-interest. The point is to make groups see the long-term superiority of social contracts over simple contracts, of public policy making over mere treaty making. Unpleasant experience and a desire not to repeat it are at the root of the social contract–public policy perspective.

ON THE FALLACY "WHATEVER THE NEGOTIATORS AGREE ON WILL BE ACCEPTABLE"

What I have just been saying can be summarized in two more general statements. The first is that constitutive policy decisions really matter. The second is that mode of decision and content of decision are related.

Some provisions are more conducive to intergroup accommodation than others, and some procedures are more likely to produce these provisions.

Previously, I called attention to a contrast between Malaysia and Sri Lanka that illustrates the first of these statements very well. I said that the Malaysians had acted early on their ethnic problems, whereas the Sri Lankans had acted late. What the Malaysians did and the Sri Lankans did not do are every bit as important. Here I have in mind, not the Malaysian constitutional bargain, which later largely unraveled (for reasons to which I have already adverted), but the interethnic coalition that Malaysians formed even before independence. That coalition ran a single electoral slate, and it was flanked by ethnically based political parties. The coalition was the location for interethnic compromise and, in some modest measure, still is. By contrast, the Sri Lankans opted for ethnically based parties and Sinhalese-majority governments; and they implicitly opted against interethnic coalitions and interethnic compromise. These contrasting approaches are heavily responsible for the Malaysians' capacity to moderate a very difficult ethnic problem and the Sri Lankans' capacity to exacerbate a much less difficult ethnic problem.

To underscore the second proposition—that mode of decision and content of decision are related—I hardly need to say more than that, if we are in a deal-making mode, we shall probably make a deal, if we make anything at all. Deal making is common in divided societies—and not merely in ethnically divided societies but in societies divided along class lines as well.[77] Lack of consensus, even active dissensus, among the component groups, together with spheres of complementarity or ethnic divisions of labor, can make the quid pro quo seem a natural solution. Trades also are attractive for political leaders in building support, for they can show constituents the palpable gains they have made right at the moment of agreement.

By the same token, serious public policy making for interethnic accommodation is rare, for some of the converse reasons and for some other reasons as well. If deal making is attractive because of immediate, palpable gains—because one immediately knows what one has received and has given up, at least for the time being—the very unforeseeability

---

77. See Guillermo O'Donnell and Philippe C. Schmitter, "Tentative Conclusions about Uncertain Democracies," in Guillermo O'Donnell et al., eds., *Transitions from Authoritarian Rule: Prospects for Democracy* (Baltimore: Johns Hopkins University Press, 1986), pt. 4, pp. 37–47.

of gains and losses is what makes public policy making less attractive, absent the Nigerian sobriety induced by bitter experience. Serious public policy making, embodied in constitutions, is also rare because constitutional documents have so often been sold to countries in need of them as so much parchment and so many lofty (albeit irrelevant) phrases required by every self-respecting state in the world community. They have been sold by provision merchants who, more often than not, have only a superficial acquaintance with the problems of the buyer countries. They are sold to politicians who have, in any event, their own agendas.

I do not mean to denigrate deal making in severely divided societies. On the contrary, an exchange, a treaty, a deal, is usually better than simply letting nature take its course in such societies, for that course is generally the course of serious, destructive conflict—or worse. All I want to emphasize is that the results that follow from the public-policy-making mode are different. For the reasons I have given and for some additional reasons that I shall identify later, they are also likely to be superior.

If I am correct about this, there is an important corollary for interethnic negotiation. There is now a large body of literature on negotiation, including interethnic negotiation, for such societies as Cyprus and Zimbabwe. That literature is almost entirely processual: it documents why and how parties reach, can be induced to reach, or fail to reach, agreement.[78] The tacit assumption has been that, if the parties agree and can live with the agreement, they must have arrived at something like the market-clearing price. Perhaps they have, but the notion that, if an agreement clears the market, the resulting commodity will produce interethnic peace down the road is entirely specious. There are many designs for living together in a severely divided society. Evidence that the parties to a conflict have agreed on one such design only shows that this one was among those acceptable at the moment. It does not show that it was the best or that it will be durable.

There is a powerful bias toward process operating in world affairs. Parties to conflicts are supposed to talk to each other. If they talk earnestly and long enough, it is thought, they will understand each other's

---

78. For a typical sampling, see Diane B. Bendahmane and John W. McDonald, Jr., eds., *Perspectives on Negotiation* (Washington, D.C.: Center for the Study of Foreign Affairs, 1986). See also I. William Zartman, "Negotiations and Prenegotiations in Ethnic Conflict: The Beginning, the Middle, and the Ends," in Montville, ed., *Conflict and Peacemaking in Multiethnic Societies*, pp. 511–33.

concerns and solve their problems. The South African literature on negotiation is, unfortunately, suffused with the same notions. It emphasizes the "communication process"[79] between adversaries, the "chem-
istry of negotiation"[80] and its ability to produce unforeseen outcomes.
"If the process is a reasonable one," claims a proponent of this view,
"people will naturally be reasonable with each other."[81] Such an approach begs the question of what is reasonable for a divided society, as
it begs a host of other questions related to agreements, including the
one alluded to in Chapter 1—namely, the problem of feigned assent to
an agreement as a prelude to achieving hegemonic, rather than democratic, aspirations.

INCENTIVES VERSUS CONSTRAINTS

The more enduring and effective arrangements to reduce intergroup
conflict are fortified by internal incentives, not external constraints. For
present purposes, a constraint is a rule that binds only because it was
agreed to at the outset. It has no continuing binding force based on
present interest (except, of course, the interest in keeping one's word or
in abiding by the law). It can readily be seen that most of the approaches reviewed in this chapter—group rights, consociationalism,
binationalism—are based on constraints. An incentive, on the other hand,
binds because it is in the continuing interest of the actors. The approaches just mentioned do not attend to the problem of incentives to
accommodative behavior. If they create any such incentives, that is entirely accidental. The incentives of greatest concern are, of course, those
that operate on politicians and their followers, that harness their self-
interest to the cause of intergroup conflict reduction, regardless of their
personal feelings, that, in a word, make moderation pay.

The exigencies of certain electoral systems do this, and certain political coalitions that result from particular competitive and electoral settings do the same. The genius of the Malaysian coalition arrangements
that I referred to previously was that they forced Malay and Chinese
politicians, in heterogeneous constituencies, to rely in part on votes de-
livered by politicians belonging to the other ethnic group. Those votes

79. Hendrik W. van der Merwe, *Pursuing Justice and Peace in South Africa* (London:
Routledge, 1989), pp. 65, 94.

80. Clem Sunter, *The World and South Africa in the 1990s* (Cape Town: Human &
Rousseau Tafelberg, 1987), p. 99.

81. Ibid., p. 105.

would not be forthcoming unless leaders could portray the candidates as moderate on issues of concern to the group that was delivering its votes across ethnic lines. Consequently, compromises at the top of the coalition were supported by electoral incentives at the bottom. At various times, the Lebanese, Nigerian, and Sri Lankan electoral systems—or parts of them—have offered comparable electoral inducements.

The division of territory has sometimes had moderating effects on intergroup conflict. Before the "linguistic states" that were put into effect by Jawaharlal Nehru's government in India in the 1950s, intergroup conflict seemed to be growing. The advent of linguistically homogeneous states, however, impelled politicians seeking power in those states to compete with other politicians belonging to the same group, rather than different groups, and the effect was to reduce intergroup political rivalries and conflict.

All of this is what I mean by internal incentives built by constitutional engineers into the structure of the selfish calculations of politicians. Sometimes, however, the engineering is inadvertent. Like some other Indian nationalists, Nehru was initially opposed to linguistically homogeneous states, because he thought they constituted a capitulation to the forces of linguistic parochialism and a challenge to national unity.[82] He did not foresee that linguistic states would tend to reduce separatism and intergroup tension, rather than foster them.

To frame the utility of incentives in terms of their ability to affect the selfish calculations of politicians, harnessing self-interest to the cause of peace, is, of course, to reject the perhaps-loftier aspiration of dealing with the so-called root causes of conflict. It is to resort to an approach that does not seek or need to change hearts and minds in order to succeed. That is not to say that significant periods of accommodative behavior will not soften up what seem now to be intractably difficult conflicts. Perhaps they will, but the efficacy of incentives does not depend on that; it depends instead of changing behavior. In this case, what needs changing is the behavior of the key actors who turn polities toward either conflict or accommodation: the politicians.

By contrast, consider the more usual and generally much less effective approaches, which rely on external constraints. Unlike incentives, the lure of which consists in their being rewarding, constraints are to be obeyed even if they are not rewarding. They are rules from outside.

---

82. Hugh Tinker, *India and Pakistan: A Political Analysis,* rev. ed. (New York: Praeger, 1967), p. 136.

It should not be thought that only minorities insist on constraints. One set of superficially attractive constraints consists of prohibitions relating to party composition. No party may be registered unless it provides lists of officers and members that demonstrate its multiethnic, multiracial character. Disturbed by the prospect of ethnic claims, a large number of African states outlawed ethnically based parties.[83] In so doing, they managed to cast a pall over the political process but did not succeed in ending ethnic claims. Such prohibitions are futile where they are not draconian. Many parties are able to provide the appropriate spread of names on their lists of officers, members, and candidates without changing the character of the party at all. Formal legal regulations of this sort can produce a great deal of window dressing without altering the ethnic base of any party. As I shall indicate later, however, there are ways to induce ethnically based parties to alter, if not their membership base, their posture and their behavior on ethnic issues.

Despite their successful experience with electoral incentives, which I shall describe in Chapter 5, and their unsuccessful experience with an attempt to force parties to transcend ethnic lines, Nigeria's military rulers, planning a second return to civilian rule, have created a mandatory two-party system. Each of the parties is to be government created and ethnically balanced.[84] Although they are not necessarily apt for democracy in plural societies, the two-party ideal and the nonethnic-party ideal are strongly held in much of Africa.[85]

The ANC's *Constitutional Guidelines* similarly imply that advocacy of ethnic exclusivism might be unlawful in a nonracial, nonethnic South Africa.[86] This would mean that ethnically based political parties would be unlawful. "During talks with an ANC delegation in Dakar in July 1988 it was made clear that racially or ethnically based mobilisation in

83. For the early Ghanaian version of this, see David R. Smock and Audrey C. Smock, *The Politics of Pluralism* (New York: Elsevier, 1975), pp. 229–30.

84. See Diamond, "Nigeria: Pluralism, Statism, and the Struggle for Democracy," p. 78. For the military directive for officials to set up the two parties, see *St. Louis Post-Dispatch*, November 23, 1989.

85. For an explanation of why two-party systems tend to extremism in divided societies, see Robert A. Dahl, "Some Explanations," in Robert A. Dahl, ed., *Political Oppositions in Western Democracies* (New Haven: Yale University Press, 1986), pp. 375–76.

86. Paragraph I of the ANC's *Constitutional Guidelines for a Democratic South Africa* would place the state and "all social institutions" under an obligation to eradicate racial discrimination, while paragraph K provides that the "advocacy or practice of racism, fascism, nazism or *the incitement of ethnic or regional exclusiveness* or hatred shall be outlawed." Paragraph M states that "parties which conform to the provision[s] of (I) to (K) above shall have the legal right to exist and to take part in the political life of the country." *Weekly Mail* (Johannesburg), October 7–13, 1988 (emphasis supplied).

a hypothetical future dispensation under the ANC would be met with 'liberatory intolerance,' as it was put." [87] Such prohibitions would affect some of the strongest likely participants, representing potential minorities, in a future democratic system. These might include the largely-Zulu Inkatha and the National Party. [88] With such a step, so heavily reminiscent of the suppression of ethnically based opposition by Kwame Nkrumah, Sékou Touré, Milton Obote, and other post-independence African leaders, there is a strong sense of déjà vu. In no African case did such measures reduce ethnic conflict. In every one, however, such measures stifled democracy. Ethnically based parties are a serious problem, but outlawing them and depriving their constituencies of representation is not the answer. A much better answer, as I shall point out in Chapter 5, is to provide them with incentives to dilute the exclusivity of their appeals.

Constraints, then, consist of prohibitions as much as they do of guarantees. Neither necessarily has any payoff in inducements to accommodative behavior.

Occasionally, of course, constraints are part of a larger bargain. If the parties are unusually lucky at the outset, the resentment at what was given up is mitigated in the first instance by the knowledge that something else was gained. In the case of Cyprus, the Turkish guarantees, seen as Greek losses right from the beginning, were not offset by Greek gains. But even if they had been, the bargain would have been vulnerable to being undermined in the long term by all the forces that conspire against such contracts. These I have reviewed earlier in this chapter. In South Africa, there might well be a temptation to enact group political guarantees for Whites in exchange for an affirmative action program in education and employment for Blacks. Affirmative action may be desirable, [89] but the asymmetrical character of the likely returns in this exchange counsels against making it part of a constitutional bargain. Group political rights may be conferred by a stroke of the pen, but the fruits of affirmative action may take years to appear. Differential rates of return, such as these, tend to undermine constitutional bargains. In Malaysia, precisely such a trade—of Chinese citizenship at once in return for a promise to help the Malays progress economi-

87. Schlemmer, "Requirements for and Possibilities of Successful Constitutional Negotiation in South Africa," p. 29.
88. See Simkins et al., *The Prisoners of Tradition and the Politics of Nation Building*, p. 28. In 1990, both parties announced their intention to become multiracial.
89. Cf. Charles Simkins, *Reconstructing South African Liberalism* (Johannesburg: South African Institute of Race Relations, 1986; mimeo.), pp. 55–57.

cally—tended to undermine the bargain a dozen years later, when Malays expressed discontent at what they had received.[90] The lesson seems to me generalizable.

Another constraint-based approach consists, not of explicit group guarantees, but of ostensibly neutrally framed bills of rights and other legal requirements, often to be enforced by independent judiciaries. These rights and requirements may then provide shelter for groups seeking areas of autonomy or influence as groups.

There is nothing wrong with bills of rights or with judicial review of legislation. There is certainly an increasing tendency to regard both as useful, if not essential, to democracy. The Canadians have adopted a Charter of Rights and its concomitant, judicial review. In Australia and even in Britain, the seat of legislative supremacy, there have been serious discussions about the adoption of a bill of rights. Proposing a bill of rights, the report of the South African Law Commission on group and human rights is, in most ways, a remarkable and forward-looking document.[91] The report endorses principles of universal suffrage and nondiscrimination and recognizes the need for wholesale law reform on these matters.[92]

Although denominated a report on "group and human rights," the report of the commission puts the accent on human rights, rather than group rights. The sole exception is the provision of article 2 of its proposed Bill of Rights, which would permit positive discrimination in order to improve, "on a temporary basis," the position of groups that have been disadvantaged "for historical reasons."[93] It does not require such affirmative action; it merely allows political bodies to resort to it. For the most part, the commission's work is markedly individualistic.

The problems arise, not from bills of rights or from judicial review per se, but from an effort to solve the problems of severely divided societies through the entrenchment of guarantees for particular groups and the commitment of enforcement to the independent judiciary. This, it seems to me, puts too heavy a weight on constitutional law, evolved

90. See Donald L. Horowitz, "Cause and Consequence in Public Policy Theory: Ethnic Policy and System Transformation in Malaysia," *Policy Sciences* 22, nos. 3–4 (November 1989): 249–87.

91. South African Law Commission, "Report on Group and Human Rights" (1989; mimeo.). For some cogent reservations about its security aspects, see A. S. Mathews, "Law Commission Report on Group and Human Rights: Analysis of Security Law Aspects" (April 17, 1989; unpublished paper).

92. See especially South African Law Commission, "Report on Group and Human Rights," pp. 471–91.

93. Ibid., p. 471.

through the courts, rather than on constitutional practice, evolved through elected politicians; and it confers an unsustainable task upon a precariously placed judiciary.

The recent history of independent judiciaries in severely divided societies is, with some exceptions, not an especially happy one. The discord of the larger society may creep into their deliberations and undermine their independence. Even if it does not, self-interested politicians may find ways to achieve the same result, by reducing the jurisdiction of the courts or refusing to obey judicial decrees.[94] When the overthrown prime minister Zulfikar Ali Bhutto, a Sindhi, was sentenced to death in Pakistan, his appeal was heard by the Supreme Court, which divided along ethnic lines. Sindhi judges voted in Bhutto's favor; Punjabi judges voted against him.[95] When Turks walked out of the Cyprus parliament, Greek legislators passed a statute creating a Greek-dominated Supreme Court, contrary to the Cyprus Constitution. The Greek majority of the new court upheld the law on grounds of "necessity."[96] When some Chinese in Malaysia went to court to force governmental permission to open a Chinese-language university, Malay judges were not sympathetic to their constitutional claim, whereas a Chinese judge was.[97] And, finally, there is a well-known example in South Africa itself. In the mid-1950s, Cape Coloured voters were stricken from the electoral roll, in spite of an entrenched provision of the Constitution, by increasing the size of the Appellate Division that would hear a challenge to the law and by increasing the size of the Senate to insure the requisite two-thirds majority.[98]

It is doubtful that a rights and requirements approach to divided

---

94. For one of many steps in the political emasculation of the Malaysian judiciary, the withdrawal of internal security cases from judicial review, see *Far Eastern Economic Review* (Hong Kong), July 6, 1989, p. 19. For the common tendency of Tanzanian party and government functionaries to refuse to respect court orders, see Chris Maina Peter, *Human Rights in Africa: A Comparative Study of the African Human and People's Rights Charter and the New Tanzanian Bill of Rights* (New York: Greenwood Press, 1990), p. 92.

95. *Bhutto v. The State,* [1979] I P.S.C.R. 1.

96. *Attorney General v. Ibrahim,* 1964 Cyprus Law Reports 195. For comment on this and similar cases, see Mark M. Stavsky, "The Doctrine of State Necessity in Pakistan," *Cornell International Law Journal* 16, no. 2 (Summer 1983): 341–94. The Cyprus issue appears on pp. 355–58.

97. *Merdeka University Berhad v. Government of Malaysia,* [1982] 2 M.L.J. 243 (Fed. Ct.).

98. The story is told in full by Gwendolen M. Carter, *The Politics of Inequality: South Africa since 1948,* 2d ed. (New York: Praeger, 1959), pp. 118–44. On the general problem discussed here, see Otto Kircheimer, *Political Justice* (Princeton: Princeton University Press, 1961).

societies can survive the fragile state of judiciaries in those societies. All it is likely to do, when politicians are opposed to the claims, is to put undue pressure on a nascent institution that might otherwise evolve traditions of genuine and useful independence.

Given a choice between betting on the solid political insulation and ethnic neutrality of judiciaries in most divided societies or betting on the self-interest of politicians, prudent gamblers would put their resources on the latter. Give politicians a reason to be moderate, and they will find a way. But give them the Cyprus Constitution of 1960, with its heavy burdens and absolutely no political incentives for the majority to accept its minority protections, and the politicians will do just what Archbishop Makarios did—overthrow it.

PLANS, PERFECT AND IMPERFECT

The Cyprus experience to which I have referred supports an insight of Pierre du Toit about divided societies. Based on experimental evidence with respect to bargaining, du Toit suggests that the more an outcome of bargaining between parties departs from the principle of equality between those parties, the harder it is for the more powerful party to justify such an outcome and for the less powerful party to accept such an outcome in the long term.[99] This point is related to the earlier one that, for consociational plans to survive, roughly equal-sized segments are preferable to lopsided proportions. If du Toit is right, that does not mean that unequal outcomes will not emerge from bargaining processes, but it does imply that such provisions will not be durable. The Cyprus experience is consistent with both the adoption and the durability point.

It is not necessary to be a purist in these matters. For two reasons, severely divided societies can survive some measure of explicit Cyprus-type protection.

The first is that, without such protection, some agreements, some moves forward, will simply be precluded. If we take an absolute stand on this, we may not maximize interethnic accommodation as a value, because we may raise the threshold too high for some agreements and consign some groups in some states to a conflict-prone status quo. South Africa may be among those states.

99. Pierre du Toit, "Consociational Democracy and Bargaining Power," *Comparative Politics* 19, no. 4 (July 1987): 419–30.

The second, related reason is that, although the best-designed structures, filled with incentives to accommodation, may produce the best results, mixed structures may still produce mixed results. That is to say, if a given structure consists of components, some of which reduce conflict and some of which exacerbate it, there may still be a net reduction of conflict—not as great a reduction as might have been obtained had the parties to the conflict chosen a better design, but a reduction nonetheless. As I shall note later, the Nigerian Second Republic had some new, incentive-based features that reduced conflict, and it had some features that perpetuated conflict; the latter were copies of the conflict-fostering institutions of the First Republic. Still, the Second Republic did rather well overall. In terms of ethnic relations, it had mixed results, which were far better, in the aggregate, than were obtained in the First Republic.

The point, then, is not to be pure or entirely right about institutional design in the end. The point is to attempt to think clearly about the matter at the beginning, to urge apt institutions on the designers, and indeed to urge maximum incentives for accommodation in every body and at every level, but not to persuade the designers to reject anything other than the perfect plan. The perfect plan will not come along.

Far from it. Negotiating their way through a maze of conflict into an uncertain future, leaders of the respective groups have every reason to devise plans that do not point in a mixed direction but point in the wrong direction. So the real problem becomes, not one of accepting a less-than-perfect plan, but of being vulnerable to a plan that succumbs to all the pitfalls without possessing accommodative components. Major benefits accrue to polities that start out with accommodative institutions, rather than trying to build them later.

FOUR REASONS FOR PESSIMISM

Consider how many forces conspire against decisions at critical junctures that will operate to reduce intergroup tensions. The forces are at work in most divided societies, and they are at work in South Africa.

First, and very likely, it is already late. Bad things have happened, and good opportunities have been missed. That is assuredly the case in South Africa.

Second, decisions are likely to be taken in a crisis atmosphere, and too little attention will be paid to the distinctions I have been making—between incentives and constraints, as well as between contracts and social contracts and between reaching any agreement and reaching a genuinely accommodative agreement. Certainly, in South Africa, these distinctions have not been a prominent part of political debate.

Third, since an agreement will be necessary, a deal may be sought, and it will be easy and natural for the parties to slide into the contractual form, with its many disadvantages. Again, in South Africa, the talk has fairly consistently referred to an undifferentiated "negotiated settlement."

Fourth, because the situation at the moment of settlement is likely to be grave, or at least serious, groups will fear to rely on internal incentives, although they are more effective. They will probably demand hard-and-fast guarantees—external constraints—that are far more frail and easy to undo. For years, the atmosphere has been rife with discussions of group rights in a future South Africa.

Because much is known about how to do better, crises in divided societies do not have to come out wrong. Thus far, most of them have. The question is whether South Africa will be in the one category or the other.

CHAPTER FIVE

Electoral Systems for a Divided Society

The electoral system is by far the most powerful lever of constitutional engineering for accommodation and harmony in severely divided societies, as indeed it is a powerful tool for many other purposes.[1] Unfortunately, one would hardly sense the potential of electoral innovation for conflict or accommodation from reading the standard literature on electoral systems. Most of that literature is concerned with the impact of various electoral systems on the number of political parties, the proportionality of seats to votes, the strength or weakness of party organizations, and the relationship (or its absence) between legislators and their constituents. Ethnic and racial relations are a decidedly secondary theme.[2]

Only when severely divided societies actually come up against the

1. See Giovanni Sartori, "Political Development and Political Engineering," *Public Policy* 17 (1968): 261–98.
2. For a sampling of the literature, see Arend Lijphart and Bernard Grofman, eds., *Choosing an Electoral System* (New York: Praeger, 1984); Vernon Bogdanor, ed., *Representatives of the People?* (London: Gower, 1985); Maurice Duverger, *Political Parties: Their Organization and Activity in the Modern State* (London: Methuen, 1965); David Butler, "Electoral Systems," in David Butler et al., eds., *Democracy at the Polls: A Comparative Study of Competitive National Elections* (Washington, D.C.: American Enterprise Institute, 1981), pp. 7–25; Rein Taagepera and Mathew S. Shugart, "Designing Electoral Systems," *Electoral Studies* 8, no. 1 (April 1989): 45–58. For a South African example of how the ethnic and racial implications of various electoral systems are hardly noticed, see W. H. Olivier, "Party Systems and Electoral Systems," in D. J. van Vuuren and D. J. Kriek, eds., *Political Alternatives for Southern Africa* (Durban: Butterworths, 1983), pp. 334–55.

need to innovate, the need to choose an electoral system, do they survey the alternatives. Because the literature does not respond directly to their concerns or even help them to think about the question,[3] they tend to have arbitrary or half-formed preferences. In South Africa, for example, many people continue to think the Anglo-American plurality system is the most democratic. Some others think that some form of proportional representation might be more appropriate for a divided society and sometimes rather casually recommend a version of PR for a future South Africa.[4] They rightly fear the frequent tendency of plurality systems to underrepresent minorities and to produce legislative majorities from mere pluralities—or even less than pluralities—of voters.[5] This is a phenomenon with which South Africans have had repeated experience. In 1948 and 1953, the National Party gained a majority of seats on less than half the vote. In 1948, the defeated United Party actually received more than half the vote; and in 1953, the National Party won 60 percent of the seats on under 50 percent of the vote, while the United Party won only 37 percent of the seats on nearly the same vote.[6] In 1989, suffering erosion on both liberal and conservative flanks, the Nationalists again benefited from a seat bonus attributable to the plurality system, winning a 56 percent majority of seats on only 48 percent of the vote.

"The surest way to kill the idea of democracy in a plural society," wrote Sir Arthur Lewis a quarter-century ago, "is to adopt the Anglo-American electoral system of first-past-the-post."[7] Lewis's sage discus-

3. For one of the very few notable exceptions, see J. A. Laponce, "The Protection of Minorities by the Electoral System," *Western Political Quarterly* 10, no. 2 (June 1957): 318–39. Cf. S. M. Lipset, "Party Systems and the Representation of Groups," *European Journal of Sociology* 1, no. 1 (1960): 50–85.

4. Often, the single transferable vote (discussed below) is recommended. See, e.g., Charles Simkins, *Reconstructing South African Liberalism* (Johannesburg: South African Institute of Race Relations, 1986; mimeo.), p. 79; Donald B. Molteno et al., *Final Report of the Commission Set Up by the Progressive Party to Make Recommendations on a Revised Constitution for South Africa,* vol. 1 (N.p. 1960), p. 16.

5. See M. Wiechers, "The Franchise and Alternative Electoral Systems," in L. J. Boulle and L. G. Baxter, eds., *Natal and KwaZulu: Constitutional and Political Options* (Cape Town: Juta, 1981), p. 186. See also L. Schlemmer, "An Overview," in ibid., p. 209.

6. For a table of seats and votes, see Gwendolen M. Carter, *The Politics of Inequality: South Africa since 1948,* 2d ed. (New York: Praeger, 1959), pp. 448–49. Compare the figures in Richard Hodder-Williams, "South Africa: Democratic-Centralism versus Elite-based Parties," in Alan Ware, ed., *Political Parties: Electoral Change and Structural Response* (Oxford: Blackwell, 1987), p. 25.

7. W. Arthur Lewis, *Politics in West Africa* (London: Oxford University Press, 1965), p. 71. The full discussion of electoral systems appears in ibid., pp. 69–74. Its main omission is the tradeoff between influence and representation—values assumed to be compatible. Ibid., p. 73. I shall discuss this tradeoff shortly.

sion of elections and group identity has largely been forgotten. Today, debate rarely proceeds beyond the relative fairness of PR versus plurality elections and the overall suitability of the two systems for divided societies.[8] Yet it is necessary to go much further than where the literature and most constitution makers in divided societies leave off, in order to assess the appropriateness of alternative electoral systems. The test of a good electoral system is not to be found merely in the ratio of seats to votes or in the number of parties that emerge. The test lies instead in the posture adopted by the parties with respect to other parties and with respect to voters. Concretely, does the electoral system dispose the parties to ethnic and racial inclusion or exclusion? Will one system, rather than another, encourage parties to seek intergroup compromise and accommodation? The answers to such questions are a complicated matter, because they cannot be given a priori; competing electoral systems require evaluation in context. But this much is clear. The choices are far more extensive than those implied by the simple dichotomy of proportional or plurality systems.

Not only are the choices more extensive; they are also clear-cut. There are two different goals for promoting the inclusion of any ethnic or racial group in a divided polity. One is ethnic representation, in the tangible but narrow sense of legislative office holding. The other goal also relates to representation, but in the broader sense of incorporating the concerns and interests of a given ethnic or racial group in the calculations of politicians belonging to a variety of groups. Measures that will guarantee seats to a minority group may not foster the inclusion of that group's interests more broadly in the political process—indeed, may have the opposite effect. And vice versa: measures that encourage the accommodation of group claims do not necessarily result in proportionate office holding for all groups. Those who aim at ethnic office holding tend to prefer electoral systems that make it easy for minorities to obtain their own seats.[9] If, however, the aim is moderation on divisive issues and the amelioration of intergroup conflicts, a quite different electoral system might be preferred. Lack of clarity about the tradeoff

8. See, e.g., F. van Zyl Slabbert and David Welsh, *South Africa's Options: Strategies for Sharing Power* (New York: St. Martin's Press, 1979), pp. 152–53; Political Commission of the Study Project on Christianity in Apartheid Society, *South Africa's Political Alternatives*, SPRO-CAS Publication no. 10 (Johannesburg: Ravan Press, 1973), p. 206.

9. See, e.g., Arend Lijphart, "The Power-sharing Approach," in Joseph V. Montville, ed., *Conflict and Peacemaking in Multiethnic Societies* (Lexington, Mass.: Lexington Books, 1990), p. 508; Simkins, *Reconstructing South African Liberalism*, p. 79.

between influence and office holding is responsible for much of the confusion in thinking about electoral systems for South Africa and other
divided societies.

SYSTEMS AND PARTIES: A GLOSSARY

Since I intend to discuss the impact of electoral systems on party systems and on intergroup conflict and accommodation, perhaps it is best
to insure that the terminology is clear from the outset. So I begin with
a brief narrative glossary.

First of all, there are several electoral systems. As indicated earlier,
first-past-the-post refers to plurality elections. Whichever candidate receives the largest number of votes is elected, even if that number of
votes is less than a majority. First-past-the-post or plurality systems are
generally used in single-member constituencies, those that consist of
one representative per area. *Proportional representation* refers to a variety of electoral systems designed to insure that parties receive approximately the same percentage of the total number of seats as the percentage they received of the total number of votes.

Two of the three systems to be discussed—the *single transferable
vote* (STV) and the *alternative vote* (AV)—I shall describe at the time I
introduce them into the discussion. The alternative vote is perhaps better described as a *majority system* than as a PR system, since it declares
elected only those candidates who receive a majority, rather than a plurality, of votes. But, like PR systems, AV mitigates the winner-take-all
aspects of plurality systems and generally achieves better proportionality of seats to votes than plurality systems do.[10] AV can also be described as a *preferential system,* since it enables or requires voters to list
their choice of candidates in order of preference. The third PR system—
list-system proportional representation—which we shall encounter very
soon, permits each party to put up a list of candidates. Each voter then
votes for one or another party list. Each list is numbered in order of the
party's preference for its own candidates. Candidates at the top of a list
are elected first. So a party with, say, 20 percent of the vote secures
election of the top 20 percent of its list.[11] List-system PR can operate

10. See, e.g., the rerun of the 1987 British general election under a hypothetical AV
system in John L. Old, "The Alternative Vote and the 1987 General Election," *Politics* 8,
no. 1 (April 1988): 8–13.
11. There are some variants of list-system PR that permit voters to alter the party's
rank order of candidates. One of these variations will be discussed later in this chapter.
A variation that permits voters to choose across party lists I mention in note 27, below.

either using territorially demarcated constituencies, each with its own competing lists of candidates to represent that constituency, or using a whole country as a single constituency, each party putting up just one national list. The former I shall refer to as constituency-list-system PR; the latter, as national-list-system PR.

I shall also refer to several types of party formation. *Ethnically based parties* are parties that draw their support from a single ethnic or racial group. Any ethnic or racial group, however, may give its support to one or more than one such party. *Multiethnic coalitions* are temporary or permanent alliances formed by two or more than two ethnically based parties. *Flank parties* are ethnically based parties surrounding a multiethnic coalition and typically espousing ethnically more extreme positions than the coalition, with its mixed support, is able to do.

Finally, there are a few unfamiliar terms that I shall use regarding electoral demography, numbers of parties, coalitions, and the appeals of parties to voters. Constituencies may be either *homogeneous* or *heterogeneous*, depending on whether they are composed of significant numbers of two or more ethnic or racial groups in conflict. *Party proliferation* is the growth of parties to form a *multiparty system*, usually making coalition governments necessary, as opposed to a two-party system, in which one party is able to form a government by itself, leaving the other in opposition. Coalitions are made possible as parties *pool seats* to achieve a legislative majority. *Vote pooling*, on the other hand, refers to an exchange of votes of their respective supporters by two parties. The vote pooling to which I refer takes place across ethnic or racial lines and is generally the result of agreements between parties for the exchange of electoral support. I shall say much more about vote pooling as we proceed, because—unlike the mere pooling of seats—it lies at the heart of intergroup compromise in severely divided societies.

ELECTORAL SYSTEMS: BEYOND PROPORTIONALITY

The most careful work on the South African electoral future has been done by a non–South African, Arend Lijphart.[12] Lijphart has advanced a full-blown consociational plan for South Africa, which I have commented on in Chapter 4. Here I want to focus on the electoral system he recommends, because it is assuredly the best-thought-through elec-

---

12. Arend Lijphart, *Power-Sharing in South Africa* (Berkeley: University of California Institute of International Studies, 1985).

toral scheme for South Africa and because his plan has had considerable attraction for South Africans in quest of answers to their problems. Above all, it is addressed to the problems that will likely haunt the South African future; the plan does not wish those problems away. As I shall show, however, the comparative evidence is heavily against it.

Lijphart argues for proportional representation as an integral part of a consociational constitution, according the segments of a divided society a proportional say in the running of that society. In *Power-Sharing in South Africa,* the principal justification he provides for proportional representation on specifically electoral grounds is that it is fairer than first-past-the-post.[13] Whereas plurality systems typically exaggerate the number of seats won by the largest contenders, artificially diminishing minority representation, PR can be designed so that the number of seats reflects faithfully the number of votes each party has obtained. This is true as far as it goes, but it seems a curious rationale, if that is all there is to it, for Lijphart's plan is also to give minorities—even "relatively small groups"—an "absolute veto on the fundamental issues, such as cultural autonomy, and a suspensive veto on non-fundamental questions."[14] Moreover, he wants chairs of the executive to rotate, that is, a rotating prime ministership.[15] In the face of these arrangements, small disparities in representation would seem less important than they might otherwise be.

But Lijphart has a further reason for advocating PR: it allows the constituent elements of a plural society to form into political parties. "The beauty of PR is not just that it yields proportional results and permits minority representation—two important advantages from a consociational perspective—but also that it *permits the segments to define themselves.*"[16] This is an important argument in South Africa, where the government has decided what the categories of group membership are and who belongs to each, but it should not obscure the fact that first-past-the-post and most other electoral systems also permit self-identification and self-organization. PR is not superior on these grounds.

In a later paper, Lijphart expands upon his justification for PR and argues for a specific variant: party-list-system PR, which he juxtaposes to the single transferable vote version of PR.[17] There he prefers PR be-

13. Ibid., p. 8.
14. Ibid., p. 81.
15. Ibid., p. 80.
16. Ibid., pp. 68–69 (emphasis in the original).
17. Arend Lijphart, "Choosing an Electoral System for Democratic Elections in South

cause of its tendency to encourage many parties, so that each group can have its own party if it wishes. List-system PR is better than the single transferable vote, because it generally provides closer proportionality of seats to votes and obviates the need for unduly large constituencies to avoid ethnic gerrymandering. All of this is generally true,[18] but what does it mean for a severely divided society like South Africa?

On this point, Lijphart is clear. He assumes that, with a receptive electoral system, there will be a plurality of parties in South Africa and that they will need to form a coalition in order to govern,[19] hopefully, in his view, a "grand" coalition representing all the groups.[20] This is made clear in his book on South Africa. Commenting on Zimbabwe, he says: ". . . when one ethnic group comprises a majority of the population, PR can obviously not prevent this majority from gaining a majority of seats."[21] So the assumption is that Black voters in South Africa will not be cohesive enough to form a Zimbabwe-like majority and a coalition will be necessary, once each party has gathered the support of its own group at the polls.

Even under PR, I am not certain that this would be the outcome in South Africa after the first universal suffrage elections. Given the history of White domination and the likely magnitude of the immediate post-election White threat, it is possible that Blacks, even if somewhat divided, might nonetheless line up behind a party sufficiently to give that party more than half the seats so it could form a government alone. This is what Robert Mugabe and the Shona managed in Zimbabwe, despite opposition from the disproportionately represented Whites and from Joshua Nkomo and the Ndebele. For reasons I shall explain in Chapter 7, a plurality rather than a majority of votes seems likely to me as well, but this is not a foregone conclusion.

More to the present point, there is already in existence an example of list-system PR imposed to induce fragmentation of a majority into its

---

Africa: An Evaluation of the Principal Options," Institute for the Study of Public Policy, University of Cape Town, Critical Choices for South Africa series (September 1987). As indicated above, I shall say more about these varieties of PR later in this chapter.

18. But see Michael Gallagher, "The Political Consequences of the Electoral System in the Republic of Ireland," *Electoral Studies* 5, no. 3 (December 1986): 253–75, at 258.

19. "Here we have another reason to prefer proportional representation to plurality for segmented societies: proportional representation encourages multi-partyism which in turn encourages coalition government." Lijphart, "Choosing an Electoral System for Democratic Elections in South Africa," p. 5.

20. See Arend Lijphart, *Democracy in Plural Societies* (New Haven: Yale University Press, 1977), pp. 25–31.

21. Lijphart, *Power-Sharing in South Africa*, p. 20n.

component groups so as to break its electoral hold and facilitate coalitions. The example comes from the Guyana elections of 1964, shortly before independence. The British imposed list-system PR in the hope, among others, that the majority East Indians would divide into Hindus and Muslims. British expectations were utterly disappointed. Confronted with a strong challenge from other groups, Hindus and Muslims stayed together in the party with which they had previously aligned, and the parties induced to proliferate because of PR all made such a poor showing that together they obtained 1 percent of the vote and no seats. List-system PR does assure a good measure of proportionality, but it does not guarantee party proliferation or the fragmentation of majority groups.[22]

But let us pass this point and suppose Lijphart is right that list-system PR will produce party proliferation in South Africa so that no party has a majority of seats. What motivates the formation of the coalition? Will it produce the democratic stability postulated by the consociational model? Will the need for the coalition induce the compromise Lijphart envisions as a result of the need to coalesce?

We already have clear, discouraging answers to these questions. Political parties in newly independent countries often had to form coalitions after elections, even though the elections were frequently conducted under first-past-the-post. The reasons lie in ethnic pluralism, which produced several ethnically based parties and a division of seats that left no party with a majority. The elections in Nigeria in 1959, in Uganda in 1962, in Benin (then Dahomey) several times between 1957 and 1965, and in the Indian Punjab in 1967 and 1969 all involved three main parties, and all resulted in the need to form coalitions. I have examined these elections in detail elsewhere.[23] I have called the resulting coalitions "coalitions of convenience," because they were arranged merely to aggregate the number of parliamentary seats to more than 50 percent, in order to form a government—and for no other purpose, such as interethnic compromise. No compromise took place in any of these cases.[24] The coalitions were short-lived, they fell apart over a divisive

22. I have discussed the Guyanese election of 1964 in Donald L. Horowitz, *Ethnic Groups in Conflict* (Berkeley and Los Angeles: University of California Press, 1985), pp. 643–46. For a fuller treatment of electoral engineering in conflict-prone societies, see ibid., pp. 628–51.

23. Ibid., pp. 369–78. See also the discussion of the dissolution of the Guyanese coalition that had been fostered by list-system PR. Ibid., p. 318.

24. These were not coalitions of the moderate middle. Proximity of policy positions

ethnic issue, and they left ethnic conflict worse than it was when they took office. Unless there is an incentive to compromise over ethnic issues, the mere need to form a coalition will not produce compromise. The incentive to compromise, and not merely the incentive to coalesce, is the key to accommodation.

As a matter of fact, the need to pool seats will not alone produce interethnic compromise in a severely divided society, even under conditions much more favorable to compromise. Northern Ireland has been down this road and shown where it leads. The election to which I refer took place in March 1973, after the British parliament provided for a return of self-government to Northern Ireland. It is worth recounting in some detail.[25]

It is well known that Northern Ireland contains a Protestant majority fearful of the Catholic minority. Both of these groups were represented by more than one party, so that the party proliferation envisioned by Lijphart for South Africa was already present in Northern Ireland by 1973. More than that, Northern Ireland had something there is no guarantee South Africa will have—a small but significant party of the middle, drawing votes from both major groups, polling just under 10 percent of the total vote, and expressing an aspiration for accommodation. This party was called the Alliance.

The 1973 elections were scheduled by the British parliament at a time when Britain was actively seeking compromise and even making mutual concessions on Northern Ireland with the Irish Republic. More important, the British specified that no post-election government would be permitted to take office unless it were committed to "power sharing," defined, not merely as an aspiration to interethnic accommodation, but in terms of the actual participation in government of Catholic-based parties as well as Protestant-based parties. To complete the list of favorable conditions, the election was held under the single transferable vote system of proportional representation. Like other PR systems, this

---

had, if anything, a negative role in their formation. Parties that had some ethnic policy positions in common and that had competed with each other for some part of the same voting clientele tended not to be part of these coalitions. After all, it would be difficult to justify to party activists the need to form a coalition today with yesterday's electoral competitors. The result is that lack of electoral overlap was more likely to induce formation of a coalition. As a consequence, coalition partners had opposite views on the most serious ethnic issues that divided the society. Accordingly, there was no prospect for compromise but plenty of opportunity for issues to split the coalitions apart.

25. The account here is based on Richard Rose, *Northern Ireland: Time of Choice* (Washington, D.C.: American Enterprise Institute, 1976).

was thought conducive to party proliferation, so that coalition government would be necessary.[26]

The STV system, however, has one other advantage, not possessed
by list-system PR. Voters cast their ballots for candidates, not parties,
in order of preference. In a multimember constituency with four seats
but ten candidates, a voter might cast up to ten preference votes. This
at least opens up the possibility that some of a given voter's votes might
be cast for candidates across the ethnic divide. By contrast, list-system
PR requires that votes be cast for a single party list. Where parties are
ethnically based, there is no way to transfer votes across ethnic lines. A
voter is locked wholly within his ethnic party.[27]

Under the Northern Ireland system, a quota of votes is computed by
dividing the number of seats plus one into the total number of votes
cast and adding one to the quotient. Any candidate who attains more
than this quota is deemed elected. It should be noted that the quota for
election may be far below a majority of votes cast, depending on how
many seats are at stake. If there are four seats in a constituency, a candidate could win with about a fourth of the vote. That is why STV is so
different from a winner-take-all system and so conducive to proportionality. Once a candidate receives a quota and is elected, his "surplus
vote"—that is, his vote above the quota—is "transferred in proportion
to its size to the candidates who stand next in preference among his
supporters. Once this is done, the candidate with the lowest total of
votes is eliminated, and his votes are transferred to those ranking next
in the preference of his supporters." [28] Second and third preferences are
therefore likely to count. Protestant voters may allocate them to Protestant candidates or to Catholic candidates, as they see fit, and vice
versa.

In this respect, STV permits a measure of interethnic vote pooling

---

26. Ibid., pp. 77–78.
27. This statement is not always literally true, but it is true as a practical matter.
Under the Swiss version of list-system PR, a voter may make choices across party lists. In
a severely divided society, however, where parties are ethnically based, this option is
entirely hypothetical. The lists of different parties compete in every way, so that a vote
for Party A is a vote against Party B. Voters of ethnic group B will not cast such ballots,
and the two parties will not be able to reach an agreement for such vote transfers. As I
shall explain below, the situation is different where voting is preferential (that is, under
STV or AV), for then voters are casting ballots for second and subsequent choices, to be
counted only if their first choice is eliminated (or, under STV, if their first choice does not
need their vote to make his quota). It is entirely possible for parties of different groups to
agree to exchange such lower-order preferential ballots, and voters can be induced to cast
them.
28. Rose, *Northern Ireland: Time of Choice*, pp. 76–77.

that list-system PR completely precludes. Voters of one group could provide the margin of victory for a candidate of another group, who might then be responsive to their concerns. If vote pooling of this kind occurred as a result of agreements between parties, the basis would be laid for interethnic policy compromise.

Under STV, moderate Catholic parties or candidates might have made interethnic vote-pooling agreements for the second and third preferences of supporters of moderate Protestant parties or candidates; and, of course, such agreements would be reciprocal. Presumably, such agreements could only be consummated between interethnic moderates, and therefore such agreements should also foster moderation. If the choice for a divided society is between list-system PR and the single transferable vote, STV is a far better choice than list-system PR.

Notwithstanding these conditions—which were certainly more favorable to accommodation than those envisioned by Lijphart for South Africa's first universal suffrage election—the results were a defeat for accommodation. In the first place, a new Protestant party sprung up to oppose power sharing; it and other Protestant parties that were opposed to an interethnic coalition together secured 35 percent of the vote, compared to 27 percent for the Protestant party committed to power sharing.[29] When the power-sharing cabinet was inaugurated, even the Protestant party committed to power sharing, fearful of erosion of its support, rejected the arrangement, dooming it to a short life.

A United Kingdom election, coincidentally held the next month, confirmed the erosion. In Northern Irish constituencies for the British parliament, Protestant parties opposed to power sharing gained an outright majority of votes and seats. A survey of Protestant opinion showed only 28 percent strongly in favor of power sharing. Under Protestant protest, the Northern Ireland government fell.[30] The accommodating Protestant party was vulnerable to accusations of sellout by the other Protestant parties on its flank.[31] By 1975, the accommodating party was down to 7.7 percent of the vote.[32]

Significant vote pooling across ethnic lines did not take place, either in 1973 or in subsequent PR elections.[33] The reason, explained by Richard Rose, is straightforward: "The electoral system offered parties no

29. Ibid., pp. 29–30.
30. Ibid., pp. 30–31.
31. Ibid., p. 82.
32. Ibid., p. 97.
33. Ibid., pp. 78, 93.

incentive to seek votes across the religious divide, because the chances of winning an extra seat by adding a few votes from the other community were much less than the chances of losing votes by appearing 'soft' on the issues that were of central concern within the party's home community."[34] No vote-pooling agreements were made in advance by the parties because of the same fear of a negative net result.[35] Without such agreements, the parties were never forced to confront and compromise their differences. Even with the possibility of vote pooling and a certain amount of good will at the top, plus the participation of the small Alliance party, committed to accommodation, the coalition ended up as a coalition of convenience, just like the Nigerian, Ugandan, Beninese, and Punjabi coalitions described above.

None of this is an indictment of vote-pooling incentives as a strategy of fostering accommodation. On the contrary, that is the way to do it. The Northern Ireland incentives, however, were insufficient because they permitted parties to take a share of seats and even enter government, whether or not they had pooled votes. Since a fraction of the total vote was enough to reach a candidate's quota, the incentives were weak. As we shall see, there are stronger incentives to vote pooling that are possible and that promise better results.

The Northern Ireland elections are a refutation of the notion that PR can simply deliver coalitions and compromise in severely divided societies. If there are examples of this phenomenon from severely divided societies, they have yet to emerge. As the African and Asian examples show, coalition alone (based on pooling seats alone) is no assurance of compromise. As the Northern Ireland case shows, even weak vote-pooling incentives in a favorable milieu may not be enough to induce accommodation.

Lijphart, who is very clearheaded about these matters, does not say that coalition formation alone is enough. He wants coalitions in tandem with other consociational arrangements.[36] In 1986, the KwaZulu Natal Indaba, a standing conference of citizens of the two territories, took his advice and proposed a consociational scheme to govern the two regions if they should merge into a single administration.[37] The proposals em-

34. Ibid., p. 78.
35. Ibid., p. 93.
36. "Choosing an Electoral System for Democratic Elections in South Africa," pp. 3–4.
37. KwaZulu Natal Indaba, *Constitutional Proposals Agreed To on 28 November 1986* (Durban: n.p., n.d.; pamphlet).

body mutual vetoes, mandatory group representation in the cabinet, consensus decision making in the executive, cultural councils, and a bicameral legislature. The upper chamber is to be elected largely on the basis of racially reserved seats, with overrepresentation of the minorities. Both chambers are to be elected by list-system PR, the lower chamber by constituency lists and the upper chamber by treating the entire merged province as a single constituency.

This is, of course, a bold attempt to meet the problems of ethnic diversity and to foster conciliation. It is almost unkind to criticize such a plan. Nevertheless, many components of the proposals boil down to guarantees of group rights and would be vulnerable to the objections I have already stated with regard to such schemes. The electoral system would do nothing to foster vote pooling and accommodative coalitions; it would certainly not provide electoral disincentives for the strongest party or parties to dismantle the minority protections. Even if one were to favor a group rights approach, it would be necessary to design an electoral system that gives politicians electoral reasons to be supportive of their entrenchment.

Nothing I have said, of course, vitiates the importance of coalitions. Coalitions *should* be the centerpiece of accommodative arrangements. But not any coalition will do, only a coalition likely to produce compromise rather than perpetuate conflict. Absent incentives, politicians will not engage in intergroup compromise in a severely divided society. List-system PR may or may not produce enough party proliferation to require a coalition in South African conditions. Even if it does, list-system PR contains no incentives to vote pooling or compromise and will produce only coalitions of convenience that will dissolve. If politicians can, by inducing aisle-crossings or other methods, elbow coalition partners out of the coalition and govern alone, sharing the spoils with no other parties and having no longer to justify the coalition with ethnic opponents to their own supporters, politicians will prefer to govern alone.

Pooling seats, then, is not enough to provide the appropriate incentives. If, however, popular votes are actually pooled, compromise may follow, as I suggested in Chapter 4 with respect to Malaysia. Unfortunately, so far as I know, no one working on or in South Africa has emphasized the distinction between mere seat pooling and vote pooling. Vote pooling, which is the engine of compromise, has been left out of account altogether. Lijphart, for example, is opposed to presidential systems of government, because, he says, the president, being one person, "is bound to represent one particular segment to the exclusion of other segments."[38] Never does he pause to ask how a president is to be elected. Never does he note that the president of the Nigerian Second Republic, although a rather parochial Northern politician, was elected under a formula that provided him with an incentive he could not resist (if he wished to win election) to accommodate members of groups other than his own. As a candidate, he responded to the incentive to pool votes; later, as an officeholder, he responded to the desire to be reelected on pooled votes.

The emphasis here is not on statesmanship alone, but on incentives. In that respect, there is a fundamental difference of approach from consociationalism. Politicians, consociational theorists suggest, are motivated by notions of the common good. "If these leaders were exclusively or mainly motivated by a desire to survive politically, it would be much more to their advantage to fan the flames of intersegmental antagonism than to engage in the risky enterprise of striking compromises with rival segmental leaders."[39] Exactly so. Consociationalism and its electoral component come down to statesmanship, not electoral incentives. If the experience of severely divided societies shows anything at all, it is that statesmanship alone, statesmanship without tangible reasons, statesmanship without rewards, will not reduce conflict. Without incentives, statesmanship will be in short supply.

In such societies, it has been argued,[40] there is a need to choose between majoritarian democracy and consociational democracy. I do not believe this to be an accurate statement of the choices. The need is merely to choose between two kinds of majoritarian democracy: a majoritarian democracy that will produce racially or ethnically defined majorities and minorities or a majoritarian democracy that will produce more fluid, shifting majorities that do not lock ascriptive minorities firmly out of power. That is why Lijphart is right to oppose first-past-the-post in single-member constituencies. The winner-take-all assumptions of such electoral systems generally (though not always) degenerate into ascriptive majority rule. But PR alone—PR without vote pooling across group lines—will not prevent that result.

38. *Power-Sharing in South Africa*, p. 60. See also ibid., p. 80; Lijphart, *Democracy in Plural Societies*, pp. 178, 187, 210.

39. Lijphart, *Power-Sharing in South Africa*, p. 107.

40. Ibid., p. 109.

VOTE POOLING: STATESMANSHIP WITH REWARDS

To promote intergroup accommodation, the need to form a coalition is, then, a necessary but not a sufficient condition. Not all coalitions in severely divided societies are inclined to accommodation. It follows that party proliferation, which produces the need to form a coalition, is also not enough. The proliferation of parties must be accompanied by the rewards to moderation that accrue when parties are dependent, in part, on vote transfers from members of groups other than the groups they principally represent. Only coalitions that rest on intergroup vote pooling, as well as seat pooling, have reason to be accommodative.

Vote pooling makes statesmanship rewarding. Now, we have already seen that the mere theoretical possibility of transferring votes across ethnic lines is not, by itself, sufficient to induce party agreements for vote transfers or the transfers themselves. And for exactly the reason specified earlier by Rose in the Northern Ireland case: there will not be intergroup vote-pooling agreements if the number of own-group votes likely to be lost by parties contemplating such agreements exceeds the number of votes likely to be gained by transfers across the ethnic divide. The mechanism that underlies this calculation is that, to obtain votes across ethnic or racial lines by agreements with other parties to trade second or third or fourth preferences, reciprocal moderation on ethnic or racial issues is required.[41] In Northern Ireland, that moderation was likely to repel more of each group's own voters than the number of voters it was likely to attract from the other ethnic group.

Some clear conclusions emerge. Since vote pooling can only be accomplished if there is a showing of intergroup moderation by the parties seeking to exchange votes across group lines, the prospect of vote pooling with profit is the key to making parties moderate and producing coalitions with compromise in severely divided societies. Therefore, it becomes essential to reverse the calculations that prevailed in Northern Ireland in 1973—that is, to make intergroup vote pooling a positive-sum transaction for parties that participate in it. The point, in short, is to use the electoral system to induce changes in the behavior of ethnically based or racially based parties.[42]

41. On vote transferability across parties and the role of party distance, see Giovanni Sartori, *Parties and Party Systems* (Cambridge: Cambridge University Press, 1976), p. 343.
42. It is well accepted, if rarely emphasized, that electoral systems can change the behavior and posture of parties. See, e.g., Sartori, "Political Development and Political Engineering ," p. 287.

The negative-sum Northern Ireland calculations can indeed be reversed. There is an example of this, the logic of which I have explicated earlier,[43] in the case of Malaysia. There an interethnic coalition was formed and benefited from pooling votes across ethnic lines in heterogeneous constituencies so as to defeat ethnically based competitors on both flanks. The ethnically based flank parties held issue positions that were ethnically extreme and thus differentiated them from the coalition and its compromises. Those flank competitors therefore could not make any agreements to pool votes across ethnic lines, even if they had wanted to. But, it should be stressed, the moderation of the coalition parties did not predate formation of the coalition—it came into being simultaneously, precisely because it was electorally rewarding at that moment. Nor did their moderation ever produce a grand coalition of the consociational type; it produced instead an ethnically inclusive but majoritarian government, flanked by ethnic parties in opposition.

The Malaysian coalition illustrates something already implicit in my formulation of the problem of incentives for vote transfers. There are two separate components: prospective vote losses resulting from appeals to voters across the ethnic divide and prospective vote gains from such appeals. I call these separate, because they obviously come from different groups of voters, and the net is the sum of the behavior of both. The losses come from voters of one's own group who believe the party's moderation on ethnic issues constitutes a sellout of their group interests. They therefore choose to give their votes to another party representing their group. The gains come from voters of another ethnic group who are attracted by interethnic moderation and who do not have a better choice (or, in the case of preferential voting, do not have a better second or third choice) from among parties representing their own group. So the question then becomes, What choices are available to these groups of voters at the moment vote pooling could occur?

In the Malaysian case, there were no good alternatives on the flanks. The Malaysian coalition was formed at a moment when there was substantially no intraethnic competition on the Malay or on the non-Malay (Chinese and later Indian) side, so the potential losses from vote pooling were minimal on both sides. This is because the party to be defeated in the first elections that induced formation of the interethnic coalition was not an ethnically based party but a multiethnic party led by a prominent and charismatic figure, whose popularity, it was thought, made

43. See Chapter 4, pp. 154–55, above.

his party a dangerous competitor. So the Malaysian coalition was created at a rare, and never repeated, moment of exclusively centripetal—that is, multiethnic—competition. For supporters of the Malay and non-Malay parties that agreed to pool votes, the competitor multiethnic party did not hold much appeal, so the agreement could be made without the prospect of losing one's own supporters.

Thereafter the agreement, which resulted in the coalition's consistently running a single slate—that is, only one candidate (whether Malay, Chinese, or Indian) for each office—was sustained, even in the face of first-past-the-post elections, by some other favorable conditions. The first of these was the prevalence of ethnically heterogeneous constituencies. The second was the emergence of ethnically based flank parties that locked themselves into extreme positions. The electorate in most constituencies was thereafter split several ways, and the coalition, using vote transfers, could win seats on pluralities in three- or four-way contests. Even in a straight contest with one ethnic flank party, the coalition could afford to lose some votes to that flank party, if, depending on the ethnic composition of the constituency, it could compensate for those losses with support from the group whose flank party did not enter a candidate in that constituency. Most of the time, although not always, more net votes were to be had by a coalition candidate espousing interethnic moderation and practicing vote pooling than by a candidate practicing ethnic extremism in behalf of his own group.[44]

It will be noticed immediately that, under admittedly unusual conditions, even first-past-the-post can be made to serve the ends of vote pooling, intergroup coalitions, and accommodation. The mere plurality requirement means that, in a badly split constituency, only a small increment of pooled votes may be required to come out ahead of competitors. But this is not easy to engineer. In a conflict-prone society, voters will generally not cross ethnic lines. The purpose of incentives is to *create* floating voters at some level of preference, in a situation where they would ordinarily be lacking. The main point of the Malaysian illustration is simply to show the obverse of the Northern Ireland calculation, in a society divided at least as severely as Northern Ireland, as

---

44. For some estimates of vote pooling, even in the election of 1969, in which the ethnic flank parties did unusually well, see Karl von Vorys, *Democracy without Consensus: Communalism and Political Stability in Malaysia* (Princeton: Princeton University Press, 1975), pp. 302–03, 305. For the calculations of the coalition partners, see Horowitz, *Ethnic Groups in Conflict*, pp. 396–416, 424–26; Donald L. Horowitz, "Incentives and Behaviour in the Ethnic Politics of Sri Lanka and Malaysia," *Third World Quarterly* 11, no. 4 (October 1989): 18–35, at 24–29.

well as to expose the logic that supports the calculation. At a minimum, that logic requires at least some heterogeneous constituencies and party proliferation.

The example also shows the importance of sequencing. Once the Malaysian coalition and its opponents on the flanks divided up the party spectrum, the coalition's vote-pooling arrangements proved to embody the most profitable vote-maximizing strategy, certainly more profitable than going it alone on an ethnic-party basis. In other words, disintegrative options were quickly closed off. But it was sheer fortuity that vote pooling looked attractive in the specific conditions of the first election. Had the first elections simply been a contest between ethnically based parties, nothing in later elections would have produced vote pooling.[45] Constitutional engineers cannot count on fortuity. They need to build in vote-pooling incentives at the outset.

Before I turn to other ways of maximizing the chance of vote pooling, some further observations are in order. It has been argued that representing whole groups united under single leaderships, rather than fractions of groups, is superior for intergroup accommodation.[46] We can see from Malaysia the initial advantage of monopoly support for reducing the losses and maximizing the gains of vote transfers across group lines. But several caveats need to be entered. First, monopoly position is not always necessary, and in any case monopoly support is not always present at the crucial moment when an intergroup coalition is to be formed. As I said, the Malaysians were lucky. Second, there is a tradeoff between monopoly position, which provides extra latitude to make compromises, and party proliferation, which is necessary to produce the need to form any coalition in the first place. If each group is represented by only one party, there may be a danger that one party may secure a majority of seats by itself, and thus a coalition will not be necessary or at least, before the election, will not appear to be necessary. This fact may inhibit the disposition to make a vote-pooling agreement in advance. Finally, after such an agreement is made in a severely divided society, ethnically based parties will in any event position them-

45. This is the Sri Lankan case. See Horowitz, "Incentives and Behaviour in the Ethnic Politics of Sri Lanka and Malaysia," pp. 21–26.

46. Lijphart, *Democracy in Plural Societies*, pp. 25–31; Robert A. Dahl, *Polyarchy: Participation and Opposition* (New Haven: Yale University Press, 1971), pp. 114–21; cf. Eric A. Nordlinger, *Conflict Regulation in Divided Societies*, Harvard University Center for International Affairs, Occasional Paper no. 29 (Cambridge: Harvard University Center for International Affairs, January 1972), p. 118.

selves on the flanks. Therefore, intraethnic monopoly is not possible to maintain once accommodative agreements are in place.

I want particularly to underscore the first of these points—that monopoly position is not always necessary for vote pooling—by looking a bit more closely at the Northern Ireland case. The reason it is worth examining is that the Northern Ireland experience could plausibly, but I think wrongly, be read as precluding vote pooling in the absence of intraethnic party monopolies. One thing we know is that Catholics and Protestants are each represented by more than one party. What we do not know intuitively—but what turns out to be true—is that there are also significant barriers to vote transfers even between parties of the same ethnic group.

A careful study of Catholic voters aligned with the moderate Social Democratic and Labor Party (SDLP), on the one hand, and the Sinn Fein (aligned with the Irish Republican Army), on the other, shows very limited "willingness of voters of one party either to vote for the other party when their own party is not standing [in a given constituency], or to give lower-preference votes to the other party in PR elections . . . ."[47] Aptly called "Not Many Floating Voters Here," the study makes clear that the two Catholic parties are relying on quite different pools of voters, in terms of age, class, employment status, and education. Only to a small degree are the two "fishing for votes in the same pond."[48] So what looks like an intraethnic choice that might preclude interethnic vote transfers is not necessarily a choice in the eyes of the voters. As they survey the existing party landscape, voters discontented with interparty conciliation across ethnic lines may find they have nowhere better to go. Very few SDLP voters would move to Sinn Fein if the SDLP agreed to pool votes with a moderate Protestant party. Rather, the opposite: in the 1985 local government elections, more SDLP vote transfers appear to have gone to the intersectarian Alliance than to Sinn Fein.[49] Although Protestant voters were more willing than Catholic voters to transfer votes among Protestant parties,[50] nothing we know about

47. Cynthia Irvin and Eddie Moxon-Browne, "Not Many Floating Voters Here," *Fortnight* (Belfast), May 1989, pp. 7–9.

48. Ibid., p. 7.

49. Ibid., p. 9.

50. Nearly three times more willing, in fact. In the 1985 local council elections, 20 percent of all Protestant vote transfers went from the Official Unionists to the Paisleyites, compared to 7 percent of Catholic vote transfers from the SDLP to Sinn Fein. I am indebted to Cynthia Irvin for these data.

Northern Ireland supports the conclusion that the existence of more than one party per ethnic group necessarily dooms interethnic vote pooling. The point is, rather, that, in the face of intraethnic party proliferation and the possibility that some voters will shift to more extreme parties, the incentives to vote pooling need to be strong.

So far, all I have said may be interesting to analysts but is not yet useful to engineers. It comes down to this: (1) The exchange of votes by parties across group lines is essential to the emergence of coalitions that have a tangible interest in moderation and compromise on intergroup issues that can provoke severe conflict. (2) Vote exchange of this sort seems hard to arrange. Under propitious conditions, it did not occur in Northern Ireland, but it did occur in Malaysia. (3) The difference between the two cases is explicable, but the explanation rests on fortuitous, indeed nonrecurring conditions, especially the momentary fluke of entirely centripetal competition in Malaysia. (4) To underscore the idiosyncratic character of the two outcomes, it should be stressed that, because of the different party-competitive configuration in the two cases, the electoral system more likely to induce vote pooling (STV) did not do so in Northern Ireland, whereas the electoral system less likely to induce vote pooling (first-past-the-post) did do so in Malaysia. (5) To induce interethnic vote exchange, three elements are needed: (a) party proliferation, (b) heterogeneous constituencies, and (c) electoral incentives that make vote pooling politically profitable.

One could, of course, read this comparative lesson as simply discouraging for South Africa. Instead, since constitutional engineers, like all engineers, cannot quit when discouraged, constructive use can be made of the discouragement. What it argues for is a stronger dose of incentives for pooling votes than might otherwise have been thought necessary.

There is, in any case, a compelling reason for a strong dose of incentives for interethnic vote pooling, apart from the fact that an ordinary dose did not work in Northern Ireland. The compelling reason is that, whatever arrangements are ultimately agreed upon, electoral and related institutions are likely to yield, as I suggested earlier, a mixed system of incentives to accommodation and to ethnic extremism.

Wherever the system of incentives is mixed, there are always dangers that one set of incentives can outweigh the other. As I hinted with respect to the Nigerian Second Republic, such tensions existed in its arrangements. The president was elected by a system that rewarded him for interethnic accommodation, but the national legislature was elected by a system that built in no such rewards. Legislators were simply representatives of their own ethnic groups and proponents of group claims; they perpetuated conflict, even as the president damped it down.

Where the system is mixed, the incentives to accommodation can also be undone. In Malaysia, for example, periodic constituency delimitation has tended to reduce the number and impact of significantly heterogeneous constituencies. Specifically, Malay candidates of the coalition have become less dependent than they formerly were on Chinese votes for their margin of victory, although Chinese coalition candidates are still frequently dependent on Malay votes. The inequality of the exchange is a source of pro-Malay bias in policy outcomes.

It cannot be assumed, therefore, that a mixed system of incentives will always be sufficient to avert severe conflict or that it will remain in its original equilibrium in the face of pulls to change it. So there are, in the end, several reasons for strong incentives: to be sure they are adequate to induce vote pooling; to be sure the extent of vote pooling is sufficient to repel conflict-prone claims that will emerge; and to shield the vote-pooling incentives themselves from erosion.

If a strong dose can be adopted, however, it has an enormous advantage for South Africa. It will be recalled that South Africans of all racial groups agree on the need to avoid the domination of any group by another, but they do not tend to agree once various means to these ends are proposed. The attraction of working on ameliorating conflict through a system of incentives lies in their self-renewing character. If the incentives are strongly built in, the politicians will generally behave in accordance with the rewards structured by those incentives.[51] To put the point more sharply, in a divided society like South Africa, the polity that adopts the strong incentives approach need only agree on one set of means at the outset. It can then let political interest take its course. This is no small advantage where consensus is hard to find once the question shifts from abstract goals to concrete means.

---

51. There are no guarantees, of course, that politicians will play by these rules, but that argument proves too much—it is true of all rules. The point about these is that they probably need to be put in place only once. Of course, all of this assumes that South Africa can, in the first instance, surmount the hegemonic aspirations attributed to its main participants. This problem I have described in Chapter 1 and shall return to in Chapter 7.

ELECTORAL PATHS TO ACCOMMODATION

If South Africans decide that the promise of intergroup coalitions committed to accommodation is worth pursuing, as I obviously hope they will, South Africans will have to work out an appropriate institutional design. Since such coalitions are dependent on vote pooling by parties across ethnic lines, it is time to provide ideas about how a strong dose of incentives can be built in to induce the exchange of votes.

There are at least three approaches. The first is to enact distribution requirements for electoral victory, over and above plurality or majority requirements. The second is to opt for preferential voting, and here there are two main varieties, the alternative vote and the single transferable vote. The third is to require or nearly require ethnically mixed slates, along the lines of the Malaysian or Lebanese practice.

The Nigerian formula for the election of the president, put into effect for the 1979 and 1983 elections, had a double set of requirements. The victorious candidate needed to obtain the largest number of votes (a majority if there were only two candidates, a plurality if more than two). He also needed geographic distribution: at least 25 percent of the vote in no fewer than two-thirds of the then-nineteen states in the Nigerian federation. To reach the 25 percent threshold, given the geographic distribution of the various ethnic groups, it would not be enough for any two of the three largest groups to unite behind a single candidate, even though the three largest groups together formed nearly two-thirds of the population. This was a system put in place deliberately to broaden the support required by a president and to protect minorities.

As I have already noted, the system worked well. But, of course, it has an obvious problem. It is possible that no candidate will meet the requirements of the formula. In 1979, this difficulty nearly came to pass. And so there must be a reliable backup formula to elect a president if no candidate secures the 25 percent distribution.[52]

Two observations are in order. First, since these are competitive elections, candidates and their parties have every incentive to reach out

52. In my discussions with members of the Nigerian Constituent Assembly in 1978, delegates—especially Ibo delegates—were much concerned with the prospect that, under a distribution formula, no candidate might meet the dual set of requirements. They feared the instability that might follow upon an uncertain outcome. Such concerns make it imperative to adopt an effective and definitive backup formula, so that some candidate is declared elected by a process that is rapid, authoritative, and clear-cut—in short, incontestable. For the 1978 calculations, see Donald L. Horowitz, "About-Face in Africa: The Return to Civilian Rule in Nigeria" *Yale Review* 68, no. 2 (Winter 1979): 192–206.

effectively to attain the 25 percent distribution threshold. They certainly cannot sit supine, because competing candidates must be presumed to be reaching out. As a result, there is less chance of failure to elect than might at first be thought. Still, there is some chance, and my second observation relates to the backup formula. That formula is likely to be based either on plurality alone or on a runoff, either by direct election or, as in the Nigerian case, by indirect election. In a federation, the indirect election could involve either central or state legislatures, or both. But note that, if distribution is the only incentive to interethnic cooperation, and the backup formula confers the power to elect on officials who themselves have been chosen by a system with different incentives, then these, too, will figure into the calculations of candidates and their parties, thereby likely weakening the accommodative effect of the distribution requirement.

In Nigeria, since federal and state legislatures, unlike the president, were elected without any incentives to interethnic accommodation, the backup formula did not reinforce the distribution requirement. Observers of the Nigerian preparations for the return to civilian rule in 1992 have, in fact, called for a system of legislative election different from first-past-the-post in largely homogeneous constituencies, a system that will reinforce the incentives for multiethnic distribution.[53]

One such possibility might be to elect legislators by a formula requiring plurality plus distribution within legislative constituencies. The distribution principle of election need not be limited to a presidential system. But distribution requirements for legislative elections would have an accommodative effect only if constituencies were heterogeneous. Even then, the requirements would raise new problems, for there would have to be a backup formula for legislative elections, probably providing for a runoff or for indirect election by a lower tier of legislators. All of this is feasible, but it may seem unattractive or complex. If a president is to be elected on the basis of distribution, it is quite possible that legislatures will be elected by some other formula that provides a different set of accommodative incentives. The main objective is to build in accommodative incentives strongly for every office in each branch and each level of government.

The party system produced by the mixed Nigerian incentives was itself mixed. The same three ethnically based parties as prevailed in the

53. Larry Diamond, "Nigeria: Pluralism, Statism, and the Struggle for Democracy," in Larry Diamond et al., eds., *Democracy in Developing Countries,* vol. 2, *Africa* (Boulder, Colo.: Lynne Rienner, 1988), p. 77.

First Republic reconstituted themselves, but they also broadened out to embrace minorities around the edges. Fairly clearly, this broadening was induced by the presidential electoral formula (and, in the north, by the effect of new federal states). No interethnic coalition emerged in the national legislature, except a coalition of convenience, based only on seat pooling. This is not surprising, since the presidency, with its unique mode of election, was only one piece of the system.

In South Africa, it is not clear whether a single principle of distribution could be made to work in legislative elections. The Nigerian technique uses geography as a rough proxy for ethnicity. It depends upon territorial concentration of groups—that is, a certain level of homogeneity within areas but heterogeneity between areas. The spatial distribution of all but the White group [54] in South Africa, however, is uneven. Some areas, such as Natal and the Cape, have strong concentrations of large groups: Zulu and Indians in Natal, Xhosa and Coloureds in the Cape. Others, notably the Transvaal, have a good deal more ethnic heterogeneity. In the heterogeneous areas, it might be possible to impose distribution requirements in single-member parliamentary constituencies, using the standard of plurality plus distribution thresholds in some percentage of the total number of wards or electoral subdivisions. In more homogeneous areas, however, a party and its candidate in a single-member constituency could probably meet a low distribution threshold without making any commitment to intergroup moderation. Consequently, to make distribution work, complex electoral formulae in large multimember constituencies might be required. This might not be an altogether bad thing, because it might well produce ethnically mixed slates in those multimember constituencies. Since all voters would vote for all candidates, candidates could not win without relying on the votes of groups other than their own. Vote pooling among candidates would be essential to victory. The result would be to maximize intergroup conciliation. [55]

Of course, if all that concerned us were distribution across racial (as opposed to ethnic) groups, the Group Areas Act has so segregated the groups for the time being (and will probably continue to do so for some time after its abolition) that geographic distribution requirements within

---

54. Leaving aside, for the moment, distinctions between Afrikaans and English speakers.

55. The rather clear analogy here would be the former Lebanese system of ethnically mixed lists in multimember constituencies, which produced exactly this result. See Horowitz, *Ethnic Groups in Conflict*, pp. 633–35.

multiracial constituencies would be easy to arrange. But the areas in which single racial groups predominate are so extensive that, again, large multimember constituencies would be required.

Although distribution requirements worked well in Nigeria, they are rather unusual. It bears mention, therefore, that analogous requirements have been proposed previously in Uganda and in South Africa itself.

The Uganda proposals were made shortly before Milton Obote was overthrown in 1971. They would have required each member of parliament to represent his own area plus three others. For victory, a candidate would need the highest vote in all four constituencies taken together.[56] While this is not strictly a distribution requirement, it has the same aim of requiring panethnic support.

The South African proposals were made by the Molteno Commission that reported to the former Progressive Party in 1960. At the height of Verwoerdian apartheid, the commission recommended a bicameral legislature for a future South Africa seeking to alleviate its racial problems. It proposed that the upper house be elected by plurality vote in single-member constituencies, provided that the winning candidate obtain "at least one-fifth of the total votes cast by members of each [racial] community" in the constituency.[57] The commission candidly acknowledged the important drawback that racial distribution would require "racial classification of voters for the purpose of Senate elections"[58]—which, of course, would not be true for geographic distribution—but it urged distribution requirements because candidates "would know in advance that success depended on racial moderation and the support of some proportion, at all events, of all communities."[59] The restricted franchise recommended by the commission drew several dissents, but the distribution provisions were recommended unanimously. Thereafter, the functions of distribution requirements were forgotten until the Nigerians discovered geographic distribution requirements independently in 1978.

If geographic distribution requirements are well designed, as in the Nigerian presidential election, they can produce an altogether benign

56. Fred M. Hayward, "Introduction," in Fred M. Hayward, ed., *Elections in Independent Africa* (Boulder, Colo.: Westview Press, 1987), p. 9.
57. Molteno et al., *Final Report of the Commission Set Up by the Progressive Party to Make Recommendations on a Revised Constitution for South Africa,* vol. 1, p. 19. Fallback provisions were also recommended. Ibid., p. 20.
58. Ibid., p. 26.
59. Ibid., p. 24.

impetus to ethnic inclusion. But it is easy to imagine quite different consequences in South Africa. Consider two hypothetical responses of electoral engineers to multiracial constituencies containing a heterogeneous array of Black groups.

To achieve maximum political inclusion of all the Black groups, the temptation might be to set the distribution thresholds so high as to produce recurrent uncertainty about whether any candidate could meet them. In the Nigerian presidential elections, distribution thresholds were only 25 percent and, at that, only in two-thirds of the states. Even so, a president was almost not elected in 1979. Even absent that uncertainty, if distribution requirements are set high, they might have the effect of consolidating the bonds among Black voters but exacerbating the cleavages between Black voters, on the one hand, and White voters, on the other. That is, parties and candidates might respond to the requirement of well-distributed support by securing their standing among all the Black groups. The way to do this is to emphasize racial issues.

If, however, distribution requirements are left very modest despite ethnic heterogeneity, those requirements might be satisfied even if parties broke cleanly along ethnic lines. If, for example, the requirements are plurality plus 20 percent support in two-thirds of the wards, that is something a party may well be able to achieve even if it appeals only to, say, Xhosa or Zulu. In short, distribution requirements can be so supereffective or so ineffective that they still leave many groups out in the cold.

Of course, this could be a problem with distribution requirements for a presidential election as well. But the likely effects of a distribution formula are easier to calculate for one whole country than they are for a multitude of individual constituencies. And so it is probable that distribution requirements for a presidential election can be designed to work as intended, just as they did in Nigeria.

Preferential voting may be more promising for the legislature. There are many varieties, but two are worth distinguishing. The single transferable vote we have seen at work—or, rather, not at work—in Northern Ireland. It is also utilized in composing the parliament of the Irish Republic and in composing several Australian bodies, including the federal Senate. Alternative voting is a system in which second and subsequent preferences of those voters whose first preference is not one of the top two candidates are reallocated until a candidate attains a majority.[60] AV is used in composing other Australian bodies, including the

---

60. Under another variant of AV, if no candidate wins an absolute majority of first

lower federal house, and in electing the president of Sri Lanka. It is generally regarded as a modest reform of first-past-the post, a sound way of diminishing the arbitrariness of the plurality system without yielding to the dominance of central party officials in candidate selection that tends to accompany list-system PR.[61]

Quite obviously, both STV and AV give weight to second and third choices and open up the possibility that parties will bid across ethnic lines for the second preferences of voters whose first choice stands no real chance of election. This is especially true of alternative voting, since it is based on a majority threshold for election. The majority requirement necessarily disqualifies the first choices of a fair number of people whose candidate could meet a lesser standard. Indeed, an objection to alternative voting is precisely this: "If one party has, say, forty percent of the first preference votes, but those who do not rank the party first rank it last, then it may fail to win any seats." [62] If it does win seats, it may be represented less than proportionately. This is labeled by critics "a major disadvantage of the AV system." [63]

But notice that what is labeled a disadvantage can be turned to the service of moderation in a society in need of moderation. Why, after all, did the party with 40 percent of first preferences not succeed in negotiating across party lines to obtain the second and third preferences of voters who gave their first preferences to other parties? If the 40 percent party had done so, it would have come out better. But to do so, it would have had to compromise with supporters of those other parties.

Transfer this issue to a severely divided society with ethnically based parties, and the conclusion reads as follows: Under alternative voting, with a majority threshold for victory, many elections will turn on second and third preferences. Parties that succeed in negotiating for second and third preferences will be rewarded. The price of a successful negotiation is intergroup accommodation and compromise. The exchange of second and third preferences, based on reciprocal concessions on ethnic issues, is likely to lead to an accommodative interethnic coalition if no party can form a government alone. Under conditions of party proliferation, therefore, AV is likely to produce governments committed to

---

preferences, the bottom candidate is dropped out, and that candidate's votes are redistributed in accordance with the second preferences of his supporters, and so on, using subsequent preferences, until one candidate attains a majority.

61. Butler, "Electoral Systems," pp. 8, 20.

62. R. J. Johnston, "Seats, Votes, Redistricting, and the Allocation of Power in Electoral Systems," in Lijphart and Grofman, eds., *Choosing an Electoral System*, pp. 63–64.

63. Ibid., p. 63.

accommodative policies. To dislodge such governments at the polls, at least some incentives will be in place for the opposition parties to outbid the governing coalition at being moderate, although other incentives may point in the opposite direction—toward differentiating those parties and giving them reason to accuse the coalition partners of selling out group interests.

Before taking this line of reasoning any further, the realism of the key steps in the reasoning needs to be underlined. That realism depends on the willingness of parties and candidates actively to work to obtain second and third preferences from voters, and it depends on the willingness of voters to think in terms of second and third best. The willingness of both has been demonstrated. In the Republic of Ireland, where STV is used, the second and third strongest parties make deals to transfer votes; between 20 percent and 25 percent of all votes in Irish elections are actually transferred at least once.[64] In Italy, where voters are permitted, even in a list system, to change the order in which they prefer candidates to be elected within party lists, it is very clear that candidates and factions set out to induce voters to do exactly that.[65] Moreover, in 1972, some 56 percent of Italian voters exercised their option to change the candidate order; the tendency was not confined to sophisticated voters but was very common among traditionally oriented voters in the south as well.[66] Experimental studies also find that voters are willing to deem acceptable a good many more candidates than they actually vote for; and, if preferential voting were in force, plurality winners in some currently first-past-the-post systems would become majority winners.[67]

Apart from parties based on ethnic cleavages in severely divided societies, we know, then, that party organizations are easily geared up for various forms of preferential voting, and voters are receptive to it. And even if voters were not prepared easily to contemplate crossing ethnic lines, that is not an insurmountable problem, because second or third preferences could be made compulsory for a valid ballot.[68]

---

64. Gallagher, "The Political Consequences of the Electoral System in the Republic of Ireland," pp. 256–57.

65. Richard S. Katz, "Preference Voting in Italy," Comparative Political Studies 18, no. 2 (July 1985): 229–49.

66. Ibid. The same is true in Australia, where voters for federal Senate seats often do not follow party-recommended preference orders. See J. F. H. Wright, "An Electoral Basis for Responsible Government: The Australian Experience," in Lijphart and Grofman, eds., Choosing an Electoral System, p. 133.

67. Gerald de Maio et al., "Approval Voting: Some Recent Empirical Evidence," American Politics Quarterly 11, no. 3 (July 1983): 365–74.

68. Cf. Wright, "An Electoral Basis for Responsible Government," p. 133, to the

One point about proportionality and party proliferation. I said earlier that party proliferation is required to make this system work for accommodation, and I shall return to the proliferation theme in a moment. As Lijphart rightly points out, party proliferation depends in some measure on degree of proportionality of the electoral system, for, if the system gives the largest parties too big a seat bonus, smaller parties can be wiped out. Both AV and STV are both considerably better at insuring proportionality than is first-past-the-post, although not quite as good at this as list-system PR is.[69] AV can provide quite enough proportionality for the requisite party proliferation. In any case, there are other ways to provide incentives for proliferation, which I shall describe in Chapter 6.

More than this, AV can provide the more rigorous incentive to vote pooling in a divided society that STV lacked in Northern Ireland. That incentive is the majority threshold. Under STV, a party could obtain representation without vote pooling. With a majority threshold, achieved by reallocated second and third preferences, it is harder to win election without vote pooling. Given party proliferation, if no one is elected without a majority and very few candidates can attain a majority without pooling second and third preferences across ethnic lines, that is about as strong a political incentive as can be devised. When supporters and leaders learn that the difference between power and no power lies in the mutual exchange of alternative votes, the sellout argument will still appeal to and motivate some voters, but it will not motivate all voters.

An analogy to the Malaysian coalition is not amiss. In the first Malaysian election, to be sure, there was only centripetal (multiethnic) competition, but in subsequent elections there was a flank (ethnic) competition exclusively. The coalition, which was rewarding because the logic of exchanging votes could win elections, stayed intact.

In 1978, the Sri Lankans adopted AV, with a majority rule, for their presidential elections. By now, therefore, we ought to know how vote pooling works under AV in actual elections in severely divided societies, but we do not. What we know, however, is still encouraging or, to put it more accurately, is not discouraging.

The two main Sinhalese parties were fairly well differentiated in their

---

effect that in Tasmania it is required to cast a ballot for as many candidates as there are seats.

69. Part of the lesser proportionality of AV in the Australian House relates to the existence of single-member constituencies. Wright, "An Electoral Basis for Representative Government," pp. 129–31. On the proportionality of STV in Ireland, see Gallagher, "The Political Consequences of the Electoral System in the Republic of Ireland," p. 255.

willingness to be conciliatory toward the Tamils. The United National Party (UNP) of J. R. Jayewardene was, overall, more moderate than the Sri Lanka Freedom Party (SLFP) of Sirimavo Bandaranaike. In 1982, the first presidential election was held under AV. Unfortunately, no second-preference test was conducted. The SLFP was in factional disarray. Mrs. Bandaranaike had been deprived of her civil rights by the Jayewardene government and was ineligible to stand for election. The SLFP leadership gave limited support to its nominal candidate. More than that, because its demands had not been met, the Tamil United Liberation Front had expressed its indifference to the election in the Tamil areas and put forward no candidate. For the most part, legitimate Tamil party politics was no longer functioning by then.[70] No arrangements for vote pooling were made. (Indeed, a defect of the system is that second preferences are not required for a valid ballot, and few voters cast any second preferences.) Under the atypical competitive circumstances of that election, second preferences were unnecessary. The UNP candidate won on a 52 percent majority of first preferences. In effect, since two main parties were far below their usual strength, party proliferation was insufficient to require vote transfers.[71]

By the next presidential election, in 1988, conditions were worse. A civil war was being fought in the Tamil areas, and a reasonably effective boycott was conducted there. Again, the UNP candidate won on a small absolute majority of first preferences (50.4 percent).[72] If and when the Sri Lankan Tamils (a 13 percent minority of the whole population) come back into the system, the Sinhalese parties will have every reason to bid for valuable Tamil second preferences. Since the Tamils' first choice, a Tamil presidential candidate, will have no prospect of winning, Tamil second preferences will be available for transfer. From the very narrow margins of first-preference victory under the most abnormal conditions, it seems perfectly clear that, under even modestly normal conditions,

---

70. The rival Tamil Congress did put forward a candidate, who received 2.7 percent of the total vote.

71. The election is described in full in C. R. de Silva, "Plebiscitary Democracy or Creeping Authoritarianism? The Presidential Election and Referendum of 1982," in James Manor, ed., *Sri Lanka in Change and Crisis* (London: Croom Helm, 1984), pp. 35–50.

72. By now, however, the UNP quite clearly had majority support among all the minorities taking part in the poll—Indian Tamils (as opposed to the Sri Lankan Tamils in the war zone), Muslims, and Sinhalese Christians—as well as the support of a substantial minority of Sinhalese Buddhists. S. W. R. de A. Samarasinghe, "Sri Lanka's Presidential Elections," *Economic and Political Weekly* (Bombay), January 21, 1989, pp. 131–35; Sunil Bastian, "Two Elections," *Thatched Patio* (Colombo) 2, no. 2 (April 1989): 1–21.

no Sinhalese candidate will have a majority of first preferences, and elections will surely be decided by second preferences.

To illustrate just how AV would work and how it would produce conciliatory results, consider an imaginary conversation between party leaders seeking the presidency in Sri Lanka. Suppose two main Sinhalese candidates are contesting the election. The first estimates 40 percent first-preference support, and the second estimates 35 percent. There is also a Sri Lankan Tamil candidate, who can count on perhaps 10–12 percent of all first-preference votes. A meeting is convened between the first Sinhalese candidate and the Tamil candidate. Since no candidate will have a majority of first preferences, the discussion quickly turns to the subject of Tamil second preferences. The Tamil leader is asked whether he would be willing to urge Tamil voters to give their second preferences to the first Sinhalese candidate. He replies that his ability to do so depends on the Sinhalese candidate's willingness to be hospitable to Tamil aspirations. Otherwise, his appeal to Tamil voters to cast second-preference ballots for a Sinhalese candidate would be futile. Before long, concrete policy issues are being discussed. By the end of the negotiations, the first Sinhalese candidate has emerged as decidedly more accommodating on Tamil issues than the second Sinhalese candidate.

Now this conversation has reverberations. The second Sinhalese candidate will probably seek to differentiate himself from the first, by becoming less accommodating on Tamil issues, in order to attract hardline defectors who are displeased by the compromise commitments of the first Sinhalese candidate. For this reason, accommodation of Tamil interests will lose the first Sinhalese candidate some Sinhalese first preferences. He cannot go overboard in accommodating the Tamils, if he is to have a net gain from the transaction. But he can compensate, to some extent, for the loss of hard-line Sinhalese votes by appealing to the other minorities in Sri Lanka as well. They, too, can offer votes to conciliatory Sinhalese candidates. The 50 percent threshold means that, every time there are more than two candidates, parties need to search hard for pockets of votes to reach a majority. If there were more than two Sinhalese candidates, the majority threshold would be harder to reach, the extreme Sinhalese vote would be more divided, and the votes of minorities would be both more valuable and less risky to attract. In an AV system, then, intergroup compromise can become useful in getting elected, whereas in most other systems compromise makes it more difficult to get elected.

This transaction will not necessarily be limited to one election only. If reelection is to be sought later, the current commitments will be kept, and the partners will have found joint rewards in the arrangement. The defecting voters will likewise remember the concessions unfavorably, and the party of the second Sinhalese candidate will find rewards in continuing to attend to their concerns. In other words, a party spectrum, based on willingness or reluctance to compromise, will begin to differentiate itself.

Translating these parochial circumstances into general lessons about alternative voting, one point stands out. It was Sri Lanka's strong tendency toward party proliferation that led it to adopt a majority threshold and alternative voting to reach that threshold in the first place.[73] Without party proliferation, AV is of less utility. If a party can win on first preferences, second preferences are irrelevant. The peculiar conditions that undid Sri Lanka's customary and long-standing party proliferation also undid, for the time being, some—but, as I shall note below, not all—of the conciliatory impact of AV.

If there is reason to think AV would generally encourage intergroup accommodation, is this likely to be true for South Africa? It will be recalled that a problem with applying Nigerian-style distribution requirements to South African parliamentary elections is that, for distribution to work and still provide certainty that someone will be elected, distribution thresholds must be kept at least moderately low. But modest distribution thresholds would afford no guarantee of inclusiveness. The same would not be true for alternative voting. With party proliferation and the need to get over the 50 percent threshold, there would be no real danger of not electing anyone. The reallocation of preferences takes care of that automatically. There would also be little danger of Black-White polarization. Just as all groups could make arrangements with each other, Whites could help elect a Black president, if AV were used in conjunction with a presidential system. And the same would be true for parliamentary seats. The whole notion of AV would be that voters of all groups could help elect parliamentarians of other groups, even if parties break along ethnic or racial lines. Not that any group could unilaterally dictate terms as the price of second preferences, for the simple reason that the party being dictated to is also in a competitive game for first preferences. The system fosters compromise but not surrender. Across the board, AV, with majority requirements, should en-

73. Horowitz, *Ethnic Groups in Conflict*, p. 639.

courage intergroup conciliation and coalition in a major way. Indeed, as we shall see in Chapter 7, the percentages used in the Sri Lankan example above may not be so far removed from the South African electoral numbers when parties compete under universal suffrage.

There is, however, one qualification. Parliamentary constituencies would have to be heterogeneous. To achieve this, the constituencies may have to be large, and they may therefore need to be multimember constituencies. Alternative voting in multimember constituencies creates a complicated ballot. This is a major disadvantage, but the promise of alternative voting for intergroup compromise is so considerable that it is worth thinking long and hard about how to make it work.

There are certainly simpler systems, such as approval voting, which allows voters to cast ballots indiscriminately for all candidates they deem acceptable.[74] In some circumstances, approval voting flushes out second choices. However, it will not produce conciliatory results in divided societies. Since approval votes are, in form, first preferences, voters are not likely to include candidates of other ethnic groups in their list. To induce the exchange of votes across ethnic lines, interparty agreements are necessary, and these are unlikely to be consummated without a preferential ballot.

This brings me to a third set of innovations, which can be dealt with quickly: ethnically mixed slates. The Malaysian example is the quintessential case in practice but not in prescription, for nothing in Malaysia requires mixed slates. The coalition partners simply found the single slate to be to their advantage, and they pursued that advantage. The Malaysian example shows how vote pooling can be accomplished with profit—it illuminates the mechanism—but, as indicated previously, because of the idiosyncratic formative conditions of the coalition, it does not show us how to get to that result.[75]

The Lebanese had a way to achieve the same result through the electoral system, and it served Lebanon well from 1943 to 1976. The system consisted mainly of (1) seats reserved by ascriptive group, (2) in mixed, multimember constituencies, (3) on the basis of a common electoral roll. Because seats were reserved, competition for them was intraethnic, but because everybody voted for each seat, irrespective of the

74. See Steven J. Brams and Peter C. Fishburn, *Approval Voting* (Boston: Birkhäuser, 1983). I am indebted to Akhil Amar for suggesting the potential relevance of approval voting.
75. However, in Chapter 7, I shall describe the emergence in South Africa of some patterns resembling those in Malaysia, and I shall point to some possibilities for coaxing them along.

voters' identity, there were inescapable incentives for candidates in the multimember constituencies to exchange with each other the votes of their supporters and thus to put up what were tantamount to mixed lists. Otherwise, each candidate might have been limited to the support of members of his own group and defeated by an opponent who had obtained support from other groups.

It was an ingenious system,[76] but there is no need to consider it further, because, as I said in Chapter 1, it would be completely unacceptable in South Africa. A good many South Africans have made clear their determination not to have official group designations taint their electoral system. Reserved seats, balanced lists, communal rolls,[77] and the like are all precluded. Even if an agreement were struck at the outset to create reserved seats or communal rolls, it would suffer from dubious legitimacy and might not prove durable. Were it not for the metaconflict, in short, a Lebanese-type system might have been considered to mitigate the conflict.

Apart from the Lebanese system, nothing I have discussed here rests on any official designation of group identity. The innovations I have considered should help mitigate group tensions, and yet all of the systems analyzed here are ethnically and racially neutral. As we have seen, several are used in more or less homogeneous (or at least not severely divided) countries.

ELECTORAL ENGINEERING: MECHANISMS AND CONSEQUENCES

The approach I have advocated is to adopt an electoral system that will make moderation rewarding by making politicians reciprocally dependent on the votes of members of groups other than their own. The dependence is only marginal, of course, but it will sometimes be the margin of victory. Since the parties must pool votes rather than pool merely seats, they must find ways before the election to communicate their ethnically and racially conciliatory intentions to the voters. After the election, they must deliver on those commitments or risk electoral retribution.

76. I have described the Lebanese system and its conciliatory effects in *Ethnic Groups in Conflict*, pp. 633–35.
77. For the Fijian electoral system, using communal and common rolls, see Ralph R. Premdas, "Fiji: The Anatomy of a Revolution," *Pacifica* 1, no. 1 (January 1989): 67–110, at 80–83.

This approach could hardly be further from that of consociational democracy. Two sharp differences should be underscored.

The first relates to the much-contested question of groups and alignments in South Africa. Consociational arrangements, it is true, do not require specification of group identities in advance of party formation and elections. But consociation assumes ascriptive groups will emerge; and, once they do, it requires a certain entrenchment of their rights to autonomy, mutual veto, and the like. (The fact that the formal holders of the rights in some schemes may be political parties, rather than ethnic groups, matters not at all, once there are ethnically based parties.) The electoral mechanism of vote pooling, on the other hand, makes no such provisions. It only assumes that, if distribution requirements are laid down, parties will seek to find well-distributed support; or, if alternative voting is adopted, parties will seek second preferences to assure a majority. The policies pursued by governments will reflect the exigencies of building support; they will flow from incentives, not constraints.

Quite obviously, it is my view that ethnic and racial divisions will be a prominent part of the South African political system. But if I am wrong and they are not, no harm will be done. These electoral systems will still encourage conciliation along whatever lines of difference emerge in the polity—including, but not limited to, differences based on policy, ideology, class, or region. Consequently, to adopt these innovations is not at all to bias the future political system in favor of ethnic and racial politics. It is only to take some precautions against the most severe polarization of any kind. And so these provisions will ameliorate the metaconflict as well as the conflict. One can hardly overemphasize the utility of incentives to conciliation in post-apartheid South Africa.

The second difference from consociation is that these mechanisms work at the voter level, not at the elite level. They contemplate no elite cartel, no monopoly control over the groups. Political leaders must act, of course, to take advantage of them; but, in acting, party leaders are responding to the political market in votes. They are not conspiring against the electorate. And, for this reason, we need make no assumptions about the politicians' own beliefs and whether they are more moderate than those of the voters. All we need assume is that politicians are rational electoral actors, that they like being elected and reelected—not exactly farfetched assumptions.

If these mechanisms work as they should, they will provide some modest boost to the moderate middle, on whatever issue dimensions emerge, at the expense of the extremes. But they do not, by any means, rule out the extremes. On the contrary, they simultaneously provide a raison d'être for the extremes, for those extremes react to the compromises made by politicians to secure well-distributed support or second preferences. Those voters who are against vote pooling or conciliation will gravitate to those parties that do not advocate or practice it. It will be recalled that the emergence of the multiethnic Malaysian Alliance gave a fillip to parties on the Malay and Chinese flanks. Similarly, if a United National Party presidential candidate in Sri Lanka were conciliatory to the Tamils, in order to secure his margin of electoral victory on Tamil second preferences, the Sri Lanka Freedom Party would, no doubt, denounce the underlying interparty agreement that attracted Tamil votes. In short, the parties will sort themselves out by their willingness to compromise, and the center will be surrounded by less conciliatory flanks. But the rules of the game will generally favor accommodation—an enormous advantage in a divided society.

Sometimes, of course, if parties start out by being ethnically based, interethnic coalitions will emerge, not just to govern, but to contest elections. The Malaysian Alliance was such a coalition, which put forward a single slate. All of the electoral devices that might foster conciliation make pre-election agreements between parties electorally rewarding. That is how the devices will be brought to life.

It will be noted that, in advancing these electoral ideas, I have practically ignored the major conventional arguments for first-past-the-post and for list-system PR.[78] The seat bonus typical of first-past-the-post systems is said to provide stable governments by converting pluralities of votes into majorities of seats and also to make those governments moderate. Ruling parties become risk averse, for if they offend marginal voters, small swings of votes can produce large swings of seats and thus alternation in office. In the case of ethnically or racially divided societies, however, these advantages are nullified by the common identification of party with ascriptive group and the concomitant tendency of majorities to shut out minorities.[79] Floating voters are less important.

---

78. For a good, concise statement, see Butler, "Electoral Systems," pp. 11–22.

79. There is no evidence whatever that plurality systems minimize the role of ethnic parties in divided societies. Compare Kader Asmal, "Electoral Systems: A Critical Survey" (paper presented at the In-House Seminar, African National Congress, Lusaka, Zambia, March 1–4, 1988), p. 5. Quite the contrary, such parties can flourish in plurality systems, as they did, for example, in the Nigerian First Republic or in Zimbabwe before the one-party state was declared. The most plurality systems will generally provide is an incentive to reduce the number of ethnic parties. By so doing, they decrease multipolar fluidity and increase bipolar rigidity and conflict. Cf. Horowitz, *Ethnic Groups in Conflict,* pp. 360–62. The Malaysian coalition, which grew up in a plurality system, is an unusual case.

Similarly, list-system PR is generally advocated on grounds of fairness, because it reduces the disparity between seats and votes; parties receive little or no seat bonus. But, again, in divided societies, list-system PR is as conducive to racial or ethnic exclusion as first-past-the-post is. The only difference is that, unlike first-past-the-post, list-system PR may compel formation of a coalition government before the ascriptive minority or minorities can be excluded.

And so these conventional arguments for plurality or proportionality are irrelevant to the problem of divided societies, which is the problem of exclusion and inclusion. As a matter of fact, close attention to the conventional arguments, mainly formulated in homogeneous societies, can produce harmful effects in heterogeneous societies. Two excellent illustrations, related to list-system PR, are at hand.

List-system PR, with the whole country as a single constituency, is, as we have seen, conducive to proportionality. However, there are two conventional objections to this form of national-list-system PR that have been noticed in South Africa,[80] as they have elsewhere, and in some places have produced modifications of the system.

The first objection is that the relations between individual representatives and constituents are attenuated or fictitious when the whole country is a single constituency. This objection can be met by a change from national lists to separate lists for each multimember territorial constituency. Then, even if a constituency has several representatives, they are accountable to it.

The second objection is that voting by party-determined lists of candidates, with no voter ability to alter the order of candidates elected from the list, accords too much power to central party authorities and too little power to individual voters. This objection can be met by empowering voters to determine the order in which candidates on a party list will be elected. The mechanism is a simultaneous double ballot: the voter first votes for a party list and then votes for the order of candidates within his preferred list. In counting ballots, parties are first allocated percentages of seats, and candidates are then deemed elected or not according to voter preferences. As we have seen, candidates, party factions, and voters in Italy are actively mobilized in the process of altering the order of the party lists.

Both of these objections and both modifications are customarily de-

---

80. Simkins, *Reconstructing South African Liberalism*, pp. 76–79; Slabbert and Welsh, *South Africa's Options*, pp. 152–53.

bated in ethnically neutral terms, but they are not ethnically neutral. The parliament of Sri Lanka is now elected by constituency-list PR, and voters have power, by means of an additional candidate-preference ballot, to determine the order in which candidates are elected within party lists. The first results under both modifications suggest that they have the ability to reduce the representation of minorities in both senses: office holding and accommodation.

Geographically dispersed minorities will fare less well under a constituency-list system than under a national-list system, all else being equal. In a constituency with three seats, it is perfectly possible that a 20 percent minority will neither gain a representative nor be in a position to affect the outcome, since party appeals will be directed to claims made by larger groups in the constituency. This, indeed, has been the result in some Sri Lankan constituencies.[81] The same result follows from voter designation of candidate order within constituency lists. A party that generously places a minority candidate on its list will find that majority voters will change the winning order, to the detriment of that candidate. Any party tempted to go further and run a joint list and pool votes across ethnic lines will find that majority voters have undone the accommodative work of the parties by preferring majority candidates and defeating minority candidates. Again, Sri Lanka has experience on this score. Concludes C. R. de Silva, "The problem of marginalization through the system of preference voting in large electorates has to be viewed with concern by geographically dispersed minority groups."[82]

Such considerations should give considerable pause before debating any electoral innovations for divided societies in terms of the conventional criteria used to evaluate electoral systems. The problem of ethnic and racial inclusion and exclusion should induce us to think differently about desirable electoral systems. In evaluating list-system PR, for example, its formidable ability to produce proportionality is far less important than its powerful impetus to exclusion of ethnic groups not represented in the majority coalition. In evaluating distribution requirements added to plurality systems, it is hardly a cogent objection that

81. S. W. R. de A. Samarasinghe and C. R. de Silva, "The Development Council Election of 1981: Its Political and Electoral Implications," *Sri Lanka Journal of Social Sciences* 4, no. 1 (June 1981): 79–109, at 97. The elections analyzed in this article were the first conducted under the PR system also used in Sri Lankan parliamentary elections, but with seat apportionment that did not match the parliamentary apportionment.

82. C. R. de Silva, "Preference Voting: Some Remarks on the Sri Lankan Experience, 1987–1989" (paper presented at the 18th Annual Conference on South Asia, Madison, Wisconsin, November 3–5, 1989), p. 7.

they are likely to reward, not just the largest party, but also the party most widely spread across a territory, for the most widely spread may also be the most ethnically inclusive. In evaluating alternative voting, it is not an important fault that it produces less perfect proportionality than does list-system PR, if, unlike list-system PR, it produces interethnic vote pooling. And it is a virtue that AV does not provide as much of a seat bonus as do plurality systems—though it would, in South Africa, as elsewhere, accord some modest seat advantage to the largest party.

Where AV produces majority rather than coalition governments, they are likely to result, not from artificial seat bonuses, but from the considerable incentives to broaden out support that are provided by the requirement of a majority.[83] No racial or ethnic group will be permanently in office and no other group permanently out. Parties will have every reason to seek widely distributed support or to seek out the second and third preferences of many pockets of voters, enhancing the inclusiveness of the system. Since all this is the negation of apartheid—without being its mirror image, majority domination—it should be attractive to South Africans.

The broadening impact of alternative voting means it is more likely

---

83. In fact, the incentives to broadened support can be very great in alternative voting systems. Some of the modest seat bonus provided by AV is a function of constituency size. See note 69, above. Evidence from a large, multicountry sample of elections suggests that majority-threshold electoral systems—unfortunately, the category merges AV and runoff systems—overall produce one-party majority governments (rather than coalition governments) more frequently than other PR systems do, although somewhat less frequently than plurality systems do. Moreover, a large number of these one-party majority governments are the product, not of an artificial seat bonus, but of the attainment of an actual majority. This suggests that majority requirements (AV or runoff) for each seat may provide such significant incentives to broaden support that the party that ends up with the majority of seats is likely to have the support of a majority of voters in the country as a whole. A. Blais and R. K. Carty, "The Impact of Electoral Formulae on the Creation of Majority Governments," *Electoral Studies* 6, no. 3 (December 1987): 209–18.

Two important qualifications derive from the sample. First, a disproportionate number of elections conducted under majority-threshold rules took place a long time ago. Second, and more important, as indicated, the category of majority systems embraces both runoff and AV systems. There are significant differences even within AV systems, but these have not been disaggregated; nor have AV and runoff systems been separated out.

Since the Blais and Carty study does not separate out elections in divided societies, it is not amiss to note that, after AV was introduced in Sri Lankan presidential elections, the UNP proceeded to broaden out its support among all the minorities taking part in the elections. Majorities among the Indian Tamils, Muslims, and Sinhalese Christians formed part of the UNP's overall majority. See note 72, above. For reasons I have described, these were unusual elections. Nevertheless, the majority threshold is likely to induce broadening out for first preferences as well as interparty bargaining for second preferences.

to produce a government with an outright majority of seats than list-system PR or STV is. AV does not stand in the way of majoritarianism, but makes majorities responsive to the interests of others as well. This is an important conciliatory feature—and one that builds legitimacy—in a divided society.

It should be emphasized that, if the vote-pooling mechanism works as planned, it will result in *real participation in power by minorities and majorities alike*. This participation will not occur by means of rigidly specified quotas, on the Cyprus model, and it will not consist of the token overrepresentation of minorities that Whites in Zimbabwe enjoyed until 1987. The numbers are not fixed but fluid. Some governments will have more representation of some groups than of others; other governments will be composed differently. Everything will depend on the vicissitudes of elections, which is as it should be. But the elections will be structured so that parties seeking to expand their seat totals will have special reason not to neglect the interests of voters, including voters across ethnic lines, who can help them to do exactly that.

The electoral systems that are most appropriate are somewhat complex, but that is to be expected, given the tendency of plurality elections and two-party systems to intensify conflict in a bifurcated society.[84] Equally complex systems, with distribution requirements or preferential ballots, have been found workable and acceptable in other divided societies of the developing world that practice electoral democracy.[85]

The benefits that come with the costs of complexity are great. Among other things, alternative voting (like distribution requirements) would be likely to limit centrifugal tendencies in the party system of a divided society. Because of the need for interparty agreements to exchange votes, there would be a pull toward the center of the system that would help counter polarization. As Juan J. Linz has pointed out, a divided society with a polarized multiparty system—which is what South Africa would have—needs something other than a "feeble electoral system, particu-

---

84. Robert A. Dahl, "Some Explanations," in Robert A. Dahl, ed., *Political Oppositions in Western Democracies* (New Haven: Yale University Press, 1966), pp. 375–76; Lewis, *Politics in West Africa*, pp. 71–73.

85. Nigeria, of course, has had the distribution requirements for presidential elections. Sri Lanka has alternative voting for its president. Malta has the single transferable vote with a procedure for "topping up" the seats of a party with majority support grafted onto the STV system. The complexity of that system has not prevented the acceptance of electoral results in Malta's divided society. See Stephen Howe, "The Maltese General Election of 1987," *Electoral Studies* 6, no. 3 (December 1987): 235–47.

larly one with pure proportional representation [that] exercises no restraint on the voters, and . . . furthers the persistence of fragmentation." Rather, it needs an electoral law that rewards cooperation by pro-system parties, preventing the creation by anti-system parties of "a negative majority" that impedes the work of parliament.[86] The electoral systems proposed here thus avoid the problems associated with plurality systems, on the one hand, and PR systems, on the other, and build interparty cohesion. In Chapter 6, I shall argue that a presidential system would reinforce this centripetal effect in the party system.

The choice, as I have indicated, is not between racial and ethnic politics, on the one hand, and no racial and ethnic politics, on the other. The choice is between zero-sum, high-conflict contests along racial and ethnic lines—with a considerable potential for one or more actors to step in and end the democratic competition before it gets overheated or after it produces exclusionary results—and open-textured, fluid, low-conflict contests, mainly along racial and ethnic lines but with an admixture of intergroup cooperation. The challenge is to take an environment conducive to ethnic and racial allegiances in the party system and create incentives for parties to bid for floating voters who would otherwise vote their group identity. From what we know of the politics of severely divided societies, the choice may well be to see voters floating in the political system or floating in the river.

86. Juan J. Linz, "Crisis, Breakdown, and Reequilibration," in Juan J. Linz and Alfred Stepan, eds., *The Breakdown of Democratic Regimes* (Baltimore: Johns Hopkins University Press, 1978), pt. 1, pp. 67–68.

CHAPTER SIX

Designs for Democracy

Virtually everyone who writes about the future of South Africa focuses either on the need for institutions that will disperse power so as to avoid destructive conflict at the center or on the need for institutions that will concentrate power sufficiently to cope with the country's urgent problems of inequality. Is it possible to have both—to have enough dispersion to avoid mutually exclusive outcomes and enough concentration to devise and implement effective policies to ameliorate discontent?

It is possible. If South African institutions are well designed and work effectively from the outset, discontent, I shall argue, will probably be reduced, even in the face of steady but only modest reductions in inequality. To be well designed, institutions will indeed need to moderate racial and ethnic tensions at the same time as they provide sufficient governmental capacity to effect social change. If South Africa were to choose a presidential system of government, it could simultaneously use presidential elections to moderate tensions and use the presidential office to serve as a center for policy innovation. If South Africa were to choose a federal system, it could in several ways mitigate racial and ethnic conflicts without reducing governmental capacity appreciably.

To work effectively, however, these civilian institutions will need to be free of the threat of military intervention that has been so common in African politics. The configuration of institutions must obviously embrace a system of acceptable civil-military relations. While the armed forces, as an arm of the former White regime, may seem to present insuperable problems for a future regime, this need not be so. There are ways of reordering the armed forces so as to make civilian institutions more likely to endure.

THE CONSTRUCTIVE USES OF PRESIDENTIALISM

A separately elected president can perform two useful, if not vital, functions for a divided society. The first is to make intergroup power sharing more likely by making it impossible for a single racial or ethnic group to capture the state permanently by merely capturing a majority in parliament. The second is to provide another important arena for intergroup conciliation deriving from an electoral formula based on vote pooling. Africa is rich in examples of the need for both of these functions.

In a great many African countries, democracy broke down soon after one ethnically based political party gained control of parliament, leaving another in what would have been perpetual opposition. Parties had congealed into a pattern similar to the 60–40 situation described in Chapter 3. Since the party in control of the legislature was called upon to form the government and the party in opposition was left with nothing, parliament came to be seen as the decisive site of the ethnic contest. When one of the contenders gained control of parliament, the stage was set for an end to the democratic process.

Elections were replaced by violence, either by or against the opposition. If it is not possible for a minority to gain some share of power through elections, that minority may turn to a military coup if it is well represented in the officer corps. That is what occurred in the 1960s, after ethnically based parties captured parliaments in Nigeria, Congo (Brazzaville), Sierra Leone, Togo, and a number of other countries. If the excluded group is territorially separate, separatist movements become possible. Secessionist warfare on the part of the Ibo in Nigeria, Muslims in Chad, and southerners in the Sudan resulted from their being shut out of government. The disaffection of the Baganda in the south of Uganda followed the attainment of a majority by a northern-based party in parliament and the termination of Buganda's special, quasi-federal status. The unrest in Matabeleland and its brutal repression by the Zimbabwe government in the 1980s likewise followed the capture of the state by Robert Mugabe and his Shona supporters. This, then, is a recurrent pattern resulting from exclusion.

Systems in which presidents are separately elected make all political assessments more complex. A group that is excluded from power in parliament may still find ways of gaining access to the president. A group that gains the presidency may or may not also form a majority in parliament. Who owns the state? is a question no longer answered simply by looking to ascriptively based parliamentary majorities.

This first function of presidential systems—fostering inclusion by reducing the zero-sum quality of the contest to control parliament alone—cannot be performed by a presidency unsupported by an electoral formula geared to conciliation. Here I refer to presidential electoral arrangements such as the Nigerian system, which requires geographic distribution plus a plurality for victory, or the Sri Lankan system, which is based on alternative voting.[1] In both cases, and especially in the Nigerian case, the president elected under such a system became a conspicuously panethnic figure, whereas legislators, elected under first-past-the-post systems, served essentially as delegates of the ethnic groups that elected them and made conflict-producing, mutually exclusive demands in parliament.

Despite African experience with clear-cut ethnic inclusion and exclusion in parliamentary regimes, which were then quickly abandoned, and the clear benefits of presidential systems based on conciliatory electoral formulae, much conventional wisdom still holds to the view that, in South Africa, "a presidential election would be more likely to have a divisive effect on the society."[2] This might be true if the presidential election were held under a first-past-the-post system, but, as we have just seen, there is no reason to adopt such a system for the presidency. Nonetheless, Arend Lijphart has contended that presidentialism is incompatible with intergroup power sharing. Presidentialism, he asserts, "has a direct negative effect on proportionality," because "the fact that a presidential election entails the election of one person necessarily means that plurality or majority methods have to be used and that PR is logically excluded."[3] Presidentialism, he goes on to contend, "is inimical to collective and collegial decision-making and hence to compromises either on an ad hoc or regularized basis."[4] All of this is said to follow from

1. See Chapter 5, above.
2. F. van Zyl Slabbert and David Welsh, *South Africa's Options: Strategies for Sharing Power* (New York: St. Martin's Press, 1979), p. 145.
3. Arend Lijphart, "The Southern European Examples of Democratization: Six Lessons for Latin America," *Government and Opposition* 25, no. 1 (Winter 1990): 68–84, at 75.
4. Ibid., p. 76.

the fact that the president, unlike, for example, a cabinet, is a single person with a single ethnic or racial identity.

As I have argued at length, however, politicians in severely divided societies are not simply acting out their identities. Their political behavior is heavily affected by the incentives they confront, particularly the electoral incentives by which they come to office and by which their reelection will be determined.

A single dramatic contrast between two power-sharing executives, one presidential and one prime ministerial, in two severely divided societies will make the point. Contrast Shehu Shagari, elected president of Nigeria under the distribution formula utilized in 1979, with Terence O'Neill or Brian Faulkner, prime ministers of Northern Ireland cabinets that were to exemplify "power sharing" between Catholics and Protestants. O'Neill's government, supported by nothing but good intentions, tried unsuccessfully to initiate a series of reforms in the late 1960s. Although elected under proportional representation, Faulkner's power-sharing executive collapsed within a matter of months in 1974. Shagari, by contrast, was elected president under a system designed to make him more than a representative of his own group. This role he performed admirably, by, among other things, making efforts to cultivate good relations with politicians of other ethnic groups and parties. The fact that a president is a single person, whereas a cabinet is not, is irrelevant to the capacity of the two institutions to perform accommodative functions. Where the incentives are apt, even single prime ministers, presiding over conflict-prone cabinets, can find ways of transcending their own ethnic affiliations—witness the cases of Jawaharlal Nehru in India or Tunku Abdul Rahman in Malaysia. The incentives, however, are much more likely to foster accommodation where a president is directly elected by a system conducive to vote pooling and conciliation.

This brings me to arguments that have been made against presidentialism in a series of works by Juan J. Linz.[5] Linz is concerned to explain Latin American instability by reference to the presidential form of gov-

---

5. Juan J. Linz, "The Perils of Presidentialism," *Journal of Democracy* 1, no. 1 (Winter 1990): 51–70; Juan J. Linz, "Democracy, Presidential or Parliamentary: Does It Make a Difference?" (paper presented at the 1987 Annual Meeting of the American Political Science Association); Juan J. Linz, "Crisis, Breakdown, and Reequilibration," in Juan J. Linz and Alfred Stepan, eds., *The Breakdown of Democratic Regimes* (Baltimore: Johns Hopkins University Press, 1978), pt. 1, pp. 71–74. In what follows, I am drawing on my critique of Linz, "Comparing Democratic Systems," *Journal of Democracy* 1, no. 4 (Fall 1990): 73–79.

ernment so common in Central and South America. He therefore mounts
a wide-ranging attack on the institution of the presidency.

Linz begins by noting that the presidential election has a zero-sum
character. A candidate is either elected or not. In a parliamentary system, on the other hand, many outcomes are possible. Coalition governments may form; government and opposition may cooperate in the legislative process; and the opposition may make gains in later elections.
All of these outcomes, however, are possible in presidential systems as
well. The Nigerian Second Republic had both a president and a coalition in the legislature. In presidential systems, government and opposition frequently cooperate in the legislative process; the United States
Congress is notorious for this kind of cooperation. And, of course, the
opposition may make gains in later presidential as well as parliamentary elections. The two are not different from each other by virtue of
any of these features.

The presidency, says Linz, is an office that encourages its occupant
to think he has more power than he actually does. Where several candidates have contested, a president elected on, say, one-third of the vote
gains full power. That is, the president is able to make appointments,
to propose and veto legislation, and, because of the president's fixed
term of office, even to survive fluctuations in the strength of party support. Precisely because the presidential term is fixed, a crisis in government during a presidential term is fixed, a crisis in government during
a presidential term becomes, according to Linz, a constitutional crisis,
since there is generally no lawful way to bring down a failed president
in the middle of his term. By contrast, a parliamentary government that
has lost its majority in the legislature will fall, whether or not elections
are due. So conflict is routinized and need not ripen into a crisis.

At the outset, one needs to call attention to a central assumption of
the Linz analysis: that the president will be elected by a first-past-the-
post system. From this assumption follow some of Linz's complaints.
In particular, he postulates that a president who has won a three- or
four-way contest with just a third of the vote could be opposed by the
great majority of legislators and of the electorate as well. Of course, this
implies that, after the election, the president's opponents are able to
coalesce in a way that was impossible for them before the election.
Needless to say, this is improbable, but the improbability should not
distract us from the threshold point. Presidents do not need to be elected
on a first-past-the-post basis. In a divided society, such as South Africa's, they should be elected by a different system, one that insures broadly

distributed support for the president—in the case of preferential voting, majority support. This solves the problem of a plurality president who thinks, erroneously, that he has a broad mandate.

Many of Linz's other objections to presidentialism also follow from his untenable assumption about the way presidents are inevitably elected. Linz suggests that presidential candidates habitually cultivate the extremes to facilitate election. But the supposed need to make concessions to extremists for the sake of building a plurality—any plurality—dissolves if presidents are not elected in this manner. Extremists, after all, cannot provide a majority; and the way presidents are elected in Nigeria and Sri Lanka puts a premium instead on appeals to the moderate middle. In both countries, in fact, the extremists are elected to parliament, not to the presidency.

In presidential systems, cabinets are weak, typically weaker than in parliamentary systems. The weakness of cabinet ministers in presidential systems is due to the separation of powers; since the cabinet ministers are not elected legislators, they owe their office to the president. If the president is racially and ethnically conciliatory, they, too, will be conciliatory—which is more important than whether they are weak or strong.

Presidents, says Linz, are prone to abuse executive power. Yet parliamentary regimes in Africa have had more than their share of abuse of power. The abuse of power is hardly a presidential monopoly.

Now it is true, of course, that presidents serve during a fixed term of years. Unlike parliamentary governments, they cannot be removed on a vote of no confidence. Nevertheless, the fixed term of a directly elected president is not more likely than the more flexible term of a parliament to cause a governmental crisis. Most parliamentary regimes in Africa and Asia have had secure majorities. Except when a government has called an early election in order to benefit from its transient popularity, practically every parliamentary regime that was not overthrown by a military coup has served its full term. In theory, it is easier to remove an unpopular parliamentary regime in the middle of its term than it is to remove an unpopular president. In practice, the need seldom arises, so the fixed term constitutes no distinction between presidential and parliamentary systems.

Like Linz, the Sri Lankans were concerned that a directly elected president might have only a small plurality and yet think himself possessed of a popular mandate, which could only bring him into conflict with the majority of the people. This was one reason the Sri Lankans insisted on aggregating second preferences so that whoever was elected necessarily had a majority behind him.[6] The ease of devising such a system vitiates the objection.

Once we open up the electoral possibilities, it goes without saying that the zero-sum, winner-take-all outcome said to be associated with presidential elections is not at all a structural feature of presidentialism. It is a structural feature of plurality elections. It is Westminster, the Mother of Parliaments, that partakes of the winner-take-all system, for precisely that electoral reason: first-past-the-post elections generally produce a majority of seats by shutting out third-party competitors. By the same token, the assertion that presidential systems are rigid, whereas parliamentary systems are more flexible, is farfetched. The rules of the political contest are, if anything, more fixed and brittle in parliamentary systems. In presidential systems, interbranch negotiations, often inter-party and interbranch negotiations (where the branches are controlled by different parties), are the norm.

These interbranch relations can sometimes be complicated. It was precisely this complication that appealed to the Nigerians in 1978 as they adopted a constitution with a separately elected president. The Nigerians correctly understood that the Biafra civil war had been brought on by the ability of one ethnic group to gain control of parliament, thereby utterly excluding others from power.[7] That was the zero-sum game Nigerians did not want to start up again, and that is why they opted for a separation of powers and for a separately elected president. As I have suggested earlier, a presidency based upon a vote-pooling formula makes the total exclusion of those who do not win a majority of legislative seats much less likely. Norms of negotiation and inclusion are more likely to develop with a separately elected president.

There is no reason to doubt that a South African president, elected directly by the people on the basis of a vote-pooling formula, would become a barrier to racial or ethnic exclusivity and that the office would become a focal point for intergroup conciliation and compromise. Members of all groups would have reason to claim a piece of the presidency if they helped elect the president.

As a matter of fact, if a president were elected by means of a Nige-

---

6. For the details, see Donald L. Horowitz, *Ethnic Groups in Conflict* (Berkeley and Los Angeles: University of California Press, 1985), p. 639.

7. For an account, see Donald L. Horowitz, "About-Face in Africa: The Return of Civilian Rule in Nigeria," *Yale Review* 68, no. 2 (Winter 1979): 192–206.

rian-type distribution formula or a Sri Lankan—type alternative voting formula, there is reason to think that such electoral requirements might also reduce the seriousness of a problem that has frequently been manifested in the American presidency. Since the president is separately elected and his fortunes are not tied directly to those of other candidates of his party, presidential popularity can be high even when the president's party is otherwise not faring well. Impressed with their personal popularity, some presidents come to believe that they owe nothing to their party. This is not a happy result for party government. But where geographic distribution requirements must be met and, even more, where a majority vote requirement can only be met by allocation of second preferences from voters whose first preference is a candidate of a different party, the only way to secure victory is, as we have seen, through interparty agreements. The president, therefore, cannot escape his party membership—it is the key to the vote exchanges that will elect him. This is particularly the case where the legislature is elected by the same method. Then the presidential election is likely to become part of a nationwide interparty electoral arrangement that may also have the effect of building bridges between the separately elected branches of government. The presidential illusion of an independent mandate, which Linz sees as an integral part of presidentialism, is extremely unlikely under these circumstances.

The argument can be carried further. In a fully democratic South Africa, most parties will tend to follow racial or ethnic lines. I have argued in Chapter 4 that the ANC's position that such parties should be prohibited is neither in accordance with democratic practice nor necessary for the workings of nonracial, nonethnic institutions. Such parties will, in fact, reflect the affiliations and sentiments of most South Africans. To repress them would be, in the most fundamental way, to repress democratic impulses. That does not mean, however, that such parties pose no problems for the operation of democratic politics. The demands of one racially or ethnically based party may be completely incompatible with the demands of another. Even though both function within the same system, they may not compete at all for votes, given the ascriptive character of their clienteles. When anti-system parties—such as those that demand an all-Black state or those that appeal to White separatism (a *Boerestaat* or *volkstaat*) or those that aim at a dictatorship of the proletariat—are added to this mix, there is ample reason to think that race and ideology together will constitute formidable challenges. Such parties, each the negation of the other, can produce centrifugal pulls in the party system. A separately elected president, however, can be a significant centripetal force.

A party system such as the one I have just described is characterized by what Giovanni Sartori calls "polarized pluralism."[8] In such a system, competition between the parties for votes is secondary to the ideological distinctiveness of each party. Pragmatism becomes rare, and parties at the extremes do not participate in conflict resolution. Rather, they impede it by stigmatizing compromise as impurity. In such a system, the center party (or parties) has some difficulty in performing the role of independent innovator. The center is more like a sum of the opposite forces that contend. The compromises of the center, in fact, feed the claims of the extremes. Sartori's models are Italy and the French Fourth Republic, but his description can be applied to polities divided along racial and ethnic lines as well as along ideological lines.

Sartori ties party polarization to elections by proportional representation in polities in which opinion is severely divided.[9] For PR, especially by party lists, permits the representation of every conflicting tendency in a fragmented polity. Any electoral system that, contrary to list-system PR, provides links among contending parties and incentives for them to cooperate is, of course, a counter to fragmentation and a support for the center. A presidency that rests upon such links (because otherwise the president cannot be elected) will necessarily become an institution pulling moderate parties toward the center and thus providing support for interparty coherence. Such an institution can compensate for tendencies to fragmentation and the possibility of immobilism inherent in the multiparty system that could otherwise emerge in South Africa. Without institutional supports for the center, extreme fragmentation can easily produce disillusionment with politics and demands for an end to democratic competition.[10] A vote-pooling electoral system for the legislature and a presidency also dependent on such an electoral system can provide the appropriate fabric to perform centripetal functions in South Africa.

Robert A. Dahl has noted that "all the nineteenth-century competitive regimes that have managed to survive as polyarchies in the twen-

8. Giovanni Sartori, "European Political Parties: The Case of Polarized Pluralism," in Joseph LaPalombara and Myron Weiner, eds., *Political Parties and Political Development* (Princeton: Princeton University Press, 1966), pp. 137–76.

9. Ibid., p. 168.

10. See Robert A. Dahl, *Polyarchy: Participation and Opposition* (New Haven: Yale University Press, 1971), pp. 122, 223.

tieth century have developed strong executives armed with extensive capacities for action."[11] Party fractionalization, he notes, is likely, in a parliamentary system, to produce a weak executive and a chance for an undemocratic, hegemonic reaction.[12] The French solution to this problem, adopted during the Algerian crisis, is a form of presidentialism. Dahl argues that, where interests proliferate in a political system, especially interests that have previously been ignored, assembly government with a weak executive will prove inadequate to respond authoritatively to them. Without an executive armed with the ability to take "vigorous and decisive action," the likely progression is from accelerated demand to inadequate response and, "in time, a clamor for the rapid creation of hegemonic controls."[13]

This argument for a strong executive sounds very much like the argument that was made for a strong president at the United States Constitutional Convention in 1787. The framers of the Constitution debated the merits of a single executive, a plural executive, and an executive wholly responsible to the legislature—which is to say, a parliamentary system.[14] They had had experience with what Dahl calls assembly government under the Articles of Confederation, whose only executive had consisted of committees established from time to time by the legislature. They had also had experience with the generally weak governors who had succeeded the colonial governors in the states. Both arrangements they found unsatisfactory. Wary of anything that smacked of elective monarchy, the delegates to the Constitutional Convention were equally disappointed with the results of unchecked legislative supremacy. In the end, the framers adopted a presidency modeled on the one state whose governor, directly elected and armed with broad powers (including the veto power), had succeeded in establishing a vigorous executive, capable, among other things, of putting down disorder. When, in *The Federalist,* Alexander Hamilton described the new office in terms of "energy . . . [d]ecision, activity, secrecy, and despatch,"[15] he was not so much reflecting the understanding of the framers as he was describing the contours of the modern executive that was to emerge much later.

South Africa is a country that will need a strong but accountable

11. Ibid., p. 121.
12. Ibid., pp. 122–23.
13. Ibid., p. 221.
14. The debates are reviewed in Donald L. Horowitz, "Is the Presidency Failing?" *The Public Interest,* no. 88 (Summer 1987): 3–27, at 7–11.
15. Alexander Hamilton et al., *The Federalist* (New York: Putnam, 1888; originally published 1788), no. 70.

executive. A fully democratic regime will inherit large problems and accumulated expectations. Some of these problems could well be used as a pretext to establish authoritarian rule. If the new regime is to remain democratic, it will have to embody some strong repositories of problem-solving capacity. In the abstract, such an executive need not be elected separately. In ordinary circumstances, cabinet government might develop such capacity, as it certainly has in Britain. But that is, in significant measure, because Britain has developed a sharply dichotomized system of government and opposition, which in turn rests on an electoral system that disadvantages third parties. I have argued—and so have others[16]—that such a system is inappropriate for divided societies and that South Africa ought to have electoral arrangements that simultaneously foster conciliation and generate a multiparty system. But, as I have just suggested, a South African multiparty system will have great difficulty producing a coherent, powerful executive responsible to parliament. In South Africa, therefore, to have both democracy and executive authority means having a separate, directly elected executive.

THE CONCILIATORY POTENTIAL OF FEDERALISM

The government of South Africa is highly centralized and has become even more centralized in recent decades. Although there are four provinces (Natal, the Cape, the Transvaal, and the Orange Free State), these are mere administrative units. Provincial councils, which might have been transformed into instruments of decentralization, have been abolished. The multiracial Regional Services Councils, designed to facilitate the efficient delivery of services to municipalities governed separately along racial lines, report to provincial administrators, who are appointed by Pretoria. The establishment of a strong State Security Council and the involvement of army and police officers in local government under the administration of P. W. Botha also contributed to the centralizing trend. Both the cabinet secretariat and the office of the State President became important centers of policy innovation and coordination. Although the involvement of the army and police in civilian affairs was reduced after F. W. de Klerk became State President in 1989, overall there has been an accumulation of power at the center.[17] To broach

16. See, e.g., Dahl, *Polyarchy*, p. 222; W. Arthur Lewis, *Politics in West Africa* (London: Oxford University Press, 1965), pp. 71–72.

17. Mervyn Frost, "Democratization: From Below or from Above?" (Grahamstown, South Africa, September 13, 1985; mimeo.); Hermann Giliomee, "Afrikaner Politics, 1977–87: From Afrikaner Nationalist Rule to Central State Hegemony," in John D. Brewer,

the possibility of a future federalism, therefore, is once again, as in the case of electoral systems, to suggest that an inclusive South Africa needs institutions quite different from those that White South Africa seems to find eminently suitable for itself.

The very idea thus gives rise to suspicion. Consequently, as of now, federalism is an issue that, to a considerable degree, divides Whites and Blacks in South Africa. Although there has been a surge of enthusiasm for federal arrangements among Whites,[18] many Black political leaders tend to think federalism is at odds with the concept of an undivided South Africa.[19] And so it is necessary to begin by disclaiming the sort of federalism one does not espouse. That is the federalism, or devolution in general, that aims to evade the consequences of Black representation at the center by decentralization, by substituting local autonomy for democracy in the country as a whole.[20] That is not the federalism I have in mind.

Far from the struggle of South Africa, students of so-called bicommunal polities—and if one saw South Africa as divided merely between White and Black, it would qualify as bicommunal—have argued that federalism is indispensable to peaceful accommodation in such polities.[21] In Africa, the Nigerians have concluded that federal arrangements suit their divided polity, and they have several times refined those arrangements to suit it better.

Elsewhere in Africa, political leaders had an interest at the time of

---

ed., *Can South Africa Survive? Five Minutes to Midnight* (New York: St. Martin's Press, 1989), pp. 127–30.

18. See Christopher R. Hill, *Change in South Africa: Blind Alleys or New Directions?* (Totowa, N.J.: Barnes & Noble, 1983), pp. 154–75. See also South African Institute of Race Relations, *News,* June 1985, p. 1, reporting Alan Paton's strong endorsement of federalism in his Hoernlé lecture of 1985.

19. See, e.g, Pierre de Vos, "NP Shift Poses New Challenge," *Democracy in Action* (Cape Town), May 1989, pp. 1, 5, at p. 5:

> Delegates differed sharply over the desirability of a federal system of government. Some felt that a federal system with its decentralisation of power would help to prevent the abuse of power by an all-powerful government. Other delegates argued that the ANC was formed in 1912 with the goal of forming one nation and said that a federal system could create division and retard the process of nation building.

20. Compare the different orientation in Fanie Cloete, "Decentralization: Instrument for Constitutional Development in South Africa," *Politikon* 15, no. 1 (June 1988): 16–30; Nic J. Rhoodie, "Federalism / Confederation as a Means of White-Black Conflict Resolution: Conceptual Dissonance in Nationalist Ranks," *Politikon* 7, no. 2 (December 1980): 101–10. For federalism and the Bantustan strategy, see Deon Geldenhuys, *South Africa's Black Homelands: Past Objectives, Present Realities and Future Developments* (Braamfontein: South African Institute of International Affairs, 1981; mimeo.), pp. 70–75.

21. Ivo D. Duchacek, "Dyadic Federations and Confederations," *Publius* 18, no. 2 (Spring 1988): 5–31.

independence in succeeding to all the power left by the colonialists. They had no desire at any stage to share power with governmental units at lower levels. The stronger the claim to federal arrangements, the greater was the resistance to them. In Ghana, Kwame Nkrumah turned aside the demands of Ashanti; in Uganda, Milton Obote terminated Buganda's essentially federal status. The governments of the Sudan and of Ethiopia might have averted long civil wars by instituting federal arrangements, but Khartoum resisted a federation of north and south, and Addis Ababa unilaterally abrogated the federal arrangement by which Eritrea had joined Ethiopia. Despite the increasing enthusiasm for and success of federalism in Nigeria, federalism generally remains only the wisdom of hindsight in Africa.

Since hindsight frequently follows warfare, it seems likely that there will be more federal states in Africa. Ethiopia is a logical candidate, because most of the groups in rebellion against the central government would far prefer autonomy to independence. "If there were a popular referendum" in Ethiopia, "there seems little doubt that the overwhelming vote would be in favour of federalism," which "offers no threat to the country's unity and may, in fact, serve to strengthen it . . . ."[22] Since the latest round of the Sudan civil war was also precipitated by a unilateral change in the devolution arrangements that had been agreed to earlier, it is reasonable to expect that a settlement will involve a restored and reinforced system of regional governments or outright federalism. It would be yet another South African tragedy to reject federalism out of hand at precisely the time that other African states embrace federalism in order to end their bitter struggles.

It is often supposed that federalism in an ethnically divided society is simply a way of providing political space in which minorities in the country as a whole can become majorities in the provinces or states of a federal union. As I shall note, federalism can, of course, perform that function—it can devolve power to groups that would otherwise be outvoted at the center. Some theorists hold that this sort of devolution to territorially concentrated groups is the only way to mitigate the zero-sum quality of politics in divided societies,[23] that a federal regime to make democracy possible in such societies requires homogeneous units.[24]

22. Colin Legum, *Third World Reports*, no. ME / 1 (London, August 9, 1989; mimeo.), p. 3.

23. Duchacek, "Dyadic Federations and Confederations," pp. 10, 12.

24. Ibid., p. 15; Murray Forsyth, "Introduction," in Murray Forsyth, ed., *Federalism and Nationalism* (New York: St. Martin's Press, 1989), p. 5.

That is one common way of thinking about the problem, but it is not the only way. Devolution to homogeneous areas certainly cannot be the main instrument of conflict reduction in South Africa, where, at the provincial level, groups are, in large measure, intermixed. In particular, there is no prospect that any minority racial group could form a majority in any territory likely to be accorded the status of a constituent unit of a federal South Africa. Nevertheless, federalism is important for South Africa, because it performs other functions that are not generally very well recognized. South Africans can benefit from these functions of federalism without in any way conceding the utility of devolution to homogeneous units on the homeland model.

These functions can be grouped essentially into four main categories. First, federalism can furnish support for an accommodative electoral formula. Second, federal units can provide arenas in which politicians are socialized in dealing with conflict in a divided society before they must do so at the national level. Third, devolution to territorial units can reinforce a function also performed by a separately elected president—namely, to disperse conflict by proliferating the points of power vertically, as a presidency would horizontally. Fourth, federal units can support the maintenance of democracy by making hegemony more difficult to achieve. All four of these functions can be served by federalism in South Africa.

The political institutions of a severely divided society connect with each other and can reinforce each other. Although the electoral system is perhaps the central institution for accommodation, its ability to perform this function is affected by the territorial units into which the state is carved. One of the important features of a federal system is its potential impact on party proliferation. To demonstrate this, it is necessary to return once again to Nigeria.

The Nigerian First Republic consisted of three main regions, each dominated by a single ethnic group. The Second Republic consisted of 19 states, about half of them more or less ethnically homogeneous and half decidedly heterogeneous. (The Third Republic will begin with 21 states.) In the First Republic, the entire, undivided Northern Region was controlled by the Northern People's Congress (NPC), a party dominated by Hausa-Fulani. Some Northern Region minorities, such as the Kanuri, concentrated in the northeast, had a political party representing them, but it failed badly in elections.

The reasons for this failure are rather clear. By controlling the Northern Region government, the NPC had the power of patronage, the power of reward and punishment. Had the Kanuri lined up solidly behind their own party, that party would have been consigned to futile opposition in the undivided North. When, however, the Northern Region was carved into ten states, a separate party based in the Kanuri areas flourished, for now it had enough potential votes, geographically concentrated, to control a state (Borno) and to win a plurality of seats in a neighboring state (Gongola). Kanuri voters saw that the new situation was different and that they were out from under the thumb of the Northern Regional government. As the artificially induced support of the successor to the NPC in the Second Republic declined, the support of the Kanuri party expanded. Similar effects of the proliferation of states on the growth of parties could be seen elsewhere in Nigeria, notably in Kano and Kaduna states, where another formerly impotent opposition party was revived.

A principal impact of the revised federal system of the Second Republic was not to abolish ethnically based parties. Rather, it was to rearrange their building blocks and confine them to something like their proportionate share of support, which the large regions of the First Republic had artificially distorted. The NPC had benefited from a winner-take-the-whole-region rule. Now its successor could only take states in which it actually had majority support. Changes in the structure of states thus induced changes in the structure of party competition. If a party, for the first time, had a chance of controlling a state government, it had a chance of persuading voters, who might have preferred it all along to the available alternatives, that it was no longer futile to vote for it. Federalism acted as an electoral reform, setting off areas from each other, making and unmaking legislative majorities by adjusting the territories in which their votes were to be counted.

The concomitant effect of this was to proliferate parties. Five parties contested the 1979 election. It will be noted, in fact, that the division of the Northern Region into ten states did in northern Nigeria what list-system proportional representation was unable to accomplish in Guyana: fragment the electoral support of the largest group. The resulting party proliferation meant that no party could count on very widely distributed support nationally, and yet distribution was required to secure the election of the president. Since the successor to the NPC started out with a smaller base than the NPC had had in the First Republic, it had every reason to reach across group lines and across the country to secure the requisite distribution for its candidate to become president. So the new federalism and the new electoral formula worked together in the service of interethnic accommodation.

The Nigerian experience thus contains both a general point and a more concrete one. The general point is to flag a question that always needs to be asked: How will the division of territory interact with electoral provisions? The specific point is that, if a multiparty system is essential for the creation of accommodative coalitions in South Africa, then federal arrangements are likely to enhance the incentives for the requisite party proliferation. In Nigeria, parties previously suppressed by the regional system grew up, but not in unmanageable numbers. There were never more than five parties with any significant support. By creating provincial arenas for parties to control, federalism can contribute substantially to multiparty democracy.

As I have noted, half the Nigerian states were heterogeneous, and some of the remaining states also contained more than one important subgroup of the same ethnic group. Intrastate heterogeneity had a major impact on the choice of the electoral formula. In their quest for a method of electing the president that would ameliorate intergroup tensions, some delegates to the Constituent Assembly explored the electoral college system used in the United States. The American electoral college, however, is based on a winner-take-all system in most states, and this could well have created discontent among a minority in any heterogeneous state. If the minority voted for a candidate who lost in that state, the minority's votes would be considered wasted and ineffective. Recognition of this fact drove delegates back to the distribution formula that was eventually adopted.[25]

The Nigerian experience makes it clear once again that the units of a federal system need not be ethnically homogeneous. In discussions in and of South Africa, there has been great confusion about the relation of group interests to federal units. On the one hand, the homelands have created the apprehension that homogeneous units, if they could in fact be formed, would be compartmentalizing and divisive. On the other hand, it has been suggested that, in South Africa and elsewhere, *only* homogeneous units are useful in reducing divisions.[26] Neither of these views can be sustained.

If there were homogeneous units—and, as indicated above, it is hard

25. I am drawing here on consultations with delegates to the Constituent Assembly during the time the assembly was sitting, in 1978.

26. For perspectives on this question, see André du Toit, *Federalism and Political Change in South Africa,* 1974 Maurice Webb Memorial Lectures (Durban: University of Natal, 1974), p. 17; Arend Lijphart and Diane R. Stanton, "A Democratic Blueprint for South Africa," in S. Prakash Sethi, ed., *The South African Quagmire* (Cambridge, Mass.: Ballinger, 1987), p. 92.

to believe that many such contiguous units could be created, given the geographic proximity of groups in South Africa—the political struggle to control such units would take place within, rather than between, groups. The feared divisiveness of such units may not be wholly conjured, but it is certainly exaggerated, as has been demonstrated by India's linguistically homogeneous states.

In any case, heterogeneous federal units can also contribute something to the reduction of conflict, as several of the Nigerian, Canadian, and Malaysian states, among others, have certainly shown. An important function heterogeneous states perform is to bring politicians of various groups together to govern at the state level, before they meet to govern at the national level. This is a political socialization function that can help them to form intergroup ties at an early point. The people I called in Chapter 4 the "bottom-uppers"—those who advocated using existing structures to change the system as opportunities for multiracial ventures arose—do not generally point to the utility of such efforts as practical training in interracial (and interethnic) politics. But that is what the experience would be in practice. To achieve such goals, powers to be devolved on the federal units should be chosen carefully so as to maximize the chance for reciprocity and cooperation to take hold before aspiring state-level politicians need to take on more contentious issues at the national level. In Malaysia, quite fortuitously, state cabinets (called executive councils) have jurisdiction over land allocation for development. This is an issue on which there were, for a long time, symbiotic relationships between Chinese entrepreneurs, active in politics, and Malay politicians.

In light of the constructive intergroup relations that began to germinate at the local level during the period of strong United Democratic Front activity in the mid-1980s,[27] local government would seem to be a promising arena for what is sometimes called a "third tier of federalism." In post-colonial Asian and African states, even federal states, it has been quite common for central authorities to seize on any pretext to dissolve elected local councils and replace them with more malleable political allies. Responding to such problems, the Nigerian Constitution of 1978 guaranteed the maintenance of democratically elected local governments, with a 10 percent allocation of total revenue.[28] Comparable South African guarantees would provide yet another site for inter-

27. See Chapter 4, pp. 146–47, above.
28. See Martin Dent, "Federalism in Africa, with Special Reference to Nigeria," in Forsyth, ed., *Federalism and Nationalism*, pp. 200–01.

group political relations to grow, at a stage before politicians need to work with each other at the center. Local governments might become "nodes of interracial cooperation and accommodation . . . ."[29] A similar point has been made by Dahl: "Smaller representative units provide training in solving concrete, comprehensible problems for which abstract ideological solutions are less relevant. Confronting these problems may unite groups that would be antagonistic in national political life."[30]

If there is a dynamic political life at lower levels, it will in any case be somewhat easier to preserve a democratic system at the national level, against a variety of challenges. State and local politicians will have a stake, not only in working together, but also in climbing the ladder to more power. Authoritarian measures make that climb less predictable or knock the ladder down altogether. Local politicians thus have a vested interest in democratic politics at higher levels.

Another function of federalism is to make control of the center less urgent, especially if the federal units have substantial powers. This is an argument that has previously been advanced for federalism and devolution in South Africa and elsewhere,[31] and it is cogent. Unfortunately, in some plans, federalism has been tied to consociational solutions, so that the proposed devolution would be to bodies in which the various racial groups would have mutual vetoes. Consociational ideas, however, are not integral to federalism, and federal states in divided societies generally do not delegate veto powers to groups. India, Nigeria, Canada, and Malaysia are all ethnically conflict-prone federal states that have benefited from federalism without any practice of mutual vetoes. And, of course, federalism thrives in the adversary, nonconsociational political system of the United States. To choose federalism, then, is by no means to choose consociationalism, which, as I have argued in Chapter 4, would not be apt for South Africa's problems.

What federalism can do in a divided society like South Africa's is to proliferate the points of power and so make control of the center less vital and pressing. A party disappointed in its quest for power at the

29. Slabbert and Welsh, *South Africa's Options,* p. 129.
30. Dahl, *Polyarchy,* p. 226.
31. Slabbert and Welsh, *South Africa's Options,* pp. 141–42; Political Commission of the Study Project on Christianity in Apartheid Society, *South Africa's Political Alternatives,* SPRO-CAS Publication no. 10 (Johannesburg: Ravan Press, 1973), pp. 201–07; Masipula Sithole, "Zimbabwe: In Search of a Stable Democracy," in Larry Diamond et al., eds., *Democracy in Developing Countries,* vol. 2, *Africa* (Boulder, Colo.: Lynne Rienner, 1988), p. 253.

center might still capture control of a state or might at least gain influence, position, or patronage at the state level that is denied to it at the federal level. National politics in a great many African countries has been intensely fought, because of the zero-sum quality of the stakes. An inestimable benefit of federalism inheres in its capacity to lower the high temperature of politics at the center by reducing the all-or-nothing nature of the stakes at that level.

A related function, not at all dependent on homogeneity—indeed, heightened if the units are heterogeneous—is to identify issues on which states, rather than groups, may disagree because the interests of states may differ from each other. This has certainly been a prime benefit of federalism in Nigeria, where some states discovered that they had common interests—on issues of resources and revenue, for example—and others discovered that they had disparate interests, all irrespective of common ethnicity.[32] The less issues run along a single intergroup axis, the more complex the issue agenda is, the less likely a political system is to move toward unrestrained intergroup conflict.

A crucial function of federalism for South Africa resides in the ability of federal units to help counter drives toward hegemony by any one group over the entire state. Consider how much more difficult it would have been for the South African state to become the exclusive preserve of Afrikaners had a federal system been adopted, instead of a unitary government, in 1909. Natal, where there was, among Whites, an English-speaking majority, would not readily have acquiesced in Afrikaner domination.[33] Changing political balances in the other provinces, despite their Afrikaner majorities, might also have complicated the task, which, in the event, was made so simple that it entailed merely gaining a plurality of votes at the national polls in 1948.

There is no prospect that any minority racial group could constitute a majority in any likely federal unit in a new South Africa. Coloureds might well form a plurality in a federal unit or units in the Cape; but, in a vote-pooling electoral system, plurality support would not translate into one-race control. It is quite likely, however, depending on how federal units are constructed, that large African ethnic groups, such as Zulu or Xhosa, could form a majority of the electorate in some federal units. If this should happen, there would still be conflict-reducing ben-

32. For the Nigerian case, see Horowitz, *Ethnic Groups in Conflict*, pp. 602–13.
33. See David Welsh, "Federalism and the Problem of South Africa," in Forsyth, ed., *Federalism and Nationalism*, p. 260.

efits from federalism, but not exactly the same benefits that would flow in thoroughly heterogeneous states.

Before I enumerate these benefits, it is necessary to dispel what would certainly be a significant apprehension in South Africa, if federalism were to permit a single ethnic group to gain a majority of seats in a state. It is most unlikely that any such devolution would worsen group conflict at the national level. Rather, competition to control such a unit in a federation would take place along subethnic lines, as it has in Nigeria and India, thereby mitigating the ethnic solidarity of any such group. If the large ethnic groups were spread among two or more states, those states and their populations would find that, among themselves, they had some common interests and some divergent interests. The experience of the Second Republic in Nigeria, with many heterogeneous states and many homogeneous states as well, but with none of the largest groups concentrated in a single state, makes it very clear that the mere coincidence of ethnicity with territory does not provide a foundation for insuperable ethnic conflict at the center.

On the other hand, consider the benefits. With a few exceptions, Malaysia has heterogeneous states. Malays are a majority in most of the states, but, in several, Chinese outnumber Malays. In one of these states, Penang, it became customary for the state chief minister to be a Chinese, regardless of whether the state was controlled by the party ruling at the center or by an opposition party. By such conventions, a group that felt increasingly thwarted at the center could attain a measure of political satisfaction at the state level. This is a generalizable benefit of federalism. In no complex society can it be expected that all groups will have a sense of evenly distributed participation in power at the center. If the distribution of power is different in the federal units, this can provide a modicum of compensation.[34]

Thus far, perhaps the only group predictably in this position might be Zulu in Natal. Among Charterists and Africanists, the prospect of a territorial foundation for Zulu ethnic nationalism is anathema. This particular centralizing disposition, if pursued in action, will almost surely create a self-fulfilling prophecy. If most Zulu in Natal continue to support a political party without much support outside Natal and if that party does not form part of the ruling coalition at the center, a share of power in a federal unit can mitigate alienation.

34. The same point is made for South Africa in ibid., p. 262.

The fact of the matter is that early, generous devolution is far more likely to avert than to abet ethnic separatism.[35] Where a territorially based ethnic minority is politically out of step with other groups, uncompromising centralism in the guise of democratic majoritarianism will inevitably suppress that minority and provoke a reaction. Where, however, regional autonomy or federalism—on a territorial and not an ethnic or "homeland" basis—allows such minorities nationally to form majorities locally, the result is unlikely to be an aggravation of separatism.

Unfortunately, a good many governments have proceeded on the opposite assumption—that devolution feeds centrifugal forces. The unhappy results are visible in large parts of Asia and Africa. Zulu sentiment may be strong, but it is not separatist. With large numbers of Zulu living outside Natal, territorial separatism would not be a strategy of choice. It would be entirely gratuitous to turn Natal into a region with a grievance, another Buganda, facilitating a slide to unrestrained conflict—or worse. But doctrinaire centralism or equally doctrinaire inhospitability to ethnically based party allegiance could certainly do so. Fortunately, there are at least some signs of alternative currents in Charterist thinking.[36]

To the extent that federal and state power holders are not identical— for example, if a party not in the ruling coalition at the center governs a state—one-party hegemony becomes much more difficult to impose. It is then, in the first place, implausible to claim that, by returning the same party repeatedly to power at the center, the voters have in fact cast their ballots for that party in a more elemental and permanent way. This is the usual claim of aspiring single-party authoritarians, made, for

35. For the relationship of devolution to separatism, see Horowitz, *Ethnic Groups in Conflict*, pp. 622–28.

36. See Gerhard Maré, "Inkatha: Is Your Enemy's Enemy Automatically Your Friend?" *Work in Progress*, no. 60 (August–September 1989): 26–30, at 30:

It would, however, be short-sighted to reject federalism simply because Inkatha supports it. There may well be federal options that deserve to be examined because they do not reinforce the state's ethnic fragmentation while allowing democratic decentralisation. . . .

Again, the danger of denying the strength of cultural sentiments simply because they are part of the manipulations of Inkatha must be stressed. A national identity and a national culture cannot be wished into existence. It is one of the most delicate areas of future reconstruction and present practice. The organizations of the working class, especially, have a central role to play here, despite the fact that ethnic mobilisation has featured in working-class organisations both locally and elsewhere in the world.

example, by Robert Mugabe after the Zimbabwe elections of 1990. Beyond that, where states are governed by different parties, there are focal points for opposition to undemocratic, single-party hegemony. Again, the federal experience of India, Malaysia, and Nigeria is revealing. All three have experienced recurrent divergence between ruling parties at the center and in some states, usually divergence based on ethnic politics. In India, a fair number of states have been won by opposition parties at various times. In the Nigerian Second Republic, the president came from a party that controlled only about half the states. In Malaysia, only a few states have been opposition controlled. In none of these cases has the phenomenon made efficient government impossible. In all three, the divergence has made for stronger democracy. In India and Malaysia, dominant parties at the center could not easily have aspired to a more permanent identification with the central state in the face of claims to the contrary at the level of some of the federal units. The possibilities inherent in federalism, then, constitute one small part of the answer to the problem of hegemony raised in Chapter 1.

For South Africa, therefore, the benefits of federalism are substantial, but the precise configuration of federal units requires further consideration. We know much more about this now than previously, and we are in a good position to dispel some of the former mythology. It used to be said, for example, that participants in successful federations had to "feel federal,"[37] had to belong to preexisting units and simultaneously value the wider federation for its own sake. We know now from the many new states that have been carved out in India and Nigeria that a dynamic federation does not require this kind of unity-from-the-bottom-up feeling. Far from being a prerequisite to federalism, state-level loyalties—which are not coterminous with ethnic loyalties—can actually be reinforced by federal arrangements, as they certainly have been in Malaysia and Nigeria. What this means is that there is much scope for choice in the number, powers, and location of the federal units.

Relative equality of population and power among the units is usually a sound principle, as John Stuart Mill recognized very clearly.[38] Extreme population imbalances usually cause problems of the sort the Nigerian First Republic experienced. The South African government's nine

37. See du Toit, *Federalism and Political Change in South Africa*, pp. 27–28.
38. John Stuart Mill, *Representative Government* (New York: Dutton, 1951; originally published 1861), p. 496.

regions, created for development planning, have been suggested by some pro-federalists as a starting point.[39] They crosscut a number of homeland and other political boundaries. Using those regions or units like them as federal building blocks would make clear that federalism is not a continuation of the Bantustan policy.

The functions of the units in intergroup accommodation would require that elections be conducted by means of conciliatory, vote-pooling electoral formulae. The most important link between the federal units and the center is, of course, an upper house in which the federal units are equally represented by democratically elected senators or some equivalent. This is not strictly necessary—India and Malaysia do without an upper house composed in this way[40]—but Nigeria has found the senate to be a useful body. Unlike formal or informal conferences of state chief ministers, which tend to come into being in the absence of an elected upper house, a senate consists of representatives elected exclusively to serve in the federal government.[41] Conferences of chief ministers generally signify, as they have increasingly in Canada, strong component units and a weak center—something akin to a confederation—whereas senators signify no such thing: they are not mere delegates or ambassadors from the states.

If federalism is to flourish in South Africa, the creation of the initial units and of the units demanded later—for there may be such demands—needs to take place as part of the democratic process itself. And there is the rub. Federalism is designed to take some of the zero-sum quality out of politics, as I have suggested, but the creation of a federal system depends in some measure on transcending zero-sum conceptions in the first instance. As David Welsh has noted, however, "An orientation towards politics that sees the struggle for power in zero-sum terms has become part of South Africa's political culture."[42]

39. Welsh, "Federalism and the Problem of South Africa," p. 275; Charles Simkins, *Reconstructing South African Liberalism* (Johannesburg: South African Institute of Race Relations, 1986; mimeo.), pp. 39–41, 78.

40. India's upper house is indirectly elected on the basis of state population, not equality. Part of Malaysia's upper house is indirectly elected, and part is appointed, the latter on the basis of criteria other than state origins. In both cases, the upper house functions, at best, on the model of a rather passive House of Lords rather than as an active Australian or American Senate.

41. A useful discussion of the successive Nigerian arrangements is contained in Dent, "Federalism in Africa, with Special Reference to Nigeria," p. 193. Dent remarks: "It is unusual and undesirable in federal systems to give the state governors or chief ministers a powerful voice in the federal governing body for it tends to make the national authority appear as the sum of the state authorities."

42. "Federalism and the Problem of South Africa," p. 251.

STRUCTURING THE ARMED FORCES

In a state undergoing fundamental political change, the armed forces must be considered a critical part of the governmental structure. The majority of sub–Saharan African countries have experienced successful military coups against their civilian governments. Most of the rest have experienced failed coup attempts, and several states have been immune to military takeovers only because they have no armies. The military coup d'état is a major threat to democracy in a future South Africa.

The matter is, of course, complicated by the racial composition of the South African armed forces. A White regime has had White-controlled forces. The police consists of about equal numbers of Blacks and Whites. Predictably, the number of Black commissioned police officers was very low until the late 1970s. In the period of "reform apartheid," however, this began to change. By 1980, there were 85 Black commissioned police officers and 940 Black warrant officers.[43] Of the three military services, the navy has been, in some ways, the best integrated, with a strong complement of Coloureds and Indians and, in support roles, Xhosa as well.[44] Coloured and Indian officers have served since 1978, and shipboard living quarters have been integrated.[45] The army has long had a majority of White conscripts. Of the one-quarter of the army that consists of professional soldiers, between a quarter and a third are Black or Coloured. Black soldiers have been divided between a nonethnic Black battalion and several ethnically based units (Zulu, Swazi, Venda, and Shangaan).[46] Although the training in the Black battalion was rigorous from the outset, commissions for Black line officers were slow in coming.[47] Despite a late start, however, Blacks have a foothold in the South African armed forces, including the officer corps.[48]

It goes without saying that all units have been firmly under White control and that Black officers have been either apolitical or willing to overlook the abuses of the apartheid regime for the sake of a modestly promising professional career. The question is what kind of control the

---

43. Kenneth W. Grundy, *Soldiers without Politics: Blacks in the South African Armed Forces* (Berkeley and Los Angeles: University of California Press, 1983), p. 144.

44. Ibid., p. 172.

45. Ibid., p. 189; Colin Legum, ed., *Africa Contemporary Record, 1984–85* (New York: Africana, 1986), p. B770.

46. Grundy, *Soldiers without Politics*, p. 198.

47. Ibid., p. 205.

48. See Colin Legum and Marion E. Doro, eds., *Africa Contemporary Record, 1987–88* (New York: Africana, 1989), pp. B744–45.

armed forces can be brought under and what uses apolitical profession-alism might have in a future South Africa. There are other questions as well. How to integrate a predominantly White military? What military role, if any, should be accorded to insurgent units, particularly the ANC's Umkhonto we Sizwe, which have fought the White regime, principally through sabotage? Above all, are there any measures that can be taken by a fully democratic civilian regime to prevent military intervention in politics?

Given the heavy reliance of the White regime on White conscripts for manpower, the integration of the forces should be less difficult than if there were a large professional army. Conscription is reversible, or, if necessary, it can be made universal.

More important will be the integration of the officer corps. Even if the South African Defence Force is thoroughly reconstructed, initially there will still be strong generational differences in seniority, with White officers predominating in the field grades and Black officers below. This is a quite typical cleavage in the officer corps of ethnically divided so-cieties, when sources of recruitment change over time or change as the ethnic bases of regimes change.

Imaginably, a new regime might make creative use of this cleavage to guarantee military nonintervention, but this is a dangerous course. The guarantee of civilian rule would then be that the threat of a coup would be deterred by the prospect of another coup. At least that is so when mutually suspicious officers confront each other within the armed forces. If the trip wire fails, there will almost certainly be, not one coup, but two and possibly a good deal of fighting along racial lines, all of which would set the country well on the way to pretorianism, if not civil war.

In the 1960s, countries such as Nigeria and Sierra Leone were doubly divided. The civilian regime was composed principally of members of one ethnic group, and the senior officer corps was composed dispropor-tionately of members of another. Junior officers were ethnically differ-entiated from the senior officers. Both countries did indeed experience a coup and a countercoup. All four coups were organized along identi-fiable ethnic lines. The Nigerian countercoup of July 1966 was espe-cially bloody, and it led to the anti-Ibo attacks in Northern Nigeria that were the prelude to the Biafra War. Integration of the officer corps and the prevention of military coups are thus intimately linked. A racial cleavage between junior and senior officers cannot be counted on to deter coups.

There are also perils attending the several possible strategies of dealing with former insurgent units. Hasty demobilization led to successful action by ex-soldiers against civilian regimes in Togo and Zanzibar. More skillful demobilization was carried out successfully by the newly independent government in Kenya, which chose not to incorporate the ex–"Mau Mau" guerrillas into the inherited colonial armed forces that had fought them for years. On the other hand, strategies of incorporating ex-guerrillas that leave their units more or less intact have repeatedly resulted in fighting between them and the regular army long after both were supposed to be on the same side. This was the case in Burma, in Indonesia, and—counting the internal and external units as separate forces—in Algeria as well.[49] Apart from its generally disintegrative effects, fighting of this kind is likely to make the armed forces more important to the regime and thus to constitute an argument for military rule. Skillful demobilization or skillful integration of personnel into established units is therefore the prudent course.

Even this cursory glance at the subject shows just how ticklish a task coup prevention is. In fact, there are two main approaches to coup-proofing. The first involves the performance of the civilian regime. The second involves civilian intervention in the composition of the armed forces. Neither approach is risk free.

Despite the common occurrence of military intervention in politics, a good many civilian regimes start out with a significant margin of political credit. Military officers are inclined, in the first instance, to accord legitimacy to elected governments, to be diffident about their own capacity for political judgments, and to avoid merging the civilian and military spheres. A careless or malevolent regime, however, can turn these predispositions around. Politicians who provide reason to doubt their good faith and provide evidence of their vengefulness or excessive ambition undercut the legitimacy of their regime in the eyes of officers. Civilians who continually use military force to bail them out of political conflict virtually invite officers to make their own political judgments. Regimes that use the military in politics and interfere unduly in military matters, by playing favorites in promotions and postings, breach the boundary between the two spheres and tempt armies to do the same. On all of these matters, evidence of propriety and correctness on the part of a civilian government will go a long way to induce gestures of reciprocal nonintervention.[50]

49. See Horowitz, *Ethnic Groups in Conflict*, pp. 514–21.
50. For a coup attempt precipitated by civilian imprudence in these matters, see Donald L. Horowitz, *Coup Theories and Officers' Motives: Sri Lanka in Comparative Perspective* (Princeton: Princeton University Press, 1980), pp. 183–91.

The same is true for the orientation of the civilian regime in matters of intergroup relations. A regime whose composition is ethnically or racially skewed tempts fate if it engages in predictably biased action. Policies that are discriminatory and show the regime to be the creature of some groups and not others provide motives for groups that are better represented in the armed forces than they are in the civilian government to overthrow the civilians. This is a recurrent source of military intervention in Africa.

The first set of coup prevention strategies, then, involves restraint—restraint in political activity that breaches civil-military boundaries and restraint in pursuing the untrammeled interests of some groups at the expense of others who happen to have less influence at any moment with the regime. The second strategy is, by contrast, activist. This means there is sometimes an unavoidable choice between prudence and boldness. Often it is difficult to have both.

If a civilian regime confronts a military officer corps of decidedly different racial and ethnic composition, there are possibilities for military intervention, no matter what the civilians do. If they leave the officer corps skewed, they risk an unfriendly reception when their policies or appointments disappoint the group or groups disproportionately represented among the officers. If the civilians move to alter the composition of the officer corps so as to counter the skewing, they risk a coup in reaction to or sometimes in anticipation of such measures. Every coup-proofing method involving the composition of the officer corps has carried with it, in Africa, the substantial risk that it would precipitate the very coup it was designed to avert.[51]

Here, however, the apartheid background gives a new South African regime an advantage not enjoyed by other African governments. Because apartheid consisted of discrimination and limitation of opportunity, it is very clear that the White bias of the officer corps is not the product of accident or of the differential disposition of various groups to seek careers in different sectors, as it is in many other countries; it was part and parcel of apartheid. A great constitutional change requires at the same time a compositional change in the instruments of force, and it is hardly farfetched to think that this will be widely understood as the process of change is planned. And so a new, fully democratic South African government will have a mandate to do precisely what

---

51. I have laid out the methods and assessed their effectiveness in a section called "Coup-Proofing: The Art of Prevention," in Horowitz, *Ethnic Groups in Conflict*, pp. 532–59.

other African governments could do only at substantial risk to themselves—namely, change the composition of the officer corps.

That mandate alone, of course, will not solve all problems in civil-military relations. Inevitably, there will be generational problems, for the new officers will be junior—though the generational cleavage can be reduced by the (highly selective) commissioning of a few senior non-commissioned officers to senior officers' billets. There will also be problems of which compositional strategy to adopt. One choice is to balance each unit racially and perhaps ethnically from inside. Another is to balance units from outside, creating new and differently composed units. By and large, the former is regarded by officers as more legitimate; it builds fewer resentments between units that can be seen as unequally privileged; and it creates fewer risks of fighting between ascriptively differentiated units. Perhaps most important of all, integration within units is consonant with nonracial, nonethnic ideals, whereas balance between units is not.

The armed forces are bound to be a contentious issue. But the South African situation is such that more than the usual ratio of prevention to provocation can be obtained by an agreed compositional strategy at the outset. If this is then followed by policies that respect civil-military boundaries and avoid blatant group favoritism—which should be the case if the regime is based on vote pooling—the civilian regime should have some prospect of enduring. That is not to say it will be easy to restructure the armed forces or avoid a coup, only that it is possible.

THE PROBLEM OF INEQUALITY

South Africa, it goes without saying, is an extremely unequal society. Not merely have opportunities been limited by race, but resources have been allocated unequally as well. I have suggested in Chapter 4 that it would be a mistake to make the reduction of inequality part of a constitutional bargain, since the returns from such deals are likely to be uneven and therefore disappointing. Nevertheless, in the South African context, the question of inequality, if it is not strictly a matter of political structure, necessarily has a constitutional status. Inequality is surely the one policy question that could delegitimize a new regime, and it needs to be considered at the outset.

Viewed abstractly, the dimensions of the problem are so enormous that it would be easy to succumb to pessimism. While income gaps between the races have been declining over the years, they are still large.

Average real wages for Africans doubled from 1970 to 1984, and the Black share of total personal income rose by more than 50 percent in that period. From 1985 to 1986, earnings for Africans increased by 18 percent; earnings for Whites grew by 13 percent. The ratio of White to African individual earnings was more than 4 to 1 in 1980; by 1986, it was below 3.5 to 1. The same goes for the ratio of White to Indian earnings, which went from significantly more than 2 to 1 to significantly less than 2 to 1, and for the ratio of White to Coloured earnings, which was 3 to 1 in 1980 and 2.7 to 1 by 1986.[52] Nevertheless, the ratios are very wide by any standard. South Africa's income distribution is among the most unequal anywhere.[53]

While the ratios will continue to close in the short run, the long-term outlook is much less certain. In education, the government's long-standing policy of dramatically unequal expenditure by race has combined with the political protests of the 1980s to produce some daunting challenges. These will undoubtedly affect prospects for reduction of income inequalities.

As of 1981, South Africa had a literacy rate of only 57 percent. The world rank for South Africa for male literacy was 88th, which placed it behind such poor countries as Cambodia, Zambia, Syria, Honduras, and Egypt. The South African rank for females was higher, but the country still placed 69th. Consistent with these figures, educational expenditure in relation to gross national product was 4.3 percent, which placed South Africa 87th in 1980. Since White literacy and expenditure on White education are both appreciably higher, these figures mask Black South Africa's significantly lower rank.[54] African literacy, in fact, is right around 50 percent.

Expenditures on African education have been rising rapidly. In 1987–88, they increased by 31 percent over the previous year's expenditure, compared to an increase of 16 percent for Coloured, 10 percent for Indian, and 9 percent for White education.[55] Per capita expenditure

52. The percentages and ratios in this paragraph are derived from Carole Cooper et al., *Race Relations Survey, 1987 / 88* (Johannesburg: South African Institute of Race Relations, 1988), p. 289; Carole Cooper et al., *Race Relations Survey, 1986* (Johannesburg: South African Institute of Race Relations, 1987), pt. 2, p. 717; Carole Cooper et al., *Race Relations Survey, 1985* (Johannesburg: South African Institute of Race Relations, 1986), p. 131.

53. Stephen R. Lewis, Jr., *The Economics of Apartheid* (New York: Council on Foreign Relations Press, 1990), p. 40.

54. The figures are provided in George Thomas Kurian, ed., *World Education Encyclopedia* (New York: Facts on File, 1988), pp. 1660, 1661, 1678.

55. Cooper et al., *Race Relations Survey 1987 / 88*, pp. 147–49.

ratios, although improving, were grossly unequal. Five times as much was spent on White education per capita as on African education per capita outside the so-called homelands.[56] Pupil-teacher ratios were two and a half times better in White schools than in African schools outside the four nominally independent homelands.[57]

Given time, these gaps, too, might close, as they generally had been closing in the 1980s. But, in education, time appears to have run out. One widely used indicator of educational achievement is the matriculation examination, taken upon completion of high school.[58] For several years in the mid-1980s, African pass rates hovered within 1 percentage point, on either side of 50 percent. This compared to White pass rates in excess of 90 percent, Indian rates from 85 percent to 87 percent, and Coloured rates that fluctuated between 64 percent and 73 percent.[59] Then, in 1989, the African pass rate fell to its lowest level since 1962, 42 percent, precipitating a wave of concern for the future among Black leaders.[60] It seems clear that the disrupted school years, beginning in the mid-1980s, had finally had a devastating effect on academic achievement. The results were notably worse in centers of political protest, such as Soweto, where pass rates were typically 15 and 20 percentage points lower.

Many different forces may have contributed to these results. More African students have been enrolled in secondary school in recent years. To some extent, declines in pass rates may reflect a larger number of poorly prepared students. When school boycotts were called in the mid-1980s, many affluent Black pupils abandoned township schools for homeland schools, for integrated but predominantly White schools, or for overseas schools.[61] Consequently, as more poorly prepared students were entering high schools, better prepared students were leaving. By the late 1980s, when the boycotts ended, education had not returned to its former state. Absenteeism, tardiness, and disorder became the norm. Little learning took place in high schools in Soweto and other politically active townships. By early 1990, disruption was so great that virtually

56. Ibid., p 151.
57. Ibid., p. 158.
58. For a critique of matriculation examinations as an indicator of academic achievement, see C. S. Potter and A. N. Jamotte, "African Matric Results: Dubious Indicators of Academic Merit," *Indicator South Africa* 3, no. 1 (Winter 1985): 10–13.
59. Cooper et al., *Race Relations Survey, 1987 / 88*, p. 165.
60. *New York Times*, December 31, 1989.
61. Nomavenda Mathiane, *South Africa: Diary of Troubled Times* (New York: Freedom House, 1989), pp. 137–38.

no instruction was being conducted in some 40 percent of all Black schools. In the Johannesburg townships, the schools were simply not functioning. Teachers, dispirited, sought other opportunities, and the morale of those who stayed was low.[62]

At universities with Black students, learning also became a sporadic phenomenon. Troops were deployed to counter protests at some African campuses. At the University of Durban–Westville, newly admitted African students were in conflict with Indian students, for whom the apartheid regime had designed the institution. Most Indians moved out of student hostels, many out of the university altogether.[63] The rector of the University of the Western Cape, a so-called Coloured institution but now with African students as well, dedicated the university to the struggle, designating it the "home of the Left."[64] Protests and mass meetings became commonplace. A new library was underutilized. Prospective speakers were vetted carefully for their political line, and the campus generally had an atmosphere of groupthink about it. Students who wanted to continue learning found progress slow. Some of these conditions were in evidence at all the English-medium campuses,[65] but the African, Indian, and Coloured institutions labored under special handicaps.

The curriculum was, in a significant way, delegitimized. "Racist gutter education" was to be replaced with such subjects as "people's history."[66] And so, at the secondary and tertiary levels, the educational system was in turmoil at the very time that education could play a significant part in the dramatic reduction of inequality.

This is obviously not the place to embark on a full-scale examination of income and education policy in a future South Africa. Nevertheless, a few observations about the political consequences of these matters are in order.

First of all, inequality will not be cured in a few years, unless, of course, draconian measures are taken, and such measures would simultaneously destroy the economy, reduce wealth, and level downward.

---

62. For an on-the-ground account, see ibid., pp. 33–37, 137–46. I am also drawing on a lengthy conversation with a Soweto high school teacher, August 5, 1989.

63. I am drawing on a conversation with a lecturer at the University of Durban–Westville, August 1, 1989.

64. See *Cape Times* (Cape Town), June 6, 1987.

65. See the account of the disruption of a meeting at the University of Witwatersrand, *Natal Witness* (Pietermaritzburg), August 1, 1989.

66. See, e.g., "The Western Cape," in Fatima Meer, ed., *Resistance in the Townships* (Durban: Madiba, 1989), p. 61.

Such measures would seem most unlikely, however, either to be taken or to be effective in meeting African aspirations. It seems perfectly obvious that Africans wish to be leveled up. Barring such draconian measures, the demand for African talent in South Africa's industrial economy is likely to be so substantial as to reduce the attractiveness of careers in teaching. Even with increased expenditure, the education crisis will not end soon.

Put together the combination of continuing, albeit reduced, inequality, a stumbling educational system, and what has become a tradition of political activism at the expense of learning in the schools. Does this combination portend a level of discontent that is incompatible with democracy or incompatible with interracial accommodation? No one can be certain, but there is still ground for very modest optimism. The evidence, such as it is, derives from the pattern of articulated Black grievances and the extent to which these might be ameliorated by the inauguration of an inclusive, democratic regime.

A revealing sample survey, conducted in all major urban areas of South Africa in 1985, inquired into levels of satisfaction in a variety of everyday domains.[67] Two conclusions emerge very clearly from the survey. The first is that Africans were far more dissatisfied with their lot than were respondents of any other group, including Coloureds and Indians. The differences were often in the range of 25 or 30 percentage points. For example, asked about personal progress at work, only 59 percent of Africans said they were satisfied or very satisfied, compared to 86 percent of Coloureds, 85 percent of Indians, and 88 percent of Whites. Second, African discontent was differentiated by subject matter. The closer to objective, impersonal matters (water supply, access to facilities, food, etc.) or to purely private life (friends and family), the higher the levels of satisfaction reported. Even on those dimensions, however, African satisfaction levels were invariably below those of other groups. The closer to politics, income, and intergroup relations, the lower were the levels of African satisfaction. Only 26 percent were satisfied with their "life compared to other races," only 27 percent with their nonexistent voting rights, 24 percent with "wages and salaries," and 20 percent with the cost of transport required to carry them from their distant Black townships to their places of work.[68] There was discontent

67. V. Moller et al., "Quality of Life and Race in South Africa: A Preliminary Analysis" (Centre for Applied Social Sciences, University of Natal, Durban, September 1985; unpublished paper).

68. Ibid., pp. 21–22.

with some aspects of housing and working conditions, but it was not in the same range as the discontent with politics, income, and transport.

In some ways, transport may be the most difficult problem. Its source is the Group Areas Act, which has segregated the races residentially and typically placed Africans far from city centers. The act, of course, will be repealed. Its enforcement in so-called gray areas (White areas to which Blacks have quietly moved) has become nearly moribund in any case. But, without massive investment, housing locations for most people will not change quickly. The cost of transportation can be subsidized in the interim, although, given the number of people transported long distances every day, this, too, would be expensive. Transport is a good example of the magnitude of the problems facing a successor regime.

Focusing on only the most severe grievances, this leaves politics and income. Even in the face of increased demands on resources, the end of apartheid will bring a "dividend" in the reduction of the costs associated with it, and the South African economy should grow.[69] Still, if Black incomes continue to rise, that is no guarantee of rising contentment. As we have seen, discontent has risen steadily with rising incomes. The intensity of frustration often increases with proximity to the desired goal.[70] But, if rising incomes are coupled with enfranchisement and fundamental political change, it seems possible that discontent can be reduced on the politics and income fronts simultaneously.

The evidence for this proposition is not very firm. In a 1978 survey of reasonably well schooled Black men in Soweto, a question eliciting respondents' projection of their life conditions in a few years' time was followed by a request for an explanation of the forecast. The most frequently invoked explanation for their assessment was "political rights for Africans," an explanation cited by 57 percent of respondents, compared to 29 percent citing housing and township conditions, 29 percent citing education, and 22 percent citing wages and salaries.[71] For this sample, then, disfranchisement was by far the strongest element in a forecast, particularly a pessimistic forecast. The evidence for the centrality of political deprivation among Black South Africans is not unequivocal. Slightly earlier surveys in Durban and even in Soweto found

69. Lewis, *The Economics of Apartheid*, p. 145.

70. For a discussion, see Ted Robert Gurr, *Why Men Rebel* (Princeton: Princeton University Press, 1970), pp. 71–73.

71. Lawrence Schlemmer, "Change in South Africa: Opportunities and Constraints," in Robert M. Price and Carl G. Rosberg, eds., *The Apartheid Regime: Political Power and Racial Domination* (Berkeley: University of California Institute of International Studies, 1980), pp. 275–76.

greater concern with the inability to make ends meet than with political rights.[72] Very likely, more educated respondents are more inclined to place political deprivation in a central position.[73] The increasing politicization that occurred in the 1980s would suggest that larger and larger numbers of Africans are focused on politics as the principal discontent. If that is so, enfranchisement should have a significant effect in reducing discontent.

An important mechanism is the ability of citizens to divorce their sentiments about the political system in general from their sentiments about what the political system produces. In their five-country study of political culture, Gabriel A. Almond and Sidney Verba found that, in Mexico, attachment to the political system was strong even in the face of low evaluations of the actual performance of government.[74] Where it exists, this discrepancy between orientations toward a system and assessments of its performance gives a regime some breathing room and some benefit of the doubt. Almond and Verba attribute the discrepancy to the continuing force of the ideals of the Mexican Revolution of 1910.

For South Africa, the relevance of such a finding is that a major, ceremonious regime change may induce a measure of political loyalty not tied directly to the ability of a new government to solve South Africa's enormous policy problems. Linz has suggested that a careful formulation of the initial agenda of a new regime, with an emphasis on its fundamental commitments, can help consolidate loyalty toward the regime.[75] In South Africa, the connection between universal suffrage and a commitment to equality could hardly go unnoticed. Dahl notes that a number of Western democracies secured the political allegiance of their deprived classes in two stages—first, by extending the franchise and, second, by responding, albeit only partially, to demands for social and

72. For Durban, see Lawrence Schlemmer, "Conflict and Conflict Regulation in South Africa," in Anthony de Crespigny and Robert Schrire, eds., *The Government and Politics of South Africa* (Cape Town: Juta, 1978), p. 167. For Soweto, see H. Lever, "Public Opinion and Voting," in ibid., pp. 145–46.

73. In the Soweto study of matriculation pupils by Melville Leonard Edelstein, "An Attitude Survey of Urban Bantu Matric Pupils in Soweto, with Special Reference to Stereotyping and Social Distance: A Sociological Study" (M.A. thesis, University of Pretoria, 1971), pp. 120, 137, 73 percent of the respondents cited political rights as their main grievance.

74. Gabriel A. Almond and Sidney Verba, *The Civic Culture: Political Attitudes and Democracy in Five Nations* (Princeton: Princeton University Press, 1963), p. 103. Some aspects of the Mexican findings have been challenged. See Ann L. Craig and Wayne Cornelius, "Political Culture in Mexico: Continuities and Revisionist Interpretations," in Gabriel A. Almond and Sidney Verba, eds., *The Civic Culture Reconsidered* (Boston: Little, Brown, 1980), pp. 325–93.

75. "Crisis, Breakdown, and Reequilibration," pt. 1, pp. 40–41.

economic equality. Democratic regimes, he argues, can survive less inequality than undemocratic regimes can—which should, of course, be chastening for a democratic South Africa—but democratic regimes can still survive a considerable measure of inequality. "When demands for greater equality arise, a regime may gain allegiance among the deprived group by responding to some part of the demands, though not necessarily all of them."[76] No South African regime will be able to respond to all of the demands it will confront, but that will not necessarily doom stable democracy.

76. *Polyarchy,* p. 89.

CHAPTER SEVEN

The Transition to Democracy and the Problem of Hegemony

Since 1967, power has never passed from one elected government to another in Africa. Before 1967, although several states held free elections won by incumbents, almost no civilian government ever handed over power to a duly elected government from among the former opposition. There were, to be sure, two short-lived cases of peaceful alternation. In Benin, from 1957 to 1965, several civilian coalitions alternated in office, although usually with one of the coalition partners constant from one government to another, until a military coup ended the process. In the Sudan, power passed peacefully in 1956 from one party to a coalition of two others. In the elections that followed in 1958, a new coalition—including one party that had served in the former government—formed a majority. A coup later in the year put an end to that government and to alternation in office. There was also an aborted attempt at alternation in Sierra Leone in 1967. A new government had barely been sworn in when it was overthrown by the military. After that, alternation ended. No African political party has ever again moved from the opposition to the government benches after an election.

Rather than turn power over, elected governments transformed themselves into single-party regimes. In several countries, continuing opposition electoral strength precipitated the declaration of a one-party state. As we have seen, in those few countries where an opposition functions and free elections are held—Senegal, Botswana, and the Gambia—the structure of cleavages is such as to give the ruling party a dominant position, free of any real prospect of losing power at the polls. If democracy includes the possibility of participation or alternation in office, as it does in most conceptions—including Nigerian conceptions [1]— the African background against which South Africans write is not propitious.

As a matter of fact, three of the five long-standing Asian democracies, Japan, Malaysia, and India, have also been one-party-dominant systems through most of the post-colonial period. The other two, Sri Lanka and the Philippines, have had more difficulty maintaining stable

1. Democracy is "a political system characterized by competitive elections, civil liberties, and the toleration of significant 'loyal oppositions.' " Robert R. Kaufman, "Liberalization and Democratization in South America: Perspectives from the 1970s," in Guillermo O'Donnell et al., eds., *Transitions from Authoritarian Rule: Prospects for Democracy* (Baltimore: Johns Hopkins University Press, 1986), pt. 3, p. 100. Democracy generally refers to "concepts of representation, majority rule, opposition, competition, alternative government, control, and the like . . . ." Giovanni Sartori, "Democracy," in *International Encyclopedia of the Social Sciences*, vol. 4 (New York: Macmillan and Free Press, 1968), p. 112. Democracy "denotes a system of government that meets three essential conditions: meaningful and extensive *competition* among individuals and organized groups (especially political parties) for all effective positions of government power, at regular intervals and excluding the use of force; a highly inclusive level of *political participation* in the selection of leaders and policies, at least through regular and fair elections, such that no major (adult) social group is excluded; and a level of *civil and political liberties*— freedom of expression, freedom of the press, freedom to form and join organizations— sufficient to ensure the integrity of political competition and participation." Larry Diamond et al., "Preface," in Larry Diamond et al., eds., *Democracy in Developing Countries*, vol. 2, *Africa* (Boulder, Colo.: Lynn Rienner, 1988), p. xvi (emphases in the original). Democracy entails "contingent consent," such that political actors "agree to compete in such a way that those who win greater electoral support will exercise their temporary political superiority in such a way as not to impede those who may win greater support in the future from taking office; and those who lose in the present agree to respect the contingent authority of the winners to make binding decisions, in exchange for being allowed to take office and make decisions in the future. In their turn, citizens will presumably accept a democracy based on such a competition, provided its outcome remains contingent upon their collective preferences as expressed through fair and regular elections of uncertain outcome." Guillermo O'Donnell and Philippe C. Schmitter, "Tentative Conclusions about Uncertain Democracies," in O'Donnell et al., eds., *Transitions from Authoritarian Rule*, pt. 4, p. 59. Democracies hold elections "characterized by freedom of voters (universal suffrage, equal weighting of votes, secret ballots with freedom from external pressure, and accurate counting of the ballots), 'genuine' competition, and the real possibility of replacing officeholders with opposition candidates as an outcome of balloting." Ruth Berins Collier, *Regimes in Tropical Africa* (Berkeley and Los Angeles: University of California Press, 1982), p. 22. Democracy puts the emphasis "on free and universal suffrage in a context of civil liberties, on competitive parties, on the selection of alternative candidates for office, and on the presence of political institutions that regulate and guarantee the roles of government and opposition." Giuseppe Di Palma, *To Craft Democracies: An Essay on Democratic Transitions* (Berkeley and Los Angeles: University of California Press, 1990), p. 16. In planning for the return to civilian rule, the Nigerians in the late 1970s and late 1980s designed systems to open the prospect of alternation in office.

institutions. Multiparty competition with alternation has been rare, albeit not impossible.

These are chastening facts. Of course, the future of South Africa will be determined mainly in South Africa, not elsewhere in Africa and certainly not on other continents. However, some of the reasons for the failure of democracy elsewhere in Africa may also be present in South Africa.

POSSIBILITIES VERSUS PROBABILITIES

In the preceding chapters, we have oscillated between asking whether democracy is possible in South African conditions and whether it is probable. It is now necessary to examine more closely the gap between what is possible and what is probable and to consider whether anything can be or has been done to enhance the probability that democracy will emerge.

In Chapters 1 through 3, I enumerated some of the difficulties that confront democratic planners in South Africa. These include a profound dissensus about how South African society should be understood and transformed; a metaconflict that, at the very least, constrains political innovation; contenders for power who entertain hegemonic, rather than power-sharing, aspirations; ethnic as well as racial differences that will be politically significant; an array of suspicions of other players, misconceptions about the nature of majority rule, and pretensions to an exclusive place in the state; the need for change to take place rapidly; and the absence of structural features like a strong, autonomous civil society with a stake in maintaining democracy.

In Chapter 4, we reviewed a variety of proposals for a democratic South Africa, concluding that some are not apt for a racially and ethnically divided country, that some are not apt for the particular ideological divisions that sit atop the ethnic and racial divisions, and that some are not apt for either. In the process, we saw that the ideological dissensus limits South Africa to a fairly narrow band of political institutions that would have a claim on legitimacy. We also examined a number of common mistakes in negotiating arrangements for divided societies. At least some of these errors are likely to be repeated in South Africa.

The burden of much, although not all, of the material in the first four chapters suggests that inclusive democracy is improbable in South Africa. In that respect, South Africa is by no means out of line. Not only is democracy unusual in Africa, but it is also rare in ethnically and racially divided societies more generally.[2] Such societies need special precautions if they are not to be overtaken by authoritarianism.

On the other hand, Chapters 5 and 6 make it reasonably clear that democracy is possible in South Africa. Democratic institutions can be crafted that are appropriate for the divided society South Africa will be. Such institutions make no compromise on the question of majority rule and provide room for democratic pluralism to flourish. The institutions are nonracial and nonethnic. Without racially or ethnically based electoral rolls, reserved seats, group vetoes, or homeland states, the institutions meet the requirements that flow from South Africa's ideological dissensus. They could have a claim on rather wide legitimacy, which they certainly would need if they were to endure, rather than merely being accepted as interim solutions, to be scrapped at the first opportunity.

The electoral systems that were recommended are premised on the crucial importance of a single question: Are there sufficient incentives to intergroup accommodation? This puts the accent on how institutions actually work, rather than on acquiring a particular kit or inventory of institutions. It substitutes mechanisms supportive of accommodation for prescribed devices to be used in all contexts. Most important of all, it puts the voters behind accommodation in a way that an emphasis on mere coalition formation—that is, seat pooling without attention to vote pooling—can never do. Putting the voters back into the center of the calculations insures that accommodation does not take place over their heads or behind their backs, that it is not just another deal. Accommodation only takes place with the voters' consent. If, in addition to measures to limit conflict, South Africa needs anything at all, what it needs most is consent.

That consent is by no means assured in South Africa. Among the other systemic features a democratic South Africa will enjoy is a fragmented, potentially polarized party system. Institutional design needs to take account of this feature. Like electoral rules that encourage vote pooling, a central political officer, a president, elected on such a formula, would reinforce the centripetal pulls of the system. And just as

2. See Robert A. Dahl, *Polyarchy: Participation and Opposition* (New Haven: Yale University Press, 1971), pp. 108–11; Robert A. Dahl, "Some Explanations," in Robert A. Dahl, ed., *Political Oppositions in Western Democracies* (New Haven: Yale University Press, 1966), p. 368.

the electoral system changes the incentives, federalism would change the context of politics, so that state arenas, state loyalties, and substate competition would be activated. Unlike a unitary system, with a single arena in which intolerance can be writ large—which is roughly the situation from which South Africa is emerging—a federal system would permit a variety of local adjustments and might impede a single pattern of domination from emerging. The institutions that have served White interests, or narrower Afrikaner interests, are, in short, not appropriate to the heterogeneous polity South Africa must and will become if it is to escape a new domination. Fortunately, a new set of utterly group-neutral institutions is available.

Attractive as these institutions are, there is no blinking the difficulties attending their adoption and implementation. Vote-pooling electoral systems and interparty competition for votes are not easy to envision in the many townships where, in the 1980s, one or another organization—generally the ANC, AZAPO, or Inkatha—claimed exclusive control and ran its opponents out.[3] Perhaps peaceful competition is not altogether impossible. There have been some spontaneous street committee elections, in effect revolts against the bullying rule of young comrades. But people have become accustomed to local tyrannies.[4]

Or consider the persuasion it will take to convince the extraparliamentary opposition that federalism is not just a cleaned-up version of the homelands policy. The bias against federalism is so strong that, according to a sophisticated UDF leader who concedes its possibilities, it is not worth the immense effort it would take to change minds.[5] Many such innovations, it is thought by some UDF leaders, could be adopted at a later stage.[6] However, where a great disjunction exists between one regime and the next, "attitudes toward the legitimacy and efficacy of the new regime are quite likely to be permanently shaped by the initial steps."[7] Moreover, once new institutions are in place, political actors

3. Typical of descriptions is this letter to the editor of *Argus* (Cape Town), April 26, 1990: "The trouble and the slaughter going on in Natal at the moment is that ANC gangs have been attempting to get all black people to join their organization; if they refuse outright and dare to express anything against them, they are visited by the ANC's many forms of revenge." The same has been said of the efforts of other organizations.

4. For the elections, see Nomavenda Mathiane, *South Africa: Diary of Troubled Times* (New York: Freedom House, 1989), p. 62. For tyranny in the townships, see ibid., pp. 3, 36, 40, 44–45, 59–62, 101.

5. Interview, Durban, August 3, 1989. I have previously encountered strong resistance among UDF leaders to even the idea of federalism. Interviews, Durban, September 16, 1985; Johannesburg, September 17, 1985; Johannesburg, September 20, 1985.

6. Interview, Pietermaritzburg, August 1, 1989.

7. Juan J. Linz, "Crisis, Breakdown, and Reequilibration," in Juan J. Linz and Alfred

adapt to them. After political parties are established, for example, it will be difficult to alter their position by attempting to change the electoral rules. "The party strategists will generally have a decisive influence on electoral legislation and opt for systems of aggregation most likely to consolidate their position . . . ."[8] The same, of course, goes for federalism, presidentialism, and other measures reallocating powers. Seymour Martin Lipset and Stein Rokkan speak of "the freezing of political alternatives"[9] in the formative phase of new regimes. In short, since interests will crystallize quickly around the first set of institutional innovations, it is a chimera to think that much flexibility will be retained thereafter.

If there is one proposition that commands wide assent among theorists of democracy, it is that democracy is no single form of government but "an array of possibilities," a "system of processing and terminating intergroup conflicts" without foreordained outcomes, a way of "institutionalizing uncertainty," an arrangement in which many people can pursue "widely varying goals over time."[10] This is, of course, one reason why rigidly predetermined ascriptive majorities and minorities can hardly be said to be conducive to democratic rule. The indeterminacy prescribed by these conceptions of democracy implies that no group should indefinitely be denied the opportunity to participate in government.[11] But to assure that opportunity, to make the system fluid, requires a configuration of institutions that South Africans have not yet embraced across the many cleavage lines that divide them.

Reviewing all this evidence, then, the conclusion is inescapable that democracy is possible but improbable in South Africa. The institutions for democracy are available, but they are not likely to be adopted or, if adopted, made to work. Can these conditions be altered? Is it feasible

---

Stepan, eds., *The Breakdown of Democratic Regimes* (Baltimore: Johns Hopkins University Press, 1978), pt. 1, p. 41.

8. Seymour Martin Lipset and Stein Rokkan, "Cleavage Structures, Party Systems, and Voter Alignments: An Introduction," in Seymour Martin Lipset and Stein Rokkan, eds., *Party Systems and Voter Alignments: Cross-national Perspectives* (New York: Free Press, 1967), p. 30. See also Rein Taagepera and Mathew S. Shugart, "Designing Electoral Systems," *Electoral Studies* 8, no. 1 (April 1989): 49–58.

9. "Cleavage Structures, Party Systems, and Voter Alignments," p. 54 (emphasis omitted).

10. The quotations in the text are derived, in sequence, from Robert A. Dahl, *After the Revolution* (New Haven: Yale University Press, 1970), p. 59; Adam Przeworski, "Some Problems in the Study of the Transition to Democracy," in O'Donnell et al., eds., *Transitions from Authoritarian Rule*, pt. 3, pp. 56, 58; Linz, "Crisis, Breakdown, and Reequilibration," pt. 1, p. 12. See also Di Palma, *To Craft Democracies*, pp. 53–56.

11. Dahl, *Polyarchy*, p. 115.

to convert possibility into probability or at least to reduce the gap between the two?

Clearly, some conditions are not alterable in the short run. The need for rapid change, for example, is a given. A weak civil society cannot be strengthened overnight. Fundamental cleavages cannot be abolished, and they certainly should not be wished away. Yet, proponents of democracy need not be content with all aspects of the environment they confront. It is plainly inadequate for constitutional engineers to produce an appropriate design and let it languish in inhospitable conditions, some of which might yield to deliberate effort.

An analogy to inhospitable international conditions is suggestive. In the struggle to create international cooperation in the face of rewards for noncooperation, international actors have worked to change the structure of the situation—to provide incentives for cooperation and penalties for noncooperation, to engage in reciprocally rewarding behavior, to create international regimes with more stable rules and procedures, and to gain acceptance for new, cooperative norms.[12] What we have for South Africa is a set of new norms thus far awaiting actors who are willing to put them into practice by committing themselves to appropriate political behavior. Can anything be done, comparable to what has been done internationally, to enhance the prospects for cooperation and democracy, rather than conflict and authoritarianism, in South Africa?

The crucial conditions in need of alteration concern the aspirations of the main political actors and the prospects for the longevity of apt new institutions. Although these two are related, the first brings us back to the difficult problem of hegemony raised in Chapter 1, and the second focuses particularly on the process by which agreement is reached.

GENERAL MODELS OF DEMOCRATIC COMMITMENT

The willingness to share power in a democratic regime cannot be taken for granted. Some actors may see the choice as simply to dominate or be dominated. Some may not value democracy, including the prospect of alternation in office. They may think that they have earned the right to rule, or they may believe democracy is too cumbersome a framework

---

12. Robert Axelrod and Robert O. Keohane, "Achieving Cooperation under Anarchy: Strategies and Institutions," *World Politics* 38, no. 1 (October 1985): 226–54.

in which to achieve transformative objectives. In any of these cases, they may aim at hegemony rather than democracy.

In South Africa, it has been suggested that one "contending regime model" is essentially authoritarian,[13] and so the hegemony problem exists. (A problem also exists, in a different way, with respect to the White right wing, about which I shall say a little more later.) The problem is, of course, exacerbated by the prevalence of undemocratic, single-party or military regimes in most southern African countries, with the exception thus far of Botswana, Swaziland (a monarchy), and Namibia (a dominant-party system but not yet a single-party system). For all the contending organizations in South Africa to forswear hegemonic aspirations is for them to renounce what has become nearly normal in most of the region and, for some of them, as we saw in Chapter 1, also to renounce a strand in their ideological commitment to socialist dictatorship. For the African National Congress, the matter is compounded by the overlapping composition of much of its leadership and that of the South African Communist Party (SACP), a party that has not been enthusiastic about the transformations toward liberal democracy in the Soviet Union and Eastern Europe.[14] And, for all of the extraparliamentary opposition, there is a further problem. If there has been a "liberation struggle" in South Africa, it may seem at best an ironic result to have to share power with those from whom liberation has been won. Not surprisingly, revolutionary turnovers are not likely to lead to democratic outcomes.[15]

The prospect of hegemony is, then, to be taken seriously, as nervous calls for multiparty democracy suggest.[16] Perhaps the first thing that needs to be said about this is that single-party systems are not democratic. Such a view is held even by those few who think that democracy is a system that can grow up only in certain limited historical periods,

13. See Chapter 1, p. 33, above. Apprehensions about authoritarianism derive in large part from the ANC's expressed doubts about "classical liberal democracy" and from the skepticism of the PAC and AZAPO about multiparty democracy.

14. For the overlapping membership of the ANC and the SACP, see *Africa Confidential* (London), January 12, 1990, pp. 1–4; ibid., May 4, 1990, pp. 1–2. See also Belinda Barrett, "A Profile of the African National Congress (ANC)" (Inkatha Institute of South Africa, May 1989; mimeo.). Although ANC funds came, in large measure, from the Swedish Social Democrats, social democracy was regarded, in Leninist terms, as a form of heresy.

15. O'Donnell and Schmitter, "Tentative Conclusions about Uncertain Democracies," pt. 4, p. 11.

16. Such as the call by Bishop Stanley Mogaba, president of the South African Institute of Race Relations and past president of the Methodist Church of Southern Africa. *SA Dialogue* (Cresta), January 1990, p. 2.

such as early capitalism.[17] The obvious reason for the undemocratic character of one-party states is that contestation, the prospect of alternation, and even the possibility of exchanging opinions in an autonomous organization are all denied.[18] Many African single-party rulers have stayed in office for decades. The less obvious reason is that, in ethnic terms, such regimes tend not to be inclusive and are sometimes narrowly exclusive, because they no longer need to build electoral majorities.[19] For South Africa, there are straws in the wind: the strong affinities of some contenders with other one-party regimes, the climate of fear that has overtaken many townships, the frequent critiques of liberal democracy, and even the defense of summary executions of collaborators against criticism from human rights organizations.

An examination of the conditions that prompt the creation of one-party regimes in Africa suggests that those conditions may also be present in South Africa. In much of Africa, the single-party state emerged in response to party competition along ethnic lines. A ruling multiethnic party was threatened with erosion of its clientele. Ethnically based parties grew on one or both flanks of the ruling multiethnic party as sentiment polarized. Fearful of both the polarization and the shrunken base, the ruling party then declared a one-party state, outlawed the competitor parties, and thereafter purported to represent the interests of their former adherents.

Needless to say, such moves do not abolish ethnic conflict—they only mask and silence it.[20] Among other reasons, the former opposition parties and the ethnic groups they represent are rarely well integrated into the single party that ostensibly welcomes them. Established party functionaries make sure of that. What Fred M. Hayward and Jimmy D. Kandeh conclude for one-partyism in Sierra Leone is apt more gener-

17. Collier, *Regimes in Tropical Africa,* p. 26.
18. Dahl, *Polyarchy,* pp. 30–31; T. B. Bottomore, *Elites and Society* (Harmondsworth, Eng.: Penguin Books, 1966), pp. 118–19. See also Fred M. Hayward and Jimmy D. Kandeh, "Perspectives on Twenty-five Years of Elections in Sierra Leone," in Fred M. Hayward, ed., *Elections in Independent Africa* (Boulder, Colo.: Westview Press, 1987), p. 55. Contrast Robert H. Jackson and Carl G. Rosberg, "Democracy in Tropical Africa: Democracy versus Autocracy in African Politics," *Journal of International Affairs* 38, no. 2 (Winter 1985): 293–305.
19. Donald L. Horowitz, *Ethnic Groups in Conflict* (Berkeley and Los Angeles: University of California Press, 1985), pp. 433–37. See also Theodor Hanf, "The Prospects of Accommodation in Communal Conflicts: A Comparative Study," in Hermann Giliomee and Lawrence Schlemmer, eds., *Negotiating South Africa's Future* (New York: St. Martin's Press, 1989), p. 102.
20. See Horowitz, *Ethnic Groups in Conflict,* pp. 429–37.

ally: "The multiparty system, as a mechanism for electoral competition and change, has been viewed in many cases in Africa . . . as responsible for the intensification of ethnic and communal conflicts. As this [Sierra Leone] case demonstrates, the creation of a one-party state does not necessarily diminish such conflicts and may in fact intensify them by eliminating mechanisms designed to prevent such conflicts and the abuses leading to them."[21] Under the cloak of one-partyism, ethnic groups and cliques within groups are able to attain hegemonic influence that would probably be checked in openly democratic systems, where narrowing of a base of support would incur an electoral penalty.

To be sure, at least the Charterist contenders in South Africa, particularly the African National Congress, are multiracial and multiethnic. But so were many anti-colonial movements. After independence, some groups, often those less well represented in the umbrella movement, fell away, forming their own flank parties and eventually precipitating the end of party competition. South Africa already has several competing parties, with varying ethnic bases, and is as plausible a candidate as any other for a one-party, hegemonic regime.

How, then, should those who are interested in a democratic South Africa think about restructuring the situation to render hegemony less likely? With few exceptions, none of the major bodies of literature on transitions to democracy confronts the problem of hegemony from inside the regime. Retrospective explanations are available for why and how regimes become democratic.[22] Theories have also been devised for returning to democracy by inducing the military to withdraw from power and then keeping it out during the transition to democracy. Others are concerned with the ability of regimes to prevent oppositions from turning against the democratic system as well as to prevent anti-system opposition parties from taking over the system from the outside.[23] Backsliding to authoritarian rule has not been ignored, but much of the prodigious work on democratization in Latin America and southern Europe focuses principally on keeping the armed forces out and secondarily on keeping the opposition loyal.

On few other issues of comparative politics have interregional differences in focus been as much in evidence. Despite the prevalence of au-

21. "Perspectives on Twenty-five Years of Elections in Sierra Leone," p. 55.
22. E.g., Dankwart A. Rustow, "Transitions to Democracy: Toward a Dynamic Model," *Comparative Politics* 2, no. 3 (April 1970): 337–63.
23. Linz, "Crisis, Breakdown, and Reequilibration," pt. 1, pp. 33–37. I am indebted to Robert R. Kaufman for helping to clarify my thoughts on the emphases in the literature.

thoritarian tendencies within new regimes and despite the African single-party state, hegemony from the inside is the least systematically treated issue of the transition to democracy.[24] The principal obstacle to democracy in Africa is thus hardly noticed in the transitions literature. The commitment of a new regime to democracy is the very thing that often cannot be taken for granted.

Ideological, racial, or ethnic polarization, on the South African model, is an unfavorable condition for democracy, but polarization can also lead to democratic accommodation. In Dankwart A. Rustow's model of transitions to democracy,[25] the decisive step to a democratic regime is preceded by a long period of struggle and polarization. Then, either at one decision point or several, leaders of the contending forces agree to accept what divides them and live with it in a democratic framework. In Sweden, this decision was facilitated by a great compromise. Universal suffrage, sought by the challengers, was accepted by those already within the system, in exchange for an electoral system that confined the former outsiders to a proportionate share of seats.

As Rustow and other writers suggest,[26] a democratic accommodation entails the creation of institutions to prevent vulnerable social forces from losing out to a new authoritarian regime. But what decides the participants on a commitment to the new democratic system? What cements the accommodation and overcomes hegemonic aspirations? Here we are truly in terra incognita. The possible models are many, and each suggests a different strategy.

One possibility is a *deterrence* model.[27] If power is located in several places, actors may hesitate to use their share of power in ways that are contrary to their commitments. In Portugal, for example, the armed forces, which held independent power during the transition to democracy, from 1976 to 1982, served as a guarantor of the transition.[28] A variant of this can be put in cost-benefit terms. Democracy may be permitted to the extent that a regime believes the attempt to coerce the

---

24. But cf. Di Palma, *To Craft Democracies*, pp. 65–73.

25. "Transitions to Democracy."

26. E.g., Przeworski, "Some Problems in the Study of the Transition to Democracy," pt. 3, p. 61.

27. Larry Diamond thus argues for constraints on the executive, constitutional guarantees of decentralization, and high thresholds for modifying the constitution. "Introduction: Roots of Failure, Seeds of Hope," in Diamond et al., eds., *Democracy in Developing Countries*, vol. 2, *Africa*, pp. 27–29.

28. Alfred Stepan, "Paths toward Redemocratization: Theoretical and Comparative Considerations," in O'Donnell et al., eds., *Transitions from Authoritarian Rule*, pt. 3, pp. 77–78.

opposition will either fail or be too costly to justify the attempt.[29] To prevent retrogression to authoritarian rule, therefore, one strategy might be to make the success of any such attempts problematic and to make even small breaches of democratic norms transparently obvious.

A second way of thinking about the matter involves *habituation.* If democratic institutions can be made to work to the common advantage of the major actors across the divide between government and opposition for a long enough period for democratic habits to take hold, those habits will render backsliding less tempting and, should it occur, more aberrational and less legitimate than it would otherwise seem.[30]

A third model is premised on *reciprocity.* The literature on transitions to democracy in Latin America and southern Europe is suffused with discussions of the utility of "pacts," agreements among crucial actors that commit them to democracy. The pacts contain guarantees of mutual security and tangible rewards for cooperation in the process—in some formulations, rents to participating organizations, which are privileged over their rivals, so that democracy is underpinned by a form of corporatism.[31]

A fourth view emphasizes changing *belief* through learning. Hegemony is a problem, because not all the actors believe in democracy. They need to learn that the consequence of a failure of democracy (and power sharing) in a divided society is a long period of destructive conflict. Learning therefore focuses on the advantages of cooperation and the costs of trying to secure hegemony.[32] In contrast to habituation, which also involves learning, the changes in belief envisioned by this view take place at the inception of the new democratic regime.

All of these models are ideal types, and there is overlap among them. It is well known in learning theory that the acquisition of knowledge proceeds more readily when learning is rewarding. The internalization of democratic norms may thus be reinforced when deterrence makes

29. Robert A. Dahl, "Preface," in Dahl, ed., *Political Oppositions in Western Democracies,* p. xiv.

30. Rustow, "Transitions to Democracy."

31. On pactology, see O'Donnell and Schmitter, "Tentative Conclusions about Uncertain Democracies," pt. 4, pp. 41–45; Stepan, "Paths toward Redemocratization," pt. 3, pp. 79–81. Schmitter sees pacts as involving rents and therefore envisions the inclusion of some favored participants, to the exclusion of others, whereas Stepan sees pacts as inclusive. For a more skeptical view of pacts, see Di Palma, *To Craft Democracies,* pp. 86–90.

32. Pierre du Toit, "Contending Regime Models and the Contest for Hegemony in Divided Societies" (University of Stellenbosch, 1989; unpublished paper).

resort to undemocratic behavior dangerous and reciprocity provides a payoff for conformity to democratic norms. In spite of the overlap among the models, however, none of these models—not even all of them together—can provide a sure path or even a probable path to democracy in South Africa. All of them set up fences higher than can be scaled, quite possibly higher than need to be scaled. Later in this chapter, I shall suggest a less demanding set of possibilities.

FROM HEGEMONY TO DEMOCRACY: BLOCKED PATHS

The one model that can be pushed to one side for the moment is habituation. Democratic habits take hold as democratic practice proceeds. Habituation is therefore cement that binds democracy at a later stage, perhaps even in a later generation than in the formative generation.[33] For the formative period, the question is whether actors will commit themselves to the "act of alienation of control over outcomes of conflicts that constitutes the decisive step toward democracy."[34] This is a difficult step to take, because all the forces seeking to bring down an undemocratic regime want simultaneously to create conditions that will favor their specific interests in the regime that replaces it.[35] But democracy embodies a large measure of indeterminacy. Habit, then, cannot solve this problem, because pre-democratic habits are, by definition, not democratic and because the impulses of so many actors in the process are to restrict the uncertainty that democracy brings.

Of course, deterrence, reciprocity, and learning do have something to contribute to securing commitments to democracy. The existence of powerful forces with the ability to retaliate if democratic norms are breached might induce a degree of conformity to democratic norms. The commitment of other actors to forswear the use of undemocratic methods might elicit a reciprocal promise to do likewise. Learning the hazards of conflict and the possibilities of cooperation might reduce the temptation to high-risk, hegemonic strategies. It is, therefore, worth taking a closer look at each of these approaches.

33. Rustow, "Transitions to Democracy," pp. 358–59.
34. Przeworski, "Some Problems in the Study of the Transition to Democracy," pt. 3, p. 58.
35. Ibid., p. 61.

Deterrence can be produced by the structure of forces already in existence or by deliberate design. In South Africa, the Congress of South African Trade Unions (COSATU), a strong union that has enjoyed close relations with the UDF and the ANC, might be wary of an attempt to establish a one-party state. Such regimes have generally not been receptive to expensive wage demands emanating from trade unions or even to the principle of free trade unionism. The disciplined power of COSATU, whose members have shown their cohesion in strikes and protests, could act as a deterrent. In this case, a force with some checking power is thus already in existence.

Not many such forces can be identified, however. I have suggested in Chapter 6 that a decision in favor of federalism would produce more such forces and raise the costs of a potential move to authoritarianism. This would be deterrence by design. The problem is that the argument is circular. Knowing that federalism creates a more complex system that makes authoritarianism problematic implies that those not yet committed fully to liberal democracy will resist creating a federal state or will attempt to convert it into a sham federalism, precisely to reduce its inhibiting power.

And so we are back where we began. South Africa does have some potential counterforces. Were they to be given scope to operate, there might be enough pluralism to sustain democratic complexity. But potential hegemons will oppose providing the requisite scope right from the beginning.

The same goes for reciprocity in the form of pacts, guarantees of mutual security, and institutional compromises. There is no doubt that, in some settings, agreements have been forged in circumstances that, without them, would have been uncongenial to moving forward to a consolidation of democracy. Sweden's great compromise, mentioned earlier, is an example. Another was consummated in Portugal in 1975, when revolutionary attempts to redistribute land provoked a right-wing reaction that threatened to reverse the democratic process. At that point, the Socialist-led government of Mario Soares crafted an agreement returning most of the seized property to its former owners and ending rural anarchy, but ratifying state ownership of already-nationalized industries. The effect was to provide a new sense of security to the threatened right and to consolidate democracy at the expense of redistribution. Not only did such an agreement work in Portugal, but, suggests Nancy Bermeo, in every case where a transition to democracy was successful, "dramatic redistributions of property were postponed, circumscribed, or rolled back."[36] The agreement, explicit or not, was to trade more mass democracy for less mass economic welfare.

Again, such conclusions may reflect the European and Latin American focus of most studies of transitions to democracy. In Europe and Latin America, the main threats to democracy, albeit not the only threats, have come from the right. The assumption has been that force is not controlled by the left in a transition situation, so that the left is, by default, committed to the democratic path to achieving its objectives.[37] That has largely been true in Europe and Latin America, but it is not uniformly true.

Explicit agreements to protect weaker elements in the polity and to prevent authoritarianism have been recommended in general, and they have been recommended for South Africa.[38] The United States also managed a regime change from a troubled confederation to a strong federal union in 1787 by means of, among other devices, some great compromises, especially those between small states and large states.

In the United States, however, and arguably elsewhere, there was an underlying consensus on the utility of liberal democracy, even though there was no consensus on the institutional forms it should take or the extent to which various interests should be protected. In South Africa, that underlying consensus is the very thing in issue. What Guillermo O'Donnell and Philippe C. Schmitter call "contingent consent,"[39] or agreement to compete so that temporary winners do not use their power to impede those who win election in the future from taking office, is the object of a possible exchange that would indeed provide mutual security. But if one party to such a transaction thinks it can find equivalent or better security without making such an agreement, is that belief not an insuperable obstacle to consummating the transaction?

I have discussed the pitfalls of deals and contracts in Chapter 4, and I shall return to the subject in connection with the negotiation process. Lying in wait, years down the road, are many more hazards to the contractual mode of arranging political affairs than have been appreciated

36. Nancy Bermeo, "Rethinking Regime Change," *Comparative Politics* 22, no. 3 (April 1990): 359–77, at 365.

37. O'Donnell and Schmitter, "Tentative Conclusions about Uncertain Democracies," pt. 4, p. 69.

38. Przeworski, "Some Problems in the Study of the Transition to Democracy," pt. 3, p. 61. For South Africa in particular, see Charles Simkins et al., *The Prisoners of Tradition and the Politics of Nation Building* (Johannesburg: South African Institute of Race Relations, 1988), p. 29.

39. "Tentative Conclusions about Uncertain Democracies," pt. 4, pp. 59–61.

by the proponents of pacts. Some of the same pitfalls have been identified in connection with reciprocity as a strategy for achieving international cooperation.[40] But, whatever their ultimate advantages and disadvantages in the democratization process, it seems clear that such exchanges cannot by themselves cause democracy to be seen as the best alternative.

Before we leave deterrence, reciprocity, and habituation, perhaps we should consider the possible efficacy of a combination of all three. Suppose agreements are struck that embody some of the characteristic payoffs that are said to accompany pacts and also that those pacts include strong, publicly stated commitments to liberal democracy. Suppose further that the accompanying constitutional arrangements embody powerful elements of deterrence, including a Madisonian system of checks and balances, interim guarantees of democracy (perhaps involving the armed forces, on the Portuguese model), and clear rules of the political game that would make departures from democratic norms embarrassingly and dangerously obvious. If we postulate adoption of these arrangements, along with appropriate institutions to mitigate racial and ethnic conflict, would we be warranted in speculating that habituation could then take over and propel the regime into a democratic future?

My own view is that even this configuration would not be enough. It is one thing to ask committed socialists to understand the advantages of the free market, particularly when the social costs of a market economy can be reduced with welfare policies. A remarkable number of seemingly committed socialists have been willing to make this conversion. But the equivalent conversion to the political market is more farfetched for committed authoritarians or even weakly committed democrats. For one thing, the indeterminacy of the political market can oust them from power altogether. Economic policy may produce the same result, but such a possibility is not an intrinsic part of the policy choice, as it is with democracy. For another, the benefits of democracy are simply not as palpable as are the benefits of the free market. Political freedom does not have quite the same feel to it as economic welfare does, and politicians are less certain that they can claim credit for liberty than they are that they can reap rewards from prosperity. This is particularly the case in a society where people value their own liberty but are ambivalent about the liberty of other social groups. And so the arrangements hypothesized here, entailing interlocking parts of deterrence and

40. Axelrod and Keohane, "Achieving Cooperation under Anarchy," pp. 245–46.

reciprocity, with a hope of habituation, seem altogether too contrived, too confining, perhaps too open to insincere assent, to produce democratic habits.

If strong medicine is probably insufficient to overcome deficiencies of belief, perhaps we are back to learning. Can the dangers of a quest for hegemony be learned? Can the utility of contingent consent be impressed upon the participants? When and how?

Interpreting the findings of studies in southern Europe and Latin America, Bermeo emphasizes "value change,"[41] by which she means that the experience of authoritarianism often—though not always—inclined many voters and many politicians to moderation, to self-limiting compromise, when the time came for a transition to democracy. Political actors had learned that extreme demands and unsettled conditions might prompt renewed military intervention. Lessons like these may be essential to democratization, which can only be brought about with "heroic forms of restraint and cooperation," to use Robert R. Kaufman's language.[42]

Whatever opponents of authoritarian regimes may have learned in many Latin countries, the opponents of colonial authoritarianism in Africa obviously learned something quite different. The point is so transparent that it is rarely stated: most post-colonial African leaders have had only a shallow belief in democracy. Quite accurately, Naomi Chazan describes Ghana's brief experiment with democracy after the British departure as "half-hearted and short-lived. Ghanaians had had little practical experience with this model under colonial rule until the postwar period. . . . In Ghana, as elsewhere on the continent, a British style of parliamentary democracy retreated quickly along with its colonial originators because the new leaders had little commitment to uphold its precepts."[43]

To be sure, independent South Africa has had far more experience with parliamentary democracy, but it has been democracy for Whites only. There is little reason to think that the excluded majority has somehow been able to overcome the knowledge that parliamentary institutions have been the source of discriminatory legislation and instead managed to develop an affinity—a positive preference—for a now-

---

41. "Rethinking Regime Change," pp. 371–73.
42. "Liberalization and Democratization in South America," pt. 3, p. 106.
43. Naomi Chazan, "Ghana: Problems of Governance and the Emergence of Civil Society," in Diamond et al., eds., *Democracy in Developing Countries*, vol. 2, *Africa*, p. 98.

inclusive democracy of the very sort that has been so conducive to the experience that is to be transcended. As I have shown in Chapter 3, survey data indicate that a great many South Africans want a racially and ethnically inclusive polity, but the data provide no evidence of commitment to any particular arrangement of democratic institutions.

Neither is there any reason to think that, confronted by recalcitrant White authoritarians, the extraparliamentary opposition has internalized the lessons so well learned in Latin America—that restraint and cooperation, commitment to mutual guarantees, moderation and compromise, are preferable to confrontation with former oppressors. A finding that value change *preceded* successful transitions to democracy is actually a pessimistic omen for the many cases in which such a transition has not taken place and in which democratic values have not yet become preeminent. Learning may still be the appropriate model, but, for South Africa, it will not be the learning that took place during the period of exclusion. That learning does not seem particularly congenial to the position that democracy and power sharing constitute the preferred alternative. Instead, if learning is to play a role, the relevant value change is that which takes place during the democratization process itself. This need not be fatal. Perhaps, as Giuseppe Di Palma says, "genuine democrats need not precede democracy . . . ."[44]

One thing that could be learned during the planning for inclusive democracy is that the price of a regime change is a commitment to democratic institutions on the part of all contenders for power, since the White regime will not change without such a commitment. I have suggested earlier that this is not likely to be a fruitful way to proceed. Standing alone, such a condition will encourage, not a change of heart, but a change of tactics. South Africa needs more than paper guarantees.

On the other hand, as I mentioned in Chapter 1, the problem can be cast in terms of learning just how explosive and inimical to everyone's interests intergroup conflict and violence can be in a divided society. Advocates of consociational democracy have argued that the path to such an agreement begins with a recognition of mutual vulnerability, facilitated by "a glimpse into the abyss of violence . . . ."[45] As I have argued earlier, the best time for the appreciation of mutual vulnerability is after serious violence, when vulnerability has been demonstrated clearly. The Nigerians and Ugandans are witnesses to the point. Nevertheless,

---

44. *To Craft Democracies*, p. 30.
45. F. van Zyl Slabbert and David Welsh, *South Africa's Options: Strategies for Sharing Power* (New York: St. Martin's Press, 1979), p. 119.

the requisite learning about vulnerability, it is said, can occur during negotiations.[46] The key, then, is enlightened self-interest. But how is "enlightenment" to take place if an actor is "unenlightened," that is to say, unconvinced?

The negotiating table is an unlikely setting for learning. The time frame is too short for the requisite shifts to take place. Furthermore, what we know about cognition suggests that "people assimilate new information to existing beliefs; they are 'cognitive misers.' Until and unless the information is sufficiently discrepant, they are unlikely to 'learn.' Leaders are most likely to learn when they repeatedly encounter strongly discrepant information that challenges fundamental beliefs. Only then are they likely to reformulate their beliefs about others and re-frame the problem."[47] Unlike deterrence and reciprocity as models for overcoming hegemonic aspirations, the learning model does not have elements of tautology about it. Rather, it is, on empirical grounds, ex-cessively optimistic.

The process of negotiation is also likely to be inappropriate for an emphasis on danger. The whole course of negotiation is inevitably fixed on reducing differences, creating trust and good will, displaying states-manship, matching concession with concession. As a negotiation pro-ceeds, the psychology of the event is hardly conducive to an emphasis on doomsday thinking, except in the thin, rhetorical sense of holding up the specter of what will happen if negotiations fail, the better to consummate whatever transaction is on the table. A bright future to-gether is a spur to negotiation, and that is where the emphasis will be. Mediators, whose overwhelming incentive is to facilitate an agreement, cannot be expected to emphasize the disagreeable prospects that could only complicate the process. Successful mediators typically take pride in their ability to push thorny issues aside and concentrate on issues that lend themselves to resolution. For all these reasons, negotiations are unlikely to fix the minds of the participants on the sort of conflict-prone polity to which they belong and on the sort of hostility toward which they might be headed. Negotiation is simply not structured to serve the purpose of changing values.

Theorists of negotiation do distinguish two phases: the tentative phase

46. Ibid. See also ibid., p. 150.
47. Janice Gross Stein, "Getting to the Table: The Triggers, Stages, Functions, and Consequences of Prenegotiation," in Janice Gross Stein, ed., *Getting to the Table: The Processes of International Prenegotiation* (Baltimore: Johns Hopkins University Press, 1989), p. 264.

of "prenegotiation" and the phase of negotiation proper that follows.[48] In the latter phase, a plan is formulated. First, however, distrustful perceptions of the opponent as enemy must give way to perceptions of the opponent as someone potentially able to cooperate and worthy of at least some trust. At the same time, during prenegotiation, efforts are usually made to convince the other side that concessions will be reciprocated and to prepare one's own side to accept the need for such concessions. It is true that prenegotiation is also said to be the forum for assessing risks and learning about costs.[49] But nothing so ambitious as a fundamental change of objectives or commitments is encompassed in such a formulation. On the contrary, a central function of prenegotiation is to limit the agenda for negotiation to problems that are soluble—within the actors' present frameworks—and the success of prenegotiation is said to depend on the existence of conditions that amount to an assessment, even before prenegotiation begins, that an agreement is probable.[50]

The usual negotiation, then, has modest goals compared to the goal of making completely new commitments, based on a model of changed values or new learning. Here it is instructive to compare with the two stages of prenegotiation and negotiation Pierre du Toit and Jannie Gagiano's three-stage model for reconciling differences in a divided society like South Africa.[51] Working backward, the third stage, "substantive bargaining," and the second stage, "preliminary bargaining," are recognizable as negotiation and prenegotiation. The first stage, called "bargaining about bargaining," is distinctive. The necessity for it derives from the "basic question": "whether adversaries who hate, fear and resent one another are likely to grant each other civil liberties, and whether they are likely to use their own freedoms to protect the freedoms of what they assess to be their deadly rivals. If not, how can they be persuaded to do so?"[52]

---

48. I. William Zartman, "Prenegotiation: Phases and Functions," in Stein, ed., *Getting to the Table,* pp. 3–8.

49. Ibid., p. 8.

50. Janice Gross Stein, "Prenegotiation in the Arab-Israeli Conflict: The Paradoxes of Success and Failure," in Stein, ed., *Getting to the Table,* pp. 188, 204.

51. Pierre du Toit, "Bargaining about Bargaining: Inducing the Self-negating Prediction in Deeply Divided Societies—The Case of South Africa," *Journal of Conflict Resolution* 33, no. 2 (June 1989): 210–30; Pierre du Toit and Jannie Gagiano, "Contending Regime Models and the Contest for the Middle Ground in South African Politics," *Politikon* 15, no. 2 (December 1988): 5–18.

52. Du Toit and Gagiano, "Contending Regime Models and the Contest for the Middle Ground in South African Politics," p. 12.

During the first stage, du Toit postulates a process of persuasion that the zero-sum view of the conflict is wrong, that "competing groups can do very badly together, with none emerging victorious," or "all the competitors can end up doing very well together."[53] The first stage is, then, the setting for learning all about the costs of conflict and the benefits of democratic power sharing. During this stage, the myths entertained by parties to the conflict are demolished; leaders become motivated to avoid the dangers of the conflict, and they therefore become committed to cooperation; a middle ground, a "contract zone," is created.[54]

Since there is in South Africa no consensus "over the defining characteristics of the state,"[55] particularly whether it will be a liberal democracy, this persuasion phase entails a herculean task, not comparable to the task performed during what is conventionally referred to as prenegotiation. How persuasion will be accomplished is necessarily, therefore, uncertain. The first phase is a black box.

To open this box, one possibility, as we saw in Chapter 1, is to seek analogies in the creation of international regimes in conditions of anarchy.[56] In such matters, undoubtedly, there has been learning, and there has been cooperation where there might still have been conflict. Here, too, negotiation features prominently in putting the new knowledge to work for cooperative ends. The new knowledge is exactly the sort that is necessary for divided societies. It consists of shared cognitions about joint gains that can be achieved by collaborative behavior but not by conflict behavior. Yet all of the learning does not take place during the negotiation process. Some negotiations will not yield fruit precisely because the politicians do not uniformly share the new cognitions that are underpinned by expert knowledge. In general, only where they do can the empathy that sometimes is created during negotiations help produce a zone of joint gains.[57]

Even if the lessons of international regime creation were otherwise relevant, two main caveats should be borne in mind. First, regimes are

53. Du Toit, "Bargaining about Bargaining," p. 223.
54. Ibid., pp. 224–25; du Toit and Gagiano, "Contending Regime Models and the Contest for the Middle Ground in South African Politics," pp. 5–8.
55. Du Toit and Gagiano, "Contending Regime Models and the Contest for the Middle Ground in South African Politics," p. 8.
56. Du Toit, "Contending Regime Models and the Contest for Hegemony in Divided Societies."
57. The changed cognition model of international regimes is that of Ernst B. Haas in "Why Collaborate? Issue Linkage and International Regimes," *World Politics* 32, no. 3 (April 1980): 357–405.

created sector by sector. Regulation of international financial transactions may be agreed to, even while a new regime for the oceans does not command assent. Second, the regimes are not only specialized but international. On both counts, they do not, for the most part, endanger fundamental survival interests. By contrast, a regime for the democratic governance of a racially, ethnically, and ideologically polarized society immediately implicates the core interests of its citizens. No legitimation in terms of expert knowledge will suffice.

In addition, racial and ethnic issues are often cast in terms of *relative* group advantage. Experimental evidence suggests that in such contests maximum intergroup differential is an outcome preferred to maximum joint profit, even where in-group profit in the joint profit situation exceeds in-group profit in the differential situation.[58] This is a payoff preference structure that is hardly conducive to cooperation under any circumstances[59]—which is why there is so much intergroup conflict in the world—and it is a structure that will require considerable insight into its risks for politicians to overcome the conflict behavior suggested by it.

One of the most promising strategies for enhancing prospects for international cooperation is lengthening "the shadow of the future."[60] The shadow of the future is the likelihood of continuing interaction among the players. It can strengthen cooperation, because conflict behavior can meet with retaliation when interaction extends into the future. A player with an interest in securing cooperation from another may attempt to lengthen the shadow of the future by decomposing payments (that is, paying on the installment plan) or by linking issues that are not yet linked.[61] This is, of course, another form of deterrence strategy.

The trouble with such a strategy in domestic politics is that sovereignty makes it difficult for a player without control of the state apparatus to withhold payment—difficult but perhaps not always impossible. More fundamentally, however, there is, in domestic politics, an analogue to the international strategy best calculated to limit retaliation and thus shorten the shadow of the future. In international relations, the strategy is preemptive war.[62] In domestic politics, it is the seizure of

---

58. The studies are reviewed in Horowitz, *Ethnic Groups in Conflict,* pp. 144–46.

59. Compare the preference orderings depicted in Axelrod and Keohane, "Achieving Cooperation under Anarchy," pp. 229–31.

60. Kenneth A. Oye, "Explaining Cooperation under Anarchy: Hypotheses and Strategies," *World Politics* 38, no. 1 (October 1985): 1–24, at 13.

61. Ibid., pp. 16–17.

62. Axelrod and Keohane, "Achieving Cooperation under Anarchy," pp. 232–33.

hegemony, which brightens the future up considerably for the hegemon. In a sense, then, the reasons for cooperation to avert hegemony can be rendered irrelevant by seizing hegemony. This leads us right back to the question of why a potential hegemon might nonetheless wish to eschew hegemony.

In South Africa, the question can be made much more concrete by asking why a party espousing the claims of the Black majority should act in a conciliatory fashion toward any of the racial minorities—or toward ethnic or ideological minorities among Africans—by choosing institutions that would assure them of a democratic voice. Of course, the question becomes more pointed if we assume that one party, such as the African National Congress, could count on the support of a majority or near-majority of the South African population, enough at any rate to form a government. Hegemony then might not even require the use of undemocratic methods, such as the declaration of a one-party state; an undemocratic result might be achieved using majoritarian processes. The electoral systems described in Chapter 5 are premised on the need for incentives to moderation. But there is the prior question of what incentives exist to impel actors to choose and be faithful to such an approach. What, in short, are the incentives to adopt the incentives? [63]

To put the question in these terms has three advantages. First, unlike the belief model, the incentives formulation does not depend on the sort of transformation—from lacking a certain kind of knowledge to suddenly possessing it—that is not likely to take place in the time required to bring about a result conducive to cooperation. Self-interest, rather than cognitive change, becomes the focus of the inquiry. This is appropriate, since I have already argued that incentives and self-interest form the proper foundation for thinking about institutions that can simultaneously foster democracy and conflict reduction. Second, to cast the problem in terms of incentives avoids the rather artificial choice among competing models of deterrence, reciprocity, and belief. Various features of an actor's incentive structure can be the result of differing combinations of apprehensions, desires for rewards, and cognitions. Third, to focus on incentives is to recognize the contingent and potentially reversible character of the democratic venture. There is no point speaking of value change, for example, as if democratization involves crossing a threshold once and for all.

63. This formulation of the problem owes something to the repeatedly expressed concerns of Pierre du Toit.

It is instructive to compare White and Black incentives. For Whites, there will be great reluctance to move to an inclusive democracy if there are risks of undemocratic outcomes or of economic decline. The fact that many Whites appear willing to take some risks is attributable to the delegitimation of exclusively White rule among many White elites and to the likelihood that the strength of the White position will otherwise decline as time passes.[64] Now contrast Black incentives. Black rule, which, I suggested in Chapter 3, can be conflated—erroneously—with majority rule, is not yet deemed illegitimate by all those who might benefit from it. And, if the White position is likely to decline over time, the Black position shows strong signs of improving over time.

The case for a Rawlsian social contract, for blind, original-position reasoning, depends upon considerable uncertainty about one's future position. The Nigerians, for example, were willing to make neutral arrangements to counter ethnic conflict, because their bitter experience had led them, not only to an extreme aversion to the dangers but also to considerable uncertainty about who would be its next victims. The same may yet prove true for the Ugandans. But the bitter experience of apartheid might seem to some Black South African leaders to point a different moral. As the White regime weakens and the Black position improves, the future dangers to Blacks seem less menacing. (Here I should underscore the word *seem,* for, as I argued in Chapter 2, the ultimate dangers for Blacks are very much greater than they seem as the White regime begins to relent.) The appeal of a democratic institutional framework that provides for power sharing and minority inclusion is accordingly reduced. On this view, then, White and Black incentives are asymmetrical.

The picture does not appear more promising if we review incentives that have moved leaders elsewhere toward democratic conflict reduction. Eric A. Nordlinger's list of four motives—external threat, desire to gain political power, fear of economic decline, and desire to avoid bloodshed—does as well as any.[65]

External threat is a condition commonly thought to move parties closer together. Certainly the impact of externally imposed economic

64. By some accounts, the prospect of a future declining position is a classic motive for a willingness to create an inclusive democracy. Rustow, "Transitions to Democracy," p. 357.

65. Eric A. Nordlinger, *Conflict Regulation in Divided Societies,* Harvard University Center for International Affairs, Occasional Paper no. 29 (Cambridge: Harvard University Center for International Affairs, January 1972), pp. 43–52.

sanctions has had at least some force in South Africa. But it is most unrealistic to expect the prospect of adverse international reactions to prevent hegemony. After apartheid, the international salience of South Africa will decline precipitiously. International economic reactions, on the other hand, might well induce economic pragmatism. Some elements of the business community might then be persuaded to trade political hegemony for a market economy. This, of course, would reduce the incentives for potential hegemons to become democrats—the opposite of the desired effect.

The desire for power, which can only be acquired through compromise, is a possible incentive. However, that has not prevented other African leaders from altering their commitments in fairly short order by moving to single-party regimes.

The fear of economic damage from severe conflict and violence might be another motive for democratic accommodation, but political leaders in one divided society after another—among them, Cyprus, Lebanon, Sri Lanka—have been willing to risk extensive economic harm rather than take democratic precautions. And, of course, the same goes for the prospect of widespread bloodshed. Awareness of the danger is a large part of the "knowledge" I said earlier needed to be acquired. Unfortunately, that knowledge is generally acquired after the event.

No matter how we frame the question, South Africa appears to be another case in which there are more rewards for politicians to pursue both conflict and hegemony than to pursue accommodation and democracy. That does not mean that this will continue to be so under all conditions. What I shall argue for, before we are finished, is a possible model of changing incentives during the process of transition itself. This implies, first, that nothing so grand as a system of mutual deterrence or a major change in values need come into being for democracy to become more likely and, second, that the changes that take place are not preconditions to the process but integral parts of the ongoing process. At the outset, however, we need to see, concretely, how the incentives going into the process are not propitious. This, again, will underscore the long-shot character of the democratic gamble in South Africa.

PARTY INTERESTS AND PUBLIC INTERESTS

If democracy is to emerge in doubtful or unfavorable conditions, it will have to emerge out of the new configuration of interests, positions, and strategies that take shape as events unfold. During this time, as we shall see, every actor's incentives and commitments are shaped by those of every other, and so a few small changes can trigger larger changes throughout the spectrum. The process itself may unfold a new set of orientations toward the democratic regime.

To begin with, however, participation in the transition process may be grudging, and positions adopted may reflect the auspices under which the democratization process began. If the impetus comes from within the former regime, there will be, says Di Palma, "a 'left' that, even if sold on democracy (and not all will be), may not be sold yet on *this* democracy. It may fear the reappearance of the past in new guises . . . ."[66] This describes initial Black suspicion of what the South African government had in mind. On the other hand, Di Palma argues, a process begun from within the old regime has the potential for durability, since the initiators are in a position to offer reluctant sectors of the former regime an orderly transition. Moreover, initiators from within the regime may thwart the most dangerous, destabilizing reforms, provided they are able to retain the initiative and "set the agenda of democratic reconstruction."[67] All of this sounds as if it were written for—or by—F. W. de Klerk.

There is also a scenario in which the transition process is precipitated by radical mobilization and the radical left wants a "progressive" outcome, one not confined to liberal democracy but committed to a revolutionary change that obliterates the former class relations. This scenario, which, in some sense, also depicts the way the process began in South Africa, has the radicals claiming that other actors are "morally, politically, and economically bankrupt."[68] The political framework they want does not feature uncertain outcomes but rather radical socialist transformation. The democratic project is in jeopardy because, as Di Palma well puts it, "players who are reluctant to trust an open political game, preferring instead to protect themselves against their adversaries by girding democracy with their own invasive measures, may end up with a troubled democracy or worse."[69]

Between versions of these two alternatives lie South African prospects.[70] Much of the difficulty can be cast in terms of a wide divergence

---

66. *To Craft Democracies*, pp. 48–49 (emphasis in the original).
67. Ibid.
68. Ibid., p. 66.
69. Ibid., p. 71.
70. For a view that emphasizes the skepticism of the left and the incompatibility of

between party interests and public interests, if by the latter we mean the requirements of a democratic order. The aim of winning may be so central as to preempt agreement to rules that do not guarantee winning but only guarantee competing. Commitment to democratic uncertainty will then be difficult to secure. South Africa has been no exception, for this is precisely the meaning of the government's long-standing willingness to share power without losing it. Commitments to democratic uncertainty are also difficult to obtain when ideology renders some of those with whom a player must compete illegitimate participants in the game. Finally, agreement to democratic rules that assure minority interests or influence is unlikely when a player representing majority interests forecasts that such rules may impinge on its prospects. Again, at the outset of the game, this depicts the South African situation.

The reluctance of the extraparliamentary contenders to appreciate and face the dangers of racial and ethnic conflict is underpinned by a strong, genuinely held set of ideological convictions. These beliefs label race and ethnicity artificial affiliations and stamp political action based on such affiliations as manifestations of false consciousness. Were this reluctance less pronounced, there might be some disposition to regard racial and ethnic inclusion as an important political value, and this view would then be conducive to the careful construction of inclusive democratic institutions. On the contrary, however, White political behavior based on racial affinity can easily be seen as an effort to retain privilege; and Black political behavior based on ethnicity—among, for example, Zulu in Natal—can be interpreted as the product of elite manipulation designed to perpetuate historically outmoded affiliations. Consequently, departures from hegemonic aspirations are made more difficult by the racially and ethnically differentiated character of several other likely contenders, against the background of ideological commitments hostile to organization based on ascriptive group.

These ideological predispositions are shared across Charterist-Africanist organizational lines. However, the organizations differ in their orientation to electoral politics. The Pan Africanist Congress and the Azanian People's Organization are both committed to some version of revolutionary liberation and uncommitted to electoral institutions. The ANC, on the other hand, is not at all hostile to electoral paths to power.

---

goals, see Lawrence Schlemmer, "Requirements for and Possibilities of Successful Constitutional Negotiation in South Africa," in Giliomee and Schlemmer, eds., *Negotiating South Africa's Future*, pp. 28–40.

The positions of all of these organizations on this question are consistent with what is known about their share of popular support.

Of course, absent elections, it is difficult to gauge the support of organizations that might become political parties. First of all, survey respondents may express a preference for an organization that declines to participate in elections. Second, the process that eventuates in elections may change the support bases of the contenders. Third, variable electoral turnout, in rural versus urban areas, may be associated systematically with party preference. Fourth, the abstractly stated preference for one party or another may change when that preference must be translated into a choice among more and less attractive individual candidates. On all counts, South African surveys thus far have had a somewhat hypothetical character to them.

Nevertheless, virtually every survey shows stronger support for the ANC, its allies, and its leaders, than for any other organization. The ANC's support grew steadily through the 1980s. In 1981, 40 percent of urban Africans said the ANC would be their first choice in a parliamentary election. Inkatha would have been the first choice of 21 percent; the Black Consciousness organizations, of 11 percent; and the PAC, of 10 percent.[71] By 1985, another urban survey of Africans found that 49 percent of those asked who would make the best president for South Africa gave Nelson Mandela's name. Bishop Desmond Tutu had 24 percent, and Chief Mangosuthu Buthelezi had 6 percent. Again, the ANC-UDF forces emerged ahead of the others.[72] Comparable results were reached in another urban survey, in which Black support for Mandela, the ANC, the UDF, Tutu, and the Reverend Allan Boesak totaled more than 50 percent, compared to 8 percent for Buthelezi and Inkatha and 1–2 percent each for AZAPO and the PAC (including affiliates).[73] By early 1989, urban Africans gave Mandela 41 percent of their popularity preferences (interestingly, they gave P. W. Botha and F. W. de Klerk together 22 percent),[74] and careful observers attributed to the

71. *Star* (Johannesburg), September 23, 1981. This survey was regarded as accurate by the ANC. See African National Congress of South Africa, Observer Mission to the United Nations, "Recent Developments in South Africa (1981–1982)," (New York; mimeo.), p. 7.

72. *Sunday Times* (London), August 25, 1985.

73. Mark Orkin, *Disinvestment, the Struggle, and the Future: What Black South Africans Really Think* (Johannesburg: Ravan Press, 1986; pamphlet), p. 35.

74. These are the results of a Markinor survey, reported by Hermann Giliomee and Lawrence Schlemmer, *From Apartheid to Nation-Building* (Cape Town: Oxford University Press, 1989), p. 200.

ANC and its internal affiliates at that time a majority of African support.

The ANC's increasing support came clearly at the expense of Inkatha, the PAC, and the Black Consciousness organizations. Inkatha's fortunes outside Natal declined steadily as the ANC's improved. In 1977, Inkatha support was even with ANC support in the industrial Pretoria-Witwatersrand-Vereeniging (PWV) area. Each had about a third of Black support. By 1988, Inkatha's support in the PWV was below 5 percent, while the ANC's was 50 percent, even higher if affiliates are counted.[75] On the other hand, Inkatha remained strong in Natal, particularly in rural areas. In the late 1970s, after the Soweto killings of 1976, the fortunes of Black Consciousness organizations had risen dramatically. In suveys, students in Transvaal townships, including Soweto, chose Black Consciousness organizations and leaders over the ANC and Mandela by margins of 2 or 3 to 1.[76] After the UDF emerged dominant in the township protests of the mid-1980s, Black Consciousness was eclipsed. But the fortunes of all these organizations have fluctuated, and their leaders do not assume they are necessarily fixed.

All these surveys are of urban respondents only. Rural and homeland people, who constitute a majority of the African population, are harder to reach with sample surveys and have hardly been heard from in politics. In the few surveys in the 1980s with rural as well as urban coverage, the ANC remained ahead, but by a smaller margin; predictably, Buthelezi and Inkatha improved the showing they made in urban surveys, but to nothing like their former strength nationwide.[77] It bears emphasis also that the survey respondents were Africans. Coloureds and Indians, some of whom are found in all the extraparliamentary camps, are nevertheless, on the whole, decidedly more conservative. Many fewer Coloureds and Indians than Africans are likely to support the UDF or the ANC or, for that matter, any other Charterist or Africanist organization.[78] And, of course, the same is true to a greater extent for

75. J. W. W. Aitchison, "The Pietermaritzburg Conflict—Experience and Analysis" (Pietermaritzburg: Centre for Adult Education, University of Natal, July 7, 1989), p. 10.
76. Mark Orkin, " 'A Divided Struggle': Alienation, Ideology, and Social Control among Black Students in South Africa," *Journal of Intercultural Studies* 4, no. 3 (1983): 69–98, at 72.
77. See, e.g., *Times* (London), August 3, 1986; Colin Legum, ed., *Africa Contemporary Record, 1986–87* (New York: Africana, 1988), p. B742.
78. See, e.g., Fatima Meer and Alan Reynolds, "Sample Survey of Perceptions of the Durban Unrest—August 1985," in Fatima Meer, ed., *Resistance in the Townships* (Durban: Madiba, 1989), pp. 262, 264, 270.

Whites. After de Klerk announced the legalization of the ANC and the release of imprisoned ANC leaders in 1990, surveys of Africans outside rural Natal suggested that the ANC would have the support of more than half of all African voters in a universal suffrage election.[79] When rural Natal and non-Africans are added in, the ANC would have a plurality but not a majority of the vote.

Such estimates bear on the incentives the ANC might have to attempt hegemony or democracy. The ANC's preference for first-past-the-post is perfectly consistent with its position as the likely plurality choice of the South African electorate. Party interests may or may not converge with public interests. To take the clearest example, a party's position on electoral reform is a function of whether it will gain or lose from it. In Britain, where third parties habitually demand proportional representation, the two main parties speak of the plurality system in reverential terms. In Israel, where extreme proportional representation has had major adverse effects on the political system, the two largest parties may collaborate on a reform that benefits them and the political system while it harms small parties. It is infeasible to set aside party interests; and "exhortations to reach mutually desirable outcomes are often beside the point," for "undesirable yet 'rational' outcomes"[80] are distinctly possible.

A party with the plurality support the ANC might enjoy would inevitably benefit from a substantial seat bonus in a plurality electoral system. With 48 percent of the total vote in a first-past-the-post system, a party is virtually guaranteed a majority of seats, and a majority of seats is possible even on a 40 percent share of the vote.[81] With widespread electoral support and a fair number of three- or four-way contests, a party like the ANC could secure a very substantial majority of seats on a mere plurality of votes. These interests provide a strong foundation for the ANC's willingness at the outset to pursue an electoral route and also for its hostility to changes from first-past-the-post.

Similarly, the expectation of a large seat majority nationwide makes the ANC hostile to federalism. The regionally concentrated support of organizations like Inkatha means that federalism could only detract from the favorable prospects the ANC contemplates.

79. The surveys are summarized in *Argus,* July 23, 1990.

80. David D. Laitin, "South Africa: Violence, Myths, and Democratic Reform," *World Politics* 39, no. 2 (January 1987): 258–79, at 268.

81. See Douglas W. Rae, *The Political Consequences of Electoral Laws,* rev. ed. (New Haven: Yale University Press, 1971), pp. 75–76.

Here, then, there is a classical coincidence of interest and behavior. The extraparliamentary organization with the most support chooses a strategy of negotiation. The organizations that find themselves weak oppose negotiation, the results of which might entrench their weakness. As the ANC becomes more flexible, therefore, AZAPO and the PAC remain revolutionary, initially opposing negotiation with "the white minority settler government" (AZAPO) as a "sell-out" (PAC).[82] What each organization wants is consistent with its competitive position. As Jeremy Bentham said, "Interest smooths the road to faith."

Since I have already argued that a society like South Africa's should not have plurality elections and should have federalism, it is scarcely necessary to emphasize that the coincidence of party interest and behavior makes negotiation a perilous mode of institutional design. The same goes for the National Party's advocacy of group rights, which might also involve the equivalent of reserved White seats that the National Party, as the largest White party, could then capture. Group rights and reserved minority seats are, as I explained in Chapter 5, less valuable than is genuine influence in the political system. Once again, whatever the negotiators agree to is not necessarily what the society ought to have, because of the clear disjunction between party interests and public interests. Risk-averse actors prefer certainties that reinforce the favorable elements in their present position to the fluidity that a divided society needs and to the uncertainty of outcome that a democracy demands.

Party interests, however, are almost all we have to work with. Therefore, the issue is whether party interests can be harnessed to public goals—in this case, democratic goals. On this score, more interesting conclusions can be extracted from the ANC's interests and position.

First of all, a party with a strong preference for the seat bonus provided by plurality elections will probably find alternative voting to be its second choice. As I have noted, AV is usually seen as a modification of plurality elections, and many plurality parties are able to convert that plurality into a majority of votes through second and third preferences. Likewise, a party with widely distributed support may be receptive to electoral distribution requirements. These are hopeful signs for the ultimate arrangements that could emerge in South Africa.

Less hopeful, however, is another prospect associated with ANC i

82. The quotations are from, respectively, *Sowetan,* May 4, 1990, and *SA Dialogue,* May 1990, p. 1. For more on AZAPO, see *SA Dialogue,* May 1990, p. 6. For the PAC subsequent second thoughts, see *Argus,* June 11, 1990.

terests. The ANC's willingness to follow an electoral path may imply that what it contemplates is a secure ANC government, with a stable majority of seats, tolerating at the margins several powerless opposition parties: the National Party, perhaps even the Conservative Party, possibly Inkatha, the PAC, and AZAPO, if they should take the electoral path. The presence of active White parties could only enhance the ANC's base of support, by reactive mobilization. With periodic elections but no prospect of losing office, perhaps the ANC could comfortably run a dominant-party system on the model of Botswana, Senegal, and the Gambia—all of which survive as semidemocracies because the opposition cannot become the government. Indeed, those few other African states that held more than one free election after independence were also disproportionately of the dominant-party type. Among them were Somalia in the 1960s, Madagascar in the 1960s and early 1970s, and Burkina Fasso (then Upper Volta) in the early 1970s. (All of these regimes were ended by military coups.)

A South African dominant-party quasi-democracy, however, would not be likely to endure. Leave aside the possibility of military intervention. As we have seen, the reason Senegal's system endures is that opposition is compartmentalized. Confined especially to the Casamance region, it is not likely to spread. Botswana's opposition is ascriptively limited—largely to the non-Tswana Kalanga and Bayei groups and to dissident Tswana subgroups, notably the Bangwaketse. Ascriptive minorities cannot become majorities, so elections are safe. It might be thought that Inkatha support, limited to Natal Zulu, creates a similar situation, but it does not. There would be a continuing struggle for the allegiance of the Zulu. Inkatha claims, based on the desire to recapture a glorious Zulu past, would be ideologically jarring to the ANC and, if successful, potentially dangerous to the regime because of their demonstration effect for other ethnic groups. But even if all this were not so, the challenge from an unrestricted PAC and AZAPO, whose support is thus far not confined to any single ethnic group, would be potentially very dangerous. The danger is especially credible, since support for the various Black movements already has a history of fluctuation.[83]

The short of the matter is that a South African dominant-party regime would not resemble that of Senegal, Botswana, or the Gambia, and it certainly would not resemble the fluid, dominant-party systems

83. If the PAC or AZAPO could credibly make the accusation of Xhosa dominance against the ANC, that would make the PAC or AZAPO much more dangerous.

of India and Israel from the late 1940s to the late 1970s.[84] The South African version would be disinclined to tolerate what it saw as mortal competition from other Black parties. Such a regime, therefore, would be very likely to declare a single-party state, outlawing the opposition. As I said earlier, this is the way single-party regimes originally came into being in states such as Kenya, Guinea, Chad, Uganda, Zambia, Sierra Leone, Mali, Burkina Fasso, and Mauritania. Such regimes do not wait until the competition actually threatens to become a majority. Volatility of support, not really present in Senegal, Botswana, and the Gambia—especially volatility coupled with rising ethnic tension—is quite enough to induce the declaration of a one-party state. In South Africa, these concerns would be particularly exigent if the tension were not merely intra-African but also involved the well-armed, extreme right-wing White organizations that grew increasingly numerous, militant, and menacing after the ANC was legalized.

THE TRANSITION PROCESS AND THE CHANGING STRUCTURE OF INCENTIVES

There is a more promising but still very uncertain vision of durable democratization. What makes it promising is that it is also solidly anchored in party interests. The central feature of such a vision is that incentives can change, and change dramatically, as the process of democratization is under way. The decision by each actor to commit or not to commit itself to the process induces reactions on the part of every other actor. Before long, a different spectrum, with different alignments, is visible, and a new structure of opportunities and constraints can present itself. The outcome is not assured by any means, but new probabilities can be assigned to some of the possibilities.

The matter is best put concretely by returning to the process in South Africa. The early phases of prenegotiations, begun in 1990, resulted in surprising collaboration between the ANC and the National Party (NP) government, which quickly discovered that they had some common interests. Both were opposed by potentially strong rivals who hoped for the failure of the negotiations. Consequently, the partners developed a common interest in making the negotiations succeed. Both also stood

---

84. See W. H. Morris-Jones, *The Government and Politics of India,* 2d ed. (London: Hutchinson, 1967), pp. 199–200; Rajni Kothari, "The Congress 'System' in India," *Asian Survey* 4, no. 12 (December 1964): 1161–73; Alan Adrian and Samuel H. Barnes, "The Dominant Party System: A Neglected Model of Democratic Stability," *Journal of Politics* 36, no. 3 (August 1974): 592–614.

to gain from order and lose from disorder, although the ANC's interest was in demonstrating its ability to create order or, if necessary, disorder, whereas the NP government's interest was in showing that its control was intact. As a result, they found themselves collaborating to some extent in the maintenance of order. So quickly were these common interests acted upon that close observers suggested, with some hyperbole, that there already was a de facto ANC-NP coalition government, that the negotiations were really about how to finalize their relationship for the future, or at least that the ANC and NP would be the main pillars in a new regime.[85]

One conception of such a relationship, well described by Hennie Kotzé,[86] involves an ANC-NP joint executive, dominating parliament and avoiding the full implications of majority rule for quite some time. This model depends on the ANC's possible desire to escape the dysfunctional demands of some of its more activist constituents for establishment of a full-blown—and unproductive—socialist state. On this view, electoral politics would bind the ANC to restructure the economy in ways that would actually prevent it from delivering on its promises for Black welfare. As a result, the two parties would agree to have multiracial government but without democracy.

Such a model depends on some very doubtful assumptions, and it is not the only model of an emerging ANC-NP coalition. It is just as easy to envision such a relationship emerging out of a more open process of constitutional consultation. This is the sort of process considered here.

Now if indeed an ANC-NP coalition were consummated in the process of moving toward electoral politics based on universal suffrage, this would produce major repercussions in the rest of the political system. On the White side, the Democratic Party would favor the coalition and find ways to join it, but parties to the right of the NP would either benefit from the electoral support of Whites unprepared for an interracial coalition or would withdraw from electoral politics into armed resistance.[87] On the Black side, determined to remain a player, Inkatha

85. Mervyn Frost, "Who Governs?" *Leadership* (Cape Town) 9, no. 3 (April 1990): 101–04; Hugh Roberton, "Thinking the Unthinkable—Part 2," *Argus*, May 3, 1990; Hermann Giliomee, "ANC, NP Alliance in View?" *Cape Times* (Cape Town), February 22, 1990.

86. Hennie Kotzé, "Wat ís die Regering se plan?" *Rapport* (Johannesburg), April 1, 1990.

87. Initial right-wing White reactions to ANC-NP conversations were divided. The Conservatives did not withdraw from electoral politics, but vigilante organizations organized traditional Boer "commandos" and raided arsenals for weapons. *SA Dialogue*, May 1990, p. 3. See also *Africa Confidential*, February 23, 1990, p. 3.

would feel obliged to solidify its support among Natal Zulu. This is exactly what it did after the unbanning of the ANC. In a speech to Zulu chiefs, the king of the Zulu became an Inkatha partisan, accusing the ANC of being anti-Zulu: "They want no proud Zulus left. They only want subservient black Africans who say, 'yes sir, no sir, anything you like sir,' to the ANC."[88] As indicated in Chapter 2, the inception of inclusive democracy will promote the acceleration of intra-African ethnic conflict. On the other hand, the PAC and AZAPO, rejecting the ANC's interracial conciliation, would also profit.[89]

The White and Black organizations flanking the ANC and the NP would thus provide mirror-image responses. Without any doubt, they would have some ability to siphon off support, based on sellout arguments. Perhaps, in the aggregate, the ANC might suffer relatively more electoral erosion than the NP, especially if parts of the White opposition stay out of the electoral game while parts of the Black opposition join the game. It would be possible for ANC factions to take different positions on the linkage with the National Party and for the dissenters to find the Black opposition preferable to a conciliatory ANC.

The system would then consist of three differentiated sectors: a moderate, interracial middle, flanked by racially exclusive extremes. The relations of the three incipient sectors are already dynamic. As White politics polarizes, as the Conservative Party is pulled to an extreme position, and as armed White vigilante organizations threaten violence, the PAC and AZAPO are furnished further evidence for their contention that negotiations are premature and futile. With each act of moderation by the ANC and the NP, the extremes are provoked against the middle. Negotiations create support for both flanks. Each sector rebounds off the others.

If this dynamic keeps up, it has the potential to drive the middle partners closer together. By drawing the partners closer together, the extremes do the work of the moderate middle. Especially if the extreme Black flank grows in support and is ultimately willing to test its rejection of accommodation at the polls, it will then be impossible for any actor to gain electoral power alone. For this purpose, an ANC-NP coalition would be essential, as it might also be essential to the NP in its

88. Quoted in *Cape Times*, May 7, 1990. See also *Natal Mercury* (Durban), May 5, 1990. For the ANC leadership's endorsement of a Transvaal affiliate's decision to keep Inkatha members out of the area, see *City Press* (Johannesburg), July 29, 1990.

89. Mutual hostility between the PAC and AZAPO could limit the potential electoral impact of their uncompromising positions. For PAC-AZAPO tensions, see *Weekly Mail* (Johannesburg), April 5–10, 1990. For PAC-ANC violence, see *Argus*, June 11, 1990.

competition with the White flank. In these competitions, each partner—perhaps joined by Coloured and Indian partners—could help the other out at the crucial margin needed for victory. There would be an interdependent middle.

Such help is not farfetched on either side. It is worth remembering that Black survey respondents have often given surprisingly large percentages of support to White politicians like de Klerk. (De Klerk's approval ratings among Blacks soared after the legalization of the extraparliamentary opposition in 1990.) Now such dispositions would be underpinned by genuine compromise. And it goes practically without saying that such a coalition would have a strong interest in preferring vote-pooling electoral systems, which give an advantage to parties or coalitions able to appeal across racial or ethnic lines—although, given the threefold division of the spectrum, such a coalition might prevail under a number of electoral systems. (For example, it might even win some seats with pluralities in three-way contests.) Moreover, mutual help may extend beyond elections. If, for example, the armed White organizations endanger the new democracy, suppression by a largely Black government risks a race war. Suppression by a government with a strong White component does not.

This would not be the first time a three-sector party spectrum developed in a divided society. Where incentives to compromise exist in a society with two main groups, the accommodating middle can be set off from the respective extremist flanks, which, by their continuing threat, provide the middle with its raison d'être. In fact, this is the way the Malaysian party system developed, partitioned as it was between Malay and non-Malay sectors, with a coalition of the two in the middle, fending off claims from both flanks. It was a system conducive to both democracy and interethnic conflict reduction.

The differentiation of the spectrum in Malaysia was initially the product of the exigencies of electoral politics, for the coalition came into being to contest a difficult election, but it was then solidified by the need to negotiate a constitution.[90] Electoral politics locked the coalition in place between the extremes, because the single slate the coalition put up made clear its commitment to moderation. The negotiation bonded the participants to each other. In South Africa, the negotiation might precede the election, but an electoral component, with rewards for mu-

90. For the electoral origin and negotiational solidification of the Malaysian coalition in a three-sector spectrum, see Horowitz, *Ethnic Groups in Conflict*, pp. 398–416.

tual cooperation, is indispensable. Even with an electoral component, a South African coalition, operating in a polarized society, might not survive.

This is a speculative, but not wholly improbable course for the parties to take in South Africa. It may not be the only course conducive to eliciting democratic commitments from aspiring hegemons. I mention it, not to demonstrate its inevitability or even its probability, for there are a great many stumbling blocks along the way, but to reveal its plausibility and also to display the mechanism that underlies it. That mechanism is perhaps best described as transformation of the structure of incentives as the result of differential commitment of various parties to the initial democratization process.

Since this is not the only course by which hegemony can be abandoned, the point deserves to be put more generally. Di Palma speaks of political actors who "trespass, intentionally or not, into new behavior (for instance, holding free or nearly free elections)," and he goes on to add that "the first and contingent choice of trespassing can induce the trespassers to yet other behavioral commitments, with further unanticipated consequences of their own. In this way, actors come to comply with the results of actions that they had taken earlier in the process with other intents and expectations."[91] This is a felicitous, if indeterminate, way of describing the larger democratic entailments that sometimes flow from ostensibly more limited commitments.

These entailments are recurrent phenomena. The Malaysian coalition itself illustrates this, for the desire to win a single set of elections preempted for many years a Malay claim to untrammeled hegemony in the polity. Parties committed to hegemony were confined to the flanks. With the passage of time—shades of habituation!—"one-race government" or an undemocratic regime came to be regarded in Malaysia as a great leap into a very dangerous unknown. The temptations, often great, were resisted.

A comparable episode blunted Hausa claims to hegemony in Nigeria in 1967. A Hausa commitment to restructure the federal system was secured, and it resulted in a new balance of power.

In the early 1960s, Nigeria, it will be recalled, was divided into three main regions. The Hausa dominated the largest of them, using it also as a springboard to pursue hegemony at the center. In 1966, however, things went very wrong in Nigeria. The so-called Ibo coup of January

91. *To Craft Democracies*, pp. 111–12.

was followed by terrible anti-Ibo violence in May and by a bloody northern countercoup in July. The July coup, however, involved two groups of northern officers: Hausa, mainly Muslim, and "Middle Belters," mainly Christian. When the attempted Biafra secession was imminent in 1967, the unity of the north had to be consolidated if the impending war were to be won. This required fulfillment of the aspirations of northern minorities for separate states, to be carved out of the Northern Region. Simultaneously, the Ibo secessionists would then be confronted with claims from their own dissident minorities aiming to control the new states to be created in the East. The regions were thus divided into twelve states (six of them in the north), later into nineteen and then into twenty-one.[92] Without the undivided Northern Region as an artificially powerful base, the Hausa could no longer dominate Nigeria, for reasons I have explained in Chapter 6. By these means, then, a Hausa quest for hegemony was turned into something altogether more benign and cooperative.

The new states were not reversible, and neither was the decline of Hausa hegemony. A commitment to power sharing was a by-product of a commitment to a unified Nigeria, threatened by the civil war. Equally, the three-sector spectrum could not soon be altered in Malaysia, and so commitment to accommodation there was a by-product of initial and quite idiosyncratic electoral exigencies. In each case, what could not be done directly was done, with equal effect, indirectly. In each case, an insecure future prompted risk-averse behavior that inadvertently exchanged hegemonic possibilities for immediate gains of a qualitatively different sort. In each case, potential hegemons were enticed into becoming cooperators and democrats in spite of themselves. Not deterrence, not learning, not even reciprocity—because hegemony was not overtly traded but lost as a by-product of a different transaction—explains the change. The entailments of the transaction hemmed the parties into a new structure of constraints.

That they find themselves in this position does not mean that the coalition partners like it. In Malaysia, many Malay politicians in the coalition came to regret the compromises it required, and they took every opportunity to pursue narrow ethnic interests. If the Malaysian case is any guide, the center-versus-flanks configuration makes for a most imperfectly realized democracy. Something similar could very eas-

---

92. A helpful brief account is contained in Ruth First, *Power in Africa* (Harmondsworth, Eng.: Penguin Books, 1972), pp. 341–43.

ily appear in South Africa—which is another reason for reinforcing happenstance commitments with institutions appropriate for democracy in a divided society.

There is one implication of the Malaysian model in particular that bears on the tasks inherent in the transition to democracy. There is some uncertainty about whether everyone needs to be brought along on the same bandwagon. Di Palma suggests that there needs to be "one coalition of consent for democracy," a coalition "reaching the peripheries of the political spectrum." [93] The Nigerian experience in 1978 suggests that this is possible after a disaster, such as a civil war. But the Malaysian example and the hypothetical South African course that has been described both render this approach doubtful as a general proposition in divided societies. If democratic commitments arise out of a repartition of the political spectrum into three, then it is the center, struggling against the extremes, that carries the consent. The extremes, rejecting the compromises of the center, are essential to the power of the new incentives, but they are assuredly not part of an inclusive coalition. That renders the task of governing much more difficult than it might otherwise be, but governing a divided society is always a precarious venture. At least it is comforting to know that not everyone needs to be brought along for an effective change to occur. If everyone needed to join the bandwagon, change in a divided country like South Africa would wait forever.

No doubt, as the process moves along, others, initially reluctant, may well be coopted into participating in the democratic arrangements, lest they be left behind. One could easily imagine the Conservatives, the PAC, and AZAPO participating as electorally oriented parties on the flanks. Yet, that would still be consistent with their opposing the institutions and the compromises that underpin them. In a spectrum divided as I have hypothesized, the actors on the flanks cannot concede the legitimacy of the arrangements of the middle. [94] I do not know of any severely divided society, including those functioning along more or less democratic lines, in which the political system enjoys a large measure of broadly distributed legitimacy.

I said earlier that the belief and learning paradigm would not explain the differentiation of the middle that I have depicted. If the process

---

93. *To Craft Democracies*, pp. 40, 56.

94. That does not mean that the anti-system character of the opposition should be reinforced when in fact it can be mitigated. See Linz, "Crisis, Breakdown, and Reequilibration," pt. 1, p. 34.

solidifies, there will be learning later, as participants protect what they have created. What they learn during the initial course of the transition process, however, are no big lessons about the dangers of conflict or the rich rewards of cooperation. Continuing to conduct themselves in accordance with self-interest, all they "learn" is that their self-interest has changed incrementally—hence the minimalist quality of what might be required for a democratic commitment.

Since the process I have postulated depends on the reactions of a variety of actors to a series of initiatives, the process can scarcely be guided step by step. Nevertheless, the situation is amenable to some deliberate action to alter the unfavorable incentives with which the transition begins. Differentiation of the players depends upon their having an invitation to negotiate, to which they can respond in one way or another. In a sense, everyone has been asked a single question: Who wants to live in the same polity, on more or less equal terms? By giving different answers, the participants have changed the structure of the situation confronting each of them. By starting the process, a South African government or comparable actor can initiate the differentiation of the spectrum at both ends. Then those in the middle can take deliberate steps to solidify their coalition by making their commitments public. Predictably, this generates the flank reactions that give the spectrum its clear, emerging configuration. Central among the coalition's commitments are the new constitutional rules, which need to be crafted carefully, with an eye on both intergroup accommodation and inclusive democratic outcomes. Thereafter, the need to justify the constitutional product can and should be a new source of mutual democratic commitment. As I shall suggest in a moment, the rejection of the extremes can be helpful here, too.

This, then, is a process that can, in part, be shaped to make it more promising, but it can still be derailed at many points. The possibilities for thwarting democratic evolution in South Africa are multiple. The conflict between emergent Xhosa and Zulu ethnic claims, the reluctance of any opposition movement to live in peaceful coexistence locally with any other, and the threat of violence from several sources comprise only some of the dangers.[95]

If, despite the dangers, an interdependent center emerges, it can still make hegemony recede as a strategy and democratic power sharing ap-

---

95. See Hermann Giliomee, "Analysing the Reef Violence," *Natal Witness* (Pietermaritzburg), August 23, 1990.

pear more promising. In particular, these developments may create interests that are congruent with the successful operation of the political institutions most conducive to democratic conflict reduction, especially electoral institutions. Democracy then has, for the first time, a reasonable chance—certainly nothing more, but perhaps nothing less either.

IMPROVING THE ODDS: CONSTITUTION MAKING AND DEMOCRATIC COMMITMENT

Timing is a key issue in any transition to democracy. The advantages of gradualism—in permitting the growth of new elites, of interests with a stake in democracy, of forces that can check each other, of new expectations and modes of cooperation—have been stated repeatedly.[96] In general, the advantages of gradualism—many of which, restated, actually come back to deterrence, belief, reciprocity, and perhaps especially habituation—cannot be achieved in the still short time frame of any realistic delay. On the other hand, following from what I have just argued, it would be wise to move along while the incentive structures of the actors are pro-democratic. Delay may unintentionally signal retrenchment of the democratic project. An optimal strategy therefore aims to capture the benefits of speed and decisiveness rather than the longer-term benefits of gradual change.

With two important qualifications, however. Both derive from the fact that, if the transition is to entrench interests supportive of democratic competition, neither it nor the negotiation can be regarded merely as a process, a stage to be passed through. First, since the substance of the actual rules that are adopted to govern a divided society is a matter of great importance, the process must be subordinate to getting the substance right.[97] A good process and a good negotiating atmosphere are not substitutes for good institutions. Second, the process by which agreement is reached has a latent function for the institutions that emerge from it. Along the way, participants may become more or less solidly committed to arrangements they shape. Commitment is not a foregone conclusion. They may also become committed to each other, across

96. See ibid.; Maria do Carmo Campello de Souza, "The Brazilian 'New Republic': Under the 'Sword of Damocles,' " in Alfred Stepan, ed., *Democratizing Brazil: Problems of Transition and Consolidation* (New York: Oxford University Press, 1989), p. 381; Bolivar Lamounier, "*Authoritarian Brazil* Revisited: The Impact of Elections on the *Abertura*," in Stepan, ed., *Democratizing Brazil*, p. 45; Bermeo, "Rethinking Regime Change," p. 362.

97. Process and substance are closely related in negotiations. For an example, see Stein, "Prenegotiation in the Arab-Israeli Conflict," p. 183.

cleavage lines, if they are then obliged to defend their product against attack from outsiders or dissenting insiders. Both commitments are more likely if what has been produced is a synthesis, not a swap. If a party exchanges one thing for another, that party is generally committed to what was received, rather than to what was given. Commitment to the whole product is preferable, and that is, of course, a further argument for a social contract, rather than an ordinary exchange.[98]

Several implications follow. Getting the institutions right will take time, and the social contract mode is more difficult than trading horses. Trying to convince doubters is also time-consuming. All of these aims are more likely to be achieved in a multilateral constitutional convention than in a bilateral negotiation, but consummating the arrangements becomes more difficult as participants are added.[99] Yet, the credibility of the product as a constitution is greater if it cannot be made to look like a deal that benefits those few parties who happened to be in on it. The process therefore needs to be open to wider participation, but some may decline to participate, and the end product need not embrace every shade of opinion.[100]

The skepticism that would attend the efforts of a narrow band of participants to craft an agreement could be well founded. Parties to a negotiation may be able to consummate a deal, once they sit down, but there is no assurance that what suits their interests at the moment will be conducive to the democratic stability of a severely divided society over the long term. I indicated that the middle of the South African spectrum might benefit from vote-pooling electoral systems, but the partners might or might not prefer federalism and presidentialism. Whatever their preferences, it remains true that a severely divided society needs a heavy dose—on the engineering analogy, even a redundant

98. The Namibian Constitution, forged by a process watched closely in South Africa, seems to me vulnerable to this line of criticism. Agreement was reached, but the document left ethnic party bifurcation intact and provided little in the way of conciliatory institutions.

99. This certainly is a lesson that emerged from the negotiations of Black township organizations with White employers or White city councils in the mid-1980s. They tended to break down when the interests of third-party actors had to be taken into account. See Doreen Atkinson and Chris Heymans, "The Limits and Possibilities of Local Initiatives for Change: The Case for Participatory Planning," *Politikon* 15, no. 1 (June 1988): 31–44.

100. While expertise needs to be used, and used well, the idea that experts could do the actual negotiating, while leaders join only at the end to finalize the document, is at odds with the sort of instrument that is being forged and the need for commitment to it. Compare Clem Sunter, *The World and South Africa in the 1990s* (Cape Town: Human & Rousseau Tafelberg, 1987), p. 107.

dose—of institutions laden with incentives to accommodation. Malaysia did not have the panoply of such institutions. Consequently, both its democracy and its interethnic accommodation have experienced slippage over time. Negotiation inevitably requires both trades and tradeoffs. (That is what the theorists of negotiation like about it: compared to the hostility and stalemate of the past, any horse-trading is an improvement.) A possible result, which needs to be countered deliberately, is a conglomerate set of institutions that can work against each other in unfortunate ways, as those of Nigeria did in the Second Republic. An institutional patchwork is a likely product of an agreement reached by a few participants.

Beyond that, the deal that is done by a narrower than necessary band of participants invites a special kind of opposition. Besides opposing the substance of the institutions, or even the need for compromise, this opposition could extend, root and branch, to the procedure that produced a private accommodation masquerading as public policy. There is, then, no escaping the possible disjunction between the institutions that are needed and the procedures that may be called upon to bring them into being, especially if the political spectrum is partitioned in the way I have described, if the participation of the extremes is grudging or absent, and if the middle parties are the moving forces of democratization. There is a need for caution at this point.

This is not to denigrate the model I have advanced of a moderate middle, drawn closer together by the opposition of the extremes. It needs to be reiterated that this model is functional in a severely divided society. But the model invites oligopolistic constitutional procedures that can delegitimize its constructive work.

That the process itself can produce some especially valuable side benefits needs to be underscored. The American Constitutional Convention, with its innumerable compromises, fostered an enduring political culture of accommodation.[101] Despite the reservations urged against the document, the ratification process, carried on separately in each state, produced a degree of constitutional convergence and commitment that Americans had not previously displayed toward their institutions.[102] These processes were not rapid; they were deliberate. The pro-

101. See Donald L. Horowitz, "The Constitution and the Art of Compromise," in J. Jackson Barlow et al., eds., *The New Federalist Papers* (Lanham, Md.: University Press of America, 1988), pp. 37–38. On constitutional conventions, see Dahl, *Polyarchy*, pp. 169–71.

102. Michael Allen Gillespie and Michael Lienesch, "Introduction," in Michael Allen Gillespie and Michael Lienesch, eds., *Ratifying the Constitution* (Lawrence: University

cess in Malaysia also drove coalition leaders of all ethnic groups closer together. They drew the lesson that many of their differences could be accommodated in a spirit of good will, and they joined to defend the arrangements they reached against forces that attacked them from both sides.[103] The result was an enhanced degree of intimacy between the partners that supported the durability of the coalition. Later they were able to argue that what differentiated them from the extremes was their realism and their commitment to compromise. Their departure from hegemony became ideologized. If a speedy conclusion to constitutional negotiations risks losing such benefits, then speed is not an unmitigated virtue.

After a democratic regime begins its work, it will not be possible to sit supine. Even if there is a rush of formerly reluctant participants to take part in the new arrangements, the democratic game will not necessarily be secure. That is why the bonds that grow up among the founding generation are so important, as is the rapid use of the accommodative mechanisms of the new arrangements. With their repeated use over time, alternatives should look less and less plausible. The probability may then recede that one person, one vote, one value, and one state will degenerate into only one legal party and one last election.

Press of Kansas, 1989), p. 22; Michael Allen Gillespie, "Massachusetts: Creating Consensus," in ibid., pp. 147, 156–57.

103. See Gordon P. Means, *Malaysian Politics,* 1st ed. (New York: New York University Press, 1970), p. 194.

Index

Compositor: Maple-Vail Book Manufacturing Group
Text: 10/13 Sabon
Display: Sabon
Printer: Maple-Vail Book Manufacturing Group
Binder: Maple-Vail Book Manufacturing Group